RATIONAL CHOICE IN AN UNCERTAIN WORLD

*In memory of Hillel Einhorn, whose decision
to work in the field of behavioral decision theory
under unfavorable circumstances made such a difference;
of Clyde Coombs, whose lifetime of accomplishments in this field
was based on his thorough enjoyment of the work; and
of Amos Tversky, whose brilliance illuminated every facet
of the field of judgment and decision making.*

RATIONAL CHOICE IN AN UNCERTAIN WORLD

The Psychology of Judgment and Decision Making

Reid Hastie ▪ Robyn M. Dawes

Sage Publications
International Educational and Professional Publisher
Thousand Oaks ▪ London ▪ New Delhi

For information:

Sage Publications, Inc.
2455 Teller Road
Thousand Oaks, California 91320
E-mail: order@sagepub.com

Sage Publications Ltd.
6 Bonhill Street
London EC2A 4PU
United Kingdom

Sage Publications India Pvt. Ltd.
M-32 Market
Greater Kailash I
New Delhi 110 048 India

Printed in the United States of America

Library of Congress Cataloging-in-Publication Data

Hastie, Reid.
   Rational choice in an uncertain world: The psychology of judgment
and decision making / by Reid Hastie and Robyn M. Dawes.
      p. cm.
   Includes bibliographical references and index.
   ISBN 0-7619-2275-X
   1. Judgment.   2. Decision making.   I. Title: Psychology of judgment and
decision making.   II. Dawes, Robyn M., 1936–   III. Title.
   BF447 .H37   2001
   153.8'3—dc21   00-012061

             05   06   07   7   6   5

Acquiring Editor:	Jim Brace-Thompson
Editorial Assistant:	Shannon Helm
Production Editor:	Diana E. Axelsen
Editorial Assistant:	Candice Crosetti
Typesetter/Designer:	Lynn Miyata
Indexer:	Mary Mortensen
Cover Designer:	Michelle Lee

CONTENTS

PREFACE

The greatest enemy of truth is very often not the lie—
deliberate, contrived, and dishonest—but the myth—
persistent, pervasive, and unrealistic.
—John F. Kennedy

In this book, we have attempted to present basic theories and research findings from the field of judgment and decision making in as nontechnical a way as possible. Students have liked this approach in the classroom and we hope that readers of this book will as well. We have been teaching this material of more than 30 years (15 years for each of us, please) to students at Carnegie Mellon University, University of Colorado, University of Oregon, Northwestern University, and Harvard University. We have found not just that the responses from students are enthusiastic, but that these courses are comparatively more popular with students than any of the other topics that we teach.

A primary motivation for writing this book is our belief that an understanding of the principles of rational decision making can help people improve the quality of their choices and thus their lives. The material is not only of scholarly interest but practically useful as well. Again, students recognize this potential value and have frequently told us, years after they completed our courses, that what they had learned was useful and made a difference in their everyday life (a greater difference than knowing that their anterior cingulate is part of the mesocortical system or that hebephrenic schizophrenics are the silly ones).

The book is divided into six conceptual sections. Chapters 1 and 2 provide some history and introduce the main themes of rational versus descriptive approaches to judgment and decision making. Chapters 3 through 7 review the psychology of judgment. Chapters 8 and 9 focus on the accuracy and rationality of our habits of judgment. Chapters 10 and 11 review what we know about where our basic values come from and how we make choices when there is little uncertainty about obtaining outcomes but often much uncertainty about how much we will like them. Chapters 12 and 13 review the major theory of rational decision making, subjective expected utility theory, and the major descriptive psychological theory, prospect theory. The last chapter reviews our major themes and conclusions, with an exhortation to appreciate the positive aspects of living with uncertainty. Finally, the Appendix provides a brief introduction to the concepts from mathematical probability theory that we rely on in earlier chapters.

Throughout the book, we compare basic principles of rationality with actual behavior in making decisions. There is a discrepancy. Moreover, this discrepancy is due not to random errors or mistakes but to automatic and deliberate thought processes that influence how decision problems are conceptualized and how future possibilities in life are evaluated. The overarching argument is that our thinking processes are limited in systematic ways, and we review extensive behavioral research to support this conclusion.

We attempt to present as clearly and forcefully as possible the implications of the research we describe. Subsequent research will doubtless show that some of the conclusions reached in this book are incorrect or that they require modification, but we take the position that research—not anecdotes, not "plausible beliefs," not common sense, and not our everyday experience—should be the basis for understanding and evaluating our decision-making achievements and defeats.

Nevertheless, we have also used anecdotes as a teaching device. Although we believe that anecdotes are of little value in scientific discovery and verification, anecdotes are a powerful way of conveying information and making it understandable, believable, and memorable. We have tried, however, not to reason from anecdotes to conclusions ("My great-aunt Matilda was once told she had terminal cancer and then went for a walk by the lake on a moonlit night and the cancer went into remission; therefore . . . "); rather, we try to use anecdotes to reinforce the conclusions supported by more substantial theory and research.

The theme of limited cognitive capacity conflicts with our preconceptions about how smart we are. Although many of us are willing to accept the idea that our unconscious (for Freud) or "animal" (for Plato and Aristotle) or "hotheaded" natures may interfere with our reasoning when we are faced with an important decision, the idea that thinking per se is a fundamentally flawed and limited process is an unpleasant one. Moreover, many people rebut the view that thinking is flawed on the grounds that our dominant species status on this planet is related to our cerebral capacity and evidenced by our technologically advanced civilizations. This commonsense argument is flawed in several respects.

First, although evolution is often phrased in terms of the "survival of the fittest," its actual mechanism is better described as "survival of the fitter." Animals that have a higher probability than their competitors of surviving to adulthood and reproducing in a particular environment have a higher probability of dispersing their genes to future generations. Successful animals need not be optimal when compared to some physical or mathematical criterion of optimality, but only "one up" on competing animals and their forebears. Even that comparative superiority is defined relative to the particular demands and survival tasks of an environment. If indeed the human cerebral cortex is responsible for our ascendance over competing species, that does not imply it is the optimal thinking device, just that it is a better one.

Second, our technological development does not attest to the brilliance of our thinking as individual human beings. Rather, it is evidence for the human ability to communicate knowledge within and across generations. A single human could not have created a map of the human genome sequence, a symphony, or a hydrogen bomb without building on knowledge borrowed and inherited from living others and from the past. Such borrowing involves recognizing what is useful—but recognizing a valuable intellectual result is far easier than creating it. When faced with an important decision in our lives, in contrast, we are often "on our own" to think through what we might do and what are the probable consequences of the behaviors we might choose. And when we must make important social decisions, it is important that we be able to communicate with one another precisely and fluently. (In fact, many of the most convincing success stories told to us by ex-students involve the use of concepts from our courses to clarify and communicate during collaborative decision making.)

We must also counter the misconception that decision making is important simply because of the vastness of the choices with which we as individuals and as a species are faced today in the modern world. It is true that few of our great-grandparents seriously considered the option of divorce and that few of their political leaders considered risking the annihilation of the human race to achieve an international political objective. Nor were engineers of that day asked to produce energy by constructing complicated plants that could poison vast areas of the earth as a result a single operator's bad judgment. But despite the larger set of options available to us than to our ancestors, our decisions are probably not more difficult than were theirs. We adapt to whatever decisions must be made and to their consequences. Such adaptation is both a blessing (as when an individual in the worst prison camp can experience near ecstasy over eating a single crust of bread or cultivating a single weed) and a curse (as when people who appear to "have it made" adapt to their riches and find themselves on an unsatisfying "hedonic treadmill"). The subjective weight of decision making has always been a heavy one; philosophers throughout the centuries have discussed the process of decision making and suggested ways in which it is good or bad. The new knowledge that underlies the field of decision making is simple principles that define rationality in decision making and empirical facts about the cognitive limits that lead us not to decide rationally.

A word about format: We have avoided footnotes; subordinate explication and commentary has been incorporated in the text. Each chapter is followed by a bibliography of all the of materials cited in that chapter. We have attempted to rely on sources that discuss basic ideas in a nontechnical manner. When we refer to material that is presented elsewhere in this book, we provide section headings that point to a section within a chapter (e.g., a reference to Section 3.4 points to material in the fourth section in the third chapter).

We are intellectually and emotionally indebted to too many colleagues and friends to dare list their names, for we would surely neglect someone important and deserving. But we want to thank Mike Doherty, Baruch Fischhoff, Pat Larkey, Gary McClelland, Elke Weber, and several anonymous reviewers who provided advice to us (and to the publishers who asked them to evaluate the manuscript) that directly improved this version of the book. Our agent, Gerard McCauley, reluctantly accepted our plea for help in navigating the shoals of the textbook publishing business. We probably have no idea how much we owe to him. Anna Howland and Jim Brace-Thompson at Sage Publications have been competent, tolerant, and pleasant to work with.

Robyn Dawes would like to thank his research secretaries, Annette Romain and Amy Colbert, for their indefatigable labors on his behalf; the Swedish Research Council in the Humanities and Social Sciences for support via the Olof Palme Visiting Professorship at the Universities of Stockholm and Göteborg; and the Charles J. Queenan, Jr., University Professorship at Carnegie Mellon University.

Reid Hastie is grateful to the University of Colorado at Boulder for providing him with interesting colleagues, fine students, *and* a reduced teaching load, not to mention a year-round delightful off-campus environment in which to get away from "The Book" (and away from those fine students and interesting colleagues). And finally, Reid Hastie wants to thank Mary Luhring, his secretary and friend for the past 12 years, whose skills, good judgment, and sense of humor made this book and many other professional achievements possible and even enjoyable.

1

THINKING AND DECIDING

*Life is the art of drawing sufficient
conclusions from insufficient premises.*
—Samuel Butler

1.1 DECISION MAKING IS A SKILL

Humans evolved from ancestors hundreds of thousands of years ago who lived in small groups and spent most of their waking hours foraging for sustenance. When we weren't searching for something to eat or drink, we were looking for safe places to live, selecting mates, and protecting the offspring from those unions. Our success in accomplishing these "survival tasks" did not arise because of acute senses or especially powerful physical capacities. We dominate this planet today because of our distinctive capacity for good decision making. This same skill has allowed us to leave the planet for brief periods, but of course the skill has allowed us to develop technologies and weapons that could render the planet uninhabitable if we make a few really bad decisions. Human beings have an exceptional ability to choose appropriate means to achieve their ends.

This book is about decision making, but it is not about *what* to choose; rather, it is about *how* we choose. Most of the conclusions in this book follow from research conducted by psychologists, economists, and biologists

1

about how people actually make choices and decisions—people ranging from medical and financial experts to college students participating in psychological experiments. The important finding is that diverse people in very different situations often think about their decisions in the same way. We have a common set of cognitive skills that are reflected in similar decision habits. But we also bring with us a common set of limitations on our thinking skills that can make our choices far from optimal. These limitations are most obvious when we must make judgments and decisions that are not like those we were "selected" to make in the ancestral environments where we evolved.

But our decision-making capacities are not simply "wired in" following some evolutionary design. Choosing wisely is a *skill*, which like any other skill can be improved with experience. We can draw an analogy with swimming. When most of us enter the water for the first time, we come with a set of muscular skills that we use to keep ourselves from drowning. We also have one important bias: We want to keep our heads above water. Because the orientation of the head in large part determines the orientation of the rest of the body, that bias leads us to assume a vertical position, which is one of the few possible ways to drown. Even if we know better, in moments of panic or confusion we attempt to keep our heads wholly free of the water, despite the obvious effort compared to that of lying flat in a "jellyfish float." (Decisions, too, are sometimes made in moments of panic or confusion.) The first step in helping people learn to swim, therefore, is to make them feel comfortable with their heads under water. Anybody who has managed to overcome the head-up bias can survive for hours by simply lying forward on the water either prone or with arms and legs down—and crooking his or her neck only when it is necessary to breathe (provided, of course, the waves are not too strong or the water too cold). Ordinary skills can be modified to cope effectively with the situation by removing a pernicious bias. (To overcome the head-up bias in swimming, one of us—Dawes—invented a game in which children were to tell him the number of fingers he held up beneath the surface.)

This book describes and explains these self-defeating thinking styles and then suggests other strategies that will improve the decision maker's skill. This book reflects the spirit of Benjamin Franklin, whose 1772 letter of advice about a pressing decision to his friend Joseph Priestley began, "I cannot, for want of sufficient Premises, advise you *what* to determine, but if you please, I will tell you *how*" (1772/1975, pp. 299-300). We will attempt to detail pernicious modes of thought in order to provide advice about how to improve choices. We will not suggest what your goals, preferences, or aspirations ought to be when making these choices. The purpose of this book is not to improve tastes or preferences or ethics—or to provide advice about how to implement decisions once they have been made. Nor (unlike many other books written in this style) does it offer advice about how to feel good about yourself. Rather, this book's purpose is to increase skill in thinking about decisions and choices. Our emphasis is on *how*, not what, but we do not wish to derogate the importance of *what* is chosen or of values. In fact, as is pointed out in Chapter 10, one goal of our choices may be to discover our own value system or even to create it. In addition, to understand the decision process and to identify the situations in which our choices are less than optimal, we introduce a second perspective on the decision process, namely, analyses of the nature of rationality by philosophers and mathematicians.

1.2 THINKING: AUTOMATIC AND CONTROLLED

What is thinking? Briefly, it is the creation of mental representations of what *is not* in the immediate environment. Seeing a green wall is not thinking; imagining what that wall would be like if it were repainted blue is. Noting that a patient's skin is yellow is not thinking; hypothesizing that the patient may suffer from liver damage is. Listening to a suicidal client is not thinking; attempting to establish the similarity between that client and previous ones who have or have not made suicide attempts is. (As is indicated later in this book, matching with specific memories is usually not a very productive way of thinking, at least not for nonexperts who do not possess a rich memory store of useful specific memories.)

Sir Frederick Bartlett (1958), whose work 50 years ago helped create much of what is now termed cognitive psychology, defined thinking as the *skill* of "filling gaps in evidence." Michael Posner (1973) defines it as the achievement of a new representation through the performance of mental operations. Thinking is probably best conceived of as an *extension of perception*, an extension that allows us to fill in the gaps in the picture of the environment painted in our minds by our perceptual systems and to infer causal relationships and other important "affordances" of those environments. (Steven Pinker, 1997, provides an instructive analysis of the assumptions that we *must* be using as "premises" to "infer" a mental model of our three-dimensional world based on our fragmentary two-dimensional visual percepts.) Thinking tends to be primarily visual or verbal, and there are clear individual differences in the degree to which people use either mode.

To simplify, there are basically two types of thought processes: automatic and controlled. The terms themselves imply the difference. Pure association is the simplest type of automatic thinking. Something in the environment brings an idea to mind. Or one idea suggests another idea or a memory. As the English philosopher John Locke (1632-1706) pointed out, much of our thinking is associational. At the other extreme is controlled thought, in which we deliberately hypothesize a class of objects or experiences and then view our experiences in terms of these hypothetical possibilities. Controlled thought is "what if" thinking. The French psychologist Jean Piaget (1896-1980) defined such thinking as "formal," in which "reality is viewed as secondary to possibility" (Inhelder & Piaget, 1958). Such formal thought is only one type of controlled thinking. Other types include visual imagination, creation, and scenario building.

To distinguish these two broad categories of thinking, we can give an example that we discuss at greater length in a later chapter. Many of our clinical colleagues who practice psychotherapy are convinced that *all* instances of child abuse, no matter how far in the distant past and no matter how safe the child is at the time of disclosure, should be reported "because one thing we know about child abuse is that no child abusers stop on their own." How do they know that? They may have seen a number of child abusers, and of course none of those they have seen have stopped on their own. (Otherwise, our colleagues wouldn't be seeing them.) The image of what a child abuser is like is automatically associated with the abusers they have seen. These known abusers did not "stop on their own," so all child abusers do not. The conclusion is automatic.

Controlled thinking, however, indicates that the logic of this conclusion is flawed. With a moment's reflection, it becomes clear that the child abusers who are currently in therapy are only a subsample of the complete population of all child abusers. There *could* be a set of child abusers who stop on their own, but they are not referred to psychologists (by definition, those referred would not have "stopped on their own"); consequently, the experience of clinical psychologists seeing child abusers is inadequate for determining whether any child abusers stop on their own. A critic pointing out the flaw in his or her colleagues' reasoning does not do so on the basis of what comes to mind (the clients he or she is seeing), but quite literally *pauses* to ask "What if?" Such thinking corresponds to Piaget's definition of formal. The sample of people who are observed (child abusers who have not stopped on their own) is regarded as one of two possible sets, and the practicing psychologist does not have the people in the other set available for observation.

Nor can that set be available for systematic observation; given our extremely negative attitudes toward child sexual abusers, most of those who are not caught would be loath to provide information about themselves, particularly the type of systematic observation required for a conclusion about how many of them there are. Conversely, we might *want* to know whether any stop on their own—and hence how many do so—but our logical conclusion must be "We don't know." Thus the playing field is not level when such logical specification of all possibilities is pitted against automatic thought. (Unfortunately, it often is in legal settings, where automatic thought can "win.") In these examples and many others that follow, this logical conclusion of "don't know" is supported, much to the distress of some readers and often to our own personal distress.

The prototype of automatic thinking is the thinking involved when we drive a car. We respond to stimuli *not* present in the environment—for example, the expectation that the light will be red before we get there. Our responses to the stimuli are so automatic that we are usually unaware of them. We steer the car to reach a desired position without being aware that what we are doing is turning the steering wheel a certain amount so that the car will respond as we desire. It is only when we are learning to drive that we are aware of the thought processes involved, and in fact we have really learned to drive only when we cease being aware of them. Although much of driving involves "motor programs" as opposed to "mental representations," we nevertheless do think. This thinking is so automatic, however, that we can carry on conversations at the same time, listen to music, or even create prose or music in other parts of our head. When automatic thinking occurs in less mundane areas, it is often termed intuition (e.g., we admire the intuitive wisdom of a respected medical diagnostician, financial analyst, or business leader).

In contrast, a prototype of controlled thought is scientific reasoning. Although the original ideas may arise intuitively, they are subjected to rigorous investigation by consideration of *alternative explanations* of the phenomena the ideas seem to explain. (In fact, one way of characterizing Piaget's idea of formal thought is that it is scientific thinking applied to everyday situations.) *Conceivable explanations* are considered, and most of them are systematically eliminated by experimentation, observation, or logical reasoning. (There are historical instances of ideas later regarded as correct being eliminated as a result of poor experimentation. Schroedinger's equations describing the behavior of the hydrogen atom are an example. The physicist Paul Dirac later claimed that Schroedinger had paid too much attention to the experiments and not enough to the intuition that his equations were "beautiful.")

Occasionally, the degree to which thinking is automatic rather than controlled is not clear until the process is examined carefully. The situation is made more complicated by the fact that any significant intellectual achievement is a mixture of both automatic and controlled thought processes. For example, business executives often claim their decisions are intuitive, but, when questioned, demonstrate that they have systematically thought through the relevant alternatives quite deliberately before deciding which intuition to honor. At the other extreme, the thinking of chess grand masters has been shown to be much more automatic than most of us novices believe it to be. When a grand master's visual search across the chess board is traced by a camera following eye movements, it often shows that the grand master looks at the best move first. The subsequent eye movement pattern indicates the grand master is checking out alternative possibilities, most often only to come back to the original and best one. Moreover, the grand master is not distinguished from the mere expert by the number of moves he or she "looks ahead" (anticipates); the eye movement camera indicates that *both* experts and grand masters look ahead only two or three moves, with a maximum of five. Additionally, masters and grand masters can look at the 20th position in a typical chess match for 5 seconds and then reproduce that position almost perfectly. But mere experts and novices cannot do that, and no one can do it for pieces randomly placed on the board. (Thus the ability has nothing to do with the general skill at visual memory per se.) The conclusion is that grand masters are so familiar with positions in sensible chess games that in 5 seconds they can automatically encode entire patterns of pieces as being ones familiar to them—with perhaps a displacement or two—and that they know from experience (estimated at 50,000 hours for master-level players) what constitute good and bad moves from such patterns. As Herbert Simon and William Chase (1973) summarized their findings, "The most important processes underlying chess mastery are . . . immediate visual-perceptive processes rather than the subsequent logical-deductive thinking processes." Such immediate processes are automatic, like the decision to brake to avoid a collision.

One fundamental point of this book is that we often think in automatic ways when making judgments and choices, that these automatic thinking processes can be described by certain psychological rules (e.g., heuristics) and that they can systematically lead us to make poorer judgments and choices than we would by thinking in a more controlled manner about our decisions. This is not to say that deliberate, controlled thought is always perfect or even always better than intuitive thought. In fact, we hope the reader who finishes this book will have a heightened appreciation of the relative advantages of the two modes of thinking.

1.3 THE COMPUTATIONAL MODEL OF THE MIND

There has been a modest revolution in the sciences of the mind during the past half century. A new field has emerged, named cognitive science, with a new conceptual paradigm for theorizing about human thought and behavior (Gardner, 1985; Pinker, 1997). The computational model of the mind is based on the assumption that the essence of thinking can be captured by describing what the brain does as manipulating symbols. (Note we state described; we do not wish to imply that the brain itself literally manipulates symbols or—more extreme yet—that the brain is a "symbol-manipulating machine.") The computational model is obviously inspired by an analogy between the computing machine and the computing brain, but it is important to remember that it is an analogy. The two devices, brains and computers, perform similar functions, relating input information to output information (or actions) in a strikingly flexible manner, but their internal structures are quite different.

The central concept in the notion of a computational model is the manipulation of symbolic information. Perhaps the classic example of a cognitive process is the performance of a mental arithmetic task. Suppose we ask you to solve the following addition problem in your head: 434 + 87 = ???

If we asked you to think aloud, we might hear something like the following: "Okay, I gotta add those numbers up, uh . . . 4 + 7, that's 11 . . . write down the 1, and let's see, carry the 1 . . . ummmm . . . so 3 + 8 equals 11, again, but I gotta add the carry, so that's 12, and uhhhh . . . write down the 2, and I gotta carry a 1 again. Now 4, that's 4, but I have to add the carry, which was 1, so that's 5, write down the 5. So that's 521, does that look okay? Yeah, the answer is 521."

Another controlled, deliberate method that one of us (Dawes) uses is to work down from the highest multiples of ten while making a list of remainders in "another part of the head." Thus 434 + 87 is equal to 400, with 34 and 87 remaining. The 87, being larger, is attacked first as 100 minus 20, with a 7 left over. So we now have 400 + 100 − 20 = 480. We now attack the 34, which is larger than the other remainder of 7. It is basically 20 + 10, with a remainder of 4. Because we are already 20 short of 500, we reach it with a remainder or 10 + 4, to which we add the previous remainder of 7 to obtain 21. The answer is 521. Although the second algorithm may appear complex on first being stated, it has the advantage of avoiding silly errors that lead to large mistakes (e.g., as a result of not aligning what is to be carried over). But a little practice can also lead to speed that absolutely amazes salespeople.

It is tempting to try to create a theory of performance of cognitive tasks by summarizing the contents of thinking aloud reports as a sequence of pieces of information (e.g., "the sum for the right-most column is 11") and operations on that information to create new information ("plus" means looking up the sum of two digits in your long-term memory of arithmetic facts). Such a theoretical endeavor was unsuccessful until we had an appropriate theoretical language in which to express all these complex representations and operations.

Either of these computational strategies is a good illustration of what we mean by symbol processing: Information goes into your brain through the eyes (or another sense); it is converted to some kind of internal, symbolic code that retains the essential information from the digits; and then we perform mental operations to compare, manipulate, and transform that information, including combining the information from the external problem with our knowledge of arithmetic facts and algorithms we have learned in school. When we believe we have achieved the goal we set for ourselves when we started thinking about the problem, we respond to report the answer. (Note that behavioral scientists do not usually attempt to describe these internal codes and operations in neuroscientific terms, although eventually we will have neural computational theories intertwined with or linked to the computational information-processing theories.)

It is tempting to try to create a theory of performance of cognitive tasks by summarizing the contents of thinking aloud reports as a sequence of pieces of information (e.g., "the sum for the right-most column is 11") and operations on that information to create new information ("plus" means looking up the sum of two digits in your long-term memory of arithmetic facts). Such a theoretical endeavor was unsuccessful until we had an appropriate theoretical language in which to express all these complex representations and operations.

The cognitive revolution in psychology really got under way in the 1960s when the first generally useful computer programming languages were applied to the task of summarizing and mimicking the mental operations of people performing intellectual tasks like chess playing, logical deduction, and mental arithmetic. For example, the studies of grand masters' chess playing we mentioned above were part of a research program at Carnegie Mellon University aimed at describing human cognitive skills (including novice and expert levels) precisely enough so that computational models could be written in computer programming languages to simulate and compete with human players. As Allen Newell and Herbert Simon (1972) put it:

> The programmed computer and the human problem solver are both species belonging to the genus "Information Processing System." . . . When we seek to explain the behavior of human problem solvers (or computers for that matter), we discover that their flexibility—their programmability—is the key to understanding them. Their viability depends upon their being able to behave adaptively in a wide range of environments. . . . If we carefully factor out the influences of the task environments from influences of the underlying hardware components and organization, we reveal the true simplicity of the adaptive system. For, as we have seen, we need to postulate only a very simple information processing system to account for human problem solving in such tasks as chess, logic, and cryptarithmetic. The apparently complex behavior of the information processing system in a given environment is produced by the interaction of the demands of that environment with a few basic parameters of the system, particularly characteristics of its memories. (p. 870)

The first conclusion we want to emphasize is that many aspects of human thinking, including judgment and decision making, can be captured with computational models. The essential parts of these models are symbols (e.g., a theoretical representation of the idea of "yellow" or "rook" or "11") and operations that compare, combine, and record (in memory) the symbols. Thus, in the chess playing example, symbols represent the board, the pieces, and the rules and, at more complex levels, goals and strategies to win. One of the fundamental and ongoing research projects in cognitive science is to conduct an analysis of the contents of these representations, some say to describe the natural "mentalese" in which we think and to relate it to the biological substrate in which it must be implemented. For purposes of the present book, we can rely on rudimentary descriptions of mental representations to characterize the knowledge part of cognitive models of decision processes.

The other half of cognitive theory is a description of the elementary information processes that operate on the representations to store them, compare them, and transform them in productive thought. Again, for present purposes we can rely on a rudimentary theoretical vocabulary to convey the essentials of cognitive models of decision making. The first insight from cognitive science is that we can think of intellectual achievements, such as judging and deciding, as computation and that computation can be broken down into symbolic representations and operations on those representations. (We emphasize that *both* automatic and controlled modes of thinking can be modeled as computations in this sense.)

The second insight we use from cognitive science concerns the nature of the mechanism (the brain) that performs the computations. Since about 1970, there has been considerable agreement on a general "cognitive architecture" of the human mind. The basic outline of the cognitive system includes three kinds of memory stores: sensory "input buffers" that hold and transform incoming sensory information over a span of a few seconds; a limited short-term working memory where most of conscious thinking occurs; and a capacious long-term memory where we store concepts, images, facts, and procedures (see Figure 1.1 for an overview; a good introduction to the computational, information processing approach is provided by John Anderson, 2000). Over the past quarter century, there have been many modifications of the specific characteristics of each of the stores, but for our purposes the general outline suffices.

Two properties of these memory stores play major roles in our explanations for judgment and decision-making phenomena. First, the limited capacity of working memory is used to explain many departures from optimal, rational performance. As Newell and Simon wrote (see quote above), "The apparently complex behavior of the information processing system in a given environment is produced by the interaction of the demands of that environment with a few basic parameters of the system, *particularly characteristics of its memories* [italics added]." James March and Herbert Simon (1958) introduced the concept of "bounded rationality" in decision making, by which they meant approximately optimal behavior, where the primary explanation for departures from optimal is that we simply don't have the capacity to "compute" the optimal solutions because our working memory imposes limits on how much information we can use. Second, we often refer to the many facts and procedures that we have learned and stored in working memory. For example, we would explain the differences between a grand master and a novice chess player with reference to stored knowledge about past chess games, good moves,

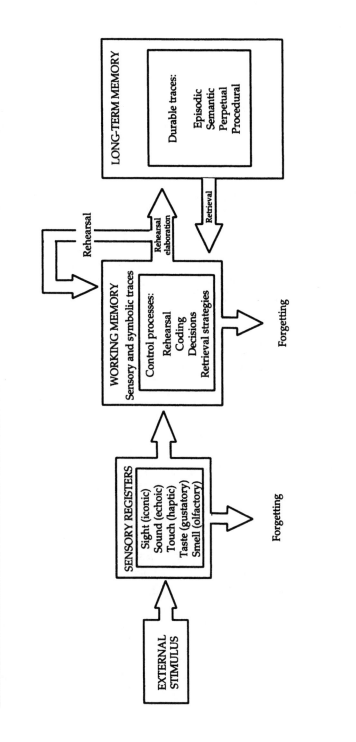

FIGURE 1.1. An Overview of the Human Information-Processing System (arrows indicate the flow of information and control from one component of the system to another)

and so on and with reference to special analytic skills (analogous to an educated person's knowledge of arithmetic algorithms), all stored almost permanently in long-term memory. (Remember, we did not use working memory differences to explain the differences in chess skill as a function of expertise. Research showed that novices and grand masters had similar working memory skills; what the grand masters seem to have that the novices lack is knowledge about chess stored in their long-term memories.)

The sheer amount of information to consider—and the limits that working memory places on our ability to consider information—is not the only source of bounded rationality, however. The type of automatic association discussed earlier (e.g., the association of characteristics of child abusers in general with those of child abusers seen in therapy) often provide impediments to rational thought in the simplest of situations. Information overload can be a sufficient condition for limited (bounded) rationality, but it is not a necessary condition.

1.4 THROUGH DARKEST PSYCHOANALYTIC THEORY AND BEHAVIORISM TO COGNITION

Most of the work discussed in this book has been done in the past half century. Why? Until the 1950s, psychology was dominated by two traditions: psychoanalytic theory and behaviorism. Neither of these traditions—which became preeminent in the early 1900s—treated thought as an important determinant of human behavior.

Unconscious needs and desires were the primary stuff of psychoanalytic theory; even defense mechanisms, by which these unconscious impulses could be channeled into socially acceptable—or neurotic—behaviors, were largely unconscious and hence outside of the awareness of the individual. (People who claimed to be aware of their own defense mechanisms were said to be denying their problems through intellectualization; only the psychoanalyst could really understand such mechanisms.)

Although dogmatic acceptance of psychoanalytic theory still lingers in some settings, skepticism was enhanced by its failure to explain one of the most important psychopathologies of the 20th century, Nazism. A strong implication of the theory was that the Nazi leaders, who engaged in monstrous activities, *had* to be suffering from the types of pathologies postulated by the theory. Moreover, these pathologies had to be related to pathologies and traumas of childhood, which—according to the theory—

are crucial to the development of adult disorders: "The child is father to the man." In fact, a 1943 U.S. Office of Strategic Services report by Walter C. Langer (1943/1972) was devoted to an analysis of Adolf Hitler and a prediction of his future actions based on his "psychosexual perversion," which was later found not to exist. Supposedly incapable of normal sexual intercourse, Hitler was believed to achieve sexual release through urinating and defecating on his mistress. Moreover, Langer wrote that Hitler survived World War I by granting homosexual favors to his officers. There is no historical evidence of any such behaviors. In fact, applying his philosophy of the insignificance of the individual human life to his own life as well as to others, he served without hesitation in the particularly dangerous position of "runner" (battlefield messenger), declining promotion to a safer position.

Psychoanalytic interpretations made no mention of Hitler's basic cognitive assumptions about the world, his thinking style, the ways in which he framed problems, or the heuristics he used for solving them. Instead, the future of the world was to be predicted on the basis of his ambivalent hatred of his brutal father and his unconscious identification of Germany with his mother. Except for making the somewhat obvious prediction that Hitler wouldn't succeed, this psychoanalytic approach didn't work. Moreover, careful study of the defendants at the Nuremberg war crimes trials—complete with Rorschach inkblot tests—failed to reveal any extraordinary psychosexual disorders or childhood problems. These men and women were ordinary people, much too ordinary. Years later, studying Adolf Eichmann, the SS officer who served as the director of the Central Office for Jewish Emigration and was responsible for the deaths of millions of Jews under the Nazi regime, the philosopher Hannah Arendt (1963) coined the phrase "the banality of evil."

A strategic retreat was called for in the psychoanalytic camp. Apparently, the Nazis suffered not from blatant pathologies but from a subtle "intolerance of ambiguity," one nurtured in the German character by the strict, authoritarian, paternalistic upbringing allegedly prevalent in German families. Scales were developed to assess such intolerance so that these ambiguity-intolerant people ("authoritarian personalities") could be distinguished from the rest of us. That didn't work either. Although scores on authoritarian personality scales were correlated to behavior that might be termed "fascistic," the relationship was weak. Then, in 1963, Stanley Milgram published his striking and controversial experiments on destructive obedience; in them he demonstrated that *a variety* of people would administer extremely painful and potentially lethal shocks to strangers as part of a psychological experiment, provided that they were urged to do so by an authority figure who took responsibility and that the victim was physically distant from them. (The shocks were not actually administered to the stranger, but the experimental participants thought that they were.) In effect, Milgram asked not, "How were the Nazis different from us?" but, "How are we like the Nazis?" He was able to answer the latter question better than others had answered the former.

According to the behaviorist approach, in sharp contrast to psychoanalysis, the reinforcing properties of the rewards or punishments that follow a behavior determine whether the behavior will become habitual. Awareness—as in the psychoanalytic tradition—is unimportant; at most it is an epiphenomenon. As B. F. Skinner (1984), probably the most famous behaviorist of all time, put it, "The question is not whether machines think, but whether men do" (p. 953). Again, as with psychoanalytic theory, the failure of behaviorism can be attributed to its failures to account for important phenomena rather than to any direct disproofs. For example, there are no useful analyses of everyday speech and communication, intellectual achievements like mental arithmetic, or behavior in modestly complicated gambling decisions from a behaviorist perspective. In fact, to address these phenomena, behaviorists have become so cognitive that it would difficult to separate them from psychologists who more comfortably march under that banner (Rachlin, 1989).

Accounts of even the most elementary learning processes seem to require more structure than is provided by basic behaviorism. For example, people and other animals cannot be conditioned to avoid or fear just any food or danger. Children are distinctively nervous about snakes and spiders; rats (and children) are exceptionally sensitive to the pairing of smells and nausea (Garcia & Koelling, 1966 Mineka & Cook, 1993; Seligman, 1971). We are prepared (probably via some form of evolutionary selection) to learn certain associations, especially causal associations, and not others; the laws of behaviorist conditioning are not general across stimuli and responses. A related finding is that our conscious understanding of contingencies is a significant moderator, maybe even a necessary condition, for many forms of learning to occur. A number of ingenious experiments (e.g., by Don Dulaney, 1968) demonstrated not only that awareness of "reinforcement contingencies" was important in determining whether behavior would be repeated, but that in many areas—notably verbal behavior—such awareness was crucial. This finding contradicted the general "law of effect," which maintains that the influence of consequences is automatic.

Ingenious experiments by Marvin Levine, Gordon Bower, Tom Trabasso, and other early cognitive psychologists illustrate the necessity of postulating an active human mind to understand behavior (see Levine, 1975, for the history of this revolutionary research). The experiments involve a task termed *concept identification* in which participants are presented with stimuli that vary on many attributes, most often geometric figures that vary in size, shape, color, and pattern characteristics. The participant's task is to sort these stimuli into two categories and by so doing identify the rule (or concept) that the experimenter has used as the basis for classification. For example, the rule may be that red patterns are to be placed on the left and green ones on the right. Participants are simply told "correct" or "incorrect" when they sort each stimulus, and they are judged to have identified the concept (or rule) when their sortings are consistently correct (e.g., 10 correct sorts in a row).

Behavioral analyses of responses to this task focused purely on the reinforcement (being told "correct" or "incorrect") for the participant's choices. Awareness, to the degree to which it exists, was assumed not to affect sorting choice. Some early results appeared to support such analyses. For example, some participants were able to achieve perfect sorting without being able to verbalize the experimenter's rule (although it turned out that they could if pressed, their earlier reluctance apparently resulting from being unsure of themselves), and in some tasks participants did not achieve the perfect learning that would be predicted from intellectual insight (but the experimenter's rules themselves may have been ambiguous, e.g., "unitary" designs versus "multiple" ones). Moreover, *average* success in concept identification *across participants* appeared to increase gradually, much like the learning of an athletic skill.

Clever experiments demonstrated that learning in such tasks was in fact not gradual but "all or none," the type of learning predicted on the basis of an active hypothesis-testing mind that continually searches for the correct rule whenever the experimenter indicates that an incorrect sorting has been made. First, these investigators analyzed each participant's responses separately and determined the pattern of correct and incorrect sortings *prior to the last error*. If learning was gradual, as predicted by most reinforcement theories, the probability of a correct sort "within" a single participant's learning trials should increase gradually from .50 (the chance probability of being "correct"). Instead, it was *stationary* at .50. The gradual increase found earlier was an artifact of averaging across participants who had identified the correct concept at different points of time in the experiment. Moreover, an error was, in the terminology of Frank Restle (1965), a *recurrent event*. Patterns of sorting after each error were indistinguishable regardless of the point in the experiment at which the error occurred. By making an error, the participant indicated that she or he "didn't get the concept"; hence performance was at the chance level prior to each error. An error indicated that the participant had no knowledge of the experimenter's rule.

Marvin Levine demonstrated that participants' conscious beliefs were virtually perfect predictors of their responses, particular error patterns, and time to learn. In an especially ingenious experiment (1971), he showed that participants failed to learn very simple concepts (e.g., to sort all stimuli to the left) over hundreds of trials if this concept was unexpected or "absent from their hypothesis set." Gordon Bower and Tom Trabasso (1963) devised a procedure they termed the *alternating reversal shift* procedure. Every *second* time the participant made an error, the rule was reversed. For example, participants who had initially been told "correct" when they placed red figures on the left and green ones on the right were told they were correct the second time they put a green figure on the left (or a red one on the right) and were subsequently told correct or incorrect according to this reversed rule—until they again made a second error, at which point the rule was reversed again. Except for participants lucky enough to identify the concept without making two errors, all participants would be reinforced a roughly equal number of times for placing red figures and green figures on the same side. If the effect of reinforcement were automatic, participants should never identify the concept. But in fact they did. As a group, they identified the concept after being told they were incorrect (falsely "called errors") roughly the same number of times as did those in comparison conditions where the rule was never reversed. Performance prior to the last error is stationary, and "called errors"—as well as "real errors"—are recurrent events.

It is almost impossible to explain these results without postulating an active, hypothesis-testing mind mediating between the reinforcement provided by the experimenter and the behavior in the sorting task. Moreover, the mind we hypothesize is a limited mind. For example, participants who perfectly recalled all their previous choices and the experimenter's responses to them would be totally confused by the alternating reversal shift procedure in the Bower and Trabasso experiments (and suspicious that the experimenter was doing something bizarre, because they were told they were wrong much less than half the time before identifying the concept). It is precisely such a limited, hypothesis-testing mind that this book is written about and for.

Neither the psychoanalytic nor the behavioral tradition regarded individuals or groups as decision makers who consciously weighed the consequences of various courses of action and then chose from among them. And neither tradition has contributed useful explanations of moderately complex behaviors. Most psychologists today accept the compelling assumption that ideas and beliefs cause behavior and that cognitive theories are the best route to understanding and improving important behaviors. If we want to understand why the juror said the defendant was a murderer, how the doctor diagnosed the patient with a blocked kidney duct, or why the pilot diverted to another airport for an unscheduled landing, the best way to proceed is to find out what they were thinking before they emitted each of these behaviors. It is now legitimate for psychologists to talk about thinking, choice, mental representations, plans, goals, mental hypothesis testing, and "cognitive biases." This book uses such concepts to better understand judgment and choice.

1.5   QUALITY OF CHOICE: RATIONALITY

If we aspire to give advice about how to make good decisions, we need to say something about what we mean by bad decisions. The quality of a decision cannot be determined unambiguously by its outcome. For example, most of us believe it would be silly to accept an even-money bet that the next time we throw a pair of unloaded dice we will roll "snake eyes." (The actual chance of throwing two ones, "snake eyes," is 1 in 36.) Moreover, we would regard the person who accepted such a wager as foolish—even if he or she happened to roll snake eyes. On the other hand, if that person were in danger of physical harm or death at the hands of a loan shark, and if the wager were the only way to raise enough money to avoid that harm, then the person might not seem so foolish. What this example illustrates is that it is the potential outcomes, their probabilities, and their values to the decision maker *at the time the decision is made* that lead us to judge a particular choice to be wise or foolish. A general who is losing a war, for example, is much wiser to engage in a high-risk military venture than is a general who is winning a war. The failure of such a venture would not reflect unfavorably on the decision-making ability of the losing general; it is more rational for the losing general to take a risk.

So what is rationality? Often, the term is used in a purely egocentric evaluative sense: "Decisions I make are 'rational'; those of which I disapprove are not." Occasionally, we adopt a broader perspective and judge rationality not just in terms of approval but in terms of the "best interests" *of the person making the decision*—but with best interests still defined by *us*. As we said at the outset, good decisions are those that choose means available in the circumstances to achieve the decision maker's goals. Thus, for example, some of Adolf Hitler's decisions may be viewed as rational and others as irrational, despite the fact that we may disapprove of all of them.

In this book, rationality has a narrow technical meaning; it will nevertheless provide the criteria by which we will judge the wisdom of choices. A *rational* choice can be defined as one that meets four criteria:

1. It is based on the decision maker's current assets. Assets include not only money, but physiological state, psychological capacities, social relationships, and feelings.

2. It is based on the possible consequences of the choice.

3. When these consequences are uncertain, their likelihood is evaluated according to the basic rules of probability theory.

4. It is a choice that is adaptive within the constraints of those probabilities and the values or satisfactions associated with each of the possible consequences of the choice.

Don't we make all our decisions like that? Decidedly not. Chapter 2 details how it is that we are affected not only by our present state but by *how we got to it*. The past is over and cannot be changed, but we often let it influence our future in an irrational manner. In Chapters 10 and 12, we show how we are sensitive not just to the possible consequences of our decisions but also to the way in which we *frame* these consequences. Chapters 4, 5, 6, and 7 are devoted in large part to the cognitive heuristics ("boundedly rational mental rules of thumb") we use to judge future likelihood, heuristics that systematically violate the rules of probability theory. Chapters 10 and 11 discuss many examples of confusing and even self-defeating value judgments, including non-optimal heuristics that we often rely on when combining elementary values to evaluate complex objects and events. Finally, Chapters 8, 9, and 12 describe some ways of reaching decisions that avoid the problems specified in the previous sections.

In fact, there are common decision-making procedures that have no direct relationship to these criteria of rationality. They include

1. Habit, or choosing what we have chosen before

2. Conformity, or making whatever choice (you think) most other people would make or imitating the choices of people you admire (Robert Boyd

and Peter Richerson, 1982, have pointed out that imitation of success can be adaptive in general, although not, for example, if it is imitation of the drug use of a particular rock star or professional athlete.)

3. Religious principles or cultural mandates, choosing as we have been taught by parents and other authorities

The four criteria of rationality have a philosophical basis. If any are violated, the decision maker can reach contradictory conclusions about what to choose—even though the conclusions are based on the same preferences and the same knowledge. That is, the person violating these principles may decide that a course of action is simultaneously desirable and undesirable, or that choice A is preferable to choice B *and* choice B is preferable to choice A. For example, a business executive who attends not just to the current assets of the company but to the fact that they have been increasing or decreasing in the past could conclude that it is both wise and unwise to continue to finance a losing venture. A doctor whose probabilistic reasoning follows automatic thinking principles rather than the rules of probability could decide that a patient both should and should not have an operation. Or a juror could decide that a defendant is both guilty and innocent. Because reality cannot be characterized in contradictory ways, contradictory thinking is irrational thinking. A proposition about reality cannot be both true and false.

1.6   THE INVENTION OF MODERN DECISION THEORY

Where does this idea of rationality come from? In the Western world, it began in Renaissance Italy (e.g., in the analysis of the practice of gambling by scholars such as Geronimo Cardano [1501-1576], a true Renaissance man who was simultaneously a mathematician, physician, accountant, and inveterate gambler. He tended to lose, though, because his insightful analyses of the numerical structure of random situations were accompanied by a habit of counting incorrectly.) The most recent impetus, however, comes from the book published in 1947 titled *Theory of Games and Economic Behavior* by the mathematician John von Neumann and the economist Oskar Morgenstern. (The first publication in 1944 omitted some of the most important analyses of decision making, so we cite the 1947 edition.) Von Neumann and Morgenstern provided a theory of decision making according to the principle of maximizing *expected utility*. The book does not discuss behavior per se; it is rather a purely mathematical work that discusses utility theory's relevance to optimal economic decisions. Its relevance to noneconomic decisions was ensured by basing the theoretical development on general *utility* (we prefer the term *personal value*) rather than solely on monetary outcomes of decisions.

This criterion of expected utility may most easily be understood by analyzing simple gambling situations. Because gambles are familiar, well-defined situations, we rely on them heavily (as have most scholars in this area) to illustrate basic concepts, though we try to provide a diverse collection of nonmonetary, everyday examples as well. Consider, for example, a choice between two gambles:

(a) With probability .20, win $45, otherwise nothing.

(b) With probability .25, win $30, otherwise nothing.

The *expected value* of each is equal to the probability of winning multiplied by the amount to be won. Thus the expected value of gamble (a) is .20 × $45 = $9; that of gamble (b) is .25 × $30 = $7.50. People need not, however, prefer gamble (a) simply because its expected value is higher. Depending on their circumstances, they may find $30 to have more than $4/5$ths the *utility* of $45, in which case they would—according to the theory—choose gamble (b). For example, an individual may be out of money at the end of a week and simply desire to have enough money to eat until the following Monday. In that situation, the individual may find the difference in utility between $30 and $45 to be negligible compared to the difference between a $1/4$th and a $1/5$th chance of receiving any money at all. Such a preference is represented in the von Neumann and Morgenstern theory by the conclusion that .25 times *that individual's utility* for $30 is greater than .20 times *that individual's utility* for $45. Let the utility of $30 be symbolized U($30) and the utility of $45 be symbolized U($45); then by simple algebra: .25 × U($30) > .20 × U($45), which is true if and only if U($30)/U($45) > .20/.25 (which is equal to 4/5).

In point of fact, most people, when asked, prefer gamble (a). But when faced with the choice between the following two gambles, most prefer (b'), the one with the $30 payoff:

(a') With probability .80, win $45, otherwise nothing.

(b') Win $30 for sure.

An individual who preferred (a) to (b) yet (b') to (a') would *violate* the von Neumann and Morgenstern principle of choosing according to expected utility. Using the same algebraic symbolism as before, a choice of (a) over (b) implies that $.20 \times U(\$45) > .25 \times U(\$30)$, or $U(\$45)/U(\$30) > .25/.20 = 5/4$. But a choice of (b') over (a') implies that $.80\, U(\$45) < U(\$30)$, or $U(\$45)/U(\$30) < 1/.80 = 5/4$. Thus there is a logical (algebraic) contradiction between the two choices.

Another possible violation of expected utility theory would occur if a person were willing to pay more for one gamble than another, yet preferred the other gamble when given a choice between the two. Such a person might prefer the sure $30 of alternative (b') yet—realizing that (a') has a higher expected value ($36 vs. $30)—be willing to pay more to play it than to play (b'). The theory equates the utility of each gamble with the utility of the maximal amount of money paid for playing each. The result is that by preferring the gamble for which he or she was willing to pay less, this hypothetical individual has implicitly indicated a preference for less money over more. Assuming any positive utility at all for money, that is irrational—because the greatest amount of money is equal to the lesser amount plus some more. The conditions that lead to such contradictions are discussed in Chapters 12 and 13.

What is important here is not just that some choices can contradict expected utility theory, but that the four criteria of rationality listed here are *preconditions* for the development of expected utility theory. Thus choices that violate expected utility theory can also violate very simple, fundamental, and plausible criteria for choice, criteria that almost all of us would say we would like to follow when we make important decisions. Again, there is nothing in the theory that mandates what desires a decision maker should wish to satisfy, that is, the theory does not prescribe *what* the utilities for various outcomes should be.

Theory of Games and Economic Behavior inspired a lot of interest in utility theory; many mathematically oriented researchers published work that drew out consequences of maximizing expected utility that were not present in the initial formulation. Others suggested that the basic formulation might be in error, but they did not advocate abandoning the four criteria of rationality; instead, often supported by examples that were intuitively compelling, they suggested that rational decision makers might choose according to some rational principle other than maximizing expected utility. These initial works focused on the *normative* question of how decision makers *should* choose. Soon, however, people became interested in the *descriptive* question of how decision makers—people, groups, organizations, and governments—*actually* choose. Do actual choices conform to the principle of maximizing expected utility?

The answer to this question appears to depend in large part on the field of the person asking it. Traditional economists, looking at the aggregate behavior of many individual decision makers in broad economic contexts, are satisfied that the principle of maximizing expected utility does describe what happens. As Gary Becker (another Nobel Prize-winning behavioral scientist) puts it: "All human behavior can be viewed as involving participants who maximize their utility from a stable set of preferences and accumulate an optimal amount of information and other inputs from a variety of markets" (1976, p. 14). Becker and many of his colleagues have taken this assertion seriously and have provided insightful analyses of nonfinancial, nonmarket behaviors including marriage, education, and murder.

There are good reasons to start with the optimistic hypothesis that the rational, expected utility theory and the descriptive—how people really behave—theories are the same. After all, our decision-making habits have been "designed" by millions of years of evolutionary selection and, as if that weren't enough, shaped by a lifetime of learning experiences. Surely, truly maladaptive habits have been eliminated by the pressures of evolution and learning and maybe, we might optimistically conclude, only the rational tendencies are still intact.

Psychologists and behavioral economists studying the decision making of individuals and organizations tend to reach the opposite conclusion. Not only do the choices of individuals and social decision making groups tend to violate the principle of maximizing expected utility, they are often patently irrational. (Recall that irrationality as discussed here means that the chooser violates the rules of rational decision making and chooses contradictory courses of action. We are not talking about the nature of the *goals* of the decision maker; we are talking about the failure to pursue those goals consistently, whatever they might be for the individual.) What is of more interest is not just that people are irrational, but that they are irrational in *systematic* ways—ways related to their automatic or "bounded" thinking habits. Chapters 4 through 9 of this book are devoted to a discussion of these systematic irrationalities.

Those behavioral scientists who conclude that the rational model is not a good descriptive model have also criticized the apparent descriptive successes of the rational model reported by Becker and others. The catch is that by specifying the theory in terms of utility rather than concrete values (such as dollars), it is almost always possible to *assume* that some sort of maximization principle works and then, ex post, to define utilities accordingly. This is analogous to the assertion that all people are "selfish" because they do, *by definition*, what they want to do. (As James Buchanan, 1978, points out, many aspects of standard economic theory tend to be vacuously true when phrased in terms of utilities, but demonstratively false if money is substituted for utility. And Herbert Simon, 1959, defending his more psychological approach, has identified some of the explanatory contortions that are necessary to make expected utility theory work descriptively.) But the best evidence that these principles don't work descriptively comes from demonstrations of out-and-out irrationality according to one or more of our four criteria for rational individual decision making (see above).

This book reflects the mixture of approaches to judgment and decision making that have characterized this complex field since its beginnings—the rational, normative hypotheses (often accompanied by the optimistic notion that we approximate the rational in our actual behavior) versus the cognitive, descriptive hypotheses about how we really behave. In our view, both the top-down normative view and the bottom-up descriptive approach are necessary to understand the ideal of adaptive rationality and the reality of human decision-making processes.

REFERENCES

Anderson, J. R. (2000). *Cognitive psychology and its implications* (5th ed.). New York: Worth.

Arendt, H. (1963). *Eichmann in Jerusalem: A report on the banality of evil.* New York: Viking.

Becker, G. (1976). *The economic approach to human behavior.* Chicago: University of Chicago Press.

Bower, G. H., & Trabasso, T. (1963). Reversals prior to solution in concept identification. *Journal of Experimental Psychology, 66,* 409-418.

Boyd, R., & Richerson, P. J. (1982). Cultural transmission and the evolution of cooperative behavior. *Human Ecology, 10,* 325-351.

Buchanan, J. M. (1978). *Cost and choice: An inquiry in economic theory.* Chicago: University of Chicago Press.

Dulaney, D. E. (1968). Awareness, rules, and propositional control: A confrontation with S-R behavior theory. In T. R. Dixon & D. R. Horton (Eds.), *Verbal behavior and general behavior theory* (pp. 98-109). Englewood Cliffs, NJ: Prentice Hall.

Franklin, B. (1975). *The papers of Benjamin Franklin* (W. B. Willcox, Ed.). New Haven, CT: Yale University Press. (Original letter written September 19, 1772, and contained in Vol. 19, pp. 299-300)

Garcia, J., & Koelling, R. A. (1966). The relation of cue to consequence in avoidance learning. *Psychonomic Science, 4*, 123-124.

Gardner, H. (1985). *The mind's new science: A history of the cognitive revolution.* New York: Basic Books.

Inhelder, B., & Piaget, J. (1958). *The growth of logical thinking from childhood to adolescence.* New York: Basic Books.

Langer, W. C. (1972). *The mind of Adolf Hitler: The secret wartime report.* New York: Basic Books. (Original work published 1943)

Levine, M. (1971). Hypothesis theory and non-learning despite ideal S-R reinforcement contingencies. *Psychological Review, 78*, 130-140.

Levine, M. (1975). *A cognitive theory of learning.* Hillsdale, NJ: Lawrence Erlbaum.

March, J. G., & Simon, H. A. (1958). *Organizations.* New York: John Wiley.

Milgram, S. (1963). Behavioral study of obedience. *Journal of Abnormal and Social Psychology, 67*, 371-378.

Mineka, S., & Cook, M. (1993). Mechanisms involved in the observational conditions of fear. *Journal of Experimental Psychology, 122*, 23-38.

Newell, A., &, Simon, H. A. (1972). *Human problem solving.* Englewood Cliffs, NJ: Prentice Hall.

Pinker, S. (1997). *How the mind works.* New York: W. W. Norton.

Posner, M. I. (1973). *Cognition: An introduction.* Glenview, IL: Scott, Foresman.

Rachlin, H. (1989). *Judgment, decision, and choice.* New York: W. H. Freeman.

Restle, F. (1965). The significance of all-or-none learning. *Psychological Bulletin, 64*, 313-325.

Seligman, M. E. (1971). Phobias and preparedness. *Behavior Therapy, 2*, 307-320.

Simon, H. A. (1959). Theories of decision making in economics and behavioral science. *American Economic Review, 49*, 253-280.

Simon, H. A., & Chase, W. G. (1973). Skill in chess. *American Scientist, 61*, 394-403.

Skinner, B. F. (1984). The shame of American education. *American Psychologist, 39*, 947-954.

von Neumann, J., & Morgenstern, O. (1947). *Theory of games and economic behavior* (2nd ed.). Princeton, NJ: Princeton University Press. (Original work published 1944)

WHAT IS DECISION MAKING?

Why don't you move your truck over here? It'll be easier.

Yeah, but then I'd be blocking people who want to get out of the alley.

Somebody did it yesterday.

Okay, I'll be right over.

—overheard

2.1 DEFINITION OF A DECISION

A good image of what we mean by decision making is a person pausing at a fork in the road and then choosing one path to reach a desired goal or to avoid an unpleasant outcome. The most important evolutionary situations that selected our basic decision-making capacities probably involved physical approach or avoidance: which mate, which waterhole, which field, which stranger, which fruit tree, which cave to approach and which to avoid? With bad decisions punished in a dramatic manner, as the philosopher Willard Van Orman Quine (1969) commented: "Creatures inveterately wrong in their inductions have a pathetic but praiseworthy tendency to die before reproducing their kind" (p. 126; in other words, animals that make bad predictions of the future tend to die before they can pass their genes on to the next generation).

A decision in scientific decision theory terms is a response to a situation that is composed of three parts: (a) There is more than one possible course of action under consideration, "in the choice set" (e.g., taking the right or left path at the fork in the road); (b) the decision maker can form expectations concerning future events and outcomes following from each course of action, expectations that are often described in terms of probabilities or degrees of confidence (e.g., indicating the degree of belief that the right-hand path becomes impassable a kilometer up the trail and that the left-hand path leads to a scenic lake with a good campsite); and (c) consequences, associated with the possible outcomes, that can be assessed on an evaluative continuum reflecting personal values and current goals.

There are countless situations that fit this definition that all of us encounter everyday: what college course to enroll in next semester; whether the defendant is innocent or guilty of committing a crime; whether to marry our current boyfriend or girlfriend; which car to purchase; whether to have a knee operation or not. . . . The problem with this definition is that it includes so many situations that it might alternatively be used as a definition of "all behavior," not just "decision behaviors."

One way to distinguish between decisions and other behaviors is to give some examples of prototypical, representative decision situations. Definition by example is a perfectly respectable method of being clear about our subject matter, and it may be the most useful solution to the problem of defining the varied collection of behaviors that are properly called decision making. Figure 2.1 is compiled from several surveys of examples of decisions reported by students, retired persons, academic historians, and decision textbook authors (see Allison, Jordan, & Yeatts, 1992, for a systematic study). (We present these examples exactly as they were stated by the subjects—without any editorial changes.)

It is worth noting that all of these decisions are deliberate, conscious accomplishments. Although technically we might want to analyze some highly automatic mental processes as decisions (e.g., a recent spate of scientific papers analyzes the microsecond saccadic movements of the eyes as decisions; Newsome, 1997), we focus on more deliberate, controlled decision processes in this book. We also do not attempt to analyze the extended, long-term sequences of behaviors that we sometimes call decisions in everyday conversation. For example, we might refer to the decision someone makes to lose weight or to exercise more often, including long-term, self-control efforts as part of the decision. Issues involved in implementation and adherence to decisions lie outside the scope of our discussion in this book.

Decisions by Older Adults

Whether to buy a new or used car.

Whether to move into a retirement community or to live alone in my house.

To retire early or to work for another ten years.

Whether to choose cremation or burial after death.

Which heir to leave my money to.

How much money to give to which charities.

Whether to have a knee operation.

Whether to travel by plane or bus.

Which presidential candidate I should vote for.

What church to join.

Whether to get married.

Decisions by College-Age Adults

To go to college.

What career or job to choose.

To work while my children were preschoolers.

Whether to fix my car or "junk" it.

To get a job vs. go to graduate school.

Whether to have my tongue pierced.

Religious preference.

To vocally defend some of my controversial viewpoints or to just keep quiet.

To abstain from all drugs.

To have my dog put to sleep.

To confront my father about his drinking.

Which parent to live with after a divorce.

Whether and when to sever a relationship.

Which college courses to take

Where I want to live next year.

To visit an old roommate or not.

(continued)

FIGURE 2.1. Examples of "Decisions" Generated by Four Samples of Respondents

Scholars' Examples of Significant 20th-Century Historical Decisions

Johnson's decision to escalate involvement in Vietnam in the 1960s.

Hitler's invasion of Russia (1941).

Supreme Court decision: *Brown vs. Board of Education* in 1954 (desegregation of public schools).

Rosa Parks's decision not to give up her seat on the bus in 1956.

Supreme Court decision: *Roe vs. Wade* (to legalize abortion).

U.S. Public Health Service decision to put the birth control pill on the market, 1950's.

King George's appointment of Churchill in 1940.

U.S. election of Franklin Roosevelt (1932).

Truman's decision to support the Marshall plan (1947).

Decision to establish the common market in Western Europe (1958).

Decisions of leaders to sign the Treaty of Versailles (1919)

Chamberlain's and Dadalier's decision at Munich to "appease" Hitler (1938).

Decisions Appearing as Examples in a
Popular Decision-Making Textbook

Judging which high school program a class was selected from.

Estimating the risks associated with nuclear war.

Which medical treatment to use on a patient.

Which lottery ticket to purchase.

Which casino gamble to play.

Whether to buy car insurance.

Whether to support building a nuclear power plant.

Deciding between two different financial (stock market) investments.

Which classes to take.

Which consumer product (e.g., television set) to buy or which apartment to rent.

FIGURE 2.1. Continued

The examples in Figure 2.1 fit the three-part definitional template we extracted from utility theory: two or more courses of action, uncertainty about events, and evaluations of consequences contingent on the events. The examples illustrate the central characteristics of decision-making phenomena in that they involve thoughts and behaviors about the external world, about what events will happen and what has happened, and about the "internal" consequences of those events (i.e., what the decision maker likes and dislikes). It is this integration of beliefs about the objective events and our subjective reactions to those events that is the essence of decision making.

2.2   PICTURING DECISIONS

It is very helpful to have a method of describing decision situations in a clear and consistent notation. We use schematic "decision tree" diagrams to summarize decisions throughout this book. One of the major uses of these diagrams is to describe personal or public decision situations in order to apply the principles of decision theory systematically to choose the best course of action. We introduce this "decision analysis" in Chapter 12. But for the moment, we want to explain the method of constructing the diagrams so that we can use them to describe the tasks and situations that are important in research on decision-making behavior.

The conventions of the decision tree diagram are that the situation is represented as a hypothetical map of choice points and outcomes that lead to experienced consequences, like a road map representing forks in a road and the objects that are located along the roads. For example, we might summarize a medical situation concerning a knee injury, as in Figure 2.2. On the left is a choice point (we use squares, □, to indicate "choice points" at which the decision maker chooses a course of action). The lines indicate the outcomes that follow from choosing each course of action. In the medical example, we imagine two possible courses of action: have a knee operation or do not have the operation. Events that are out of the decision maker's control, indicated by circles (O), are often associated with uncertain outcomes; we don't know for sure, nor can we control, which path we will take "out" of a circle. In the medical example, the upper path ("do not operate") is associated with two possible outcomes: The knee improves on its own (it was "normal") versus the knee remains in bad shape (it was truly injured). The lower path, representing the "have the operation" course of action, is also associated with two outcome paths: The operation

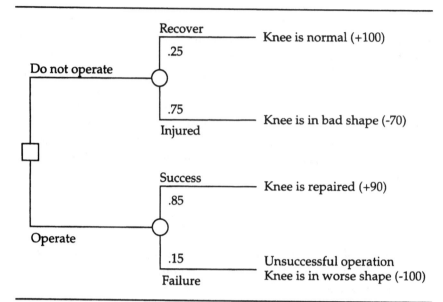

FIGURE 2.2. A Hypothetical Medical Decision Situation: An apparent
knee injury requires a decision between having an
operation or not.

is successful (for whatever reason—maybe the operation was unnecessary or maybe the operation was necessary and fixed the problem) versus
the operation is a failure.

On the far right-hand side of the diagram, we list the consequences
that are associated with choice points and events in the decision tree. We
often summarize the decision maker's evaluations of those outcomes with
numbers (traditionally they are called "utilities," but we prefer to call
them "personal values"). Sometimes, a decision problem is stated with
numbers associated with the consequences (e.g., money payoff gambles
with dollars, life-and-death medical and policy problems with "lives
saved—lives lost" tabulations). In these problems, we may use the numbers in the problem statement as summaries of consequences—but keep
in mind that the subjective "personal values" of quantities like dollars do
not bear a direct, linear relationship to the predicted or experienced "personal values" (we discuss the issues of valuation of such consequences in
Chapters 9 and 10). When the consequences are not already quantified, we
use −100 (worst) to +100 (best) scale for simplicity. We assign −100 to the
worst outcome we can foresee (in the decision tree) and +100 to the best. In

the medical example, the worst outcome would be to "have the operation and the knee is still in bad shape" (–100), the best outcome would be "no operation and the knee recovers" (+100). We might assign +90 to the outcome "operation is a success" and –70 to "no operation and the knee is still in bad shape." (In this age of health maintenance organizations—HMOs—and various forms of governmental and private health insurance, the task of scaling value of life under various medical conditions, e.g., as "quality life years," is enormously important—and controversial.)

We also express the decision maker's degrees of uncertainty in judging the possible outcomes that occur at the event nodes in the diagram in numerical terms. Here we use a probability scale (0.00, could not possibly occur . . . 1.00, certain to occur). For example, if the decision maker judges that the probability the knee will recover with no operation is .25, we assign that number to the corresponding path from the event node. In this simplified example, we assign .75 as the probability that the knee will remain in bad shape if there is no medical intervention. Since we expect that the chances of recovery are higher if the patient has the operation, we might assign .85 as the probability the knee will recover if the patient decides to have an operation; thus .15 is the probability of no recovery even after the operation.

We use probabilities (in the range from 0 to 1) to represent beliefs about what will happen. Usually, we mean to summarize people's subjective beliefs about those events. Although we use numbers that might be interpreted as formal probabilities by a mathematician, we do not assume that these numbers necessarily "behave" like true probabilities; Chapter 9 summarizes many of the ways in which our judgments under uncertainty violate rules of formal probability theory. When we mean to refer to mathematical probabilities we will make sure the context is clear. (The Appendix in this book is an introduction to the mathematical laws of probability.)

We will not spend much time in this book on how these numbers summarizing consequence values and outcome uncertainties might be extracted from people's thoughts about decision situations. But psychologists and economists have developed many practically useful "scaling methods" to solve these measurement problems. To spare the reader a lot of technical details, we just present plausible numbers. The reader who wants to understand these methods, can find this information in many other sources (e.g., Dawes & Smith, 1985).

We often use simple gambles to illustrate decision-making principles and habits. Gambles are the most popular experimental stimulus in

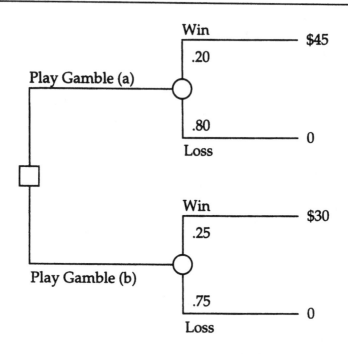

FIGURE 2.3. Decision Tree Representation of a Simple Money Gamble That Might Be Used as an Experimental Stimulus

research on decision making, and they provide well-defined, easy-to-understand decision dilemmas. Let's work through the representation of a typical experimental gamble in terms of the decision tree diagrams. Consider the choice between two gambles we described in Chapter 1:

(a) With probability .20, win $45, otherwise nothing.

(b) With probability .25, win $30, otherwise nothing.

Figure 2.3 summarizes this situation in a decision tree diagram, which is a common representational format for gambles and for everyday decisions. An interesting question, which is of practical importance for judgment researchers, concerns the extent to which human thinking is the same for both kinds of situations. We frequently ask ourselves, do the results from research in which people are asked to make choices among artificial money gambles generalize to everyday decisions? If we know how a person chooses in an artificial gambling task, can we predict how that person will choose in an analogous naturally occurring decision situation?

2.3 DECISION QUALITY REVISITED

The decision tree diagrams remind us that the crucial first step in understanding any decision is to describe the situation in which the decision occurs. That step may sound trivial, but the attempt to construct a summary diagram forces us to answer difficult questions about what to include and—more difficult—what to exclude. The diagram also prompts us to solve the challenging problem of quantifying the uncertainties and values that define the decision. Solving the problem of inferring how another person has conceptualized a decision situation is usually the toughest part of psychological research or applied decision analysis. (Much of the craft of research design involves creating experimental situations in which the researcher restricts the subject's thought processes and understands the effects of those restrictions on the subject's "mental model" of the experimental situation.)

If we believe that we have captured our subject's "situation model" in a decision tree diagram, it is relatively easy to calculate the decision that leads to the highest expected outcome by applying a rule that follows from decision theory (the four rational assumptions introduced in Chapter 1). This rule is called the "rational expectations principle" and it is usually summarized as an equation:

$$\text{Utility} = \Sigma \, (\text{probability}_i \times \text{value}_i)$$

The equation prescribes that for each alternative course of action under consideration (each major branch of the decision tree), we need to weight each of the potential consequences by their probabilities of occurrence and then add up all the component products to yield a summary evaluation, called an *expected utility*, for each alternative course of action (each initial left-hand branch). In our example of a medical decision (Figure 2.2), the calculations specify the expected utility for "operate" as +61.50 and for "do not operate" as –27.50, implying that the rational decision would be to have the operation. In the case of the gamble (Figure 2.3), if we assume that the dollar values represent the decision maker's true personal values for those consequences (an assumption that needs to be carefully examined), the expected utility for gamble (a) is $9.00 and for gamble (b) is $7.50, implying the decision maker should choose to play gamble (a).

Note that these calculations assume we can describe the decision process in terms of numerical probabilities and values and that arithmetic operations (adding, multiplying) describe the decision maker's thought processes. The calculation also assumes that the decision maker thoroughly considers all (and only) the options, contingencies, and consequences in the decision tree model of the situation. As we will see, most everyday decision processes are not as consistent or thorough as they would need to be to fit the rational expectations principle. But the decision tree representation and calculations are a good place to start in creating a descriptive model, and even if the representation is not descriptively accurate in all details, it may be useful as a model to analyze and improve our decision processes.

2.4   INCOMPLETE THINKING: A LEGAL EXAMPLE

Let's consider a complex decision that is made by many citizens in our county, the acquit-convict decision that a criminal trial juror is asked to make. Figure 2.4 summarizes the contingencies and the consequences for a simple version of a juror's decision where there are only two verdicts, acquit versus convict. (We ignore the possibility that the decision maker will "decide not to decide" and refuse to commit to a verdict, and we avoid the complexities of multiple verdicts, e.g., innocent, guilty of manslaughter, guilty of second-degree murder, or guilty of first-degree murder.) According to decision theory, a rational juror should think through all four right-hand consequence terminals of the diagram, carefully assess his or her evaluation of each consequence, and then weight those consequences by their probabilities. In the diagram, we have inserted numbers to represent a juror's beliefs and feelings, and if we accept those numbers and perform a rational expectations principle calculation, this juror should acquit.

What is interesting is that people do not appear to engage in the thorough, consistent thought process that is demanded by the decision tree

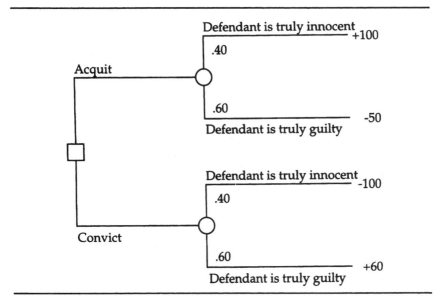

FIGURE 2.4. Idealized Juror Decision in a Criminal Trial

representation when they make these kinds of decisions in everyday life, even when they are in the jury box in a trial where their decision will have serious consequences. They do not appear to think through each of the options, to evaluate and weigh every one of the terminal consequence nodes in even a simple four-node tree like our example. Rather, people seem to focus on one or two nodes and reason extensively about those, but incompletely about the whole tree (Pennington & Hastie, 1991). Typically, people focus on the gains and losses associated with the decision they initially believe is most attractive, but ignore the gains and (especially) the losses associated with the other alternatives. Thus jurors who form an early impression that the defendant is innocent usually evaluate only the consequences that might ensue if they make that decision.

This form of incomplete thinking is similar to the thinking of the clinician (discussed in Chapter 1) who was trying to assess the validity of the claim that child abusers never stop on their own. The clinician's thinking was dominated by his available experience. More generally, a decision maker's thoughts are dominated by his or her initial impression, a phenomenon referred to as a "primacy effect" or "confirmatory hypothesis testing" (Nickerson, 1998). Baruch Fischhoff (1996) has reached a similar conclusion about people's thinking in more informal everyday decisions, such as teenagers' decisions about school, social, and family life (including some decisions about matters with serious consequences such as drug use, contraception, marriage, self-defense against criminal assaults, and career choices). Fischhoff observed a general tendency to focus on a few *most salient* possibilities and consequences and to ignore others, resulting in incomplete analysis.

For the moment, we just want to make the point that people usually do not exhibit the systematic kind of reasoning demanded by decision theory and summarized in the decision tree representation. Although we may have an initial reaction that many of the decision tree analyses we see in this book and elsewhere are oversimplified, the truth is that these trees are still more complex and balanced than our thoughts usually are, even in consequential situations. For researchers whose goals are to describe, predict, and enhance people's decision-making behavior, the critical first step in any psychological analysis will be to study how our subjects comprehend and represent the decision situation in their minds.

2.5   OVERINCLUSIVE THINKING: SUNK COSTS

Suppose that you and a companion have purchased discount ski tickets, rented skis, and driven to a resort. When you arrive the conditions are rotten; it's cold, it's icy, and several of the best ski lifts are not operating because of the wind. In addition, both you and your companion feel lousy physically and out of sorts psychologically. *Your assessment of the situation is that you would have a much better day if you just turn around and drive home rather than stay and attempt to ski.* Your companion says it is too bad you have already paid for the one-day-only tickets and the nonrefundable ski rental, because you both would much rather spend the time at home, but you can't afford to waste $70. You agree. But you agree that given the way you both feel, it is unlikely you will have a better time at the resort than you would at home. Do you stay and ski or return home?

Look at the problem another way. The moment you paid the $70, your net assets decreased by $70. That decrease occurred before your drive to the resort. Is the fact that your net assets have decreased by $70 sufficient reason for deciding to spend the day at a place you don't want to be? The point is, you reiterate, that if you go home you will have *wasted* the $70;

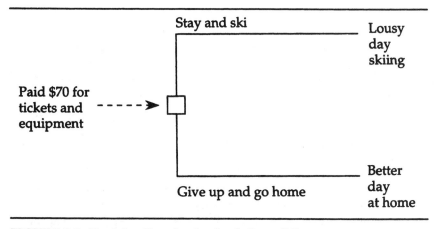

FIGURE 2.5. Decision Tree for the Sunk Costs Dilemma

waste not, want not. Perhaps you are slightly obese due to the same reasoning. Once you have paid for your food, you feel compelled to eat it all to avoid wasting it—even though the outcome of that particular policy is to decrease your dining pleasure *and* to make you fat.

The $70 you *have already paid* is technically termed a *sunk cost*. Rationally, sunk costs *should not affect decisions about the future*. If we draw a decision tree diagram summarizing your situation as you stand in the ski resort parking lot wondering whether or not to use your lift ticket, we see that the $70 does not appear in the diagram (Figure 2.5). (Or you might include it in every consequence node, since it has already been spent; decision theorists—and most people—agree that a consequence associated with every possible outcome is useless in discriminating between alternatives and therefore irrelevant to a decision.)

When we behave as if our nonrefundable expense is equivalent to a current investment, we are *honoring a sunk cost*. Now the only choice available that avoids the contradictions specified earlier is the one you judge to be the more valuable—turning back. Honoring sunk costs is irrational. (We exclude the possibility that you have motives *other* than personal enjoyment for going to the resort or that you wish to create the impression you are at the resort when you actually are not. The information presented in the examples in this book is to be taken as the total information available to the decision maker. Naturally, if there is other information or if there are other reasons for engaging in a behavior that are not specified in the examples, then the choices might be different.)

The following are examples of people honoring sunk costs:

"Finally, the day has finally come. You've got to think logically and realistically. Too much money's been spent, too many troops are over here, too many people had too many hard times not to kick somebody's ass."—Sergeant Robby Felton on the first day of the Gulf War (*San Francisco Chronicle*, January 16, 1991, p. A1); and more generally, many remarks attributed to proponents of continuing the U.S. involvement in the Vietnam War: " . . . our boys shall not have died in vain" (quoted in Dawkins & Carlisle, 1976).

"Completing Tennessee-Tombigbee is not a waste of taxpayers' dollars. Terminating the project at this late stage of development would, however, represent a serious waste of funds already invested."—Senator James Sasser, arguing for further investment in a project that, if completed, would be worth less than the amount of money yet to be spent to complete it, November 4, 1981.

"I have already invested so much in the Concorde airliner . . . that I cannot afford to scrap it now."—Businessman (quoted in Dawkins Brockmann, 1980).

If these arguments are taken on face value as compelling rationales for their conclusions (invade Iraq, invest further in the Tennessee-Tombigbee Waterways project; pay more to develop the Concorde airplane), the irrationalities are clear. Massive amounts of resources have been invested in mounting the war; therefore we can't stop now, no matter what the current situation. The federal budget deficit was already $1.1 billion more than it would have been had the project not been started—that is, used as a justification for spending money to create something worth less than the money yet to be spent. Like lost lives, dollars must not be spent in vain. But limiting concern to the *future* consequences of choices, which is made clear when a decision tree is constructed, starting from the "present" on the right-hand side and running to the future, is the best way to avoid honoring sunk costs. Conversely, honoring sunk costs violates the first criterion of rationality—that decisions should be based only on future consequences. As illustrated by the example, such violations yield contradictions.

We should note that there is some ambiguity about the irrationality of these arguments. Perhaps they are really rationalizations or are motivated by ulterior considerations: The soldier was quoted on the day the Gulf War started. He was about to risk his life anyway, with little choice about the matter. Why not think of a logical and realistic reason for doing so? The senator was advocating further federal investment in his state, which would provide employment and other benefits to his constituents. Nonetheless, it is still puzzling that the speakers would expect others to find these sunk costs arguments convincing if they themselves did not accept their validity.

The descriptive, psychological point is that we have a habit of paying too much attention to past losses and costs when we make decisions about the future. Even in the context of our discussion of justifications of sunk cost thinking in terms of future consequences, there is ample evidence that we overweight sunk costs in many practical decisions (Staw & Ross, 1989; Teger, 1980). With reference to self-improvement, the message is that we need to deal with the possibility of social disapproval as a potential future consequence of our decisions.

But consider some real-world *counter*examples: Hirohito, the emperor of Japan, who on August 15, 1945, announced Japan's surrender at the end of World War II: "The war situation has developed not necessarily to Japan's advantage. . . . In order to avoid further bloodshed, perhaps even the extinction of human civilization, we shall have to endure the unendurable, to suffer the insufferable" (see Butow, 1967). And he lived to see his country recover from the war and subsequent occupation to become one of the most prosperous nations in the world today. The Ford Motor Company wisely abandoned the Edsel as not suitable to American tastes and later replaced it with the popular Mustang. In the 1964 presidential elections, the Republican candidate, Barry Goldwater, publicly chided the former president of Ford, then the Secretary of Defense, for having first promoted and then abandoned the Edsel—even though it could equally well be maintained that the Edsel venture provided Ford with invaluable information that led to the tremendous success of the Mustang. This same secretary of defense showed a much greater commitment to a sunk cost in Southeast Asia, as did the subsequent secretary of state, who wrote, "We could not simply walk away from an enterprise involving two administrations, five allied countries, and thirty-one thousand dead as if we were switching off a television channel." The kindest interpretation of these commitments is that because the leaders of *other* nations honor sunk costs, the United States would have suffered a severe blow to its prestige had it failed to do so.

There is a defense against the label "irrational" for some examples of sunk costs reasoning. In some situations, it is likely that the decision makers are choosing actions that appear to honor sunk costs to project and

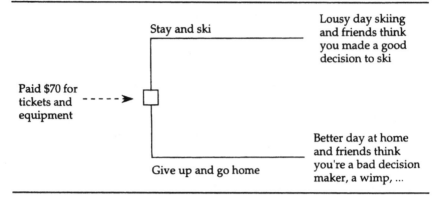

FIGURE 2.6. Sunk Costs Decision Tree With Reputational and Self-Concept Costs Included

preserve their reputations for being decisive or for not being wasteful. Just as the person who orders too much food might be labeled a poor judge of his or her own appetites and wasteful, these decision makers might be trying to protect their *future* reputations as morally consistent individuals or good decision makers. If, indeed, abandonment of a sunk cost negatively affects *future* reputation, then it may be wise not to do it. Reputational damage can lead to *future* problems, and it is only with respect to such future consequences that honoring sunk costs should make a difference. The automaker who abandons the Edsel may be derided for making a "gutless" decision and lose future clout and actual power in his or her organization. The skier who gives up after having already paid $70 may be regarded not just as financially wasteful but as confused or silly and lose his or her friends' respect and loyalty (see Figure 2.6). Such *future* costs are perfectly reasonable factors to consider in determining whether or not to abandon a particular course of action. But the sunk cost per se should not be a factor. As long as other people believe in honoring sunk costs, the person who does not may be regarded as aberrant. (A student once stated that after taking a course on decision making she found it more difficult to discuss decisions with her friends and sometimes her friends thought her something of a kook.)

Some of these subtleties of interpretation were revealed in efforts to explain parental investment behaviors in human and nonhuman species. In a landmark, and still controversial, article on this topic, anthropologist Robert Trivers (1967) defined parental investment as "any investment by the parent in an individual offspring that increases the offspring's chance of surviving (and hence reproductive success) at the cost of the parent's ability to invest in other offspring" (p. 1872). Trivers used the concept of parental investment (e.g., differential feeding of young, defense or abandonment of a nest) to explain diverse phenomena, such as differential mortality rates between males and females, promiscuity, competition for mates, and nurturing strategies. Trivers's original explanation for the tendency of males to be more likely than females to abandon their offspring and mates exhibits a misapplication of a sunk costs principle:

> At any point in time the individual whose cumulative investment is exceeded by his partner's is theoretically tempted to desert, especially if the disparity is large. This temptation occurs because the deserter loses less than his partner if no offspring are raised and the partner would therefore be more strongly tempted to stay with the young. (p. 1872)

Later analyses by biologists Richard Dawkins (famous for popularizing the "selfish gene" concept from evolutionary biology) and Thomas Carlisle (1976) showed that it was more plausible that the phenomenon of mate desertion was explained by the deserter's sensitivity to *future* consequences (an explanation that Trivers later endorsed): The offspring who had already accrued the greatest parental investment were also the most likely to survive to *future* reproductive maturity and would require less parental investment in the *future*. Interestingly, there appear to be no known examples of "sunk cost fallacies" in the life survival decisions of nonhuman animals. Hal Arkes and Peter Ayton (1999) point out that this summary observation is consistent with an interpretation of human examples of sunk cost reasoning as resulting from humans' tendency to overgeneralize rules for conduct, such as "Waste not, want not." Further confirmation is provided by the finding that younger humans (who are less likely to have internalized everyday truisms like "Waste not, want not") are less likely to demonstrate sunk cost behaviors than adults. As Arkes and Ayton conclude, maybe the adults are "too smart for their own good."

The subtleties of the sunk cost phenomenon have another message for those of us who favor controlled experimental methods as a primary scientific method. Experiments allow us to create refined situations in which other considerations can be eliminated. Hal Arkes and Catherine Blumer (1985) arranged for three different theater ticket subscriptions to be sold to people who bought season tickets to the Ohio University Theater series. The experimenters arranged it so that, randomly, one third of the patrons paid the full $15 price for the tickets, one third paid $13 for the same package, and one third paid $8. Compared to those who paid full price, those who purchased at a discount attended fewer plays during the subsequent 6-month season. Apparently, those who "sunk" the most money into the tickets, were most motivated to use them. The experimental demonstration eliminates most of the interpretive ambiguity that is present in the also important, naturally occurring examples.

To conclude on a practical note, the social problems that arise after abandoning a sunk cost can be ameliorated by a type of framing. The framing consists of explaining that one is not forsaking a project or enterprise but, rather, wisely refusing "to throw good money after bad." Rationally, that is exactly what is involved in abandoning a sunk cost, and of course it involves forsaking a project or enterprise. Using this phrase, moreover, tends to enhance the credibility of the speaker, who is then relieved of the necessity to explain in any detail the irrationality of honoring such sunk costs.

This "good money after bad" framing focuses the listeners' attention on the *present* as the status quo and phrases the abandonment of a sunk cost as the *avoidance* of a sure loss (which is good). In contrast, honoring a sunk cost involves framing a *past* state as the status quo and abandoning it as the *acceptance* of a sure loss (which is bad). The person who abandons a sunk cost benefits from behaving rationally, and if the present is effectively framed as the status quo, he or she also enjoys the approval of others. Remember that President Kennedy achieved the height of his popularity shortly after he abandoned the Bay of Pigs venture.

2.6   THE RATIONALITY OF CONSIDERING ONLY THE FUTURE

The notion of ignoring sunk costs has arisen only with modern decision theory, which in turn is based on probabilistic thinking that arose in the Italian Renaissance. This thinking is based on the idea that probabilities can be assessed properly only with reference to *future* events. For example, consider a fair coin that has been tossed four times and is to be tossed a fifth time. The probability of its landing heads is 1 in 2. The pattern of previous results is irrelevant because they have already occurred and do not affect the way in which the coin is handled when it is tossed for the fifth time. Four previous heads do not make a fifth head unlikely—even though in general four heads and a tail is an outcome five times more likely than five heads. Given that four heads have already occurred, a fifth head is as likely as a tail.

That the idea of limiting such probability assessments to future possibilities was not intuitively obvious prior to the Italian Renaissance (and may not be obvious today to most people who do not understand probability theory) can be inferred from answers proposed to a famous problem in Fra Luca dal Borgo's (also known as Paccioli) *Summa de arithmetica, geometrica, proportioni e proportionalita,* published in 1494 (see David, 1962, for a discussion of the history of this problem). The problem: "A and B are playing a fair game of *balla.* They agree to continue until one has won a total of six rounds. The game actually stops when A has won five rounds and B three rounds. How should the stakes be divided?" Paccioli's answer was 5:3.

One objection to this answer—dividing the stake proportionally to the number of games already won *in the past*—is that it implies A should get the same amount (the entire stake) whether he or she has won one, two, three, four, or five games in a row against no wins by B, although A clearly is in a much better position the more games he or she has won. Moreover, it implies that A is more deserving when ahead 2 to 1 than when ahead 5 to 3, even though it is clear that A has a much better chance of winning six games from the latter lead. Joachim Krueger (2000) has shown that college students, especially those with no training in probability theory, intuitively prefer the past-oriented proportional distribution rule.

It was not until 64 years later that G. F. Peverone proposed a solution that doesn't have any of the problems listed above (or others) and is consistent with the principle of thoroughly considering only future events. According to Peverone's solution, the more consecutive games won the higher the proportion of the stake, and a player ahead 5 to 3 receives a higher proportion of the stake than does a player ahead 2 to 1.

The solution is based on two principles. First, where p is the probability that A will be the first person to win six games *looking forward* from the current situation, p is the proportion of the stake that should be given to A. Second, p is computed by analyzing all of the possible games *remaining* (in the future) before A or B wins a total of six. The correct computation begins by noting that when A is ahead 5 to 3, the only way B can win six first is to win three consecutive games. Since the game is fair, that probability is $(1/2) \times (1/2) \times (1/2)$, or $1/8$ (regrettably, Peverone actually miscalculated p; as the statistician Maurice Kendall [1956] commented, Peverone's error "must be one of the nearest misses in mathematics," p. 8). Hence, because B's probability of winning is 1 in 8, B should receive 1/8th

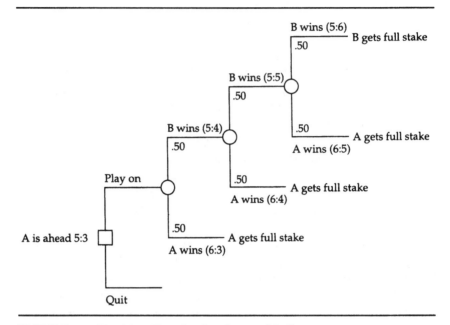

FIGURE 2.7. Decision Tree for the Game of *Balla*

of the stake and A should receive 7/8ths. Similar calculations can be used to determine A's proportion of the stake when A has won five consecutive games, when A is ahead 2 to 1, and so on. When A has won six, A has the probability of 1 of having won and, of course, receives the whole stake (see Figure 2.7).

In general, the past is relevant, but only for estimating *current probabilities* and the desirability of *future states*. It is rational to conclude that a coin that has landed heads in 19 of 20 previous flips is probably biased, and that therefore the probability it lands heads on the 21st flip is greater than 1 in 2. It is not rational to estimate the probability of a head on the 21st toss by assigning a probability to the entire pattern of results *including those that have already occurred*. (Again, the probability of five straight heads when tossing a fair coin is 1 in 32; in contrast, the probability of a fifth head *given* four heads in the past is 1 in 2.) Rational estimation of probabilities and rational decision making resulting from this estimation are based on a very clear demarcation between the past and the future.

Rational decisions are based on a thorough assessment of *future* possibilities and consequences. The past is relevant only insofar as it provides information about possible and probable futures. Rational decision making demands the abandonment of sunk costs, unless such abandonment creates *future* problems outweighing the benefits of abandonment (e.g., the reputational costs discussed in the ski trip example). Today really is the first day of the rest of our lives.

2.7 THE REST OF THIS BOOK

Two very general questions about decisions have dominated psychological research on this topic: What makes a decision good? And, what makes a decision difficult? The answer to the first question has traditionally been with reference to principles of rationality: A decision is a good one if it follows the laws of logic and probability theory and their implications for behavior summarized in traditional decision theory. We will see that this standard is still the dominant one in professional evaluations of "goodness," although there has been a shift to include other measures of goodness. How robust is the decision process, can it prevail over challenging conditions such as limited computational capacity ("brain power") or missing information or in a chaotic, "nonstationary" environment? And how stable or "survivable" is the decision process in a competitive, "zero-sum" environment where it is pitted against other antagonistic "decision strategies"?

The second question is more psychological and has achieved less consensus in behavioral research. But there are many intellectual aspects of a decision that make it difficult: the number of alternatives under consideration; the potential for loss if a bad choice is made; the degree of uncertainty about the outcomes that will occur if different choices are made; and, especially, the number and difficulty of the trade-offs that must be made on the way to selecting just one from many courses of action. And there are more emotional aspects as well: the degree to which cherished values are involved and even threatened by the choice alternatives, the intensity of the emotions associated with the choice process or evoked when evaluating the possible consequences of the alternatives, and the presence of time pressure and other threats to a smooth decision process.

The rest of this book presents the best answers we know to these important questions. We begin with a review of the psychology of the judgment process, the extensions of our perceptual systems that let us go beyond the information given to us through our senses (Chapters 3 through 9). Then we cover the rapidly advancing and still controversial subject area of the psychology of personal values and utilities (Chapters

10 and 11): How do we know and predict what we like? We conclude with an introduction to modern rational decision theory and some of its more psychologically valid modern descendants (Chapters 12 and 13).

REFERENCES

Allison, S. T., Jordan, A. M., & Yeatts, C. E. (1992). A cluster-analytic approach toward identifying the structure and content of human decision making. *Human Relations, 45,* 49-72.

Arkes, H. R., & Ayton, P. (1999). The sunk cost and Concorde effects: Are humans less rational than lower animals. *Psychological Bulletin, 125,* 591-600.

Arkes, H. R., & Blumer, C. (1985). The psychology of sunk cost. *Organizational Behavior and Human Performance, 35,* 129-140.

Butow, R. J. C. (1967). *Japan's decision to surrender* (5th ed.). Stanford, CA: Sanford University Press.

David, F. N. (1962). *Games, gods, and gambling: The origins and history of probability and statistical ideas from the earliest times to the Newtonian era.* New York: Hafner.

Dawes, R. M., & Smith, T. L. (1985). *Attitude and opinion measurement. In G. Lindzey & E. Aronson (Eds.), Handbook of social psychology* (3rd ed., pp. 509-566). New York: Random House.

Dawkins, R., & Brockmann, H. J. (1980). Do digger wasps commit the Concorde fallacy? *Animal Behavior, 28,* 892-896.

Dawkins, R., & Carlisle, T. R. (1976). Parental investment, mate desertion and a fallacy. *Nature, 262,* 131-133.

Fischhoff, B. (1996). The real world: What good is it? *Organizational Behavior and Human Decision Processes, 65,* 232-248.

Kendall, M. G. (1956). Studies in the history of probability and statistics: II. *Biometrika, 43,* 1-14.

Krueger, J. (2000). Distributive judgments under uncertainty: Paccioli's game revisited. *Journal of Experimental Psychology: General, 129,* 546-558.

Newsome, W. T. (1997). Deciding about motion: Linking perception to action. *Journal of Comparative Physiology, Series A, 181,* 5-12.

Nickerson, R. S. (1998). Confirmation bias: A ubiquitous phenomenon in many guises. *Review of General Psychology, 2,* 175-220

Pennington, N., & Hastie, R. (1991). A cognitive theory of juror decision making: The story model. *Cardozo Law Review, 13,* 519-557.

Quine, W. O. (1969). Natural kinds. In *Ontological relativity and other essays* (pp. 114-138). New York: Columbia University Press.

San Francisco Chronicle. (1991, January 16). P. A1.

Staw, B. M., & Ross, J. (1989). Understanding behavior in escalation situations. *Science, 246,* 216-220.

Teger, A. I. (1980). *Too much invested to quit.* New York: Pergamon.

Trivers, R. L. (1972). Parental investment and sexual selection. In B. Campbell (Ed.), *Sexual selection and the descent of man* (pp. 1871-1971). Chicago: Aldine.

A GENERAL FRAMEWORK
FOR JUDGMENT

The causes of the disaster are not due to faulty organization,
but to misfortune in all risks which had to be undertaken. . . .
We took risks, we knew we took them; things have come out
against us, and therefore we have no cause for complaint, but
bow to the will of Providence, determined still to do our best
to the last.

> —From the diary of explorer
> Robert Scott, quoted in
> Savours, 1975, p. 157)

3.1   A CONCEPTUAL FRAMEWORK
FOR JUDGMENT AND PREDICTION

British explorer Robert Scott, who lost the race to the South Pole and then
perished from starvation and exhaustion only 11 miles from his return
supply depot, describes himself and his men as heroes defeated by the

implacable, enigmatic natural world. But history has not been kind to Scott, and most commentators now attribute Scott's failure to repeated episodes of poor judgment as much as to unpredictable adverse events during his trek to and from the South Pole (Diamond, 1989; Huntford, 1999). It seems that Scott made many bad judgments, for example, about where to locate his supply base; about the endurance of his men, pack animals, and machines; and about numerous other details of his expedition.

This chapter is an introduction to the psychology of judgment, the human ability to infer, estimate, and predict the character of unknown events. As the excerpt from Scott's diary suggests, our judgment faculties are subject to certain systematic flaws; perhaps the most prominent of these is simple overconfidence.

The human mind has been designed by nature to go beyond the information given by our senses and to go further beyond "the given" than does the nervous system of any other organism on this planet. Even the apparently effortless perception of a three-dimensional physical scene involves inferences that are mathematically impossible if based on only "the information given" to our retinas (Pinker, 1997). Nonetheless, evolution has endowed us with a cognitive system that has the right assumptions built into it to do an excellent job of navigating through our three-dimensional environment without bumping into major landmarks. Our visual system is so good at making these "unconscious inferences" that it is impossible for us to figure out how we make them by examining our conscious experience. In some unusual cases of brain damage, a phenomenon called "blindsight" reveals that we are still able to make these judgments even when due to damage to our primary visual cortex, we have no conscious awareness of the perceptual experience itself. This chapter is about the process of judgment, including a broad range of accomplishments from the intuitive visual cognition involved in anticipating the path of a fly ball to the deliberate inference strategies of an internist reasoning through the nuances of a patient's endocrine system.

For the moment, we will focus on the psychology of judgment processes in which the goal of the judgment is to infer the nature of some condition that does or could exist in the world (we will ignore issues concerning judgments of internal events associated with evaluated consequences and personal values; we discuss these topics in Chapters 10 and 11). In psychology, a conceptual framework has been developed to deal with our judgments and expectations concerning events and outcomes of possible courses of action. The framework and its associated terminology may seem antiquated today, but the basic concepts still provide an excellent organizational scheme to summarize judgments made under *irreducible uncertainty*. By irreducible uncertainty, we mean uncertainty that cannot be eliminated before a decision about what action to take must be made.

The framework, called the *lens model*, was invented by an Austrian-American psychologist named Egon Brunswik (Brunswik, Hammond, & Stewart, 2000). The model gets its name from the notion that we cannot make direct contact with the objects and events in the world outside our sense organs, but only perceive them indirectly through a "lens" of information that mediates between the external objects and our internal perceptions (Pepper, 1942). The framework is divided into two halves, one representing the psychological events in the mind of the person making a judgment and the other representing events and relationships in the "real world" in which the person is situated. The framework forces us to recognize that a complete theory of judgment must include a representation of the environment in which the behavior occurs. We refer to it as a framework because it is not a theory that describes the details of the judgment process, but rather it places the parts of the judgment situation in a conceptual template that is useful by itself and can be subjected to further theoretical analysis.

Let's take an example judgment and work our way through the conceptual diagram (Figure 3.1) for the lens model. Suppose we are trying to estimate the biological age of a man encountered on the street (judgments of the gender, ethnicity, and age of other people are usually automatic). The lens model frames this judgment as a process through which we, the judges, are trying to "see" a "distal" true state of the world (the person's age) through a "proximal lens" of items of information, called "cues," that are available to us. In the case of an age judgment, we probably observe and rely on cues such as characteristics of the man's hair (Is it gray? Is he balding?), his skin quality (Is it wrinkled or smooth?), his body (How fit does he appear to be? Does he exhibit the gait and posture of a youthful or aged man?), his clothes (Is he dressed like an older person or younger?), his voice (Is it childish, adolescent, harsh, faint?), and other signals that might support inferences about his age. Note that for an intuitive judgment (like the age judgment), even the person making the judgment may not be able to provide a complete report of the cues.

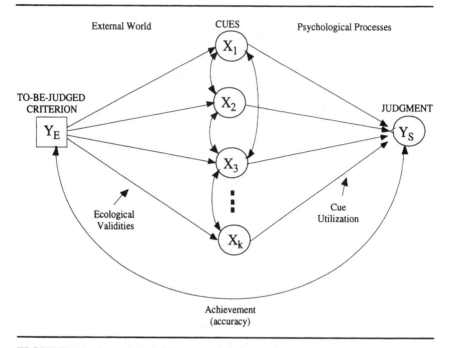

FIGURE 3.1. Lens Model Framework for Judgment

The left side of the lens model diagram summarizes the relationships between the true, to-be-judged state of the world, called the criterion (the man's age), and the cues that may point to that state of the world. In the case of the age judgment, physical anthropological studies would address the relationships on the left side of the diagram: What are the true relationships between biological age and the visible cues or signs it produces? Those relationships are often conceptualized as causal—the criterion state or outcome causes the cue, or maybe the criterion state produces or moderates the cue values where the relationships are not directly causal. In the middle of the diagram is the "lens" of cues that connect the judgment to the criterion or goal of the judgment. The right-hand side of the lens diagram is the psychological, judgment process part of the framework. It refers to the inferences that a person makes to integrate information conveyed by the cues to form an estimate, prediction, or judgment of the value of the criterion. The overarching path in the diagram (labeled "achievement") represents the judge's ability to estimate the to-be-judged criterion accurately.

The lens model is a useful framework to conceptualize any judgment task. We could use it to summarize the situation in which a physician makes intuitive estimates of the severity of damage to a patient's knee or the longevity of a cancer patient, and we could apply the same framework to summarize the operation of an assembly line machine that uses an X ray to assess the structural integrity of a metal automobile frame. Or we could consider a unique historical event, such as Robert Scott's misjudgments about his capabilities and the location of his supply depot, and analyze the information available to Scott, infer weights to describe his reasoning, and elucidate his judgment process.

3.2 RESEARCH IN THE LENS MODEL FRAMEWORK

The lens model was invented by psychologists for use in research; it can be interpreted as a blueprint for an empirical analysis of judgment processes. Once a judgment has been selected for study, the first step for the researcher is to identify and measure the cues on which the judge relies. This is often a laborious task, requiring several rounds of measurement and testing before all of the effective cues have been discovered. Obviously, this task is especially difficult for more intuitive judgment processes, where the judge can't tell the researcher what cues he or she is using. Often, this situation arises in important decisions made by experts. It is very difficult for a physician, an engineer, or a financial analyst to "unpack" his or her highly practiced, automatic judgment process and explain how he or she does it. In the case of the age judgment, we would probably start with our own intuitions, maybe consult with other people about how they make the judgment, maybe do a little research in the anthropometric literature on actuarial facts about human aging, and come up with an initial set of candidate cues. Then we would conduct a study of the age judgment, keeping open the possibility that the initial cue set may need to be enhanced to include additional cues that are used by people to make the judgment.

The second step in the analysis is the creation of a model of the events on the left side of the diagram. Often, a linear regression model can be used to summarize the criterion-cue relationships in terms of the correlations between the criterion and each of the cues that are related to it and might be used by a judge to infer the criterion (see a good introductory statistics text for an introduction to linear equations; e.g., Freedman, Pisani, Purves, & Adhikari, 1991; Glenberg, 1996). In this analysis, the correlation coefficient (or a related statistic) is used to summarize the strength of the relation between the criterion and a cue (the "ecological validity" of the cue) and between the cue and the judgment (the "cue utilization" coefficient, or more informally the psychological impact of the cue on the judgment). Sometimes, the modeler recognizes that the linear model is a simplified abbreviation of those "external environment" dynamics, although in many domains linear equations provide a surprisingly complete summary of the environment. Our subjectively experienced world is dominated by approximately linear relationships.

The third step in research shifts over to the right-hand side of the diagram and involves inventing and testing models of the psychological process of cue utilization: How do people use the cues to make inferences about the criterion state? Here again researchers have often found the linear statistical model to be a good description. The usual research tactic is to collect a sample of to-be-judged stimuli, for example, a sample of videotapes of men of various ages, to present to an experimental subject for judgments of the age of each stimulus person. The judge's "cue utilization" habits are "captured" in an algebraic equation that relates the judgment to a weighted sum of the cue values. (Note that this analysis depends on the researcher's ability to measure the cue values on psychologically meaningful numerical scales.) Here the research literature is clear; the most general principle to describe cue utilization processes is the linear equation. For an amazing range of everyday and expert judgments, people seem to infer the implications of cue information as though it was measured on numerical scales, weight it, and add it up.

Imagine sitting in a doctor's office watching him or her diagnose patients. Each patient comes in, has an interview with the doctor, provides the history of a medical problem, and describes some symptoms. Usually, laboratory tests are made, maybe some X rays (or other scans) are taken. Then, after reviewing all this material, the doctor makes a diagnostic decision about what is wrong with the patient. Consider recording these events for a few weeks to have a good sample of the cues (patient's history, symptoms, and test results) and diagnoses for this judgment task. Or transfer the same scenario to a busy college admissions office. Consider admissions officers reading applications—reviewing "objective" measures of achievement, such as test scores and high school grades, and more "subjective" material, such as letters of reference, lists of extracurricular activities, and a personal essay—and then making judgments about the admissibility or quality of many applicants. Again, you observe until you have a sizable sample of cases (cues) and judgments.

The lens model approach analyzes the judgment by calculating an algebraic model to provide a summary of the weights placed on the cue values for each case to predict the judge's (physician's, admissions officer's) judgments. The weights are usually based on the correlation coefficients summarizing the linear dependency of the judgment of each cue; everything else being equal, the higher the correlation, the greater the weight. The model can be extended to include nonlinear relationships (e.g., a U-shaped functional form with high judgments associated with extreme values on the cue dimension, e.g., where both extremely thin or obese patients are at high risk of injury, whereas those of average body weight are at low risk; or perhaps an admissions officer who likes applicants who either participate in many extracurricular activities or specialize in one activity but does not like applicants who participate in an "average" number—two to three—of activities). The model can also represent configural relationships where the judgment depends on combinations of cues (high levels of a hormone in the blood are bad news for female patients but uninformative for male patients; see discussion below of "interaction effects" in intervariable relationships). The simple linear model is surprisingly successful in many applications. We say surprisingly because many judges claim that their mental processes are much more complex than the linear summary equation would suggest, but empirically the equation does a remarkably good job of "capturing" their judgment habits.

If we had criterion values for our sample of judgments, we could also calculate a summary model for the left-hand side of the lens model diagram. In many applications to actual judgment tasks, however, it is difficult to obtain criterion values. In medical contexts, it is too time consuming for a physician to track the history of patients to obtain final opinions about their presenting condition or outcomes of treatment; in the academic context, we have no access to values representing success in a college for students who were not admitted. But we are usually interested in the psychology of the judgments, the right-hand side of the lens diagram, not the complete environment-behavior system encompassed by the full framework.

Hundreds of studies have been conducted of judgments ranging from medical diagnosis to highway safety, from financial stock values to livestock quality (Cooksey, 1996). There is great variety in patterns of results across judgment domains (weather forecasting is different from internal medicine is different from college admissions is different from livestock pricing) and across judges (there are big individual differences in the weights placed on different types of informational cues, and there are some, but only a few, truly remarkably expert judges, whereas there are many so-called experts who are no better than complete novices; cf. Sherden, 1998). At the risk of overgeneralization, we offer here are some conclusions about typical judgment habits that are true of both amateur and expert judgment:

1. Judges (even experts) tend to rely on relatively few cues (3 to 5). There are some exceptions to this generalization, for example, in weather forecasting and livestock quality judgments. We believe that judgments are sensitive to more cue information in these exceptional domains because training for judgment involves immediate, precise feedback to the people learning to make the judgments (unlike, e.g., training in medical diagnosis, admissions decisions, or financial forecasting, where feedback is usually delayed and often never available).

2. Few judgment policies exhibit nonlinearity—again, contrary to many judges' own beliefs about their policies.

3. Judges lack insight into their policies—they are unable to estimate their own relative "cue utilization weights" accurately, especially when they are expert and highly experienced.

4. Many studies (e.g., students' judgments of physical attractiveness, professors' graduate school admissions judgments, radiologists' judgments of tumor malignancy) reveal large individual differences in types of policies (patterns of cue utilization weights) and low interjudge agreement on the judgments themselves. In important domains like medical diagnosis, this conclusion is disturbing, because we would like our medical experts to agree with one another (and with biological theory) when they make diagnoses and write prescriptions. At a minimum, interjudge disagreements tell us someone is wrong and undermine our confidence in all judgments.

5. When associated, but undiagnostic, irrelevant information is presented to judges, they become more confident in the accuracy of their judgments, although true accuracy does not increase.

The picture of the expert painted in broad brush strokes by this research is relatively unflattering. The important message is that before we draw any conclusions about a judge's performance (whether it is the automatic acceptance of claims of wisdom and accuracy or the blanket assumption that all judges are inept) we need to take a careful look at that performance and we should be prepared for surprises. Vaunted experts with extensive credentials and impressive demeanors may be no better than college sophomores at their specialty judgments, but there are some true experts who are certainly worth heeding or hiring.

3.3 CAPTURING JUDGMENT IN STATISTICAL MODELS

Historically, some of the earliest psychological research on judgment addressed the question of whether trained experts' predictions were better than statistically derived weighted averages of the relevant predictors. Employing multiple regression analyses in the lens model framework, we can ask the question, which is better, a linear statistical model summarizing the left-hand side of the lens model diagram or the human judgment on the right-hand side of the diagram? This question has been studied extensively by psychologists, educators, and others interested in predicting such outcomes as college success, parole violation, psychiatric diagnosis, physical diagnosis and prognosis, and business success and failure. In the initial studies, the information on which clinical experts based their predictions was the same as that used to construct linear models. Typically, this information consisted of test scores or biographical facts, but some studies included observer ratings of specific attributes as well. All of these variables could easily be represented by (coded as) numbers having positive or negative relationships to the criterion outcome to be predicted. (Higher test scores and grade point averages predict better performance in subsequent academic work; a higher leukocyte count predicts greater severity of Hodgkin's disease; more gray hair and more wrinkles predict more biological years.)

In 1954, Paul Meehl published a highly influential book in which he reviewed approximately 20 such studies comparing the clinical judgments of people (expert psychologists and psychiatrists in his study) with the linear statistical model based on only relationships in the empirical data on the events of interest (the left side of the lens model). *In all studies, the statistical method provided more accurate predictions, or the two methods tied.* About 12 years later, Jack Sawyer (1966) reviewed 45 studies comparing clinical and statistical prediction. Again, there was *not a single study* in which clinical global judgment was superior to the statistical prediction (termed "mechanical combination" by Sawyer). Unlike Meehl, Sawyer did not limit his review to studies in which the clinical judge's information was identical to that on which the statistical prediction was based; he even included two studies in which the clinical judge had access to *more* information (an interview with each person being judged) but still did *worse*. (In one of these, the performance of 37,500 sailors in World War II in Navy "elementary school" was better predicted from past grades or test scores alone or in combination than from the ratings of judges who both interviewed the sailors and had access to the test or grade information used in the model.)

The near-total lack of validity of the *unstructured* interview as a predictive technique had been documented and discussed by E. Lowell Kelly in 1954 (see, more recently, Hunter & Hunter, 1984; Wiesner & Cronshaw, 1988). There is no evidence that such interviews yield important information beyond that of past behavior, except whether the interviewer likes the interviewee, which *is* important in some contexts. (Some of our students maintain it is necessary to interview people to avoid admitting "nerds" to graduate study, but they cannot explain how they would spot one or even what they mean by the term.)

A representative study of psychodiagnosis was reported by Lewis Goldberg (1968), a professor of psychology who was influential in the early history of the use of linear models to analyze judgment. Goldberg asked experienced clinical diagnosticians to distinguish between neurosis and psychosis on the basis of personality test scores (a decision that has important implications for treatment and, in current psychotherapeutic practice, for insurance coverage). He constructed a simple linear decision rule (add the patient's scores on three scales together and subtract the scores on two other scales; if the result exceeds 45, diagnose the patient psychotic). Starting with a new sample of patient cases and using the patients' discharge diagnoses as the to-be-predicted criterion value, Goldberg's rule achieved an accuracy rate of approximately 70%. The human judges, in comparison, performed at rates from slightly above chance (50%) to 67% correct. Not even the best human judge was better than the mechanical add-and-subtract rule.

Paul Werner, Terrence Rose, and Jerome Yesavage (1983) provide a truly dramatic example of the superiority of the linear statistical model to human expert judgment in the clinical people-prediction domain. Thirty experienced clinical psychologists and psychiatrists were presented with the problem of predicting the dangerousness of 40 newly admitted male psychiatric patients. The prediction of potential violence is an important and common clinical judgment in psychiatric and criminal contexts. The experts were provided with 19 cues, mostly derived from the judgments of psychiatrists who interviewed the patients on admission, as well as information about whether violent conduct was part of the behavioral pattern that led to hospitalization in the first place. The to-be-predicted criterion was the commission of a violent assault on another person during the first week of hospitalization. Using correlation coefficients to summarize accuracy, the average human judge predicted violence at a level of +.12, hardly impressive (0.00 indicates "zero" predictability), and the most accurate human scored +.36 on the correlation accuracy measure. The most interesting finding was that the linear statistical model, based on exactly the same evidence available to the clinicians, achieved an accuracy of +.82 on the correlation index. And also of interest, the humans' judgment policies were essentially linear, just not very good.

Another study of clinical versus statistical prediction was conducted by Hillel Einhorn (1972). He studied predictions of the longevity of patients with Hodgkin's disease during an era when the disease was invariably fatal (prior to the late 1960s). (Einhorn had a personal interest in the subject matter, as he had just been diagnosed with the condition, which in 1987 took his life.) A world expert on Hodgkin's disease and two assistants rated nine characteristics of biopsies (cues) taken from patients and then made a global rating of the "overall severity" of the disease process for each patient. On the patients' deaths, Einhorn correlated the global ratings with their longevity. Although a rating of "overall severity" is not precisely the same as a prediction of time until death, it should predict that. (At least, the world expert thought it would.) Einhorn found that it does not. In fact, the slight trend was in the *wrong* direction; higher severity ratings were associated with longer survival time. In contrast, a multiple regression analysis based on the nine biopsy characteristics scaled by the doctors succeeded in predicting how long the patients lived. The prediction was not strong, but it was statistically reliable and significantly more accurate than the physicians' severity ratings.

Another striking example comes from a study by Robert Libby (1976). He asked 43 bank loan officers, in banks with assets up to $4 billion, to predict which 30 of 60 firms would go bankrupt within 3 years of a financial report. The loan officers requested, and were provided with, various financial ratios (cues), for example, the ratio of liquid assets to total assets, to make their predictions. Their individual judgments were 75% correct, but a regression analysis based on the financial ratios themselves was 82% accurate. In fact, the ratio of assets to liabilities *alone* predicted 80% correctly.

These studies show that experts correctly select the variables that are important in making predictions, but that a linear model combines these variables in a way that is superior to the global judgments of these very same experts. The finding that linear combination is superior to global judgment is general; it has been replicated in diverse contexts. Not in psychology, but in some medical and business contexts, global judgment has been found to be superior; in those particular contexts, however, the people making the global judgments had access to some observational or "inside" information not available to the linear combination, and in at least one context, once this information was subsequently included in the mechanical model, its predictions again became superior (in predicting 24-hour survival on an intensive care unit; see Knaus & Wagner, 1989). Meehl has updated his classic review several times, and as recently as 1996, he and a colleague concluded, "Empirical comparisons of the accuracy of the two methods (136 studies over a wide range of predictions) show that the mechanical method is almost invariably equal to or superior to the clinical method" (Grove & Meehl, 1996, p. 293). The practical lesson from these studies is that in many clinical judgment situations, we should ask the experts what cues to use but let a mechanical model combine the information from those cues to make the judgment.

3.4   HOW DO STATISTICAL
MODELS BEAT HUMAN JUDGMENT?

Why is it that linear models predict better than clinical experts? We can explain this finding by hypothesizing a mathematical principle, a principle of "nature," and a psychological principle.

The mathematical principle is that both monotone relationships of individual variables and monotone ("ordinal") interactions are well approximated by linear models. Such interactions are illustrated in Figure 3.2. Two factors "interact" when their combined impact is greater than the sum of their separate impacts, but they do not interact in the sense that the *direction* in which one variable is related to the outcome is dependent on the magnitude of the other variable. It is not, for example, true of monotone interactions that high-highs are similar to low-lows, but that high-highs (or low-lows) are much higher (or lower) than would be predicted by a separate analysis of each variable. If high-highs are similar to

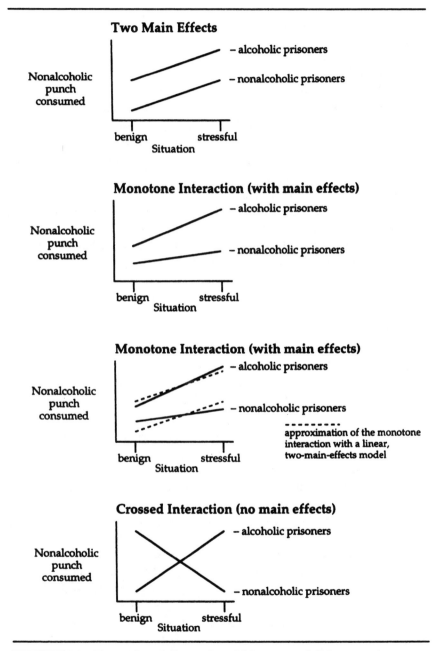

FIGURE 3.2. Examples of Crossed and Noncrossed (Monotone) Interaction Effects

low-lows, the interaction, illustrated in the lowest graph in Figure 3.2, is termed *crossed*.

For example, a doctoral student of one of us (Dawes) subjected identified alcoholic and nonalcoholic prisoners to a benign or stressful experience (Glass, 1967). He then had them spend 20 minutes in a waiting room before being interviewed by a psychologist about their experience. A nonalcoholic punch was available in the waiting room, and the behavior of interest was how much punch the prisoners consumed. The alcoholic and nonalcoholic prisoners drank virtually identical amounts after experiencing the benign situation. After the stressful situation, however, the alcoholic prisoners drank twice as much punch as the nonalcoholics did (the middle two panels in Figure 3.2). Thus a true monotone interaction was found between stress and drinking behavior of diagnosed alcoholics: You could not predict the amount of punch consumed by considering each factor independently; in the example, you make a distinctive prediction for the doubly potent alcoholism *plus* stress combination. But the data analysis indicated that this interaction could *be well approximated* by the two independent main effects, that is, alcoholics drank more punch and all prisoners drank more punch after being stressed. And they approximate main effects—a situation in which only main effects are present is a true linear situation. (A related mathematical principle is that coefficients are not as important in linear models as their signs. Thus arbitrary [with randomly chosen weights] linear models can approximate monotone interaction effects.)

To clarify our *mathematical principle*, consider the top panel in Figure 3.2. This depicts a pure main effects situation in which the two variables have simple, independent effects: Alcoholics drink more (no matter what), and prisoners in a stressful situation drink more (no matter what). A linear, weight-and-add model would fit these data perfectly. The bottom panel depicts the most complicated situation, where we imagine a crossover interaction. In benign situations, alcoholics drink the least punch; but the pattern reverses in the stressful situation, where alcoholics drink the most punch. No linear model can "capture" this pattern of effects, even approximately. But true crossover patterns of causal relationships are very, very rare. As we just noted, however, the non-crossover relationships (which are much more prevalent) can be well approximated by linear relationships (see the dotted lines in the lower "monotone interaction" panel of Figure 3.2. (See any good introduction to statistics and experimental data analysis for an exposition of the nature of interaction effects, e.g., Glenberg, 1996. Robert Abelson's 1995 *Statistics as Principled Argument* contains an especially insightful discussion of interactions and their interpretation in behavioral research.)

The *principle of nature* that partly explains the success of linear models is that most interactions that exist are, in fact, monotone. It is easy to hypothesize crossed interactions but extraordinarily difficult to find them, especially in the areas of psychology and social interactions. Because the optimal amount of any variable does not usually depend on the values of the others, what interactions there are tend to be monotone. And although a number of crossed interactions have been hypothesized in social interactions (e.g., "authoritarian" leadership is more effective in some types of situations whereas "libertarian" leadership works better in others), they tend to be supported only by verbal claims and selective post hoc data analysis. In fact, interactions of *any* sort tend to be ephemeral, as was discovered by Goldberg (1972) in his analysis of how the "match" between teaching style and student characteristics predicts student success. Of 38 interactions he thought he had discovered in the first half of an extensive data set, only 24 "cross-validated" *in the right direction* in the second half (not significantly different from the chance expectation of 19 cross-validations).

The *psychological principle* that might explain the predictive success of linear models is that people have a great deal of difficulty in attending to two or more noncomparable aspects of a stimulus or situation at once. ("separable" and "incommensurate" are other technical labels for this relationship between stimulus dimensions). Attention shifts from one aspect to another and back again. For example, when Roger Shepard (1964) asked subjects to make similarity judgments about circles of various sizes containing "spokes" at various angles (the stimuli looked like one-handed clock faces), the subjects attended to size *or* to angle but *not to both*. The experience of people evaluating academic applicants is similar. Often, they anchor their judgment on a particularly high or low grade point average (GPA) or test score and then adjust in light of less salient information in the applicant's folder. In fact, how *could* an admissions committee member rationally integrate test information and GPA information without knowing something about the distribution and predictability of each in the applicant pool? (The need for such comparisons is one reason why a purely statistical integration is superior to a global judgment. The statistical model uses valid, independent information from as many cues as convey such information, is "calibrated" to the ranges of values on all the variables available in the situation, and operates relentlessly and consistently.)

Given that monotone interactions can be well approximated by linear models (a statistical fact) *and* because most interactions that do exist in nature are monotone *and* because people have difficulty integrating information from noncomparable dimensions, it follows that linear models outperform clinical judgment. The only way to avoid this broad conclusion is to claim that training makes experts superior to other people at integrating information (as opposed to knowing what information to look at). But there is no evidence that experts *think differently* from others (remember the example of chess grand masters from Chapter 1; grand masters did *not* possess special visual or intellectual skills, but they knew much more than novices about "where to look" and they had much more knowledge in long-term memory about specific chessboard positions).

A further, more speculative conjecture is that not only is the experienced world fairly linear, but our judgment habits are adaptively linear too. Thus the linear models that are so popular to describe the right-hand, cue-utilization side of the lens model diagram convey a correct image of the human mind. The mind is in many essential respects a linear weighting and adding device. In fact, much of what we know about the neural networks in the physical brain suggests that a natural computation for such a "machine" is weighting and adding, exactly the fundamental processes that are well described by linear equations.

3.5   PRACTICAL IMPLICATIONS OF THE SURPRISING SUCCESS OF THE LINEAR MODEL

An enormous and almost unequivocal research literature implies expert judgments are rarely impressively accurate and virtually never better than a mechanical judgment rule. As Meehl (1986) put it 40 years after his "disturbing little book" was published: "There is no controversy in social science which shows such a large body of qualitatively diverse studies coming out so uniformly in the same direction as this one" (p. 373). The implication for practice seems clear: Whenever possible, human judges should be replaced by simple linear models. We put in the "whenever possible" qualification only because we also believe that some empirical observations should be made before any important decision is made in a new way. We do not advocate the simple, complete replacement of human judges. There will always be special cases and changes in the nature of the task environment (perhaps a new diagnostic method is invented) that require oversight and adjustment. We believe, however, that a substantial amount of time and other resources is squandered on expert judgments that could be made more equitably, more efficiently, and more accurately by the statistical models we humans construct than by we humans alone.

We advocate the broader use of actuarial, mechanical prediction methods. Research by one of us (Dawes) shows that it is not even necessary to use statistically optimal weights in linear models for them to outperform experts. For years, the nagging thought kept recurring: Maybe *any* linear model outperforms the experts. The possibility seemed absurd, but when a research assistant had some free time, Dawes asked him to go to several data sources and to construct linear models with weights "determined randomly except for sign." (It seemed reasonable that in any prediction context of interest, the direction in which each cue predicted the criterion would be known in advance.) After the first 100 such models outperformed human clinical judges, Dawes constructed 20,000 such "random linear models"—10,000 by choosing coefficients at random from a normal distribution, and 10,000 by choosing coefficients at random from a rectangular distribution. Dawes used three data sets: (a) final diagnoses of neurosis versus psychosis of roughly 860 psychiatric inpatients, predicted from scores on the Minnesota Multiphasic Personality Inventory (MMPI) (the same set used by Goldberg in constructing his "add three, subtract two" rule); (b) first-year graduate school grade point averages of psychology students at the University of Illinois, predicted from 10 variables assessing academic aptitude prior to admissions and personality characteristics assessed shortly thereafter; and (c) faculty ratings of performance of graduate students who had been at the University of Oregon for 2 to 5 years, predicted from undergraduate grade point averages, Graduate Record Examination (GRE) scores, and a measure of the selectivity of their undergraduate institutions. All three predictions had been made both by linear models and by human experts ranging from graduate students to eminent clinical psychologists. On average, the random linear models accounted for 150% more variance between criteria and predictions than did the holistic clinical evaluations of the trained judges. For mathematical reasons, *unit weighting* (i.e., each variable is standardized and weighted +1 or –1 depending on direction) provided even better accountability, averaging 261% more variance. Unit or random linear models are termed *improper* because their coefficients (weights) are not based on statistical techniques that optimize prediction. The research indicates that such improper models are almost as good as proper ones (and in some inhospitable judgment environments, even better; Gigerenzer, Todd, and the ABC Research Group, 1999).

Another effective, though "improper," approach is to fit a linear model to a large sample of a human judge's own judgments and then to use that model-of-the-judge instead of the original judge. This method is called *bootstrapping* (not to be confused with the "statistical bootstrap" introduced by Efron, 1988), and it too almost invariably outperforms human experts, including the person who was used as the source of judgments for the original model. Again, there are several interpretations of the success of bootstrap models, including their reliability and imperturbability (the equations are not susceptible to bad moods or fatigue) and the fact that the abstracted judgment policy may better represent the human judge's true understanding of the process than either subjective reports or case-by-case explanations. But most of the success can probably be attributed to the remarkable robustness and power of (even improper) linear models that derives from their mathematical properties and their match to the underlying structure of the events in the to-be-judged environment.

3.6   OBJECTIONS AND REBUTTALS

The conclusion that random or unit or "captured" (bootstrapped) weights outperform global judgments of trained experts is not a popular one with experts or with people relying on them. All of these findings have had almost no effect on the *practice* of expert judgment. Meehl was elected president of the American Psychological Association at a young age, but the implications of his work were ignored by his fellow psychologists. States license psychologists, physicians, and psychiatrists to make global judgments of the form "It is my opinion that . . . ," in other words, to make judgments inferior to those that could be made by a layperson with a programmable calculator. People have great misplaced confidence in their own global judgments, a confidence that is strong enough to dismiss an impressive body of research findings and to dominate predictions in our legal and medical systems.

There are many reasons for the resistance to actuarial, mechanical judgment models. First, they are an affront to the narcissism (and a threat to the income) of many experts. One common defense of expert judgment is to challenge the expertise of the experts making the global predictions in the particular studies. "Minnesota clinicians!" snorted a professor of psychology at the University of Michigan. Little did he know that most of the Minnesota clinicians in the study had obtained their PhDs at Michigan. "Had you used Dr. X," the dean of a prestigious medical school informed one of us, "his judgments would have correlated with longevity." In fact, "Dr. X" was the subject of Einhorn's (1972) study of Hodgkin's disease predictions.

Another objection is to maintain that the outcomes better predicted by linear models are all short-term and trivial (such as dying, ending up in jail, or flunking out of school?). The claim is made that "truly important long-term outcomes" can be predicted better by global judgments. But as Jay Russo points out, this objection implies that the long-term future can be predicted better than the short-term future (J. Russo, personal communication). Such prediction is possible for variables such as death (we'll all be dead 100 years from now) and rabies (after the incubation period), but those variables, which are very rare, are *not* of the type predicted in these studies. Moreover, as we come to understand processes (e.g., the existence of the rabies or the AIDS virus in the blood), "incubation period" becomes nothing more than a manner of speech, and aging is more readily predicted than is death.

A final objection is the "10,000 Frenchmen can't be wrong" one. Experts have been revered—and well paid—for years for their "It is my opinion that . . ." judgments. As James March points out, however, such reverence may serve a *purely social function* (J. March, personal communication). People and organizations have to make decisions, often between alternatives that appear equally good or bad. What better way to justify such decisions than to consult an intuitive expert, and the more money she or he charges, the better. "We paid for the best possible medical advice" can be a palliative for a fatal operation (or a losing legal defense), just as throwing the *I Ching* can relieve someone of regretting a bad marriage or a bad career choice. An expert who constructs a linear model is not as impressive as one who gives advice in a "burst" of intuition derived from "years of experience." (One highly paid business expert we know constructs linear models in secret.) We value the global judgment of experts independent of its validity.

But there is also a situational reason for believing in the superiority of global, intuitive judgment. It has to do with the biased availability of feedback. When we construct a linear model in a prediction situation, we know exactly how poorly it predicts. In contrast, our feedback about our global judgments is flawed. Not only do we selectively remember our successes, we often have *no knowledge* of our failures—and any knowledge we do have may serve to "explain" them (away). Who knows what happens to rejected graduate school applicants? Professors have access only to accepted ones, and if the professors are doing a good job, the accepted ones will likewise do well—reinforcing the impression of the professors' good judgment. What happens to people misdiagnosed as "psychotic"? If they are lucky, they will disappear from the sight of the authorities diagnosing them; if not, they are likely to be placed in an environment where they may soon become psychotic. Finally, therapy patients who commit suicide were too sick to begin with—as is easily established from an ex post perusal of their files.

The feedback problem is well illustrated by an article in praise of "intuition" by Nancy Hathaway (1984):

> Most people rarely receive intuitions so major that they change their lives. From time to time, however, it does happen. There are even legends of people following their intuitions in business decisions: the late Ray Kroc, who bought McDonald's despite evidence offered by his advisors that it would be a bad investment, did it because "I felt in my funny bone that it was a sure thing." (p. D3)

All right, so we know about Ray Kroc. But how many investors had "funny bone" feelings that led to their ruin? We don't know (absent the type of *prospective* study similar to those done of linear models). If 36 people have an intuitive feeling that the next roll of the dice will be snake eyes and are willing to bet even odds on that hunch, on the average one will win. That person is the one most likely to come to our attention; for one thing, the others probably won't talk about it much.

Another telling example is provided by a letter to "Dear Abby" published in 1975:

DEAR ABBY: While standing in a checkout line in a high-grade grocery store, I saw a woman directly in front of me frantically rummaging around in her purse, looking embarrassed. It seems her groceries had already been checked, and she was a dollar short. I felt sorry for her, so I handed her a dollar. She was very grateful, and insisted on writing my name and address on a loose piece of paper. She stuck it in her purse and said, "I promise I'll mail you a dollar tomorrow." Well, that was three weeks ago, and I still haven't heard from her! Abby, I think I'm a fairly good judge of character, and I just didn't peg her as the kind that would beat me out of a dollar. The small amount of money isn't important, but what it did to my faith in people is. I'd like your opinion.

—SHY ONE BUCK

(Taken from The DEAR ABBY column by Abigal Van Buren.
© UNIVERSAL PRESS SYNDICATE. Reprinted
with permission. All rights reserved.)

Note that Shy One Buck did not lose faith in his or her ability to predict future behavior on the basis of almost no information whatsoever but, rather, lost faith in people. Shy One Buck still believes he or she is a "good judge of character." It is just that other people are no damn good.

Hillel Einhorn and Robin Hogarth (1978) have examined the availability of feedback sources and demonstrated how they *systematically* operate to make intuitive judgment appear valid. Their prototype is of the waiter who decides he can judge whether people tip well from the way they dress. A judgment that some people are poor tippers leads to inferior service, which in turn leads to poor tips—thereby "validating" the waiter's judgment. (Not all prophecies are self-fulfilling—there must be a mechanism, and intuitive judgment often provides one; it is also a possible mechanism for some self-negating prophecies, such as the feeling that one is invulnerable no matter how many risks one takes while driving.)

In contrast, the systematic predictions of linear models yield data on just how poorly they predict. In Einhorn's study, only 18% of the variance in longevity of Hodgkin's disease patients is predicted by the best linear model (Section 3.2), but that is opposed to 0% for the world's foremost authority. Such results bring us abruptly to an unpleasant conclusion: A lot of outcomes about which we care deeply are not very predictable. For example, it is not comforting to members of a graduate school admissions committee to know that only 23% of the variance in later faculty ratings of a student can be predicted by a unit weighting of the student's undergraduate GPA, his or her GRE score, and a measure of the student's undergraduate institution selectivity—but that is opposed to 4% based on those committee members' global ratings of the applicant. We *want* to predict outcomes important to us. It is only rational to conclude that if one method (a linear model) does not predict well, something else may do better. What is not rational—in fact, it's irrational—is to conclude that this "something else" necessarily exists and, in the absence of any positive supporting evidence, is intuitive global judgment.

One important lesson of the many studies of human judgment is that outcomes are not all that predictable; there is a great deal of "irreducible uncertainty" in the external world, on the left-hand side of the lens model diagram. Academic success, for example, is influenced by whom one shares an office with as a graduate student, by which professors happen to have positions available for research assistants, by the person or people with whom one has libidinal involvement (often met on a "chance" basis), by the relative strengths of those with whom one competes for one's first job (as judged by the professors who happen to be appointed to the search committee), and so on (Bandura, 1982). Moreover, there are clearly self-exacerbating features to an academic career. A little bit of luck may lead a new PhD to obtain a position in an outstanding university (or an MD, in an outstanding hospital; or a JD, in an outstanding law firm), and the consequent quality of colleagues may then significantly reinforce whatever talents the individual brings to the job. (Conversely, a little bit of bad luck may saddle the new PhD with a nine-course-per-year teaching load, inadequate institutional resources for scholarly productivity, and "burnt-out" colleagues. Not many people move from a patent office to a full professorship after publishing a three-page paper as Albert Einstein did.)

One field in which people find linear models of judgment particularly distasteful is in assessing other people. Is it important, for example, to interview students applying for graduate school? In a word, no. What can an interviewer learn in a half hour that is not present in the applicant's lengthy past record? As Len Rorer points out, belief that one's own interviewing skills provide access to such information is grandiose self-confidence (L. Rorer, personal communication). Moreover, even if the interviewer thinks he or she has picked up some highly positive or negative quality in the interview, is it really fair to judge applicants *on the impression they make in a single interview conducted by one interviewer,* as opposed to a record of actual accomplishment (or failure) over a 4-year college career? A GPA is a "mere number," but it represents the combined opinions of some 50 or so professors over several years; some professors may be biased for or against particular students, but surely a combined impression based on actual work over time is fairer than one based on a brief interaction with a single person (who has biases and unreliabilities too). Furthermore, GPAs predict better than interviews. Is it fair to judge someone on the basis of something that does not work?

A colleague in medical decision making tells of an investigation he was asked to make by the dean of a large and prestigious medical school to try to determine why the school was unsuccessful in recruiting female students. The researcher studied the problem statistically "from the outside" and identified a major source of the problem. One of the older professors had cut back on his practice to devote time to interviewing applicants to the school. He assessed such characteristics as "emotional maturity," "seriousness of interest in medicine," and "neuroticism." Whenever he interviewed an unmarried female applicant, he tended to conclude that she was "immature." When he interviewed a married one, he tended to conclude that she was "not sufficiently interested in medicine," and when he interviewed a divorced one, he tended to conclude that she was "neurotic." Not many women received positive evaluations from this interviewer, although *of course* his judgments had *nothing* to do with gender (sarcasm intended).

3.7   THE ROLE OF JUDGMENT IN CHOICES AND DECISIONS

We have restricted our focus in this chapter to the judgment of events and outcomes. But the implications also apply to the larger framework of decision and choice between alternate courses of action. First, linear models often provide a valid description of the psychological processes of judgment of events in the external world. But they also provide an effective method to predict our own evaluations and preferences, events in the "internal" subjective world. If we wish to make choices involving multiple factors, we would do well to construct *our own* (improper) linear models. This is, in essence, what Benjamin Franklin advised (we discuss his advice more fully in Chapter 11), and his advice is echoed in popular books on decision making that recommend the deliberate listing of possible consequences of choices and of our own evaluations, weighting the consequences by their importance and likelihood, and "adding up" the totals for each alternative course of action. Decision involves predicting our future "states of mind." Given that linear models predict better than intuitive judgment in situations where the accuracy of prediction can be checked, why not this one as well?

The philosophy presented in this chapter is based on the premise that "mere numbers" are in fact neither good nor bad. Just as numbers can be used to achieve either constructive or destructive goals in other contexts, they can be used for good or ill in decision making. Research indicates that numbers in a linear model can be well used in making predictions. The implication that they can serve well also in choice and preference contexts is immediate. Using them, however, requires us to overcome a view that the "mysteries of the human mind" allow us to reach superior conclusions without relying on deliberate, controlled thought processes. The mysteries are there, but not in this context. We are, all of us, overconfident in our abilities to judge. To do well by ourselves and to treat other persons fairly, we must overcome the attitude that leads us to reject adding numbers to make judgments and to experience no more shame when we use numbers thus than when we use them in determining how to construct a bridge that will not collapse.

REFERENCES

Abelson, R. P. (1995). *Statistics as principled argument.* Hillsdale, NJ: Lawrence Erlbaum.

Bandura, A. (1982). The psychology of chance encounters and life paths. *American Psychologist, 37,* 747-755.

Brunswik, E., Hammond, K. R., & Stewart, T. R. (2000). *The essential Brunswik: Beginnings, explications, and applications.* New York: Oxford University Press.

Cooksey, R. W. (1996). *Judgment analysis: Theory, methods, and applications.* San Diego, CA: Academic Press.

Diamond, J. (1989, April). The price of human folly. *Discover,* pp. 73-77.

Efron, B. (1988). Bootstrap confidence intervals: Good or bad? *Psychological Bulletin, 104,* 293-296.

Einhorn, H. J. (1972). Expert measurement and mechanical combination. *Organizational Behavior and Human Performance, 13,* 171-192.

Einhorn, H. J., & Hogarth, R. M. (1978). Confidence in judgment: The illusion of validity *Psychological Review, 85,* 395-416.

Freedman, D., Pisani, R., Purves, R., & Adhikari, A. (1991). *Statistics* (2nd ed.). New York: W. W. Norton.

Gigerenzer, G., Todd, P. M., & the ABC Research Group (1999). *Simple heuristics that make us smart.* New York: Oxford University Press.

Glass, L. B. (1967). *The generality of oral consummatory behavior of alcoholics under stress.* Unpublished doctoral dissertation, University of Michigan.

Glenberg, A. M. (1996). *Learning from data: An introduction to statistical reasoning* (2nd ed.). Hillsdale, NJ: Lawrence Erlbaum.

Goldberg, L. R. (1968). Simple models or simple processes? Some research on clinical judgments. *American Psychologist, 23,* 483-496.

Goldberg, L. R. (1972). Student personality, characteristics and optimal college learning conditions: An extensive search for trait-by-treatment interaction effects. *Instructional Science, 1,* 153-210.

Hathaway, N. (1984, October 31). Intuition. *San Francisco Chronicle,* p. D3.

Grove, W. M., & Meehl, P. E. (1996). Comparative efficiency of informal (subjective, impressionistic) and formal (mechanical, algorithmic) prediction procedures: The clinical-statistical controversy. *Psychology, Public Policy, and Law, 2,* 293-323.

Hunter, J. E., & Hunter, R. F. (1984). Validity and utility of alternative predictors of job performance. *Psychological Bulletin, 96,* 72-98.

Huntford, R. (1999). *The last place on earth.* New York: Modern Library.

Kelly, E. L. (1954). Evaluation of the interview as a selection technique. *Proceedings of the 1953 Invitational Conference on Testing Problems.* Princeton, NJ: Educational Testing Service.

Knaus, W. A., & Wagner, D. P. (1989). APACHE: A nonproprietary measure of severity of illness. *Annals of Internal Medicine, 110,* 327-328.

Libby, R. (1976). Man versus model of man: Some conflicting evidence. *Organizational Behavior and Human Performance, 16,* 1-12.

Meehl, P. E. (1954). *Clinical versus statistical prediction: A theoretical analysis and a review of the evidence.* Minneapolis: University of Minnesota Press.

Meehl, P. E. (1986). Causes and effects of my disturbing little book. *Journal of Personality Assessment, 50,* 370-375.

Pepper, S. C. (1942). *World hypotheses.* Berkeley: University of California Press.

Pinker, S. (1997). *How the mind works.* New York: W. W. Norton.

Savours, A. (Ed.). (1975). *Scott's last voyage.* New York: Praeger.

Sawyer, J. (1966). Measurement and prediction, clinical and statistical. *Psychological Bulletin, 66,* 178-200.

Shepard, R. N. (1964). Attention and the metric structure of the stimulus. *Journal of Mathematical Psychology, 1,* 54-87.

Sherden, W. A. (1998). *The fortune sellers: The big business of buying and selling predictions.* New York: John Wiley.

Werner, P. D., Rose, T. L., & Yesavage, J. A. (1983). Reliability, accuracy, and decision-making strategy in clinical predictions of imminent dangerousness.
   Journal of Consulting and Clinical Psychology, 51, 815-825.
Wiesner, W. H., & Cronshaw, S. F. (1988). A meta-analytic investigation of the
   impact of interview format and degree of structure on the validity of the
   employment interview. *Journal of Occupational Psychology, 61,* 275-290.

JUDGMENTS FROM MEMORY

*Things seem to happen more frequently in the future
than they did in the past.*

—Anonymous

4.1 GOING BEYOND THE INFORMATION GIVEN

Our species has an unparalleled capacity to infer the attributes of objects
or events that are hidden or haven't yet occurred. This ability to "go
beyond the information given to the senses" is a natural extension of our
perceptual processes. In support of this judgment capacity, we have several truly fundamental, virtually automatic cognitive abilities: the ability
to estimate frequencies, the ability to judge similarities between objects or
events, the ability to recognize a previously experienced situation or individual, and the ability to infer causal relationships. These processes occur
with little conscious effort and are "wired into" our brains so deeply that
they do not change much across the healthy adult life span. Consider our
natural ability to estimate frequencies. Our perceptual and memory systems are tuned to automatically record the ambient frequencies of many
events as we experience them. Of course, many of these frequencies are of
little use—for example, frequencies of individual letters in texts we read,
the number of fast food restaurants we pass as we travel to work, and the
number of movies that have played on campus during the past semester.

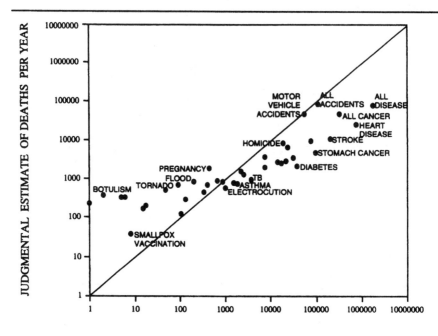

FIGURE 4.1. Frequency Estimate Curves for Two Very Different
                "Events"

NOTE: The axes of these graphs are on logarithmic scales to make the relationships more visible, but the basic pattern of overestimation of low frequencies and underestimation of high frequencies is clear in both graphs.

Others may be crucial for our survival. At least in some ancestral environments that were important in our evolution, it would have been important to notice the numbers of predators encountered at water holes, the quantities of edible plants in different parts of a forest, and other essential occurrences.

A single psychophysical function relating objective quantities to subjective memory-based estimates is characteristic of almost all frequency of occurrence estimates. At very low end of the objective scale, frequency estimates tend to be overestimates. As the to-be-estimated number of events increases, our subjective estimates exhibit a tendency to err in the direction of underestimation. The curves displayed in the two panels of Figure 4.1 summarize two very different kinds of memory-based estimates to illustrate the generality of this pattern: of the frequencies of

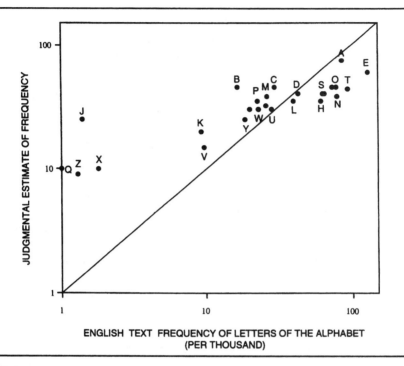

FIGURE 4.1. Continued

fatalities in various cause-of-death categories (e.g., heart attack, automobile accident, suicide) and of letter frequencies in popular texts (e.g., samples of newspaper articles or best-selling fiction). These same psychophysical curves have been observed in hundreds of other estimation situations, suggesting that we have some very general frequency estimation habits.

These estimation curves are a bit different when the to-be-judged events are presented "online," when the cues on which the estimate is based are directly available to our perception. Under these conditions, small objective frequencies (up to five events) are estimated with high accuracy. In fact, some of the earliest studies of short-term memory conducted by empiricist philosophers asked for estimates of the number of pebbles in a handful thrown down in front of the subject and then quickly covered up. The almost-perfect accuracy for estimates of up to five pebbles was taken as a measure of the "scope of apprehension." When the number of to-be-estimated events exceeds about 10 items, however, the tendency to underestimate the objective total starts to appear, as in the memory-based function. When there are more than about seven items (often cited as the capacity of short-term, immediately conscious "working memory"), a deliberate estimation strategy is used to make the judgment.

In Chapter 3, we introduced the general lens model for all judgments. In this chapter, we begin to provide more detailed "computational information-processing models" of the mental processes that link cues to judgments (the cue utilization processes on the right side of the lens model diagram). Following the insights of Amos Tversky and Daniel Kahneman (1974), we believe that a good account of the underlying cognitive judgment processes is provided by assuming that we have a "cognitive toolbox" of mental heuristics stored in long-term memory. These "tools," or judgment heuristics, are acquired over a lifetime of experience making judgments. They tell us what information to seek or select in the environment and how to integrate several sources of information to infer the characteristics of events that are not directly available to perception. We learn some of these cognitive tools from trial-and-error experience, some as folklore from our family or peers, and some through deliberate instruction. Some are primarily controlled or deliberate (e.g., the algorithm we learned in school to do long division, the strategies we use to decide whether to bet or fold a poker hand); some are automatic and mostly implicit (e.g., the unconscious habits we use to judge whether another person is lying, the intuitive rules we use to estimate how much salt to add to a dish we are cooking).

The notion is that when we encounter a situation in which a judgment is needed, we select a tool from our cognitive toolbox that is suited to the judgment (Figure 4.2). As we will see, usually there are several cognitive tools that could be used to make any particular judgment. For many everyday judgments, we use heuristic strategies because they are relatively easy in mental effort, and under most everyday conditions they provide good estimates. But as Tversky and Kahneman (1974) wrote in their classic *Science* article introducing such cognitive heuristics: "In general, these heuristics are quite useful, but sometimes they lead to severe and systematic errors" (p. 1124).

In the next four chapters, we introduce the major judgment heuristics that have been studied, describe some of the situations in which they are used to make judgments, and point out systematic biases that are introduced into estimates and predictions when we rely on them. The heuristics "explain," in cognitive detail, the cue utilization processes summarized by statistical, algebraic equations in the lens model framework.

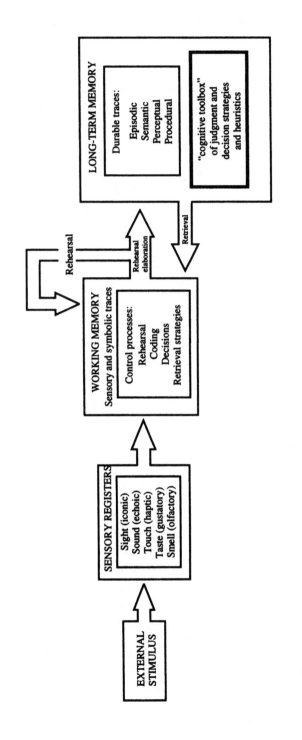

FIGURE 4.2. An Overview of the Human Information-Processing System, Highlighting the Location of a "Cognitive Toolbox" of Judgment Procedures, Strategies, and Heuristics

4.2 AVAILABILITY OF MEMORIES

Many of the judgments we make are memory-based in the sense that we don't have the "data" necessary to make the judgment right in front of us, but we have learned information in the past, now stored in long-term memory, that is relevant to the judgments. Sometimes, all we do is to rely on the ease with which information can be brought to mind to make judgments. When we think about an airplane flight, the recent, vividly remembered crash of an airliner bound for Egypt comes to mind and we overestimate the risks of air travel. We ask ourselves, is the divorce rate increasing? Several vivid memories flood our consciousness, and we judge the rate is high and increasing. This simple form of associative thinking is called the "availability heuristic" by researchers; we rely on "ease of retrieval" to make a remarkable variety of judgments.

Which is more common: murder or suicide? Statistics indicate that many more people commit suicide than are murdered (and the ratio is probably underestimated due to the tendency to err in the charitable, at least for the still living, direction of classifying ambiguous cases as death by misadventure—How many deaths in single-car accidents are truly suicides, sometimes ascribed to alcohol, even when evidence indicates the drivers may have been drinking to "get up the guts" to kill themselves?). Yet most people estimate that murder is more common. Why? The simplest explanation is that murders get more publicity. Suicides of people who are not well known are rarely reported in newspapers, whereas murders are, regardless of the identity of the victim. This explanation has been supported by the research findings of Barbara Combs and Paul Slovic (1979): People's estimates of frequency of causes of death (Figure 4.1) are correlated with the frequency with which such causes appear in newspapers independent of their actual frequency of occurrence. Thus deaths due to plane crashes; shark attacks; tornadoes; terrorism; and other vivid, much reported causes are overestimated, whereas deaths due to strokes, stomach cancer, household accidents, and lead paint poisoning are underestimated. The sample of experienced information (stored in memory and therefore available at the time of judgment) is biased in the first place.

Cognitive psychologists use flowchart diagrams to keep track of subprocesses and the relationships among them in a larger process or strategy like the availability judgment heuristic. The operations of the availability heuristic can be broken down into seven subprocesses or subroutines: (a) the original acquisition or storage of relevant information in long-term memory; (b) retention, including some forgetting, of the stored

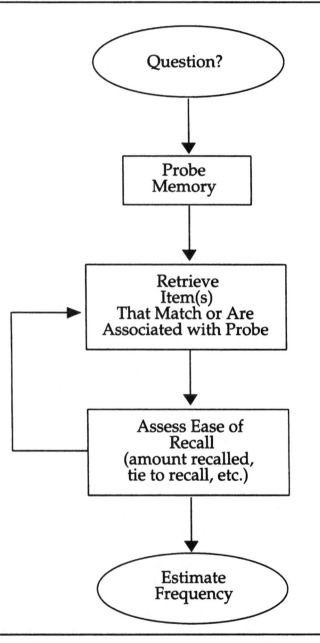

FIGURE 4.3. Flowchart Summarizing the Availability Heuristic
             Judgment Process

NOTE: Arrows indicate the temporal sequence of substages in the global process.

information; (c) recognition of a situation in which stored information is relevant to make a judgment; (d) probing or cueing memory for relevant information; (e) retrieval or activation of items that match or are associated with the memory probe; (f) assessment of the ease or retrieval (based on the amount recalled, time or quickness of recall, subjective vividness of the recalled information, etc.); (g) an estimate of the to-be-judged frequency or probability based on sensed ease of retrieval (the last five subprocesses are summarized in Figure 4.3).

There are several points in the process at which biases might perturb the final judgment: The experienced sample of events stored in long-term memory (the information that is available to be remembered) might be biased, as in our example of suicide versus homicide estimates. The memory cue that is the basis for retrieval might be biased to produce a biased "sample" of remembered events, even if the "population" of events in memory is not itself unrepresentative. Events may vary in their salience or vividness, so that some more salient events dominate the assessment of ease of retrieval. Any of these factors, individually or jointly, may introduce systematic biases into memory-based judgments.

4.3   BIASED SAMPLES IN MEMORY

What proportion of people on welfare have adopted welfare as a way of life? Once again, we must rely on the news, because we cannot know which people we see on the street are on welfare. Stories of "welfare queens" abound. But what do the statistics show? A careful study by Mary Corcoran, Greg Duncan, Gerald Gurin, and Patricia Gurin (1985) of people on government assistance (welfare) programs between 1969 and 1978 showed that only 2.2% of American families were on such programs for the *entire* 8-year period. And in April 1999, President Clinton announced that the total number of people receiving any form of welfare aid had dropped to a 30-year low (approximately 7.6 million recipients).

What proportion of crimes are committed by "ex-mental patients"? By African Americans? When a former mental patient commits a crime—particularly a violent one—the fact that that person has been in a mental hospital is often mentioned by the news media. But when someone has never been in a mental hospital, that is never mentioned: "Archibald Smith, *who has never been in a mental hospital,* was convicted of a heinous . . ." is not very likely. News reports also often mention *minority* race. For example, a news item, broadcast by the Cable News Network on November 29, 1986, described a kidnapping as follows: "Mr. Esquavale left his motor running while he paid for the gas, and a black man jumped into the car and drove off with his children." Systematic studies of media coverage show that the race of minority offenders, especially for violent crimes, is disproportionately reported ("The violent, scary world of local news" described by Franklin Gilliam and Shanto Iyengar, 2000). Wendi Walsh, Mahzarin Banaji, and Tony Greenwald (1995) provided a demonstration of these memory biases by asking college students to circle the names on a list that they recognized as known criminals. Although none of the names on the lists were associated with criminals, the students "remembered" almost twice as many African-American names (e.g., "Tyrone Washington") as other ethnicity names (e.g., "Adam McCarthy," Wayne Chan"). These effects occurred even when the participants in the research were warned, "People who are racist identify more Black than White names; please do not use the race of the name in making your judgment" (Banaji & Bhaskar, 2000, p. 151).

Sociologist Barry Glassner (1999) has documented many of the biases introduced by "if it bleeds, it leads" news reporting and by financially and politically motivated efforts to control the agenda of public fears of crimes, diseases, and other hazards. Is an increase of approximately 700 incidents in 50 states over 7 years an "epidemic" of road rage? Is it conceivable that there is (or ever was) a crisis in children's day care stemming from predatory satanic cults? In 1994, a research team funded by the federal government spent 4 years and $750,000 to reach the conclusion that the myth of satanic conspiracies in day care centers was totally unfounded; not a single verified instance was found (Goodman, Qin, Bottoms, & Shaver, 1994; Nathan & Snedeker, 1995). Are automatic weapon-toting high school students really the first priority in youth safety? (In 1999, approximately 2,000 school-age children were identified as murder victims; only 26 of those died in school settings, 14 of them in one tragic incident at Columbine High School in Littleton, Colorado.) Anthropologist Mary Douglas and sociologist Aaron Wildavsky pointed out that every culture has a store of exaggerated horrors, many of them promoted by special interest factions or to defend cultural ideologies. For example, impure water had been a hazard in 14th-century Europe, but only after Jews were accused of poisoning wells did the citizenry become preoccupied with it as a major problem (Douglas & Wildavsky, 1982, p. 7).

The original news reports are not always ill motivated. We all tend to code and mention characteristics that are unusual (that occur infrequently), and fewer people have been in mental hospitals than haven't, fewer are black than white, and fewer are left-handed than right-handed. (The last, seemingly trivial, example is interesting because there is evidence that even in describing *themselves,* left-handed people will mention that they are left-handed, whereas right-handed people will not bother to mention that they are right-handed; in fact, our moment-to-moment identities seem to be heavily determined by which of our attributes are distinctive and unusual in our current situations; McGuire & McGuire, 1980. A male on a committee composed of females identifies himself as "a man," a Broadway musical fan in a group of rock music fans thinks of herself as a "Broadway type," etc.) The result is that the frequencies of these distinctive characteristics among the class of people considered tend to be overestimated. The overwhelming majority of people on welfare are not "welfare queens"; this very fact leads to publicity for the rare welfare queens who are discovered, which produces a biased sample of welfare queens in our memories, which leads to subsequent overestimation of the number of people who are.

Social psychologists Tiffany Sia, Charles Lord, Kenneth Blessum, Christopher Ratcliff, and Mark Lepper (1997) have found that many socially important attitudes are based on the concrete images and exemplars of policy-relevant categories (we might say the "mental snapshots" of typical category members) that come to mind when a person thinks about a policy topic. Thus for many people the image of a convicted murderer is, "an inhuman beast who has 'crazy eyes,' 'kills for pleasure,' and 'will do it again at every opportunity,'" and this image seems to be the basis of their support for capital punishment. Similarly, Sia et al. found that the images of "welfare recipients," "homosexuals," "televangelists," "African Americans," and many other social categories were correlated with people's attitudes about those categories and the social policies that involved those categories.

Vicarious, vivid instances can have a profound effect even when the person supplied with them knows that they have been generated in an arbitrary or biased manner. Students shown a videotape of a prison guard talking about his attitude toward prisoners generalized to *all* prison guards when answering a questionnaire about the "criminal justice system"— even when they were told, and recalled, that the guard they had seen was picked specifically to be *different from* other prison guards. In the study demonstrating this effect, Ruth Hamil, Timothy Wilson, and Richard

Nisbett (1980) presented one of two videotapes to their subjects: one of a guard (an actor) who was compassionate and concerned with rehabilitation, the other of a guard (also an actor) who scoffed at the idea of rehabilitation and constantly referred to the prisoners as "animals." Some subjects were given no information about how the guard for the interview was chosen; others were told either that he had been chosen because he was *typical* of guards in a particular prison or because he was *different from* most of the guards—for example, that he was "one of the three or four most humane [or inhumane] out of sixty." Subsequent testing revealed that the subjects remembered how the guard was chosen in the latter two conditions. Nevertheless, their subsequent beliefs about the attitudes of prison guards *in general* were related to those expressed by the guard they had witnessed—whether he was one chosen as typical or one chosen as atypical. (There was a difference in the direction of being more influenced by the typical guard, but it was slight.)

A single instance is a poor basis for a generalization, and it is a particularly poor basis when the instance is known to be atypical. Nevertheless, such generalization occurs—often with great ease. It is especially likely to occur when the instance is salient; for example, a non-Jew who believes that he or she has been cheated by a one or two Jewish merchants may readily generalize to form a negative view of all Jews: "A young woman said to me: 'I have had the most horrible experiences with furriers; they robbed me, they burned the fur I entrusted to them. Well, they were all Jews.' But, why did she choose to hate Jews rather than the furriers?" (Sartre, 1948, pp. 11-12). As Richard Nisbett and Lee Ross (1980) point out, rationally defensible deductive logic involves a "specification" from the universal to the particular ("*All* men are mortal, therefore Robyn Dawes is mortal"), but much less reliable induction involves "generalization" from the particular to the universal ("This one Jewish merchant is dishonest, therefore *all* Jewish merchants are dishonest"). But we are prone to do the exact opposite: We "underdeduce" and "overinduce."

Finally, some experience precludes knowledge of certain instances, thus leading to a structural availability bias. In Chapter 1, we mentioned our colleagues who claim to know that no child abusers stop on their own. These colleagues do in fact have experience with abusers. The problem is that these therapists' experience is limited to those who have *not* stopped on their own, and since the therapists' experience is in treatment settings, it is of abusers who cannot *by definition* stop without therapy. Abusers who have stopped on their own without therapy do not enter it and would be unlikely willingly to identify themselves. They are systematically "*unavailable.*"

Another example: Clinical psychologists and psychiatrists in private practice often maintain that low self-esteem "causes" negative social and individual behavior. But they see only people who are in therapy. People who engage in negative behaviors and don't feel bad about such behaviors don't voluntarily seek out therapists. (And therapists in coercive settings, such as residential treatment programs for severely delinquent juveniles, do not report that their clients have low self-esteem, but in fact often the reverse.) Thus most such people seen in voluntary settings have engaged in negative behaviors *and* have a negative self-image. Therapists conclude that the self-image problem is at the basis of the behavior. It can equally well be concluded, however, that the self-image problem leads people to therapy or even that the negative self-image is *valuable* to these people because otherwise they would not be motivated to change their behaviors. Consider the assertion of a former president of the American Psychological Association in his inaugural address: "All alcoholics are obsessive-compulsive when sober." Again, who are the alcoholics with whom he has had contact?—those in a treatment setting.

4.4   BIASED SAMPLING FROM MEMORY

It is obvious that if the sample of information stored in memory is biased (perhaps because certain experiences are precluded or because the information is filtered though the popular media or just the "gossip grapevine"), subsequent memory-based judgments will be biased too. But other characteristics of the memory process can produce systematic biases as well.

How many six-letter English words have the form

$$\_ \, \_ \, \_ \, \_ \, n \, \_$$

Not many? How many six-letter English words have the form

$$\_ \, \_ \, \_ \, ing$$

More? When Amos Tversky and Daniel Kahneman (1973) asked people to make such estimates, they judged six-letter words ending in -*ing* to be much more frequent than six-letter words with -*n*- in the fifth position. (There are, of course, more six-letter words with *n* in the fifth position than six-letter words ending in -*ing*. In fact, it is logically necessary that there are more, for every word ending in -*ing* has *n* in the fifth position, whereas there are in addition six-letter words with *n* in the fifth position that do not end in -*ing*, e.g., *absent*.) It is easier to think of the six-letter words ending in -*ing*, for example, *ending*. It is even possible to go through the alphabet: *aiming*, *boring*, *caring*, and so on. It is much more difficult to think of six-letter words with *n* in the fifth position, unless the ending -*ing* "springs to mind." Moreover, it is even possible intuitively to *estimate how difficult* it would be to generate six-letter words of the two different types.

Why do many people believe that they are particularly prone to getting in the slow line at a bank when they are in a hurry, that it is more likely to rain if they do not carry an umbrella, that sportscasters have "jinxed" athletes by praising them directly prior to an error, and so on? Given that there can be no logical connection between these events, such superstitious beliefs are based on summaries of "experience." Those summaries, however, are *remembered* experience, and those instances of agitation in the bank line, getting soaked, jinxing, and other personally relevant coincidences are particularly available in our memories; we assume the other memories are "in there," just not as easily retrieved. In fact, the common belief in psychic powers (technically, "psi powers"), including clairvoyance, is often biased by our distinctively retrievable memories of coincidences such as thinking about another person whom we haven't seen for years on the same day that we receive an unexpected telephone call from the person. (Nobel laureate Luis Alvarez [1965] provides an instructive analysis of just such a personal experience, showing the inevitability of coincidences occurring to *someone*, in a large enough population of possibilities for such coincidences and of individuals: Although coincidences may be rare in each person's experience, we must remember they are "common" in a large population of individuals.)

Or consider a psychotherapist whose client threatens to commit suicide. If the best professional judgment of the therapist is that the threat is a serious one, most ethical codes require the therapist to act to prevent an attempt (regardless of the therapist's personal view about people's rights to terminate their own lives). How is a therapist to exercise that judgment? One method would be to reason by availability and to search one's memory for experiences with similar clients who have made similar threats. Which instances are likely to come to mind? Those that were serious—specifically any in which a client did attempt suicide (especially if the attempt had been successful after the therapist had not intervened).

Those instances are *salient*, and they are also most retrievable from memory, due to the circumstances that follow an attempt, particularly a successful one. Those instances in which the threats were idle or in which clients quickly overcame their self-destructive feelings are much less apt to be recalled. It follows that if the therapist estimates the probability of an actual attempt on the basis of the instances most available to memory, he or she will overestimate the frequency. But it is precisely that frequency (or perhaps more correctly the probability inferred from the frequency)—whether it is estimated explicitly or integrated implicitly by the therapist's intuition—that determines whether or not the therapist takes action. Other considerations, for example, the therapist's own views about the ethics of suicide, his or her fear of a lawsuit, concern about reputation among colleagues or potential clients, and so on, enter into the consideration of how high the probability should be before the therapist intervenes.

The point here is simply that the probability of an attempt is likely to be overestimated due to the *availability* of the instances in the therapist's memory of threats followed by attempts versus those not followed by attempts. The therapist is likely to hospitalize the client, even when the probability of a suicide attempt is low (based on the *actual* frequency of attempts following threats among the therapist's clients). Notice that in this example we assume that the collection of relevant events stored in long-term memory is representative and informative for the judgment. The bias is introduced not at the acquisition phase of the memory process, but at the utilization or retrieval phase of the process. The sample *retrieved* is unrepresentative and biased, with reference to both the actual frequencies of the events in the world and the frequencies in long-term memory.

Or consider the current widespread belief that much of the "homelessness problem" in the United States is due to the "deinstitutionalization" of mental patients, which simply releases them into the streets without the ability to obtain or hold jobs. This belief was expounded in a 1986 cover story of *Newsweek* magazine, which began with the provocative headline "Abandoned" (and subsequently failed to recount a single instance of an emotionally disturbed individual requesting psychiatric hospitalization and being denied it). The homeless are "America's cast-offs—turned away from mental institutions and into the streets. Who will care for them?" The story continues by quoting from a number of eminent psychiatrists and mental health workers: "It is true that up to 65% of the liberated mental patients have successfully adapted to life outside, but as any psychiatrist can testify, 'success' among the long-term mentally ill is a very sometimes thing" (p. 14). (Our own observation is that "success" for *all* of us is a "sometimes thing.")

What do actual surveys of the homeless show? Estimates of the proportion who are mentally ill vary from locality to locality, but the average is about one third, with the criterion for categorizing someone as "mentally ill" being either current mental distress or a history of psychiatric hospitalization. The vast majority of the homeless are poor, just plain poor. Why do so many people accept the conclusion that homelessness is due to deinstitutionalization of mental patients? Search your memory for the homeless people you saw most recently. What were they like? The unobtrusive homeless person is easily forgotten. We tend to remember the person who sings on the bus, who intrudes on passersby, who is drunk, or who is obviously high on some drug. Moreover, we prepare ourselves to behave in certain ways if such a person approaches us, such preparation being exactly the type of ancillary event that—as Willem Wagenaar (1986) points out—enhances recall of the event leading to it. Hence our view of "the homeless" is based on the *memorable* homeless, people whose emotional and physical debilitation is so severe that it suggests that poverty alone cannot be the cause of their problems. The judgment quoted earlier of "any psychiatrist" is also subject to a memory selection bias. Unlike family doctors, psychiatrists do not see their patients for periodic checkups. They see their former patients, if at all, only when subsequent emotional problems develop. This selective sampling is particularly severe for psychiatrists who work in mental institutions, because discharged patients tend to be very disturbed when a former psychiatrist sees them on readmission.

Robert Reyes, William Thompson, and Gordon Bower (1980) provide a controlled, experimental demonstration of the manner in which retrieval-biased availability affects a legal judgment. They manipulated the presentation of materials in a drunk driving case to make either the prosecution evidence or the defense evidence more vivid and more memorable. The verdict in the case hinged on whether the defendant was drunk when he ran into a garbage truck. Identically exonerating evidence about the difficulty of seeing the truck because it was gray in color was presented in (a) a "pallid" version: "The owner of the garbage truck stated under cross-examination that his garbage truck was difficult to see at night because it was gray in color"; and (b) a vivid, memorable version: "The owner of the garbage truck stated that his garbage truck was difficult to see at night because it was gray in color. The owner remarked his trucks are gray 'Because it hides the dirt, it's a garbage truck. What do you want, I should paint 'em pink?'" The same manipulation was performed on incriminating, prosecution evidence: (a) the pallid version: "On his way out of the door as he was leaving a party, the defendant staggered against a serving table knocking a bowl to the floor"; and (b) vivid and memorable: "On his way out the door as he was leaving a party, the defendant staggered against a serving table, knocking a bowl of green guacamole dip onto the floor splattering guacamole on the expensive white shag carpet" (Reyes et al., p. 4). The side of the case favored by the more vivid evidence was the side that prevailed in mock jurors' guilt-innocence ratings; the vividness advantage was especially pronounced when the verdict ratings were made 48 hours after hearing the evidence—when a memory advantage would matter more.

There is another saliency bias that seems quite general in our social cognitions: We tend to notice and exaggerate the frequencies of morally negative events. Most people who threaten to commit suicide do not make an attempt; most people who are homeless are not mentally ill. But both these availability biases are augmented by yet another factor: the particular salience of *negative* information either from one's own experience or from external sources, for example, that someone once behaved violently. The salience of negative information may be adaptive, for we must know what to avoid to survive. But still, it produces a bias to overestimate the frequencies and probabilities of negative events.

The emotion or mood invoked by an event may have a further effect on memory and, hence, availability-based judgments: When we are in a particular emotional state, we have a tendency to remember events that are thematically congruent with that state. An early demonstration of the effects of emotion on judgments was provided in a laboratory experiment conducted by Eric Johnson and Amos Tversky (1983). They asked their experimental participants to make ratings of risks and accidents (like those judged in Figure 4.1). Incidentally, some of the participants were exposed to news stories (a radio playing in the background of the experimental waiting room) that were designed to induce a feeling of anxiety and worry (stories about the death of a person similar to the participant). The negative emotion produced consistently higher ratings of the risks compared to ratings from raters who overheard happy or neutral news stories. William Wright and Gordon Bower (1992) replicated and extended the study with a stronger mood manipulation. Hypnosis was used

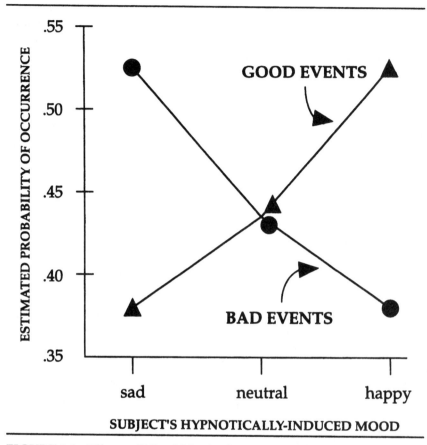

.55

.50

.45

.40

.35

ESTIMATED PROBABILITY OF OCCURRENCE

GOOD EVENTS

BAD EVENTS

sad   neutral   happy

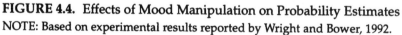

SUBJECT'S HYPNOTICALLY-INDUCED MOOD

FIGURE 4.4. Effects of Mood Manipulation on Probability Estimates
NOTE: Based on experimental results reported by Wright and Bower, 1992.

to put experimental participants in a happy, neutral, or sad mood. There was a dramatic mood congruity effect, such that participants rated events consistent with their mood as much likelier to occur, events inconsistent with their mood as less likely to occur. Thus a subject in a hypnotically induced happy mood gave high probability of occurrence estimates for good events, "blessings" (e.g., world peace, discovery of cure for cancer), and low ratings to "disasters" (e.g., being injured in a car accident, major nuclear power plant accident) (see Figure 4.4).

Many more examples could be given. The principle is simple. When we have experience with a class of phenomena (objects, people, or events), those with a particularly salient characteristic are those that most readily "come to mind" when we think about that class. It follows that if we estimate the proportion of members of that class with whom we have had experience and who have that characteristic, we tend to overestimate it. Our estimate *is* higher than the one we would make if we deliberately coded whether each member of that class did or did not have that characteristic as we encountered them (e.g., by keeping a running tally with a mechanical counter). Selective retrieval from memory can lead to a very large misestimate of proportion and a consequent misunderstanding of the nature of a serious social problem and to biases in important decisions like those required of jurors in consequential (at least for the parties) legal cases.

4.5 AVAILABILITY TO THE IMAGINATION

Imagine a group of ten people. Make an intuitive estimate of the number of pairs of people—that is, "committees of two"—that can be formed from this group. Now make the same estimate of the number of "committees of eight" that can be formed. Most subjects estimate the former number to be larger than the latter. It is much easier to imagine "picking out" pairs of people from the set of ten than from groups of eight. Once again, it is not necessary to form all such pairs mentally; it is possible to estimate the ease of doing so without an exhaustive search, and in particular to estimate that it is easier to form pairs than to form committees of eight.

In fact, there are exactly the same number of committees of eight as there are committees of two. This conclusion can be reached by pure logic. Each time a unique pair is chosen from the group, a unique committee of eight remains. It follows that there is a one-one relationship between committees of two and committees of eight; it is not even necessary to have recourse to formulas to conclude that their numbers are equal.

Or consider another example, making a judgment about the two structures depicted in Figure 4.5: A path in a structure is a line that connects an "x" in the top row to an "x" in the bottom row, and passes through one and only one "x" in each row. In which of the two structures do you think there are more distinct possible paths?

Most people will agree with our intuition that there are many more paths in structure A than in structure B, but in fact the number of paths is

Structure A	Structure B
x x x x x x x x	x x
x x x x x x x x	x x
x x x x x x x x	x x
	x x
	x x
	x x
	x x
	x x
	x x

FIGURE 4.5.   How Many Paths Can Be Drawn Through Each Figure?

the same in both structures: $8^3 = 2^9 = 512$. Why do people see more paths in A? This result reflects the differential ease of imagining paths in the two structures; a typical estimate of the number of paths for A would be 40, and for B would be 18. Again, we interpret this result as reflecting people's reliance on availability, in this case, "ease of imagining" the to-be-judged events. Note that both average estimates are *underestimates*. Imagination is often deficient (at least for judging the extent of mundane possibilities).

In these cases, availability *to the imagination* influences our estimates of frequency. The problem that arises, just as with the availability of actual instances in our experience or availability of vicarious instances, is that this availability is determined by many factors other than actual frequency. It is quite clear that some types of thinking are "easier" than others and that some ideas "come to mind" more readily than others. Moreover, it is also clear that this difference is not based entirely on past experience. (How many of us have had experience forming committees of two or eight persons or of drawing paths through "x diagrams"?) The resultant ease of availability biases our estimates of frequencies and hence our judgments of probability based on such frequencies. Currently, psychologists are limited to presenting obvious examples of this ease. A general theory about such ease of generation, a kind of creativity—and about what constitutes difficulty of thinking—does not yet exist.

4.6   FROM AVAILABILITY TO
PROBABILITY AND CAUSALITY

A theoretically important availability effect occurs when people are asked to estimate frequencies or assess probabilities for sets of events that compose exhaustive, mutually exclusive complementary sets. Donald Redelmeier, Derek Koehler, Varda Liberman, and Amos Tversky (1995) asked 52 physicians to provide probabilities for the outcomes to be experienced by hospitalized patients, based on descriptions of their cases:

- Dies during the present hospital admission

- Discharged alive but dies within 1 year

- Lives more than 1 year but less than 10 years

- Lives more than 10 years

Because the four events are exhaustive for the possible outcomes, the sum of their individual probabilities should approximately equal 1. When the outcomes were assessed separately (one per physician), the mean sum of the four judgments was equal to 1.64, much too high if the physicians were following the laws of probability theory that mandate the total probability allotted to a mutually exhaustive set of events is 1. The physicians were behaving according to the same rules as the baseball player Yogi Berra (famous for his malapropisms) when he told a reporter, "If there's a 50 percent chance we'll have a repeat American League winner, you gotta remember there's also a 75 percent chance we won't." Tversky and his colleagues explained this "subadditivity" of probabilities by proposing that support for each proposition was recruited from the physicians' memories and imaginations. The complementary subevent descriptions provide effective cues to retrieve and to generate "reasons for" the specific outcomes. For example, the description "dies during the present hospital admission" suggests several concrete, vivid ways in which the patient might die in the hospital (surgical complications, anesthesiological mishap, infection, etc.). The implicit complementary event ("does not die during the present hospitalization") is vague and does not provide effective cues or associations to the memory and imagination.

Amos Tversky and Derek Koehler (1994) have replicated this pattern of subadditivity for frequency estimates in many other domains: car troubleshooting, weather forecasting, sports predictions, and so forth. Provoked by receiving an unsolicited report claiming that posttraumatic stress caused by the aftereffects of alien abductions is a significant mental health problem (the report alleged that at least 2% of the American population is affected by this problem, implying it should be ranked above "homelessness" on our national political agenda), one of us (Dawes) became interested in subadditivity in judgments of personal events. As major support for the 2% conclusion, the authors (Hopkins & Jacobs, 1992) cite the rate of affirmative responses to a recent Roper poll question, "How often has this happened to you: Waking up paralyzed with a sense of a strange person or presence or something else in the room?" Their rationale for considering affirmative responses diagnostic of alien kidnapping involves the conjunction of the two components in the question: "A fleeting sensation of paralysis is not unusual in either hypnogogic or hypnopompic states, but adding the phrase 'with a sense of a strange person or presence in the room' forcefully narrows the scope of the question" (p. 56).

Subsequently, Matthew Mulford and Dawes (1999) asked a sample of respondents, "How often has this happened to you: Waking up paralyzed with a sense of a strange person or presence or something else in the room?" Remarkably, 40% of the people questioned about this somewhat bizarre experience answered that it had happened to them at least once. Comparable people in a (randomly) separate sample were simply asked how often they remembered "waking up paralyzed" (*without* the sense of an alien presence) (p. 48). This time, only 14% of the students and townspeople responded affirmatively. Clearly, the more detailed description including the reference to a "strange person or presence" led the respondents to "recall cases that might otherwise slip their minds" (Tversky & Koehler's [1994] description of the underlying process). Mulford and Dawes went on to replicate this subadditivity effect with other mundane personal events, such as estimates of good and bad social experiences (lying, asking for a date, feeling embarrassed).

Another, related example of "subadditivity" in judgments was studied by Michael Ross and Fiore Sicoly (1979). They asked the members of "partnerships" and teams to rate their proportional contributions to group efforts. Spouses, professor-student pairs, and basketball players all overestimated their individual contributions to the group efforts; in every case, the sums of the individual ratings greatly exceeded the ceiling value of 100%. Perhaps most interesting was the finding that these overestimates occurred for both self-aggrandizing contributions and for "negative" contributions ("causing arguments," "making errors in data analysis," "committing fouls"). The cognitive processes underlying these overestimates probably fall in the middle of the continuum from memory retrieval to imaginative generation, although, retrieval is surely part of the explanation: Follow-up studies showed that these "subadditive" estimates were highly correlated with the respondents' ability to recall specific contributions, implying that memory availability was a component of the judgment process.

Tversky and Koehler refer to the redescription of a global event (car doesn't start, patient dies, economic recession, etc.) in an explicit disjunctive list of its component subevents as "unpacking" the global event. Most studies find that subadditivity describes the relationship between the global event and its disjunctive, unpacked form. But there are examples of "superadditivity," where the global whole is larger (on the probability measure) than its parts. This seems also to happen because of the nature of the underlying availability process: When the unpacked components are difficult to think about, to imagine, to recall, then the components are judged (too?) unlikely and the whole-part relationship is reversed with the global event receiving more probability than its components. Norbert Schwarz (1996) has reported many results that demonstrate the reliance on (un)ease of retrieval to produce apparent underestimates of quantities, and Laura Macchi, Daniel Osherson, and David Krantz (1999) have provided a technical demonstration of superadditivity in whole-part probability judgments that is best interpreted as a reverse, difficulty-of-retrieval effect.

Both the subadditive and the superadditive demonstrations converge in supporting the prominent role of availability as an underlying cognitive process. Availability is a property of our cognitive systems that has ramifications for many theoretically and practically important phenomena. Some of the most important results concern the manner in which citizens (and their political leaders) "set agendas" for the investment of public resources. The cognitive availability of alienated high school students, dishonest welfare recipients, pedophilic priests, faulty airplane wiring, wild-eyed terrorists, and many other exemplars in the public imagination has major consequences for where we spend our tax dollars and how we vote on relevant legislation (see John Kingdon's 1984 classic, *Agendas, Alternatives, and Public Policies*, for a pioneering study of political agenda setting).

4.7 HEURISTIC THINKING: ADAPTIVE OR JUST PLAIN STUPID?

People rely on cognitive strategies that "work" most of the time; are cognitively economical; and are robust in the sense that they are durable in the face of incomplete information, changing situations, and momentary distraction. But most of these strategies also produce signature errors and biases; for example, we have just presented many instances of factors that make events memorable and thereby control availability, but which also introduce systematic errors under some conditions. In the case of availability, we usually identify these errors by making comparisons between true event frequencies and judgments that should correspond to those frequencies. These correspondence tests (Does the judgment hit the mark it was aimed at?) are probably the most obvious ways to talk about and measure error. But sometimes we use another measure of error, the degree to which judgments are consistent with an abstract system (logic or probability theory in this book) for making judgments, as illustrated by our discussion of subadditivity, where probability and credit judgments summed up to impossible totals. We return to this issue of how to assess the quality, accuracy, and consistency of judgments in Chapter 9, where we carefully consider the issue of rationality in judgment.

The modes of judgment summarized in the availability heuristic are so natural and so widespread that they demand explanation in terms of adaptive value. Why would such habits of thought be learned, culturally transmitted, or possibly even inherited if they did not confer some benefits or survival value? Our view is that learning from experience and evolution work by selecting *incremental improvements*—often in underlying mechanisms or general habits of thought, perhaps sometimes even at the genotype level. We prefer the expression "survival of the fitt*er*" to the traditional "survival of the fitt*est*." Eventually, over very long individual learning histories or many generations of genetic evolution, the results are visible in amazingly ingenious solutions to "problems" posed by our environments. (The human visual system is often, properly, touted as an unimaginably clever evolutionary achievement.) But the notion of *optimal* adaptation (and the phrase "survival of the fitt*est*") is misleading in the quest for an understanding of the sources of human (and nonhuman) behavior.

Almost any successful adaptation, whether learned or inherited, can be associated with weaknesses as well as with strengths, especially when the organism is in an unusual environment. Scientists capitalize on this fact that unnatural, but not impossible, environments can reveal the underlying mechanisms of thought. For example, the study of perceptual illusions reveals profound lessons about the sensory system, although the circumstances that produce most of these illusions are rare in natural environments. Thus when two physically identical length lines appear, subjectively, to be vastly different, the psychologist has a clue about how the visual system estimates length. Similarly, when people consistently misestimate or even reverse the magnitudes of two estimated quantities, it provides a clue about the workings of the judgment system.

We will return to the question of whether these judgment heuristics constitute a form of irrationality or whether they are defensible because they are efficient, sturdy, and practical (Chapter 9). But first we introduce more heuristic habits and some probability theory principles that we will need to evaluate the rationality the heuristics.

REFERENCES

Abandoned. (1986, January 6). *Newsweek*, pp. 14-16.

Alvarez, L. W. (19765). A pseudo experience in parapsychology. *Science, 148,* 1541.

Banaji, M. R., & Bhaskar, R. (2000). Implicit stereotypes and memory: The bounded rationality of social beliefs. In D. L. Schacter & E. Scarry (Eds.), *Memory, brain, and belief* (pp. 139-175). Cambridge, MA: Harvard University Press.

Combs, B., & Slovic, P. (1979). Newspaper coverage of causes of death. *Journalism Quarterly, 56,* 837-843, 849.

Corcoran, M., Duncan, G. J., Gurin, G., & Gurin, P. (1985). Myth and reality: The causes and persistence of poverty. *Journal of Policy Analysis and Management, 4,* 516-536.

Douglas, M., & Wildavsky, A. (1982). *Risk and culture: An essay on the selection of technical and cultural dangers.* Berkeley: University of California Press.

Gilliam, F. D., Jr., & Iyengar, S. (2000). Prime suspects: The influence of local television news on the viewing public. *American Journal of Political Science, 44,* 560-573.

Glassner, B. (1999). *The culture of fear: Why Americans are afraid of the wrong things.* New York: Basic Books.

Goodman, G. S., Qin, J. J., Bottoms, B. L., & Shaver, P. R. (1994). *Characteristics and sources of allegations of ritualistic child abuse.* Washington, DC: National Center on Child Abuse and Neglect.

Hamil, R., Wilson, T. D., & Nisbett, R. E. (1980). Insensitivity to sample bias: Generalizing from atypical instances. *Journal of Personality and Social Psychology, 39,* 578-589.

Hopkins, B., & Jacobs, D.M. (1992). How this survey was designed. In Bigelow Holding Company, *An analysis of the data from three major surveys conducted by the Roper Organization* (pp. 55-58). Las Vegas, NV: Author.

Johnson, E. J., & Tversky, A. (1983). Affect, generalization, and the perception of risk. *Journal of Personality and Social Psychology, 45(1),* 20-31.

Kingdon, J. W. (1984). *Agendas, alternatives and public policies.* Boston: Harper, Collins.

Macchi, L., Osherson, D., & Krantz, D. H. (1999). A note on superadditive probability judgment. *Psychological Review, 106,* 210-214.

McGuire, W. J., & McGuire, C. V. (1980). Salience of handedness in the spontaneous self-concept. *Perceptual & Motor Skills, 50,* 3-7.

Mulford, M., & Dawes, R.M. (1999). Subadditivity in memory for personal events. *Psychological Science, 10,* 47-51.

Nathan, D., & Snedeker, M. (1995). *Satan's silence.* New York: Basic Books.

Nisbett, R. E., & Ross, L. (1980). *Human inference: Strategies and shortcomings.* Englewood Cliffs, NJ: Prentice Hall.

Redelmeier, D. A., Koehler, D. J., Liberman, V., & Tversky, A. (1995). Probability judgment in medicine: Discounting unspecified alternatives. *Medical Decision Making, 15,* 227-231.

Reyes, R. M., Thompson, W. C., & Bower, G. H. (1980). Judgmental biases resulting from differing availabilities of arguments. *Journal of Personality and Social Psychology, 39,* 2-12.

Ross, M., & Sicoly, F. (1979). Egocentric biases in availability and attribution. *Journal of Personality and Social Psychology, 37,* 322-336.

Sartre, J.-P. (1948). *Anti-Semite and Jew* (G. F. Becker, Trans.). New York: Schocken.

Schwarz, N. (1996). *Cognition and communication: Judgmental biases, research methods, and the logic of conversation.* Mahwah, NJ: Lawrence Erlbaum.

Sia, T. L., Lord, C. G., Blessum, K. A., Ratcliff, C. D., & Lepper, M. R. (1997). Is a rose always a rose? The role of social category exemplar change in attitude stability and attitude-behavior consistency. *Journal of Personality and Social Psychology, 72,* 501-514.

Tversky, A., & Kahneman, D. (1973). Availability: A heuristic for judging frequency and probability. *Cognitive Psychology, 5,* 207-232.

Tversky, A., & Kahneman, D. (1974). Judgment under uncertainty: Heuristics and biases. *Science, 185,* 1124-1131.

Tversky, A., & Koehler, D. J. (1994). Support theory: A nonextensional representation of subjective probability. *Psychological Review, 101,* 547-567.

Wagenaar, W. A. (1986). My memory: A study of autobiographical memory over six years. *Cognitive Psychology, 18,* 225-252.

Walsh, W. Banaji, M. R., & Greenwald, A. G. (1995). *A failure to eliminate race bias in judgments of criminals.* Paper cited in Park, J., and Banaji, M. R. (2000). Mood and heuristics: The influence of happy and sad states on sensitivity and bias in stereotyping. *Journal of Personality and Social Psychology, 78,* 1005-1023.

Wright, W. F., & Bower, G. H. (1992). Mood effects on subjective probability assessment. *Organizational Behavior and Human Decision Processes, 52*(2), 276-291.

5

ANCHORING AND ADJUSTMENT

Give me a firm place to stand, and I will move the world.
—Archimedes of Syracuse

5.1 SALIENT VALUES

Often our estimates of frequencies, probabilities, and even the desirability of consequences are vague. In ambiguous situations, a seemingly trivial factor may have a profound effect and form an "anchor" that serves as a starting point for estimation. What happens is that people adjust their estimates from this anchor but nevertheless remain too close to it. When we follow this heuristic, we usually underadjust. For example, if we recall that a house sold for approximately $200,000, we start our efforts to infer a more exact estimate from that value and end up with estimates that are too close to the starting point. When we toss a coin, we expect two heads in four tosses (even though the probability of that particular occurrence is only 3 in 8). If we know something about an individual professional football player, we expect other professional football players to be a lot like him. If we have had a good meal in a particular restaurant, we expect the restaurant's other offerings to be equally tasty (and are often disappointed due to regression effects; see Chapter 8).

Such anchors may be entirely arbitrary. For example, Amos Tversky and Daniel Kahneman (1974) asked students to estimate the percentage of

African countries that were in the United Nations (the correct answer, in 1972 when they conducted the study, was 35%). Prior to making the estimates, the subjects were requested to make a simple binary judgment of whether this percentage was greater or less than a number determined by spinning a wheel of fortune that contained numbers between 1 and 100. Subjects who first judged whether the percentage was greater or less than 10 (selected by the spinner) made an average estimate of 25%; those who first judged whether it was greater or less than 65 made an average estimate of 45%. Thus, 10 and 65 served as anchors for the estimates *even though those numbers were generated in an apparently totally arbitrary manner.*

What happened is that the subjects' attention was focused on the anchor values at the start of the judgment process and the final estimates were insufficiently adjusted away from these anchors. (The finding of such insufficiency is general and is related to the apparent credibility of the original anchor and the amount of relevant information that the judge has *available* in memory or at hand; in this particular example, the reader may question—as we do—whether even knowledgeable subjects could be expected to know that the actual percentage of African members of the United Nations was as low as 35. The situation was cleverly contrived to be one in which the paucity of relevant information in estimators' memories would allow the arbitrary anchor leeway to exert a large effect on the estimate.)

5.2 ANCHORING AND (INSUFFICIENT) ADJUSTMENT

The serial judgment process is a natural result of our limited attention "channels" and the selective strategies we have developed to deal with that cognitive limit. Just as we can only focus on one location in a visual scene or listen to one conversation at a crowded cocktail party, we attend to one item of evidence at a time as we make estimates. We can summarize the judgment process with another flowchart diagram (Figure 5.1).

The flowchart shows that the judgment process is complex and there are many places where biases might enter the system. The most general comment is that the process is prone to underadjustments, or "primacy effects"—information considered early in the judgment process tends to be overweighted in the final judgment. But it is important to realize that availability can also perturb the ultimate output, because searching for

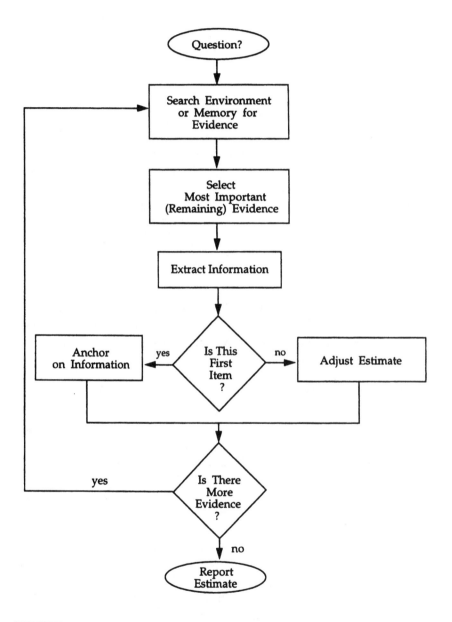

FIGURE 5.1. Anchor-and-Adjust Judgment Heuristic Flowchart

relevant information plays a major role in the overall process. The anchor not only serves as a salient starting point for the judgment, but it biases the nature of the additional information that is sought and retrieved downstream in the later stages (Gretchen Chapman and Eric Johnson, personal communication).

The anchor-and-adjust process is the most common of the deliberate human estimation habits. The closely related "weighted averaging" process model is the most frequently identified descriptive model when algebraic models are fitted to human judgments, and that equation is the basis of the statistical model most frequently used in the context of the very general lens model for judgment that we introduced in Chapter 3. When the time course of a judgment process can be mapped out, the most commonly observed sequential effect is a primacy effect, best interpreted as anchoring on the initial information considered and then underadjusting for subsequent information. In more cognitive terms, we interpret the anchor-and-adjust heuristic as a summary of the deployment of selective attention during the course of a judgment. We suspect that there is something computationally simple, robust, and adaptive about the weighted average combination rule, especially when the computation is implemented in human neurons. In fact, the linear algebraic combination rule that is the heart of the anchor-and-adjust process has remarkably robust mathematical estimation properties (see our discussion of the robust beauty of [even improper] *linear* models in Section 3.4).

The anchor-and-adjust process appears in many judgments and is especially clear when the anchor selected is obviously arbitrary (as in the original Tversky and Kahneman wheel-of-fortune demonstration described above). Another example of an arbitrary anchor, this one implicit rather than explicit, comes from a study of mental calculation. Subjects were asked, again by Tversky and Kahneman, to estimate the magnitude of "8 factorial," which means $1 \times 2 \times 3 \times 4 \times 5 \times 6 \times 7 \times 8$. The subjects did not know the answer and the problem was presented in two different ways. Some subjects were asked to estimate the product of $8 \times 7 \times 6 \times 5 \times 4 \times 3 \times 2 \times 1$, whereas others were asked to estimate the product of $1 \times 2 \times 3 \times 4 \times 5 \times 6 \times 7 \times 8$. Tversky and Kahneman hypothesized that the first number presented (or perhaps the product of the first three to four numbers) would serve as an anchor. Indeed, it appeared to be so. The median judgment of the subjects presented with the numbers in the ascending sequence $(1 \times 2 \times 3 \times \ldots)$ was 512, whereas the median estimate for those again presented with the descending sequence $(8 \times 7 \times 6 \ldots)$

was 2,250. (Note that in both formats people tended to underestimate the true factorial product, 40,320; once again, imagination underestimates the mundane.)

Even preposterously extreme anchor values are not ignored. George Quattrone and his colleages (1984) provided college students with anchors such as "Is the average price of a college textbook more or less than $7,128?" or "Is the average temperature in San Francisco greater than or less than 558° F?" (perhaps someday, but not when the studies were conducted in 1983) and still demonstrated the influence of the anchors on estimates (of course, there is a diminishing impact of extreme anchor values—plausible anchor values have a bigger impact than impossibly extreme values). But anchors need not consist of extreme values. For example, people often use an average as an anchor. We all know such people, those habitual compromisers who always say "six" when one person says "one" and another says "eleven." In fact, such habits are illustrated in the behavior personally observed by a close colleague on a subcommittee for educational funding in a state legislature. No one at the meeting could remember exactly how much money the staff had recommended budgeting for continuing education. Two members had quite discrepant ideas about the amount, but neither was sure of the figure. These amounts were simply averaged, and the committee members proceeded to discuss whether or not the resulting figure should be raised or lowered.

The most common anchor, of course, is the status quo. Although we are not constrained mentally—as we are physically—to begin a journey from where we are, we often do. Changes in existing plans or policies more readily come to mind than do new ones, and even as new alternatives close to the status quo are considered, they, too, can become anchors. This generalization is true of organizations as well as of individuals. As Cyert and March (1963) write, firms "search in the neighborhood of the current alternative." Individuals and committees tend to rely on the last or current values of costs or time-to-complete projects to decide on the allocations of resources or time to those projects. Alas, these estimates are usually unrealistically optimistic, and anchoring on previous values yields underestimates—especially for money matters, time-to-complete problems, and athletic performances, where inflation, age, and regression processes play their relentless roles.

The classic and some of the most theoretically important studies on anchoring and adjustment were conducted using pricing versus choice to express preferences between gambles by Paul Slovic, Baruch Fischhoff, and Sarah Lichtenstein (1982). They studied pricing and choice in two contexts: (a) survey experiments in which college student subjects made hypothetical choices and provided hypothetical monetary values for the gambles and (b) actual choices at a casino in Las Vegas in which gamblers played—bought or sold the gambles—for substantial amounts of real money. The results were the same.

The gambles consisted simply of probabilities to win or lose certain amounts of money. Players were requested to respond to these gambles in one of two ways: They were asked either how much money they would accept in lieu of playing the gamble (price) or which of two gambles they would prefer to play (choice). To encourage players to express the true worth of the gamble to them as their stated "selling price," the experimenters used a device that determined a random "counterbid." If this counterbid was lower than the stated selling price, the subject played the gamble; if it was higher, the subject was given the amount of the counterbid. Now consider any subjects who state a selling price that is *lower* than the true monetary value of the gamble to them. If the randomly determined counterbid falls *between* the stated selling price and the true monetary value, the subjects are given the amount of the counterbid when in fact they would prefer to play the gamble. Also consider subjects whose stated selling price is *higher* than the true monetary value to them. If the randomly determined counterbid falls between their true monetary value for the gamble and their stated selling price (which is then higher), these subjects would have to play a gamble when in fact they would prefer to receive the amount of the counterbid. Thus subjects who state a selling price that is either too high or too low can be put in a position where they receive one alternative (the privilege of playing the gamble or the counterbid) although they would prefer the other. Thus this valuation mechanism, if clearly understood, would motivate a person to state the true monetary value of the option, rather than over- or underbidding, perhaps for some misconceived strategic reason. This "sincere valuation" procedure was thoroughly explained to the subjects, and only when they understood its logic did the experiment commence.

Consider two such gambles. Gamble A has an 11 in 36 probability of winning $16 and a 25 in 36 probability of losing $1.50; gamble B has a 35 in 36 probability of winning $4 and a 1 in 36 probability of losing $1. (The expected values are both approximately $3.85; see Appendix.) Players who were asked for their selling prices produced a larger dollar equivalent for the first—after all, it has a higher winning payoff. But the same players given the choice between these two gambles had a strong tendency to choose the second, which has the higher probability of winning—after all, people like to win. The interpretation is that when people are asked to produce a monetary equivalent (through the selling price procedure), they anchor on the dollar amounts of the outcomes and insufficiently adjust on the basis of the probabilities involved. But when the same people think of winning versus losing, they anchor on the probability of success—higher probabilities are more desirable—and then they insufficiently adjust their value judgment on the basis of the dollars to be won or lost. The result is that the very same subject in different parts of the experiment or at the casino gaming table may prefer gamble B to gamble A, but state a higher selling price for gamble A.

This combination of anchor and adjust-based habits could turn such a subject into a "money pump." Suppose the experimenter "sells" the first gamble to the subject for the amount specified. Then, given a choice between the two gambles and selecting the second, the subject trades the second for the first. Now the experimenter buys back the second gamble for the selling price specified by the subject. Because this amount is less than the previous amount, the experimenter has made a profit while the subject is left with the original gamble he or she bought. Hypothetically, the experimenter can repeat the sequence to "pump" the money out of the subject's pockets; the experimenter can even begin by giving the subject one of the two gambles and still make an infinite profit (in theory, anyway). Interestingly, some people who have this pattern of preferences and selling prices will engage in this buying, choice, and selling procedure repeatedly even though they realize while doing so that the experimenter is making a profit. Comments such as "I just can't help it" and "I know it's silly and you're taking advantage of me, but I really do prefer that one although I think the other is more valuable" are common.

These subtle, but robust, *preference reversals* also provide an instructive example of how the scale on which a response is made can bias people to choose one anchor over another (favoring dollar amounts when the response is a price, but favoring probabilities when the response is a choice). Furthermore, the results challenge standard economic theory, which equates the utility (personal value) of an object with the amount of money people are willing to pay for it. Two economists, David Grether and Charles Plott (1979), rose to the challenge of these demonstrations of irrational choice and pricing behavior by conducting a series of experiments using real monetary payoffs in which they examined every "artifactual" explanation for such reversals that they could imagine. (One example: Because the study was conducted by psychologists, the experimenters could not be trusted not to cheat when playing the gambles.) They concluded that the finding was robust; they found no artifacts.

Anchor and (insufficient) adjustment effects play a role in many important everyday judgments. For example, in civil tort lawsuits, the plaintiff usually requests specific dollar amounts in compensatory and sometimes as punitive damages. Gretchen Chapman and Brian Bornstein (1996) provide one of the clearest demonstrations of the influence of these anchors in a study of mock jurors' awards in a personal injury case. The plaintiff was suing a health maintenance organization for having prescribed a birth control medication that caused her to contract ovarian cancer. The plaintiff asked for a specific damages award figure, manipulated experimentally in the range from $100 to $1 billion. These anchor values were picked to represent figures that would span the range from implausibly low to implausibly high with some representative figures near the median value ($325,000) assessed when no ad damnum request (the formal claim specifying the amount of damages requested) was made by the plaintiff. The findings were summarized in the title of Chapman and Bornstein's paper: "The More You Ask For, the More You Get." In another similar, but even more realistic, mock jury experiment conducted by one of us (Reid Hastie, with David Schkade and John Payne, 1999, p. 451), plaintiffs asserted that an award either "in the range from $15 million to $50 million" or "in the range from $50 to $150 million would be appropriate" (attorneys often ask for a range rather than a single value, because they think this is an effective trial tactic). Sure enough, the median awards were $15 million versus $50 million in the two conditions. This further demonstration is especially interesting because it was observed after the judge clearly instructed the jurors, "The attorneys' recommendations are *not* evidence."

A parallel sequence of judgments occurs on the criminal side in bail-setting and sentencing decisions. Like jurors, trial judges seem to be susceptible to anchor effects produced by attorney recommendations. For example, Ebbe Ebbesen and Vladimir Konecni (1975) sent their students into courtrooms to observe pretrial bail-setting hearings. They found that criminal court judges weighted the prosecuting attorney's recommendation for bail—the payment or financial commitment made by a defendant to guarantee appearance at a later trial—more heavily than any of the other information provided in probation reports; perhaps it is no accident that this anchor is the first piece of information presented to the judge.

Many important everyday financial situations are susceptible to anchor effects. These effects may be especially controlling in negotiations where two or more parties are trying to settle on a financial arrangement to share investments and profits. Greg Northcraft and Maggie Neale (1987) asked professional real estate agents to assess residential property values, a task that each had performed hundreds of times. The agents were provided with detailed 10-page summaries of the characteristics of houses in the Tucson, Arizona, area; they visited the properties, and then they assessed "fair market values" and predicted selling prices—all part of their day-to-day jobs. The fair market price is supposed to be objective (often governed by explicit formulas based on the location, size, and condition of the property, with inputs for the recent actual sale prices of comparable properties). Northcraft and Neale manipulated one *irrelevant* variable, the original listing prices of the properties described in the written materials, across a range of ±12% of the originally assessed fair market value. The listing price is chosen by the seller with subjective and strategic concerns in mind; although it is likely to bear an approximate relationship to the true market value, it may be higher or lower depending on the seller's goals. The listing price manipulation had consistent and large effects on the agents' appraisals.

This result—people rely on anchors—is not surprising, especially in the context of all of the other known anchoring effects. What is important though is that it appears in a consequential financial judgment, it occurs for professionals who have made the judgment many times, and it occurs in a nonlaboratory setting in which the experts are provided with as much valid information as (actually more than) they would normally have to make these appraisals—and the anchor effects are still present and still large. Northcraft and Neale also observed that most of their experts said that they would definitely notice any deviation in a listing price greater than 5% from the true value of a property; but manipulations of ±12% went unnoticed and had an impact on their appraisals.

5.3 ANCHORING THE PAST IN THE PRESENT

Anchoring and adjustment can also severely affect our retrospective personal memory. Although such memory is introspectively a process of "dredging up" *what actually happened*, it is to a large extent anchored by our current beliefs and feelings. This principle has been well established both in the psychological laboratory and in surveys. What we have at the time of recall is, after all, only our current state, which includes fragments ("memory traces") of our past experience; these fragments are biased by what we now believe (or feel) to be true to an extent much greater than we realize. Moreover, the organization of these fragments of past experience into meaningful patterns is even more influenced by our current beliefs and moods—especially if we are particularly depressed or elated.

For example, Greg Markus (1986) studied stability and change in political attitudes between 1973 and 1982. Specifically, a national sample of 1,669 high school seniors in the graduating class of 1965, along with at least one parent in nearly every case, was surveyed in 1965, 1973, and 1982. Fifty-seven percent of the parents (64% of those still living) and 68% of the students (70% of those alive) were personally interviewed all three times. All subjects were asked to indicate on a 7-point scale (with verbal anchors at the end) their attitudes toward five issues: guaranteed jobs, rights of accused people, aid to minorities, legalization of marijuana, and equality for women. In addition, they were asked to characterize their political views as generally liberal or generally conservative. Most important for analysis of the retrospective bias, Markus asked the respondents in 1982 to indicate how they had responded to each scale in 1973. The results were quite striking. For their ratings on the overall liberal-conservative scale, the subjects' recall of their 1973 attitudes in 1982 was more closely related to their rated attitudes in 1982 than to the attitudes they had *actually* expressed in 1973. Retrospectively, they believed that their attitudes 9 years previous were very close to their current ones, much closer than they in fact were. This bias was so strong that an equation set up to predict subjects' recall of their 1973 attitudes gives almost all weight to their 1982 attitudes and virtually none to the attitudes they actually expressed in 1973 (with the important exception of the students' overall liberal versus conservative ratings). In addition, what discrepancy there was between 1982 attitudes and recall of 1973 attitudes could be explained in terms of stereotypic beliefs about how general attitudes in the culture had changed; the subjects believed that they had become more conservative in general, but that (again, in general) they have favored equality for women all along. Subjects whose attitude had changed in the direction counter to the general cultural change tended to be unaware of such change. Finally, the parent group attributed much more stability to their attitudes than did the student group, which is compatible with the belief that the attitudes of older people change less. In fact, however, the attitudes of the parent group were *less* stable.

Attitudes are, of course, somewhat amorphous and difficult to determine. Linda Collins and her colleagues found quite similar results for actual behaviors when they surveyed high school students about their use of tobacco, alcohol, and illegal "recreational drugs" (Collings, Graham, Hanson, & Johnson, 1985). They repeated the survey after 1 year and again after 2½ years. At each repetition, the students (many of them then in college) were asked how much usage they had reported *on the original questionnaire.* (Collins and her colleagues had established strong rapport with this group and had reason to believe that their guarantees of confidentiality, which they honored, were in fact believed.) Again, the subjects' belief in lack of change introduced severe retrospective bias. For example, the rating of past alcohol use for those subjects whose drinking had increased over the 2½-year period was more highly related to their reported use *at the time of the current rating* than to the reports they had made 2½ years earlier.

Thus change can make liars of us, liars to ourselves. That generalization is not limited to change in an undesirable direction. As George Valliant, who has studied the same individuals for many years throughout their adult lives, writes: "It is all too common for caterpillars to become butterflies and then to maintain that in their youth they had been little butterflies. Maturation makes liars of us all" (1977, p. 28).

REFERENCES

Chapman, G. B., & Bornstein, B. H. (1996). The more you ask for, the more you get: Anchoring in personal injury verdicts. *Applied Cognitive Psychology, 10*, 519-540.

Collins, L. N., Graham, J. W., Hansen, W. B., & Johnson, C. A. (1985). Agreement between retrospective accounts of substance use and earlier reported substance use. *Applied Psychological Measurement, 9*, 301-309.

Cyert, R. M., & March, J. G. (1963). *A behavioral theory of the firm.* Englewood Cliffs, NJ: Prentice Hall.

Ebbesen, E. B., & Konecni, V. J. (1975). Decision making and information integration in the courts: The setting of bail. *Journal of Personality and Social Psychology, 32*, 805-821.

Grether, D. M., & Plott, C. R. (1979). Economic theory of choice in the preference reversal phenomenon. *American Economic Review, 69,* 623-638.

Hastie, R., Schkade, D. A., & Payne, J. W. (1999). Juror judgments in civil cases: Effects of plaintiff's requests and plaintiff's identity on punitive damage awards. *Law and Human Behavior, 23,* 445-470.

Markus, G. B. (1986). Stability and change in political attitudes: Observe, recall, and "explain." *Political Behavior, 8,* 21-44.

Northcraft, G. B., & Neale, M. A. (1987). Experts, amateurs, and real estate: An anchoring-and-adjustment perspective on property pricing decisions. *Organizational Behavior and Human Decision Processes, 39,* 84-97.

Quattrone, G. A., Lawrence, C. P., Warren, D. L., Souza-Silva, K., Finkel, S. E., & Andrus, D. E. (1984). *Explorations in anchoring: The effects of prior range, anchor extremity, and suggestive hints.* Unpublished manuscript, Psychology Department, Stanford University, Stanford, CA.

Slovic, P., Fischhoff, B., & Lichtenstein, S. (1982). Responsibility, framing, and information-processing effects in risk assessment. In R. Hogarth (Ed.), *New directions for methodology of social and behavioral science: Question framing and response consistency* (No. 11). San Francisco: Jossey-Bass.

Tversky, A., & Kahneman, D. (1974). Judgments under uncertainty: Heuristics and biases. *Science, 185,* 1124-1131.

Valliant, G. E. (1977). *Adaptation to life.* Boston: Little, Brown.

6

JUDGMENT BY SIMILARITY

*I woke up one morning and found that everything had
been replaced by an exact replica. So I called my best friend
and told him that everything in my room had been
replaced by an exact replica. He said, "Do I know you?"*
—Steven Wright

6.1 SAME OLD THINGS

Many judgments are concerned with the proper category into which to
classify an object or event. For example, we wonder whether the sore
throat we've had for 2 weeks is just a simple cold, an allergy, or something
worse, such as strep throat. We wonder if our new colleague is a behaviorist, a sports fan, or a born-again Christian. We want to listen to country-
western music tonight and are disappointed if we get more of that silly
folk rock stuff. We are looking for a low-sodium, low-fat item on the menu
in a restaurant.

Consider the following category membership judgment:

Penelope is a college student who is described by her friends as somewhat impractical, emotional, and sensitive. She has traveled extensively
in Europe and speaks French and Italian fluently. She is unsure about
what career she will pursue on graduation, but she has demonstrated

111

high levels of talent and won prizes for her calligraphy. On her boy-friend's last birthday she wrote him a sonnet as a present. What is Penelope's major field of study: Psychology or art history?

Most readers doubtless believe, as we are tempted to, that Penelope is an art history student. She just seems to fit our concept of the kind of person who would study art history. But now consider the following question: In a typical university, suppose you pick a name at random from the student directory and look up that person's major field of study. Which of the fields of study mentioned in the question is most popular? Which is least popular? What is the *probability* your random pick would be a psychology major? An art history major? (At the University of Colorado in 1999, statistics showed that approximately 300 graduates majored in psychology and 2 in art history out of approximately 4,000 graduating seniors; if we restrict ourselves to female students, the *base rate probabilities* of these majors in the entire undergraduate student body are approximately .06 for psychology and .0002 for art history, or a ratio of 300 to 1!) After answering these questions, many people change their answers. They realize that the probability would be very low that anyone, no matter what his or her "personality sketch," would be one of the two art history graduates. Moreover, some of those we questioned expressed embarrassment at their original answer. And a few expressed annoyance that they had been "tricked" by a description that sounded so much like someone who would major in an "extreme humanities" specialty when in fact they knew that they could not reasonably make this judgment given the brevity of the data and the tiny proportion of students in art history.

This example illustrates the common tendency to make judgments and decisions about category membership based on similarity between our conception of the category and our impression of the to-be-classified object, situation, or event. As in the case of availability-based judgments, similarity slips into the judgment process very early and dominates spontaneous judgments of category membership. The primary behavioral "signature" of relying on similarity is that people miss the critical statistical or logical structure in the situation and ignore relevant information (e.g., the background, or base rate, frequencies, such as the numbers of college majors in the Penelope example).

The Penelope problem appeals to our intuitions to support the claim that we ignore a critical aspect of the situation. Let's look at another example where the error is more definitely proven: Tversky and Kahneman

(1974) asked subjects to make probability judgments about the occupational categories of some men described by short personality sketches. Someone, for instance, who is described as being unsociable, disinterested in politics, and devoted to working on his boat in his spare time *sounds like* an engineer. The subjects were given explicit base rate numbers: They were told the men being judged were either engineers or lawyers, drawn randomly from a pool predominantly of engineers (70%) or predominantly of lawyers (70%). But the personality information completely overwhelmed the base rate numbers. The same probability judgment was made for a personality sketch whether the pool from which the man was purported to be drawn is 70% engineers or 70% lawyers. Only *when no description at all* was given did subjects correctly judge that someone drawn randomly from a pool of 70% engineers and 30% lawyers has a .70 probability of being an engineer, whereas someone from a 30% engineer versus 70% lawyer pool has a .30 probability. Apparently, people relied completely on the similarity between their stereotypes of the occupational categories and a two-sentence sketch of the person's background. When the same subjects were asked to rate "resemblance" or "similarity" between the categories and the background sketches they made the *same* judgments that they made when asked to assess probability. This over-reliance on similarity occurs even when people simultaneously acknowledge that the information they are using is unreliable, incomplete, or even nonpredictive (e.g., "has a wife and two children and is well liked by his friends" was rated as .50 likely to be in either category, the raters ignoring the .70 base rate of the more frequent occupation).

Base rates are not the only relevant structural information that people miss when they make judgments based on similarity. Consider another example, in which Tversky and Kahneman (1983) asked college students the following question:

> Linda is thirty-one years old, single, outspoken, and very bright. She majored in philosophy. As a student she was deeply concerned with issues of discrimination and social justice and she also participated in anti-nuclear demonstrations. How likely is it that:
>
> Linda is a teacher in an elementary school.
>
> Linda works in a bookstore and takes yoga classes.
>
> Linda is active in the feminist movement.
>
> Linda is a psychiatric social worker.

Linda is a member of the League of Women Voters.

Linda is a bank teller.

Linda is an insurance salesperson.

Linda is a bank teller and is active in the feminist movement. (p. 297)

Fully 86% of undergraduates questioned believed it more likely that Linda is a bank teller *and* active in the feminist movement than that Linda is a bank teller. The reason? Given the information about Linda, we can imagine her becoming a feminist bank teller, but it is hard to imagine her as merely an ordinary bank teller, even though feminism was not mentioned in the description of Linda. (Could she not also have been a fundamentalist Christian in college?) Even when the bank teller alternative was stated as "Linda is a bank teller *whether or not she is active in the feminist movement*," 57% of an additional 75 students still believed that "Linda is a bank teller *and* in the feminist movement" was more likely.

The logical error in this case involves missing the set relationships between bank teller and feminist bank teller. Feminist bank teller is a subset of bank tellers; but surely there are many kinds of bank tellers: "traditional female role" bank tellers, Latter-Day Saints bank tellers, anarchist bank tellers, and so forth. The set membership relations between these subsets may be unclear, but what is clear is that all are bank tellers (by definition) and some are not feminist bank tellers. So how is it possible for it to be more likely that Linda is a feminist and a bank teller than a member of the larger category of all kinds of bank tellers, which includes feminist bank tellers? The answer is that it is not logically possible, and people (like us) who judge it is more likely she is a feminist bank teller than simply a bank teller are missing the logical structure of the judgment problem.

Tversky and Kahneman (1974) called these errors illusions, because like the many popular visual illusions they persist even after we intellectually understand that they are incorrect (see also Kahneman & Tversky, 1966). Steven Pinker (1997) reports that a student confronted with a series of such illusions reported that he was "ashamed of his species." And evolutionary biologist Stephen J. Gould (1991) expressed the intuitive conflict that most of us experience: "I know that the conjunction is least probable, yet a little homunculus in my head continues to jump up and down, shouting at me—'but she can't be just a bank teller; read the description'" (p. 469). He concluded, "Our minds are not built (for whatever reason) to work by the laws of probability." What our minds do seem to work by is a basic sense of similarity, as demonstrated by the almost-perfect correlations between experimental participants' ratings of similarity and probability between the case descriptions and their stereotypes of the relevant categories.

6.2   REPRESENTATIVE THINKING

The purpose of the examples in the previous section was to demonstrate (a) that category membership judgments are often based on the degree to which characteristics are *representative of* or *similar to* schemas or categories, (b) that *representativeness* does not necessarily reflect an actual contingency, and (c) that probability estimates and confidence in judgments are related to similarity, not necessarily to the deeper structure of the situations about which we are making judgments. (In the Penelope problem and the lawyers and engineers problem, people seem to forget about the background base rates of major fields; in the Linda problem, people ignore the logical set membership relation between bank teller and feminist bank teller.)

What is representative judgment? The English empiricists such as John Locke (1632-1704) maintained that thinking consists of the *association* of ideas. (*Cognition* derives from the Latin *cognito*, "to shake together.") Although this assertion led to considerable debate about whether such ideas were primarily visual or verbal—or some "imageless" combination— and whether some ideas might be "innate" (provided to us at birth by some divine power or by evolution), the basic thesis that thought is primarily an *associative* process has gained wide acceptance. More sophisticated forms of thinking such as numeration, logical deduction, and scientific hypothesis testing are, according to this thesis, based on associations. Such a sweeping reductionistic approach has faced considerable empirical challenge, but the conclusion that a great deal of thinking is basically associative appears firm.

Another important tenet of the associationist approach was that complex ideas, as well as processes, could be reduced to simpler building block ideas, with the building block ideas glued together with associations. One of the most famous illustrations of this approach was the reduction in 1869 of the complex idea of "house" into its simple ideas by James Mill:

> Brick is one complex idea, mortar is another complex idea; these ideas, with ideas of position and quantity, compose my idea of a wall. My idea of a plank is a complex idea, my idea of a rafter is a complex idea, my idea of a nail is a complex idea. These, united with the same ideas of position

and quantity, compose my duplex idea of a floor. In the same manner my complex idea of glass, and wood, and others compose my duplex idea of a window; and these duplex ideas, united together, compose my idea of a house, which is made up of various duplex ideas. (pp. 115-116)

And in one of the most ambitious undertakings of early American psychology, Edward B. Titchener (1896) set out to complete the associationist research program of cataloging all the simple ideas (primarily derived from elementary sensations) to which all complex ideas could be reduced. (The analogy was to the chemists' reduction of all physical compounds to a periodic table of [simple] elements.) Using the method of introspection to perform countless reductions like "Mill's house," Titchener concluded that there were approximately 44,435 "elementary sensations." But for present purposes, we are most interested in a modern version of the reductionist program, the reduction of category concepts into elementary attribute or property lists.

Modern psychologists hypothesize that our concepts of categories like bank tellers and feminists, microcomputers, skunks, and all kinds of things are represented cognitively as the lists of attributes that we believe are defining and characteristic of those entities. (These psychologists acknowledge that this theory of conceptual representation is a useful, but partly fictional, simplification.) Thus, if we ask someone to tell us what is meant by the category concept represented by the word "bird," we usually get a list of the features associated with the label—for "bird": flies, has feathers, lays eggs, eats bugs, and so on; and for "art history student": sensitive, emotional, cultured, female, gentle, and so on. Notice the vestiges of the associationist approach; when we think about most everyday concepts we think (and reason) about associated, characteristic, and correlated attributes, not just the truly defining, essential attributes. And we often think about a category in terms of attributes ("flies" for birds, "cultured" for art history students) that we know do not apply to all members. Furthermore, we think about categories in terms of the *members* of the category that come to mind when we try to answer the "What does it mean?" question. Thus there is even a role for memory retrieval and availability in the category concept representation.

The last piece of cognitive theory that we need for our discussion of category classification is a model of the similarity judgment process. The most general model of this process, called the *contrast model*, says that we perceive similarity by making (usually automatic) comparisons of the attributes of the two or more entities whose similarity is being evaluated.

A useful model of this process is to suppose that our global impression of similarity arises from a quick tabulation of the number of attributes that "match" for two entities versus the number that "mismatch." The model includes provision for weighting the attribute match and mismatch pairs to reflect our experience and beliefs about what is most important. Thus, if we see a creature in the woods, the fact that it is not flying does not have as great an impact on our judgment about its "birdiness" as would the fact that it is covered with fur. In the Penelope judgment, there are so many "good matches" between attributes in the written description and in our stereotypes of art history major (retrieved from memory when we read the category name) that we respond, "art history." In the Linda problem, there are more "good matches" for feminist (and bank teller) than for bank teller alone between the sketch of Linda and the stereotypes evoked by the category labels.

In the language of cognitive psychology, characteristics access schemas, which may in turn access other characteristics (all through association). Note that this is all very reasonable in an adaptive sense; probably the major function that concepts and schemas serve is to give us information about characteristics of things or events that we cannot yet perceive. If we know that a creature we encounter in the woods is a skunk (determined by visual properties such as its size, color, and shape), we know the creature is likely to have some other (nonvisual) properties (its potent defensive scent), and we know what to do (keep our distance).

In many cases, once an object is classified into a category an association-based judgment is automatically made. In the case of skunks, the association provides a useful quick message: Avoid this creature. But sometimes our associations to categories are morally troublesome or just flat out irrational. The most carefully studied examples of this last type involve social stereotypes; our mental library of harmless stereotypes of art history students, bank tellers, and yoga teachers is also likely to include some not-so-innocent stereotypes of socially significant groups. Perhaps the most troublesome characteristics of these racial, gender, and religious stereotypes is that they automatically evoke emotional reactions that color our reasoning about (and behavior toward) members of the category. Once we've classified a person into a category with negative associations, we may not be able to help ourselves from reacting negatively to him or her. It is beyond the scope of this book, but the social psychology of stereotyped responding has revealed many uncontrolled properties of the quick deductive and analogical inferences we make when social categories are "activated" and applied to people (Hamilton & Sherman,

1994; Kunda, 1999). The many unconscious effects of stereotyped beliefs may even include rebound effects, where a well-intentioned effort to curtail stereotyped reaction is followed by an exaggerated application of the suppressed response in subsequent social interactions.

The typical sequence of processes involved in judgments by representativeness (similarity) is depicted in Figure 6.1. Usually, when a to-be-judged individual or case is encountered, related category concepts are retrieved from long-term memory. It is important to notice that both judgment by representativeness and judgment by availability (Chapter 4) involve retrieval from long-term memory. The difference between the judgment heuristics is subtle (and gets a little blurry in some situations): In the availability process, individual instances are retrieved and a judgment of amount or frequency is inferred from the ease and amount of information retrieved. In the representativeness process, information about generic concepts is retrieved and a similarity match assessment is made, comparing the original to-be-judged case with the category. The case-category similarity assessment produces a best-match "answer" for the cognitive judgment task and goodness-of-match or degree of similarity produces confidence or probability assessments.

The following description of the decision process of a college admissions committee provides an example of an automatic, but logically dubious, category activation.

> The [Brown University] admissions committee scans applications from a small rural high school in the Southwest. It is searching for prized specimens known as neat small-town kids. Amy is near the top of her class, with mid-500 verbals, high-600 math and science. She is also poor, white, and geo—she would add to the geographic and economic diversity that saves Brown from becoming a postgraduate New England prep school. While just over 20% of the New York State applicants will get in, almost 40% will be admitted from Region 7—Oklahoma, Texas, Arkansas, and Louisiana. Amy's high school loves her, and she wants to study engineering. Brown needs engineering students; unfortunately, Amy spells engineering wrong. "Dyslexia," says Jimmy Wrenn, a linguistics professor. After some debate, the committee puts her on the waiting list. (*Time*, 1979, p. 73)

What's wrong with making decisions on the basis of representative thinking? The problem is that similarity does not always reflect the underlying statistical and causal structure of the situation being judged.

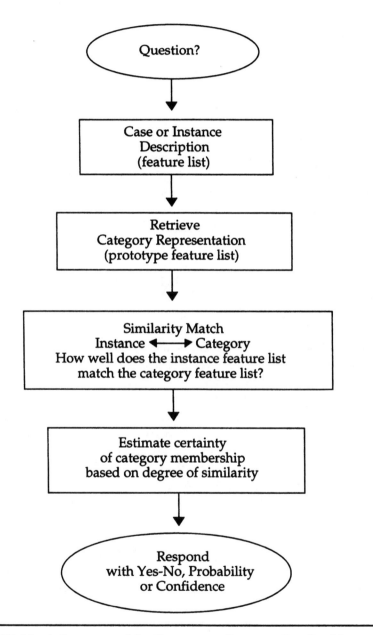

FIGURE 6.1. A Summary of the Component Processes Involved in
Categorical Similarity-Based Judgments

Misspelling *is* symptomatic of dyslexia; the schema is accessed. But of course, there are many more of us who cannot spell well who are *not* dyslexic than who *are*. Nevertheless, the schema has been accessed and Amy has been pronounced dyslexic. So much for Amy and the goal of diversity among Brown students. It is neither relevant nor ethical to consider dyslexia in making such a decision, but as members of graduate admissions committees, both of us have observed many similar judgments in admissions and fellowship assignment committees. For example, when asked for "other information that the admissions committee might find important," an applicant wrote, "Being a Capricorn, I will be a careful experimenter." "We don't want any of these astrology nuts around here!" the clinical professor on the committee snorted, and the applicant—who ranked second out of more than 700 on a linear combination of GRE and GPA—was rejected. Of course, more applicants who knew their zodiac signs *were not* "astrology nuts" than *were*, but once again, the associated schema ("astrology nut," i.e. "unreliable flake") was accessed.

The basic problem with making probability or confidence judgments on the basis of representative characteristics is that the schema accessed may in fact be *less* probable, given the characteristic, than one not accessed. This occurs when the schema not accessed has a much greater *extent* in the world than the accessed one. (The term *base rate* refers to the statistic summarizing the extent or background prevalence of category members in the context under consideration, e.g., the much larger number of psychology students than art history students on any typical college campus.) The categories "nondyslexic" and "nonflake" are much larger in reality than those of "dyslexic" and "flake"; thus the misspeller is more likely to be a nondyslexic than a dyslexic, and the applicant who knew his sun sign more likely to be a nonflake than a flake. There is, however, no corresponding mental intuition of the extent of a schema tied to the schema itself. When the category schema is accessed automatically via similarity, its base rate is not. That requires a second, self-reflexive judgment: "How prevalent is this category?" (e.g., dyslexic, astrology-flake, or art history majors). Such a judgment invites the evaluation of base rates, *independent of the characteristic*. For example, the effect of the "think again" reminder about Penelope's major was to force the reader deliberately to consider the base rates of art history and psychology majors among college students. This failure to pay attention to the statistical structure of the situation and ignoring crucial information such as relevant base rates is a behavioral "signature" of judging by representativeness. But how should we use the base rate information when making judgments?

6.3   THE RATIO RULE

In contrast to representative judgments, accurate judgments can be made by using the simplest rules of probability theory. Let c stand for a characteristic and S for a schema (category). The degree to which c is representative of S is indicated by the conditional probability $p(c \mid S)$—that is, the probability that members of S have characteristic c. (In the present examples, this conditional probability is high.)

The probability that the characteristic c implies membership in S, however, is given by the conditional probability $p(S \mid c)$, the probability that people with characteristic c are members of S, which is the *inverse* of $p(c \mid S)$. Now by the basic "laws" of probability theory,

$$p(c \mid S) = \frac{p(c \text{ and } S)}{p(S)}$$ [6.1]

that is, the extent that c and S co-occur divided by the extent of S. Similarly,

$$p(S \mid c) = \frac{p(S \text{ and } c)}{p(c)}$$ [6.2]

But $p(c \text{ and } S) = p(S \text{ and } c)$; it therefore follows that

$$\frac{p(c \mid S)}{p(S \mid c)} = \frac{p}{p}$$ [6.3]

And in general,

$$\frac{p(A \mid B)}{p(B \mid A)} = \frac{p(A)}{p(B)}$$ [6.4]

This relationship is called "the ratio rule"—*the ratio of inverse probabilities equals the ratio of simple probabilities.*

In the present context of inferring category membership, this simple ratio rule provides a logically valid way of relating $p(c \mid S)$ to $p(S \mid c)$. To equate these two conditional probabilities in the absence of equating $p(c)$ and $p(S)$ is simply irrational. Representative similarity-based thinking, however, does not reflect the difference between $p(c \mid S)$ and $p(S \mid c)$ and consequently introduces a symmetry in thought that does not exist in the world. Associations between two objects that are simultaneously presented are virtually symmetric; the world generally is not.

Statements and beliefs about the relationship between pot smoking and hard drug addiction provide a rich source of such irrationality. For example, a headline in the *Redwood City* (California) *Tribune* reads, "Most on Marijuana Using Other Drugs" (December 11, 1970, p. A1). The first line of the story that followed read, "Almost without exception, drugs are used by high schoolers in combination with marijuana when drugs are used at all, according to the findings." Whereas the text clearly states that of the students who use drugs most use marijuana, *the headline asserts the reverse.*

The ratio of pot smoking given drug usage to drug usage given pot smoking is large because the ratio of smoking pot to drug usage is large, and these two ratios are equal. Thus the survey found that the former conditional probability—smoking pot given drug usage—is quite high, in accord with our everyday observation. But that does not imply that the latter is high also. The ratio rule indicates that the latter probability—of drug use given pot smoking—is much smaller than the former, so that a large value for the former does *not* indicate that "most on marijuana [are] using other drugs." Nevertheless, 2 years previously, the Democratic candidate for president, in response to an election-eve phone call, termed marijuana, "What we in the pharmaceutical profession call a kicker."

In most writings about confusion of the inverse, authors give amusing examples. For instance, *This Week* magazine published advice on how to stay alive in a car over Labor Day weekend. In it, the author asserted that "the farther one drives from home the safer he is," because most deaths occur within 25 miles of home (Barns, 1967, p. 26; Chandler, 1948, is the source of the original statistic). This is a confusion of the probability of death given distance with the probability of distance given death; its invalidity is clear by invoking the ratio rule and noting that the probability of driving close to home is *much* greater than the probability of being killed. It is easy to make fun of that confusion. (Most deaths occur within 25 miles of people's homes because that is where they do most of their driving. By confusing the inverse, one might be tempted to tow one's car to the freeway.) When, however, identical irrationality is used as a justification—or sometimes even as a reason—for enforcing harsh prohibitions against marijuana, the confusion is not so funny. For although an individual arrested may view the arrest as a natural consequence of government by the vindictive, uptight, and exploitive, many people approve of such arrests because they believe—with the late Hubert Humphrey—that marijuana is "a kicker." Nor is it amusing when state hospitalization in a locked ward is recommended for a patient because "She gave a typical schizophrenic response; therefore, she must be schizophrenic"; or an applicant is rejected on the grounds that he or she responded like a "nut" or a dyslexic

Occasionally, people assert dependency—and its direction—without considering either base rate, as illustrated in the following item from *Management Focus.*

> Results of a recent survey of 74 chief executive officers indicate that there may be a link between childhood pet ownership and future career success. Fully 94% of the CEOs, all of them employed within Fortune 500 companies, had possessed a dog, a cat, or both, as youngsters. . . . (1984, p. 2)

The respondents asserted that pet ownership had helped them to develop many of the positive character traits that make them good managers today, including responsibility, empathy, respect for other living beings, generosity, and good communication skills.

For all we know, *more* than 94% of children raised in the backgrounds from which chief executives come had pets, in which case the direction of dependency would be negative. But perhaps a better psychological analysis can be found by relating success to tooth brushing during childhood. Probably all chief executives did so, which would clearly imply that the self-discipline thus acquired led to their business success. That seems more reasonable than the speculation that "communication skills" gained through interacting with a pet generalize to such skills in interacting with business associates.

Examples are not always so humorous. In an article titled "Airline Safety: The Shocking Truth," David Nolan presents "Some tips from experts on how to improve your chances of surviving. . . . Know where the exits are and rehearse in your mind exactly how to get to them. Harry Robertson, who has interviewed almost 200 survivors of fatal airline accidents, reports that more than 90% had their escape routes mentally mapped out beforehand" (1986, p. 58). Unfortunately, there is no evaluation of what percentage of *all* airline passengers do that (90%?), and of course, Robertson did not interview any passengers who did not survive.

Clinical psychology is not immune to such judgments. For example, Nathan Branden (1984) writes, "I cannot think of a single psychological problem—from anxiety and depression, to fear of intimacy or of success, to alcohol or drug abuse, to spouse battery or child molestation—that is not traceable to the problem of poor self-esteem" (p. 12). In other words, $p(c \mid S)$ is high, where c refers to poor self-esteem and S to problems. To state that these problems are "traceable" to poor self-esteem, however, is to assert that $p(S \mid c)$ is high, which we do not know—*clients come to Branden because they have problems.* Branden's experience is with people who want help with their problems—that is, his experience is conditional on S. Even if we found a high $p(S \mid c)$, we could not make a causal inference: Peoples' self-esteem may be poor *because* they have the problems Branden lists. Branden concludes:

> There is overwhelming evidence, including scientific findings, that the higher the level of an individual's self-esteem, the more likely that he or she will treat others with respect, kindness, and generosity. People who do not experience self-love have little or no capacity to love others. People who experience deep insecurities or self-doubts tend to experience other human beings as frightening and inimical. People who have little or no self have nothing to contribute to the world. (p. 13)

Following Branden's "I cannot think of" style, we cannot think of *any* scientific study in which the dependent variable was "nothing to contribute to the world." And it does *not* follow that since people with problems have (in Branden's experience) poor self-images that, therefore, such problems have a high probability given "deep insecurities and self-doubts"—a characteristic that may not be that uncommon. Although the word "deep" is sufficiently ambiguous that a clear statistical refutation of Branden's position is impossible, using representative thinking to communicate to a mass of people that they "have nothing to offer to the world" is intellectually irresponsible. In fact, Branden's observations are consistent with a conclusion that having low self-esteem is good for people who have problems (e.g., abuse children), for otherwise they wouldn't be motivated to seek change (e.g., enter therapy).

We will return to these issues of reasoning "coherently" about probability judgments in Chapter 9. But we don't want to convey a false sense of security. Having learned about the existence of base rate neglect is *not* sufficient to inoculate us against such errors in our future judgments. The ability to infer and correctly use base rates in judgment does not seem to be a capacity with which we are naturally endowed (Kleiter et al., 1997).

6.4   INVERSE PROBABILITIES AND BASE RATES

Fortunately, not everyone is prone to confuse inverse probabilities all of the time. For example, the great philosopher Bertrand Russell was not. His grandmother, in an effort to dissuade him from marrying his first wife, had impressed on him how much insanity there was in his family. Nine years later, he was considering having children and consulted a doctor about the hereditary component of insanity. His biographer writes,

> Four days later he saw his doctor, "who said it was my duty to run the risk of conception, the fear of heredity being grossly exaggerated. He says 50% of insane have alcoholic parentage, only 15% insane parentage. This seems to settle the matter." Settle, that is, until Russell, the potential parent, was overtaken by Russell the statistician; the footnote in his journal reads: "But he didn't say what proportion of the total population are insane and drunken respectively, so that his argument is formally worthless." (Clark, 1976, pp. 96-97)

Most of our thinking most of the time is governed by that most ubiquitous "law of thought," association, and hence we make representative connections, particularly when we assess probabilities. Even Russell, in this example, can be faulted for a degree of "mindlessness." Why, for instance, should he take the 50% and 15% figures so seriously at the outset? The problem is that to avoid such confusion it is necessary to hypothesize classes of objects or events with which one has had little experience; for example, child abusers who stop abusing without seeking help from others. Then, to estimate a conditional probability value, one must estimate the extent of this class, despite a lack of experience with its members.

Doing so involves controlled "scientific" thinking—in Piaget's terms, regarding the actual (instances have been observed) as a set of the possible (instances that *could* be observed) rather than vice versa.

Similarly, we utilize base rates more appropriately when we directly experience the elementary events that compose the relevant categories rather than learn about base rates by reading written summaries or deliberately infer an invisible base rate. For example, most of us develop impressions of the traffic congestion we will encounter when we choose particular routes to drive to work, to shop, and so on over years of experience. If we have to make an explicit route choice (e.g., which route to take to the airport during rush hour), we are sensitive to those experienced base rates (as well as to "case-specific" information such as weather reports, radio reports of traffic accidents, and knowledge about highway repairs). When studies are conducted of physicians and accountants on the job, they seem to be tuned to the relevant base rates in their locale. This is somewhat reassuring, but there is still some base rate neglect in these noisy everyday situations. Laboratory studies of mock medical diagnosis tasks have found that after substantial exposure to cases exhibiting distinct base rates (e.g., 25% of the cases turn out to be burlosis, 75% turn out to be coragia), participants are sensitive to the base rates. But, again, there are still experiential conditions under which base rates are neglected or underused (see studies by Adam Goodie and Edmund Fantino, 1995, 1996).

Another important exception to the generalization about not attending to base rates occurs if people ascribe some *causal* significance to discrepant rates. When they can see the causal relevance of the base rates, they often incorporate them in their reasoning. For example, the belief that one bus company has more accidents than another *because* its drivers are more poorly selected and trained will influence mock jurors to take this difference in accident rates into account in evaluating eyewitness testimony, but belief that a bus company has more accidents simply because it is larger will not. Study after study has shown that when these rates are "merely statistical" as opposed to "causal" they tend to be ignored. Exactly the same effect seems to occur in real courtrooms: "Naked statistical" evidence is notoriously unpersuasive (e.g., the notable failure of the DNA evidence to persuade the jury of O. J. Simpson's guilt in his criminal trial for the murder of Nichole Brown Simpson and Ronald Goldman). (Of course, *how* the $p(A)$'s and $p(B)$'s in the right-hand side of the ratio rule happened to come about is irrelevant; rationality demands their use.) But causal thinking has its own pitfalls, as we will see in the next chapter.

Unfortunately, education—at least as practiced in the United States in elementary and secondary schools—may actually train automatic thinking. The reason is that so much of what passes for education consists of memorizing connections between words, phrases, and images. These words, phrases, and images may or may not, in turn, have any mental link to external reality. ("I always just thought of fractions and decimals as two different types of numbers, but sometimes you refer to probabilities with fractions and sometimes with decimals, so I guess they're connected somehow. How do you go from a fraction to a decimal?"—college junior.)

Consider an example. In elementary school, most of us were expected to learn how to multiply one-digit numbers in our heads. A multiplication that posed some difficulty was 8 × 7= 56, or is it 57 or 54 or 53? If all that is required is memorizing the right product, there is no reason why the product should not be 57 or 54 or 53. Some fortunate students, on the other hand, are taught *not* to memorize the product, but to derive it rationally. These students are taught to think: When multiplying 7 × 8 it is easy to "get to" 5 × 8 because that's 10 × 8 = 80 divided by 2, which is 40. There's 2 × 8 "left over," which is 16. (Because 8 is "2 down" from 10, 2 × 8 must be "4 down" from 20.) So the product is 40 + 16 = 56.

In contrast, a student asked to memorize 8 × 7 = 56 is simply being asked to form an association. To the degree that education consists of merely forming such associations, we can expect "educated" people to confuse inverses, often with great ease. Consider the relegation of Amy to the college admission waiting list. Although it is never possible to be sure what would have resulted if something else had happened, it is reasonable to speculate that if the committee members had not known that misspelling is symptomatic of dyslexia Amy's fate might have been different.

The study of psychology often consists of an unclearly mixed combination of informal observation, the attempt to establish simple "theoretical" explanations or principles that work on at least a statistical basis, and controlled experimentation. This chapter has emphasized informal observation and theory. In addition, a great deal of experimentation on representative thinking has been conducted (generally with college students as subjects), and it has been uniformly confirmatory. For example, naive subjects do not distinguish between $p(A \mid B)$ and $p(B \mid A)$ in many circumstances, and when given one conditional probability, they attempt to estimate the other without reference to the base rates $p(A)$ and $p(B)$, which must be considered according to the ratio rule. Our natural habit is to think associatively about what is salient to us in the immediate situation. It takes willpower and training to escape from the "dominance of the given" and to actually *think* about events and relationships that are not salient and explicit in our experience.

REFERENCES

Barns, L. R. (1967, August 27). This quiz could save your life next weekend. *This Week*, p. 26.

Branden, N. (1984, August-September). In defense of self. *Association for Humanistic Psychology Perspectives*, pp. 12-13.

Chandler, W. R. (1948). The relationship of distance to the occurrence of pedestrian accidents. *Sociometry, 11*, 108-113.

Clark, R. W. (1976). *The life of Bertrand Russell*. New York: Knopf.

Goodie, A., & Fantino, E. (1995). An experientially derived base-rate error in humans. *Psychological Science, 6*, 101-106.

Goodie, A., & Fantino, E. (1996). Learning to commit or avoid the base-rate error. *Nature, 380*, 247-249.

Gould, S. J. (1991). *Bully for brontosaurus: Reflections in natural history*. New York: W. W. Norton.

Hamilton, D. L., & Sherman, J. W. (1994). Stereotypes. In R. S. Wyer, Jr., & T. K. Srull (Eds.), *Handbook of social cognition: Vol. 1. Basic processes* (pp. 1-68). Hillsdale NJ: Lawrence Erlbaum.

Kleiter, G. D., Krebs, M., Doherty, N. E., Garavan, H., Chadwick, R., & Brake, G. (1997). Do subjects understand base rates? *Organizational Behavior and Human Decision Processes, 72*, 25-61.

Kunda, Z. (1999). *Social cognition: Making sense of people*. Cambridge, MA: MIT Press.

Management Focus. (1984, November-December). P. 2.

Mill, J. (1869). *An analysis of the phenomena of the human mind*. London: Longman, Green, Reader, & Dryer.

Most on marijuana using other drugs. (1970, December 11). *Redwood City* (California) *Tribune*, p. A1.

Nolan, D. (1986, October). Airline safety: The shocking truth. *Discover, 7*, pp. 30-58.

Pinker, S. (1997). *How the mind works*. New York: Norton.

Time. (1979, April 9). P. 73.

Titchener, E. B. (1896). *An outline of psychology*. New York: Macmillan.

Tversky, A., & Kahneman, D. (1974). Judgments under uncertainty: Heuristics and biases. *Science, 185*, 1124-1131.

Tversky, A., & Kahneman, D. (1983). Extensional versus intuitive reasoning: The conjunction fallacy in probability judgment. *Psychological Review, 90*, 293-315.

7

JUDGING BY SCENARIOS AND EXPLANATIONS

For thousands, maybe millions of years, people have been telling stories to each other. They have told stories around the campfire; they have traveled from town to town telling stories to relate the news of the day; they have told stories transmitted by electronic means to passive audiences incapable of doing anything but listening (and watching). The reason that humans constantly relate stories to each other is that stories are all they have to relate.

—Roger Schank and Robert P. Abelson

7.1   GOOD STORIES

Ask people how likely it is that an alcoholic tennis star who starts drinking a fifth a day will go on to win a major tournament 8 months later, and they will probably answer that it is extremely unlikely. Now ask other people how likely it is that an alcoholic tennis star who starts drinking a fifth a day will join Alcoholics Anonymous (AA), quit drinking, and win a major tournament 8 months later; to most people that seems more likely.

It is logically necessary, however, that the first outcome (winning the tournament) is more likely for the alcoholic star who starts drinking a fifth a day than is the second (joining AA *and* quitting *and* winning the tournament). The probability of three events must be less than the probability of one of them alone. A moment's thought tells us there are ways in which the star could win the tournament without joining AA (e.g., quitting drinking on one's own, bribing the other players, even just being extraordinarily lucky). Hence winning the tournament must be more likely than winning it after the specific action of joining AA, which in turn is followed by the specific action of quitting. But joining AA links the parts of the story together into a plausible, coherent scenario.

Scenarios or narratives are representations of temporally ordered sequences of events glued together by causal relationships. Usually, they come in the form of simple linear causal chains: The missing nail caused the horse to throw a shoe, caused the horse to go lame, caused the message to arrive late, caused the army to be unprepared, caused the invader's victory, caused the nation to lose the war, caused the monarch to lose the throne. . . . Human beings, perhaps uniquely among all animals, create mental models of the situations they are in, and those situation models often take the form of stories (biologist Stephen J. Gould once described humans as "the story-telling primate"). And like every other fundamental characteristic of our minds, story construction plays a role in judgment and decision making.

7.2   THE CONJUNCTION PROBABILITY ERROR

Tversky and Kahneman (1983) term the belief that a specific combination of events can be more likely than parts of that combination "the conjunction fallacy." A more precise designation is *conjunction probability error*; we saw it earlier in the "Linda the feminist bank teller" representativeness-based error for category membership judgments. This same fallacy occurs in judgments of wholes like the alcoholic tennis player scenario. Another example in the context of scenario-based judgments is, again, provided by Tversky and Kahneman, who asked college students the following question (p. 306):

> John P. is a meek man, 42 years old, married with two children. His neighbors describe him as mild-mannered but somewhat secretive. He owns an import-export company based in New York City, and he travels frequently to Europe and the Far East. Mr. P. was convicted once for

smuggling precious stones and metals (including uranium) and received a suspended sentence of 6 months in jail and a large fine. Now Mr. P. is currently under police investigation again.

Please rank the following statements by the probability that they will be among the conclusions of the investigation. Remember that other possibilities exist and that more than one statement may be true.

- Mr. P. is a child molester.
- Mr. P. is involved in espionage and the sale of secret documents.
- Mr. P. is a drug addict.
- Mr. P. murdered one of his employees.

Eighty-six undergraduates ranked the events above; another sample of 86 students ranked a modified list with the last event replaced by "Mr. P. murdered one of his employees to prevent him from talking to the police." Although the addition of the specific motive reduces the extent of the event (directly analogous to the case of Linda *the feminist bank teller* compared to Linda *the bank teller*, in Chapter 6), the mean likelihood of the conjunction event ("murdered *to prevent him from talking*") was reliably higher (ranked at 2.90, on average) than the global murdered (*for any reason*) event (ranked at 3.17).

(The statement that he murdered an employee "in order to . . . " must be kept distinct from the "in order to" as a *reason* if we begin by *knowing* that he murdered an employee. Because a combination of causes can yield an effect with higher probability than each cause alone, belief that an effect is "due to" a combination does not constitute a conjunction probability fallacy. For example, believing that someone was chilled *because* the person was outside and the temperature outside was below zero is more reasonable than believing that the person was chilled simply as a result of being outside, which would include being outside in the summer.)

Legal judgments, similar to the Mr. P. judgment, are important. Tversky and Kahneman (1983) also discovered the conjunction probability fallacy when they asked medical internists questions about symptoms and diagnoses in an even more obviously life-and-death situation (p. 301).

A fifty-five-year-old woman had a pulmonary embolism (blood clot in the lung). How likely is it that she also experiences:

- dyspnea [shortness of breath] *and* hemiparesis [partial paralysis]
- pleuritic chest pain
- syncope [fainting] *and* tachycardia [accelerated heart beat]

- hemiparesis

- hemoptysis [coughing blood]

Of the 32 internists questioned, 91% believed that the combination of a probable symptom (in this case, dyspnea) and an improbable one (in this case, hemiparesis) was more likely than the improbable symptom alone. The combination of the two symptoms formed a coherent or good explanation in the minds of the medical experts.

7.3   EXPLANATION-BASED JUDGMENTS

Conjunction probability violations of rationality are widespread. For example, when we imagine the future, the content of our imaginations tends to conform to our intellectual schemas. Thus many of our scenarios are conjunctions of specific events that we believe are highly probable. Again, such belief is fairly automatic. Those of us whose thought processes are primarily visual tend to anticipate the future by seeing what we and others are likely to do, and our images may be quite concrete. Our knowledge that almost nothing turns out exactly the way we imagine does not stop us from imagining the future concretely by building vivid scenarios of sequences of likely events. It is only on reflection that we attempt to assess the probability of events in isolation and thereby become less vulnerable to the conjunction probability fallacy. (The conclusion that the likelihood of events can better be considered by viewing them in isolation—rather than as part of a meaningful, holistic, apparently probable sequence—may be jarring to some readers.)

The scenario construction process and its consequences for judgment are summarized in Figure 7.1. Story construction, at least the perception of causal relationships between events, is so natural that we would list it as an automatic cognitive capacity along with our capacities for frequency registration, memory recognition, and similarity judgments. Roger Schank and Robert Abelson (1995) have made an interesting argument that virtually all of our everyday knowledge, from arithmetic skills to the fact that a whale is a mammal, is stored in narrative formats. This is probably going too far, but an enormous amount of knowledge in our memories is represented or linked to stories. The essential cognitive function of maintaining a situation model that places us in our current context prepared for action is dominated by narrative formats. Experience is a temporal sequence of

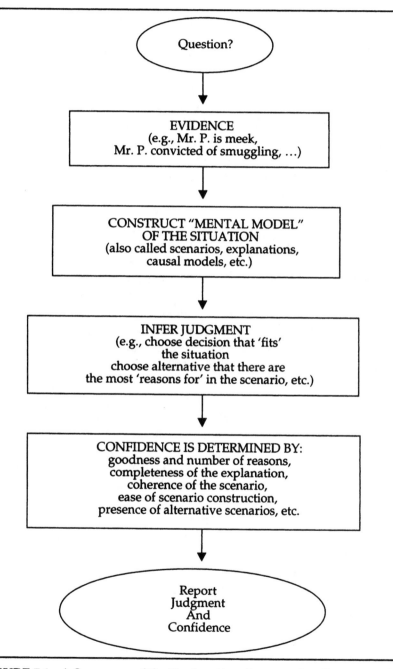

FIGURE 7.1. A Summary of the Explanation Construction Process and Its Effects on Judgments and Decisions

events, and that is the cognitive format we use to summarize the past and to project to the future.

Of course, it is no surprise that we look for good reasons for an event that we are predicting (or retrospectively diagnosing): The knowledge that a key player has been injured, that a company has a new CEO, or that a person is a drug addict is often enough cause, even if that is all we know about the situation, to make a confident prediction. But we humans have a compulsion to explain events in the world around us; this compulsion may be part of a generally adaptive habit of maintaining useful mental models of our current situations, a habit with obvious survival value. Many prefabricated scenarios are available to our imaginations either because they correspond to stereotyped scripts or because they are available through particular past experiences. (Such availability need not be based on actual frequency, as pointed out at some length in Chapter 4.) Availability here, however, must refer to availability *to our imagination* rather than availability *in fact*—because it is logically impossible for us to experience conjunctions of events more frequently than we experience the individual components of these conjunctions. Imagination is an important determinant of feelings, thought, and action. Consider again estimating the probability that a six-letter word ends in *-ing* versus the probability that it has an *n* in the fifth position. Without seeing or hearing any words, it is easier to imagine—visually or verbally—those ending in *-ing*, even though they cannot be more common.

Belief in the likelihood of scenarios tends to be associated with belief in the likelihood of their components; believable components yield believable scenarios (and often vice versa as well). Complete stories, detailed stories, and sensible stories (with reference to other stories or to our general beliefs about human motivation and natural causality) are influential stories. It is somehow plausible to us that Cleopatra's physical charms could lead two of the most powerful men in the classical world to behave like 14-year-olds or that a sexual flirtation by a 24-year-old intern could lead the most powerful man in the modern world to behave in the same manner.

Scenarios are even more believable if the components form a good gestalt because they fit into or exemplify some familiar narrative schema. We might say that the story of the alcoholic athlete who joins AA, is rehabilitated, and triumphs is a prototypical recovery narrative. Coherence leads to overestimation of the likelihood that a scenario is true or will occur. It is an overestimate for three reasons:

1. A combination of events may be improbable even though each event in it is probable; the probability of a combination of events 1, 2, . . . , *k* is,

$p_1 \times p_2 \times \ldots \times p_k$ where p_1 is the probability of the first, p_2 is the probability of the second *given* the first, p_3 is the probability of the third given the first two, and so on ($p_1 \times p_2 \times \ldots \times p_k$ may be quite small, even though each p_i in it is large, e.g., $.90 \times .80 \times .85 \times .80 \times .85 \times .90 = .37$, even though .80 is the smallest number in this sequence). To estimate the probability of the sequence on the basis of its component probabilities (average = .85) seriously overestimates this number. In fact, the probability of many conjunctions of events, even if they don't compose a plausible narrative, is often overestimated; for example, the probability of getting four cherries on a standard casino slot machine. Painstaking behavioral studies suggest that this overestimation is usually the result of an anchor-and-adjust estimation strategy; people anchor on a typical component event probability (the probability of getting one cherry) and then underadjust.

2. The same cognitive factors—such as imaginability—that lead to an overestimation of the probability of a component may also lead to an overestimation of the probability of the scenario as a whole. In fact, the imaginability of the entire scenario may lead to greater belief in the likelihood of the whole than in one of its parts, as illustrated by the belief that the sequence AA-rehabilitation-win is more probable than the single event of winning a major tournament.

3. In many domains (e.g., sports, crime, health), when dramatic coincidences occur, composed of an unlikely combination of components, they tend to draw attention and are retold and remembered, amplifying the basic conjunction overestimation effect.

7.4 LEGAL SCENARIOS: THE BEST STORY WINS IN THE COURTROOM

Like all of the heuristic judgment strategies, scenario-based reasoning underlies many casual, apparently spontaneous judgments. But it is also the strategy that we rely on when we make many highly controlled judgments. One of us (Hastie) has spent many years studying the complex strategies involved in the deliberate jury decision process. Here there seems to be little question that jurors' decisions are driven primarily by the stories they construct to comprehend and remember the evidence presented to them at trial.

Good trial attorneys know that good stories win cases. A famous trial attorney with a colorful nickname, "Racehorse" Haines, commented, "The lawyer with the best story wins." He went on to advise (defense) attorneys, "The surest way to win a murder case is to convince the jury that the best ending for the story told by the evidence is that the decedent deserved to die." Another highly successful attorney, Gerry Spence, provides more specific advice: "When I make an opening statement, I always do it as a story. But, you'd better be able to prove your story, because if jurors who believed you find out you haven't told the whole story, then they turn against you" (Spence, 1994, p. E1). And Anthony Amsterdam, another highly successful attorney, has analyzed transcripts of attorneys' arguments to the jury to demonstrate that they often tell two kinds of stories: first, stories about the evidence, the "what happened" at the crime scene; and, second, stories about the trial, with careful attention to the role that the attorney wants the jurors to play in that narrative. In the O. J. Simpson murder trial, prosecutor Marcia Clark's closing argument included a detailed summary of the prosecution crime story, complete with a time line; in contrast, defense attorney Johnnie Cochran concluded by exhorting the jurors to accept the role, at trial, of protector, even avenger, of oppressed minority defendants.

The central cognitive process in juror decision making is *story construction*—the creation of a narrative summary of the events under dispute. Thus the story the juror constructs, often quite deliberately, to "piece together the puzzle of historical truth" determines the juror's verdict. Ask any juror why he or she decided on a verdict and you will more likely than not get an answer that begins, "Let me tell you what happened . . . " Using converging measures to take "cognitive snapshots" of the contents of several hundred mock jurors' thoughts before and after rendering verdicts in a variety of cases, Nancy Pennington and Reid Hastie (1991) found that a narrative story structure was consistently the best summary of the jurors' memory structures. For example, when asked to decide a well-known civil case in which a mall employee (Kathleen Hughes) sued the mall owners (the Jardel Company) for damages after she was assaulted on her way to her car after work, the modal juror exhibited a cognitive representation of the evidence that looks like the network in Figure 7.2.

Note that the evidence at trial was not presented to the jurors in the chronological order of the events in the original crime, so the jurors must have reorganized the evidence during comprehension to produce memory structures that reflected the original chronological order of events depicted in Figure 7.2. More important, though, is the finding that jurors who choose different verdicts have reliably different mental representations. Pennington and Hastie found that jurors construct summaries of the evidence they hear and see. In legal disputes, there are usually at least two competing interpretations (otherwise the dispute would not have gotten

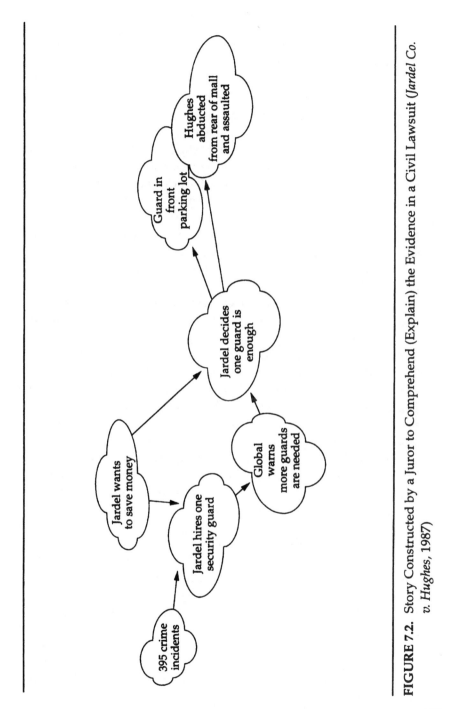

FIGURE 7.2. Story Constructed by a Juror to Comprehend (Explain) the Evidence in a Civil Lawsuit (*Jardel* Co. *v. Hughes,* 1987)

to court—over 90% of criminal cases and civil suits are plea bargained or settled before they get to court, presumably because one side or the other did not have the evidence to construct a plausible alternative story); different jurors are likely to construct different stories, and the stories lead to different verdicts. At least, after jurors reach different verdicts, they have different stories in mind. This situation is summarized in Figure 7.3 (for a criminal case): First, the juror constructs a story summary of the evidence (and there are usually only a few, at most three or four alternate culturally primed stories for a typical case); second, the juror learns something about the possible verdicts from the judge's instructions at the end of the trial; and third, the juror "classifies" the story into the best-fitting verdict category. Finally, Pennington and Hastie found that the characteristics of individual stories predicted jurors' confidence in their verdicts: Jurors with more complete, more detailed, and more unique stories were more confident.

An illustration of the power of narrative evidence summaries is provided by the dramatic differences between European American and African American citizens' reactions to the verdict in the O. J. Simpson murder trial. (There even appeared to be racial differences on the jury and within the defense team.) We believe that race made a difference in the construction and acceptance of the defense story according to which a racist police detective (Mark Fuhrman) planted incriminating evidence. African Americans, compared to European Americans, have many more beliefs and experiences that support the plausibility of stories of police misconduct and police bigotry. Many African Americans or members of their immediate families have had negative, and probably racist, encounters with justice system authorities. African Americans know of many more stories (some apocryphal, some veridical) than do European Americans of police racism and police brutality directed against members of their race. This background of experience, beliefs, and relevant stories made it easy for African Americans to construct a story in which a police officer manufactured and planted key incriminating evidence; this background makes the planted evidence story more plausible to African American than to European American jurors and citizens. (In an effort to find a European American version of the "racist cop" stereotyped scenario, one of us asked his colleagues if they knew, through personal experience, of any examples of biased or unfair authorities. The resounding answer? Internal Revenue Service officials! Almost everyone in his predominantly white, middle-class sample had had or claimed to know someone who had had a bad experience with overzealous income tax auditors.)

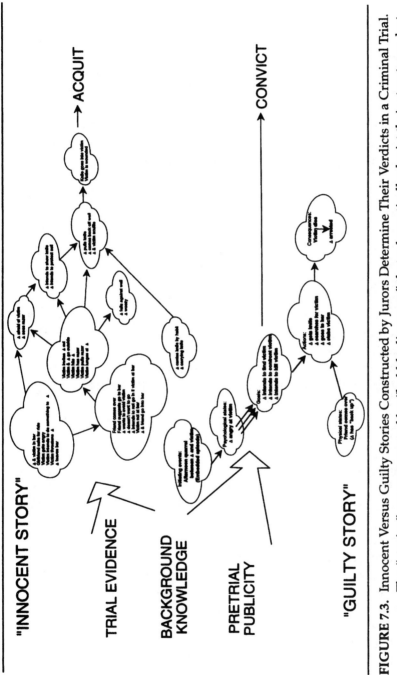

FIGURE 7.3. Innocent Versus Guilty Stories Constructed by Jurors Determine Their Verdicts in a Criminal Trial. The "stories" are represented by "bubble diagrams" that schematically depict their structures, but the "contents" of the bubbles are illegible in this figure; see Pennington and Hastie, 1991, or Hastie and Pennington, 2000, for details of the stories.

One of the most dramatic demonstrations that jurors' stories of the evidence cause their verdicts is a study of the effects of variations in the order of evidence presentation on judgments. Stories were predicted to be easy to construct when the evidence was presented in a temporal sequence that matched the occurrence of the original events (Story Order). Stories were predicted to be difficult to construct when the presentation order did not match the sequence of the original events. (The nonstory "Witness Order" was based on the sequence of evidence presented by witnesses in the original trial.) As predicted, jurors were likeliest to convict the defendant when the prosecution evidence was presented in Story Order and the defense evidence was presented in Witness Order (78% of the jurors judged the defendant guilty), and they were least likely to convict when the prosecution evidence was in Witness Order and defense was in Story Order (31% said guilty). The difference in conviction rates between the condition in which the greatest advantage was predicted for the prosecution versus for the defense was convincingly large, over 40 percentage points. (We do not claim that the "order of proof" effect will be this large in actual trials, although we do believe the effect generalizes and advise attorneys to tell good stories, when they can, as winning trial attorneys like Gerry Spence, "Racehorse" Haines, and Johnnie Cochran do.)

A more subtle aspect of scenario-based judgment occurs because stories tend to exist sui generis, without multiple interpretations or versions. In the Pennington and Hastie (1991) studies of juror decision making, the perceived strength of one side of the case depended on the order of evidence both for that side *and for the other side* of the case. This finding implies that the jurors attempted to construct more than one story summary of the evidence and that the *uniqueness* or relative goodness of the best-fitting story is one basis for confidence in their judgment. The construction of multiple stories is almost forced on the decision maker by the traditions of our adversarial trial system. We suspect that in most everyday situations when story construction is the basis for decisions, most people stop after they construct one story.

During construction and evaluation of a story, people do consider alternative versions of *parts of* the stories. This form of reasoning is called *counterfactual thinking*, or "what if" or "but for" thinking in everyday terms. In the *Jardel Co. v. Hughes* case, the crucial inference that appeared to distinguish between jurors deciding the mall owners were liable versus not liable involved the possible counterfactual effects of adding extra patrol guards to the mall security staff. Jurors who reasoned, "If there had been more guards . . . " and concluded, "the rape would have been *prevented*," went on to conclude that the mall was liable; if the owners had not been so greedy, if they'd paid to add extra guards, then the assault would not have occurred. On the other hand, jurors who reasoned, "If there had been more guards . . . the rape would still have occurred" (i.e., in a large mall, full security would require an impossibly large security force) that concluded the mall was not liable. In legal contexts, this kind of reasoning is called the "but for" test of causality; a philosopher would probably describe it as testing if a candidate cause (few security guards) is a necessary condition for an effect (the assault on Kathleen Hughes) to occur. Thus although there is a tendency for one story to dominate our mental representation of any situation, the construction of that story usually involves the consideration of alternative parts or episodes within the story. When there is uncertainty about those parts (e.g., a juror can't make up his or her mind about whether the rape would have been prevented by adding security guards), that local uncertainty is generalized to lower confidence in the whole story.

Follow-up research has addressed some practical questions about trial tactics in adversarial trials. Many criminal cases involve the presentation of only one story by the prosecution, and the defense tactic is to "raise reasonable doubts" by attacking the plausibility of that story. (Some cynical attorneys describe this defense strategy as "creating a cloud of confusion in the juror's mind and then labeling that confusion 'reasonable doubt.'") In these one-sided cases, jurors construct only one story and confidence in the verdict is determined by the coherence and fit of that single story to the verdict category. In this situation, a weak defense story is worse than no story at all. In fact, a weak prosecution story is bolstered and more guilty verdicts are rendered when a weak defense story is presented versus no defense story at all, again implicating the importance of the comparative factor when more than one story has been constructed. Another observation that reinforces the lore of trial tactics is that when a narrative strategy is used to argue a case, the attorney should set up the story in his or her opening statement to the jury. The chance of obtaining a verdict consistent with a story is increased when the story is primed to interpret the evidence in the opening statement, all other factors remaining equal.

7.5   SCENARIOS ABOUT OURSELVES

It is widely believed among psychoanalytic clinicians that clients of Freudian analysts have Freudian dreams and clients of Jungian analysts have Jungian dreams (and clients of behavior therapists have rapid eye movements, but nothing else worth mentioning). The extension that clients of Freudian and Jungian analysts have led Freudian and Jungian lives, respectively, is a bit more disconcerting, for it implies that the dearly (i.e., expensively) gained insights of these clients may be joint inventions of the clients and analysts (inventions of unknown and unknowable validity). Research on the nature of retrospective and even allegedly "repressed memory" has reinforced this possibility, for the malleability of such memory implies that mere agreement with the therapist is a poor basis for judging accuracy (Campbell, 1998). Could the therapy process be partly, or even primarily, one of inventing a good story about the client's life? If so, could this "story" hinder as well as help to foster free and responsible choice?

This notion of "narrative truth" is not contrary to the rationales behind many forms of psychotherapy. These therapies assume that clients' (narrative) representation of their life is the key to understanding their maladaptive behaviors. Reconstruction of the client's life story into a more coherent and adaptive narrative is the primary goal of therapy. The subjective nature of these life stories has gradually been recognized by therapists. (Paul van den Broek and his colleague Richard Thurlow, 1991, provide a thoughtful discussion of the role of narrative autobiographical reconstruction in psychotherapy from the point of view of laboratory-based cognitive psychology.) Freud originally believed that maladaptive behaviors were caused by actual events, but after discovering that several of his clients had manufactured memories that were impossible, he acknowledged that the crucial causal events might never have occurred. Thus the goal of therapy is not solely to recall actual events, but to reconstruct a more adaptive life story, one that may not agree perfectly with actual, historical truth. One of us (Dawes) proposed this hypothesis to a group of clinicians and was surprised to discover general agreement with the suggestion that psychotherapists, to some extent, "invent" life stories for their clients. These more adaptive life stories are aimed to help the clients to accept their past distressed behavior as a normal consequence of what had previously occurred in order to make the decision to abandon this behavior.

The problem with therapies based on reconstructing life stories was pointed out by James March (1972) in discussing the problem with "discovering" that one's adult years flow naturally—as part of a good story—from childhood:

> Belief in the model seems likely to create a static basis in personal self-analysis. Individuals who believe the "formative years" hypothesis seem quite likely to consider the problem of personal identity to be a problem of "discovering" a pre-existing "real" self rather than of "creating" an "interesting" self. The notion of discovery is biased against adult change. (p. 416)

Such discoveries can become verbal straitjackets through the attributions they create—for example, "I have come to accept the fact that I suffer from a narcissistic character disorder" can lead to self-indulgence ("What can I do, I'm a narcissist, and that's it") and unrealistic projection onto others. The art of this form of cognitively oriented therapy is to construct *adaptive* life stories. (The psychotherapist who has developed this theme most fully is Donald Spence, whose 1982 book *Narrative Truth and Historical Truth* is a landmark in modern psychoanalytic theory.)

A hint of the potentially detrimental side effects of our habit of creating and reconstructing consistent life stories is given in studies of people's biased reconstruction of what they used to be like. As we show at the end of this chapter, autobiographical memories tend to be dominated by our current attitudes, beliefs, and feelings about ourselves (see also "anchoring the past in the present" in Section 5.3).

All of the elements for belief in the high probability of personal scenarios are there when we view our lives. These include stereotypes derived from family myths, cultural beliefs, literature, plays, movies, and television and, in the case of people involved in psychology or psychiatry, prototypical case histories communicated in textbooks or through contact with others who have an interest or a professional commitment. These sources all provide prepackaged, believable, complex sequences of events for our entertainment, education, *and use.* No wonder some pop psychologists have achieved great fame through arguing that we often act out pre-selected life scripts (e.g., Eric Berne's popular 1964 exegesis, *Games People Play*).

7.6   SCENARIOS ABOUT THE UNTHINKABLE

Several small countries are working on the development of nuclear weapons. Iran, Iraq, North Korea, and Pakistan are obvious candidates. One or more of these countries may be run by a fanatic who incites his people to suicidal missions, such as that against the U.S. Marines barracks in

Lebanon in 1983. Given that H-bombs are now the size of a child's sled, it would not be impossible to smuggle one into New York or San Francisco. The suicidal fanatics all agree to die in the blast so that they cannot be traced. The city is annihilated, and there have been no missiles, no early warning, no warning of any sort. There is no reason to blame the Soviets, the Cubans, or even the Iranians. The city is simply gone, and various terrorist groups claim responsibility. (The group actually responsible will make sure there are bogus calls as well.) The civil liberties of the citizens of the United States disappear soon after the city does, and international nuclear war is not far behind.

Vivid? Yes. The terrorists are thin, swarthy, excitable young men of Arab or Asian extraction, with moustaches. (Indeed, this scenario, originally sketched out by one of us—Dawes—in 1988, is a summary of the screenplay for the 1998 movie *The Siege*.)

Likely? No, but not impossible. The point is that there are literally thousands of scenarios leading to nuclear destruction. Yet the *real* availability, accuracy, and delivery speed of nuclear weapons increase year by year while we concentrate on a few scenarios. Roughly 60% of the university students in one of our decision-making classes in 1985 believed it was more likely that there would be a Mideast crisis leading to nuclear war between the United States and an Arab nation in the next 25 years than that such a war would occur for *any* reason. Furthermore, when we concentrate on scenarios, we develop a false sense of security by taking precautions against (only) them. If the first event of a scenario (perhaps an incident that leads to a confrontation between the United States and Iraq) does not occur, we believe the rest of the scenario will not occur either (just as we were sure the tennis star must join AA and quit drinking to win the tournament). Believing events such as nuclear war can occur only in the context of specific scenarios is not thinking rationally.

How probable is nuclear war? Not very—tomorrow, next month, or this year. But the risk is similar to the risk involved in riding in cars. The probability of a person's being seriously injured or killed while riding in an automobile is less than 1 in 50,000 *on any particular trip*, but greater than 1 in 3 in a lifetime. Thus most people do not wear seat belts. Only 41% did in 1998, and 49,999 times out of 50,000 their judgment that they did not need seat belts was validated.

How high is p for a nuclear war each year? We are not claiming that it is a constant, merely that it can be approximated with a single value *given* no additional information. Let's suppose, for the sake of analysis, that the probability of nuclear destruction (which did not occur) between 1945 and 1995 was 1 in 3. That means, assuming a constant probability p and independence between years (as rough approximations to reality), that $(1 - p)^n = 2$ in 3 or $p = .01$ per year. Thus, if p remains constant, the probability of having a nuclear war sometime in the next century is 2 in 3 $(1 - .99^n)$. *But p does not remain constant.* If, for example, it were to become twice as likely in each of the next 40 years as the last—and if we accept the 1 in 3 figure—then the probability of surviving the next 40 years without a nuclear war is only .44.

The probabilistic approach to nuclear war also contains a positive message: *Whatever can decrease the probability of a war, by even a small amount, is valuable.* Assume, for example, the probability of .02 per year. As pointed out earlier, the probability of no war in the next 40 years is only .44 (assuming constancy and yearly independence). Now suppose some "small" arms agreement is reached that reduces that probability by 1/3, that is, to .0133. The probability of no war in the next 40 years would then be .58.

If that decrease does not appear important, consider this situation:

A barrel contains 100 balls, 44 of which are green, 14 of which are blue, and 42 of which are red. A single ball is drawn at random. Choose between two options:

If a green ball is chosen, you receive $10,000. If a blue or red ball is chosen, you die.

If a green or blue is chosen, you receive $10,000. If a red ball is chosen, you die.

Which option would you prefer? When the difference between .58 and .44 is viewed in this manner, the much greater desirability at .58 is evident. (Unfortunately, people tend to assess the magnitude of probability difference in terms of *ratios*—e.g., the "mortality ratio" for smokers vs. nonsmokers—rather than in terms of actual differences.)

Paul Slovic has emphasized the probabilistic approach to reducing the danger of nuclear war and other societal and personal risks (P. Slovic, personal communication). Small differences in probability for small intervals can yield large differences in broad ones. As Slovic points out, scenario thinking can once again get into the way of a probabilistic assessment. The desirable scenario for most of us would be an agreement among all countries capable of producing nuclear weapons resulting in technological control of nuclear weapons to the point that they could not be used in haste or by accident. The least desirable scenario is an international confrontation followed by war. As mental images of what could occur in the next few decades, these scenarios are understandable, vivid, and compelling. Thus we exaggerate the probability of confrontation and of total agreement while we neglect policies that would reduce the probability of nuclear war each year by some small amount.

The first step in resolving a problem is to think clearly about it. Scenario thinking grossly overestimates the probability of scenarios that come to mind and underestimates the long-term probabilities of events occurring one way or another. The big problem with scenario thinking is that it focuses the thinker on one or a few causal stories and diverts the decision maker from a broader, more systematic representation of the decision situation. Furthermore, there is a general tendency for memories and inferences to be biased to be consistent with the themes and theories underlying the scenarios. One of the main messages of this book is that rational analysis requires a systematic, comprehensive representation of situations and alternative outcomes to assess the important underlying probabilities of events.

We believe that probabilities (and some other statistics) are the best tools our civilization has developed to deal with uncertainty and other sources of confusion in decision making. In contrast to immersion in the seductive details of a few vivid scenarios, probabilistic assessments tend to be more valid. Moreover, probabilistic thinking indicates that "small" changes in likelihood can have "large" long-term effects. For example, if we must continue to play nuclear Russian roulette, putting more blank chambers into the gun is preferable to trying to (vividly) imagine which chamber the bullet is in. In Chapter 9, we return to the question of how to think more clearly and rationally in uncertain situations.

7.7   HINDSIGHT: RECONSTRUCTING THE PAST

Memory for complex events is basically a reconstructive process. As the novelist Alain Robbe-Grillet (1986) put it: "Memory belongs to the imagination. Human memory is not like a computer which records things; it is part of the imaginative process, on the same terms as invention" (p. 46). Our recall is organized in ways that make sense of the present. We thus reinforce our belief in the conclusions we have reached about how the past has determined the present. We quite literally make up stories about our lives, the world, and reality in general. The fit between our memories and the stories enhances our belief in them. Often, however, it is the story that creates the memory, rather than vice versa.

In a series of ingenious demonstrations, Baruch Fischhoff (1975) showed that people who know the nature of events *falsely* overestimate the probability with which they *would have* predicted them. (See Hawkins & Hastie, 1990, for a comprehensive review of the research on hindsight effects.) In his initial studies, Fischhoff simply asked people to predict what would happen before particular events occurred (e.g., U.S. President Nixon's visits to Russia and China in 1972) and then to recall what they had predicted. Their recall was biased in the direction of having predicted what actually happened. It follows, as Fischhoff points out, we are "insufficiently surprised" by experience. One result is that we do not learn effectively from it.

A study by David Wasserman, Richard Lempert, and Reid Hastie (1991) demonstrates the role of causality in producing reconstructive hindsight effects. These researchers followed the Fischhoff procedure of comparing foresight judgments from one group of experimental participants with informed, hindsightful judgments from a second group. They presented their subjects with short vignettes describing historical or fictional events (the outcome of a military conflict between the British colonials and native Ghurkas in India; a gold prospecting venture) and asked them to estimate the probability of various outcomes (British victory; success in the prospecting enterprise), either with or without knowledge of the "true" outcomes (they employed an experimental method, so that all possible outcomes could be presented as "true" in the hindsight condition for purposes of experimental control). Like Fischhoff, they obtained substantial hindsight effects, even when subjects were instructed to estimate the probabilities that would be given by other people like themselves in the foresight condition. But, more important, Wasserman et al. manipulated the cause that was described as primarily responsible for the reported outcome. In half of the hindsight conditions, the outcome was attributed to a causally potent event (the better equipped and trained British troops, the superior knowledge of the battle terrain by indigenous guerrilla forces, etc.), in the other half to a surprising "act of God" event (an unseasonal monsoon rainstorm disabled the British weapons and tactics, the rainstorm prevented the guerrilla forces from utilizing their superior knowledge of the terrain, etc.). The results were clear: Hindsight effects only occurred under conditions where persuasive causal explanations could be generated to glue the causes to the outcomes.

This hindsight bias is not always reducible to a knew-it-all-along attempt to appear more omniscient than we are. Sometimes, motivational factors probably apply, as when that irritating friend claims to have known that the home team was going to lose the football game or that the "dark horse" candidate was going to win the election. But people actually *make mistakes* in their recall of what they thought would happen, even when they are motivated to be as accurate as possible. A classic example was provided by the natural experiment in which President Nixon's former aide John Dean attempted to recall, before Congressional investigating committees, as truthfully as possible, events that occurred during the "Watergate scandal" (Dean tried to recall events that occurred between June 1972 and March 1973 in testimony given in June 1973). Dean exhibited detailed memory of countless events during meetings in which Nixon discussed the Watergate events and many other political matters. But subsequent to the testimony, it was discovered that many of the same conversations had been secretly tape-recorded by the president. Comparisons between the Nixon tapes and Dean's testimony revealed his memory was exceptional, but the testimony was still peppered with many examples of memory errors and illusions, almost all biased to be consistent with Dean's knowledge of the situations *at the time he testified,* not at the time the original events occurred (Ulric Neisser, 1981, conducted this analysis). Memory fits knowledge. "Creeping determinism"—to use Fischhoff's phrase—is well documented, and the major determinant of hindsight effects is our proclivity to summarize experiences as coherent narratives.

Sometimes, when we believe in change, we recall change even when it has not occurred. To make our view compatible with this belief, we resort (again, not consciously) to changing our recall of the earlier state. We can reinforce our belief in a nonexistent change for the better by simply exaggerating how bad things were before the change. Certainly, there have been times before a religious or psychiatric conversion, for example, when the individual was badly off (we all are at times), and memories of those times persist; recall can be organized around the traces of these memories. A dieter who has not succeeded in losing a single pound can certainly recall periods of time prior to embarking on a diet when he or she was heavier than when he or she completes the ineffective diet; by carefully not recording his or her weight before starting the diet, the person can (mis)recall those times as evidence for the diet's success.

Experimental evidence supports the contention that when we believe a change has occurred we are apt to distort the past in the direction compatible with the change. Michael Conway and Michael Ross (1984) randomly selected participants for a university program designed to improve study skills and a control group of students who had indicated a desire to be in the program and were on the waiting list for it. Participants and controls were questioned before the study skills program began and at its conclusion. At both times, they were asked to assess their study skills (e.g., how much of their study time was well spent, how satisfactory their note-taking skills were, etc.) and the amount of time they studied. At the second interview, they were also asked to recall what they reported during the first session concerning their skills and study time.

At the initial interview, participants and controls did not differ significantly on any measure of skill, study time, or other variables. Both groups performed equally well and—most important to the study—the program itself was *not* found to improve study skills. Nor did it improve grades. When asked to recall their situations before the program started (or before they were put on the waiting list), however, the subjects did differ. There was no difference between the two groups in their memory of the amount of time they spent studying, but their recall of their skills was markedly different. Program participants recalled their study skills as being significantly *worse* than they had initially reported, whereas, on the average, waiting-list subjects recalled their skills as being approximately the same as they had reported initially. Thus program participants exaggerated their improvement in a direction consistent with their beliefs of what *ought* to be (improved skills due to taking the course), not by exaggerating their current skills but, rather, by reconstructing their memories to fit with the expectation that they should have improved. In short, they recalled themselves as having been worse off before they entered the program than they had in fact been; they rewrote their autobiographical memories to be consistent with their current beliefs. There was no such distortion on the part of the subjects who had been put on the waiting list.

Moods also affect recall. It has been established experimentally by Gordon Bower (1981) and others that recall of material learned in a particular mood is facilitated by re-creation of that mood. Does the same principle apply to our recall of our own lives? Is our recall of events that occurred when we were in a bad mood—which are usually negative events—facilitated by a current bad mood and vice versa for good moods? The answer is yes.

Lewinsohn and Rosenbaum (1987) studied the recall of parental behavior by acute depressives, remitted depressives (i.e., people who had once been depressed and were no longer depressed), nondepressives (people who had never been depressed), and "predepressives" (people who were to become depressed) in a group of 2,000 people over a 3-year period. One focus of this research was on the relationship between current mood states and memory. Perhaps recollections of one's parents are influenced by a current state of depression or nondepression. Or people who are *prone* to depression may recall their parents differently from those who are not (the nondepressives). Theories that say depression follows from childhood problems would predict that the childhood of those of us who are depression *prone* is different from that of those who are not and hence would be recalled differently, whereas theories about the effect of current mood on past recall predict that the primary difference in recall should be between people who are *currently* depressed and those who are not. The results were consistent with the hypothesis that recollection of one's parents as rejecting and unloving is strongly influenced by current moods; it is not a stable characteristic of depression-prone people:

> Whereas the currently depressed subjects recalled their parents as having been more rejecting and as having used more negative control than the normal controls, the remitted depressives did not differ from the never depressed control in their recall of parental behavior. Similarly, the subjects who were about to become depressed shortly after the initial testing did not differ from the controls in their recollections of the degree to which their parents used negative control methods. (p. 617)

One important aspect of this study was that the subjects were drawn from the general population; they were not sampled on the basis of having any particular psychiatric problems in the first place.

This study of depression is important in that it casts doubt on the degree to which adult problems are related to childhood ones. Given a biasing effect of mood on reconstructive memory, people who are distressed as adults tend to remember distressing incidents in their childhood. One result is reinforcement of the view that the sources of the current problems lie in early life. But this view itself may serve as an organizing principle to produce even greater distortion of recall, which in a circular way reinforces the "child is father to the man" view of life.

7.8   SOMETIMES IT'S BETTER TO FORGET

One primary function of our minds is to create a model of the current situation in which we are located. When a car changes lanes in front of us, we update our mental model of the traffic situation and we don't ram into the car; when a person we once thought was reliable demonstrates that he or she is not, we adjust our mental model of that person and do not rely on him or her to come through for us in difficult circumstances. The maintenance of up-to-date situation models requires us to constantly refresh our beliefs about where we are and what is about to happen. This process is adaptive when we must make decisions about the future. Indeed, remember it is a fundamental tenet of decision theory that we should ignore "sunk costs" and focus only on future probabilities and utilities to make rational choices (see Chapter 1). But as we engage in this constant adjustment process, we lose the past and find it is difficult to recover what we used to think and sometimes even what we did.

REFERENCES

Abelson, R. P. (1985). A variance explanation paradox: When a little is a lot. *Psychological Bulletin, 97,* 129-133.

Amsterdam, A. G., & Hertz, R. (1992). An analysis of closing arguments to a jury. *New York Law School Law Review, 37,* 55-122.

Berne, E. (1964). *Games people play: The psychology of human relationships.* New York: Grove.

Bower, G. (1981). Mood and memory. *American Psychologist, 36,* 129-148.

Campbell, T. W. (1998). *Smoke and mirrors: The devastating effect of false sexual abuse claims.* New York: Plenum.

Conway, M., & Ross, M. (1984). Getting what you want by revising what you had. *Journal of Personality and Social Psychology, 47,* 738-748.

Doyle, J. K. (1997). Judging cumulative risk. *Journal of Applied Social Psychology, 27,* 500-524.

Fischhoff, B. (1975). Hindsight ≠ foresight: The effect of outcome knowledge on judgment under uncertainty. *Journal of Experimental Psychology: Human Perception and Performance, 1,* 299-299.

Hastie, R., & Pennington, N. (2000). Explanation-based decision making. In T. Connolly, H. R. Arkes and K. R. Hammond (Eds.), *Judgment and decision making: An interdisciplinary reader* (2nd ed., pp. 212-228). New York: Cambridge University Press.

Hawkins, S. A., & Hastie, R. (1990). Hindsight: Biased judgments of past events after the outcomes are known. *Psychological Bulletin, 107,* 311-327.

Jardel Co. v. Hughes, 523 A. 2d 518 (Del. Supr., 1987).

Lewinsohn, P. M., & Rosenbaum, M. (1987). Recall of parental behavior by acute depressives, remitted depressives, and nondepressives. *Journal of Personality and Social Psychology, 52,* 611-620.

March, J. G. (1972). Model bias in social action. *Review of Education Research, 42,* 413-429.

New York Times. (1994, November 29). P. E1.

Neisser, U. (1981). John Dean's memory: A case study. *Cognition, 9,* 1-22.

Pennington, N., & Hastie, R. (1991). A cognitive theory of juror decision making: The story model. *Cardozo Law Review, 13,* 519-557.

Robbe-Grillet, A. (1986, Spring). The art of fiction. *The Paris Review,* p. 46.

Schank, R. C., & Abelson, R. P. (1995). Knowledge and memory: The real story. In R. Wyer, Jr. (Ed.), *Advances in social cognition* (Vol. 8, pp. 1-86). Hillsdale, NJ: Lawrence Erlbaum.

Spence, D. F. (1982). *Narrative truth and historical truth: Meaning and interpretation in psychoanalysis.* New York: W. W. Norton.

Spence, G. (1994, November 29). Winning attorneys. *New York Times,* p. E1.

Tversky, A., & Kahneman, D. (1983). Extensional versus intuitive reasoning: The conjunction fallacy in probability judgment. *Psychological Bulletin, 90,* 293-315.

van den Broek, P., & Thurlow, R. (1991). The role and structure of personal narratives. *Journal of Cognitive Psychotherapy, 5,* 257-274.

Wasserman, D., Lempert, R. O., & Hastie, R. (1991). Hindsight and causality. *Personality and Social Psychology Bulletin, 17,* 30-55.

THINKING ABOUT RANDOMNESS AND CAUSATION

Is 2 a random number?

—Donald Knuth

8.1 MISCONCEPTIONS ABOUT CHANCE

We have been careful not to refer to the world as probabilistic or random. Probability theory is a language we can use to *describe* the world or, more precisely, to describe the relationships among our beliefs about the world—an unfamiliar language to most people, with a special symbolic vocabulary and special rules of grammar. In fact, usually we think about the world as a bunch of events and objects connected to one another with causal relationships, and many of us think about causation deterministically and in terms of degrees of causal force, but not in terms of probabilities. As we noted in Chapter 2, probability theory was not invented until recently in the history of Western civilization and words like "probability" don't seem to have entered the English lexicon until the 17th century (lexicographers believe it was derived from the expression "approvable," e.g., a *probable* husband was originally an acceptable or "morally approvable" husband).

153

Sometimes we do talk about chance, luck, probability, or randomness in everyday events. But the best interpretation of phrases like "She was lucky," "It happened by chance," and "That was a random event" is in terms of the state of knowledge or uncertainty in the mind of the person speaking. Harking back to a very wise essay on the nature of chance by the philosopher Jules-Henri Poincaré (1854-1912), most events that we refer to in everyday life are brought about by deterministic, physical processes. What singles out the events that we refer to as random, chance, or probabilistic is that the causal context is hidden, complex, or unknown to the person who describes the event as such. For example, we refer to the toss of a fair coin as a random process and assign the (ideal) probability value of .50 to the event of heads, although we (and any reader of this book, we hope) would agree that the hidden, subtle structure of biological and physical events that *cause* the outcome are all deterministic. (In fact, skilled sleight-of-hand magicians have developed their manual skills to the point where they can execute apparently uncontrolled coin tosses and almost always produce the result, heads or tails, that they desire.)

Of course, there are parts of our environment that approximate the idealized behavior of theoretical "random processes"; events in casinos and lotteries are "caused" by deterministic, physical processes, but the causal mechanism is so complex and the determinants of the events are so subtle that the best way to think about these situations is in terms of probability theory. An important message of this book is that we should use probability theory to organize our thinking about almost all judgments under uncertainty, even where we know much more (or less) about the relevant causes than we do in a casino. But we tend to deny the random components in trivial events that we *know* to be the result of chance. There is a wonderful story about the winner of a national lottery in Spain. When interviewed about how he won, the winner said that he had deliberately selected a ticket that ended with the numbers 4 and 8. He explained, "I dreamed of the number 7 for seven straight nights. And 7 times 7 is 48" (Meisler, 1977, p. D1).

In a clever series of experiments, Ellen Langer (1975) of Harvard University, demonstrated that—often without any conscious awareness—we treat chance events as if they involve skill and are hence controllable. For example, gamblers tend to throw dice with greater force when they are attempting to roll high numbers than when they are attempting to roll lower numbers. Langer conducted a lottery in which each participant was given a card containing the name and picture of a National Football

League player; an identical card was put in a bag, and the person holding the card matching one drawn from the bag won the lottery. In fact, Langer conducted two lotteries. In one, the participants chose which player would constitute their ticket; in the other, players were assigned to the participants by the experimenter. Of course, whether or not the entrants were able to choose their own players had no effect on the probability of their winning the lottery, because the winning cards were drawn at random from the bag. Nevertheless, when an experimenter approached the participants offering to buy their card, those who had chosen their own player on the average demanded *more than four times as much money* for their card as those with randomly assigned cards. On questioning, no one claimed that being allowed to choose a player influenced his or her probability of winning. The participants just *behaved* as if it had.

In another striking experiment, Langer and Susan Roth (1975) were able to convince Yale undergraduates that they were better or worse than the average person at predicting the outcome of coin tosses. The subjects were given rigged feedback that indicated they did not perform any better than at a chance level—that they were correct on 15 of 30 trials. What the experimenters did was manipulate whether the subjects tended to be correct toward the beginning of the 30-trial sequence or toward the end. Consistent with a primacy effect (or anchoring and [insufficient] adjustment), those subjects who tended to be correct toward the beginning were apt to think of themselves as "better than average" at predicting, whereas those who did not do well at the beginning judged themselves to be worse. (Of course, due to random fluctuations, the probability of success in predicting the outcome of coin tosses cannot be expected to be invariant across a sequence as short as 30 trials.) In addition, "over 25% of the subjects reported that performance would be hampered by distraction. In the same vein, 40% of all the subjects felt that performance would improve with practice." Thus not only do people behave as if they can control random events, they also express the conscious belief that doing so is a skill, which like other skills is hampered by distractions and improves with practice. It is important to remember that these subjects were from one of the most elite universities in the world; yet they treated the prediction of coin tosses as if it involved some type of ability, not just dumb luck.

And as with most everyday applications of psychology, practitioners such as the managers of casinos and lotteries already have an intuitive understanding of these principles. Commercial games of chance often contain deceptive skill elements, deliberately designed to confuse the players about the skill and opportunity for control involved in games of chance. In most states, lottery players can choose the numbers they bet their money on, and the lotteries often have skill-evoking cover stories: "Hit a home run and win major league bucks . . . ," "Just by buying a Bowling for Bucks ticket, you're a winner . . . "

8.2   SEEING CAUSAL STRUCTURE WHERE IT ISN'T

A pernicious result of representative and scenario-based thinking is that they imply structure ("nonrandomness") where none exists. This implication occurs because our naive conceptions of randomness involve *too much* variation, often to the point that we make an inference that a generating process is *not* random. Consider one of the simplest, most familiar processes we would describe as random, a coin toss. When asked to "behave like a coin" and to generate a sequence of heads and tails that would be typical of the behavior of a fair tossed coin, most people produce too much alteration, nonrandomly too many heads-tails and tails-heads transitions (exhibiting the same bias when shown sequences and asked to pick the "real coin"). Representativeness enters in because when we are faced with the task of distinguishing between random and nonrandom "generators" of events, we rely on our stereotype of "a random process" (analogous to our stereotype of a feminist or a bank teller or an art history major) and use *similarity* to judge or produce a sequence. Thus when we encounter a truly random sequence, we are likely to decide it is *non*random because it does not look haphazard enough—because it shows less alternation than our *incorrect* stereotype of a random sequence.

Many people believe airplane accidents happen in "bunches"— usually "threes." (A clinical psychologist acquaintance of one of the authors cites such coincidences as evidence for "Jungian synchronicity.") Russell Vaught and Dawes obtained data from the Federal Aviation Administration (FAA) describing all commercial airline crashes between 1950 and 1970. They examined the number of days between the occurrences of the crashes. A totally "random" model begins with the assumption that the probability of a crash on any given day is a constant, p. Hence the probability of a crash occurring the day following another crash is p. The probability that the next crash occurs on the second day subsequent to a crash is $(1 - p)p$, because there must be no crash on the succeeding day and then a crash on the next one. (Note that $(1 - p)p$ is less than p, a result that some people find counterintuitive.) Similarly, the probability that the next crash will occur on the third day following a crash is $(1 - p)(1 - p)p = (1 - p)^2 p$; and in general the probability that the next crash will occur on the nth succeeding day is $(1 - p)^{n-1} p$.

Examining all crashes and fatal crashes separately, Vaught and Dawes discovered that the fit to the theoretical prediction based on a constant p was almost perfect. Yet crashes seem to occur in "bunches." Why? Because $(1 - p)^j > (1 - p)^k p$ when $j < k$. Hence random sequences actually contain "bunches" of events. The problem is that representative thinking leads us to conclude that such random patterns are *not* random. Instead, we hypothesize positive feedback mechanisms such as "momentum" to account for them. (Those of us hypothesizing "Jungian synchronicity" are in a minority.) Although the maxim that "nothing succeeds like success or fails like failure" may be true, phony evidence for it can be found in the bunching of successes in patterns of people or organizations with high probabilities of success and of failures in those with high probabilities of failures—even when the pattern is of independent events.

A well-defined situation in which people clearly see patterns that are not in the data is the "hot hand" phenomenon in basketball. The hot hand does not merely refer to the fact that some players are more accurate shooters than others, but to the (hypothetical) positive feedback process that makes players more likely to score after scoring and to miss after missing. (Note that the same term—a hot hand—is used to describe successful crap shooters, despite general acknowledgment that in well-run games they cannot control the outcome of a roll.) Tom Gilovich, Robert Vallone, and Amos Tversky (1985) demonstrated empirically that the hot hand does not exist; a success following a success is just as likely for an individual player as a success following a failure. At least, neither the floor shots of the Philadelphia '76ers, the free throws of the Boston Celtics, or the experimentally controlled floor shots of men and women on the Cornell varsity basketball teams showed evidence of a hot hand. But the players' predictions of their success showed a hot-hand effect, even though their performance did not. More than 90% of a sample of basketball players and sports reporters queried answered yes to the question "Does a player have a better chance of making a shot after having just made his last two or three shots than he does after having just missed his last two or three shots?"

The authors do not actually prove the *nonexistence* of the hot hand, but their results strongly imply that if it exists, it is small, unreliable, or rare. The claim that any particular set of data is random is tenuous; it is more defensible to claim that a process that generates the data is random, in the sense that the observers of the data could not know the information necessary to predict the events in the data with any degree of specificity—that to these observers the best description is a probabilistic or random process. The example of the hot hand in basketball is especially surprising because it is so easy to imagine a causal process that might generate the expected (but not observed) patterns. For example, one reply to Gilovich's original claim was that they had missed the true hot hand pattern that was hidden in their data because they had ignored the timing of baskets. Patrick Larkey, Richard Smith, and Jay Kadane (1989) published a reanalysis consisting only of runs of shots occurring in close temporal proximity. They found one player, Vinnie "Microwave" Johnson of the Detroit Pistons, who departed from the random model. Microwave earned his nickname because of his reputation for streak shooting. But Gilovich (1985) in rebuttal noted that the reanalysis found only one "hot" player, and that his statistically distinctive streakiness was due entirely to a single run of seven baskets. Then they pointed out that a viewing of the original game videotapes showed that the seven-basket run had *not* occurred. In fact, Microwave had a run of four baskets, missed a shot but scored on his own rebound, and then made one more score. After correction for this data collection error, even Microwave did not depart from the random model. But the quest continues for streak performances in sports ranging from Ping-Pong to ice hockey.

Do 4 good weeks in a row indicate therapeutic success with a patient? Do 4 bad weeks indicate failure (or, more sanguinely, "coming to face the problems")? No, no more than four heads in a row in a sequence of coin tosses indicates that the coin is biased. Yet, knowing the patient's base rate for good weeks—and expecting more alternation than in fact occurs if these weeks are totally *unrelated* to therapy—makes the temptation to impute causal factors to such strings almost overpowering, especially causal factors related to therapy—that is, to the therapist's own behavior.

Why do we expect too much alternation? Daniel Kahneman and Amos Tversky (1972) ascribe this expectation to the belief that even very small sequences must be representative of populations, that is, the proportion of events in a small frame must match (be representative of) the proportion in the population. When we are tossing a fair coin, we know that the entire population of possible sequences contains 50% heads; therefore we expect 50% heads in a sample of four tosses. That requires more alternation than is found when each toss is independent. (At the extreme, 50% heads in a sequence of two tosses requires that each head is followed by a tail and vice versa.)

Consider the following question from a study by Kahneman and Tversky (1972, p. 432):

> All families of six children in a city were surveyed. In 72 families, the exact order of births of boys and girls was G B G B B G. What is your estimate of the number families in which the exact order of births was B G B B B B? What about the number of families with the exact order B B B G G G?

Almost everyone (80% or more of respondents) judges the latter birth sequences to be less likely than the first. But all exact sequences are equally likely (the probability of any exact sequence is simply $.5 \times .5 \times .5 \times .5 \times .5 \times .5$, or approximately 16 families out of 1,000 with 6 children). Why do people have the strong intuition that G B G B B G is much more frequent? Because this short sequence captures all of our intuitions about what result a random process will generate: The sequence exhibits the correct proportion (half boys, half girls), it looks haphazard, and it has lots of alternation; in short, it looks "really random." (It is also the kind of sequence we would expect a "cold hand" to generate—too many short alternating runs, so that when we see a sequence with longer runs, we are prone to say, "That can't be random . . . this player must really be 'hot.'") In contrast, the second sequence looks less likely because it violates the law of small numbers by having the wrong ratio of births (too many boys) and the third sequence is okay for proportion, but looks too orderly (three in a row, then three in a row).

Occasionally, this belief in alternation in random sequences (the "gambler's fallacy" that his or her chances of winning are "maturing" because he or she has lost the last five hands in a row or red is due to come up on the roulette wheel because the last six numbers were black) reaches ludicrous extremes. Consider the beginning of a letter to "Dear Abby":

> DEAR ABBY: My husband and I just had our eighth child. Another girl, and I am really one disappointed woman. I suppose I should thank God that she was healthy, but, Abby, this one was supposed to have been a boy. Even the doctor told me the law of averages were [sic] in our favor 100 to one.
>
> (Taken from DEAR ABBY column by Abigail Van Buren.
> © UNIVERSAL PRESS SYNDICATE.
> Reprinted with permission. All rights reserved.)

Note that the expectation that random processes will exhibit shorter "runs" and more alterations than true random processes do is the basis for beliefs in the "hot hand" and "the gambler's fallacy." It all depends on the causal model that the perceiver has of the situation. In the case of the "hot hand," perceivers believe that there is a nonrandom cause of "streak" performances and so they believe that the long "runs" they see are evidence for a "streak," even though these runs are consistent with a simple random generating process, like a coin toss. In the case of coin tosses, roulette wheel spins, or births, the perceiver believes that the process is "random" and then expects that the runs will be shorter than they will be, on average, because of the same misconception that random processes involve more "short runs," more alterations, than they do.

A "graphic" example of the tendency to see patterns (and infer causes) where there aren't any occurred during the World War II bombing of London by German V-1 and V-2 missiles. Newspapers published maps of the missile impact sites in London and citizens immediately saw clusters of strikes and interpreted them with reference to the intentions of the hostile forces (see Figure 8.1). What kind of stories did they tell to explain these patterns? The British citizens reasoned that the patterns they saw were the result of deliberate efforts to miss the areas on the city in which German spies lived. But a classic probability theory analysis demonstrated that the clusters were completely consistent with a random Poisson process generating device, and there was no reason to infer a systematic motive or cause behind the patterns (see William Feller's classic textbook, *An Introduction to Probability Theory and Its Applications*, Vol. 1, pp. 160ff., for a mathematical analysis, and Gilovich, 1991, pp. 19-21 for a discussion of the misperception).

A recent example of this tendency to infer causes for geographic patterns is part of the psychology of "cancer cluster" hysterias. During the past two decades, reports of communities in which there seem to be an unusual number of cancer incidents have soared (see summary in a 1999 *New Yorker* article by Atul Gawande). A community that notices an unusual number of cancers quite naturally looks for a cause in the environment—something in the water or the ground or the air. But investigating isolated neighborhood cancer clusters is almost always an exercise in futility. Public health agencies have deployed thousands of "hot pursuit" studies in response to reports of raised local cancer rates. But Raymond Richard Neutra, California's chief environmental health

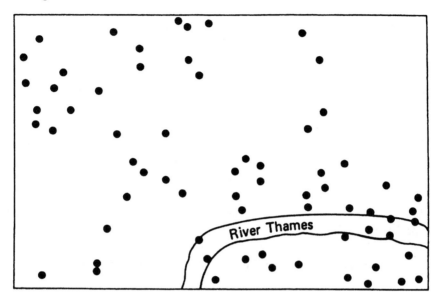

FIGURE 8.1. London V-1 and V-2 Rocket Impact Pattern
SOURCE: Based on Gilovich, 1991, p. 20; used by permission.

investigator (in 1999) notes that among the hundreds of published reports
of such investigations, *not one* has convincingly identified an environmental cause (Gawande, 1999). And only one investigation resulted in the discovery of an unrecognized carcinogen. Neutra points out that in a typical
Public Health Service registry of 80 different cancers, probability theory
predicts you would expect to observe 2,750 of California's 5,000 census
tracts to have statistically significant but random elevations of some form
of cancer. Thus, if you check to see if your neighborhood has a statistically
significant elevation in the rate of at least one of the 80 cancers, the chances
are better than .50 it will—but that discovery will be perfectly consistent
with a random model of the distribution of incidences, assuming *no* environmental causes. Commenting on the "hot pursuit" investigations that
result from neighborhood cluster alarms, Alan Bender an epidemiologist
in the Minnesota Department of Health, says, "The reality is they're a total
waste of taxpayer dollars."

    What can be done to maintain public trust and to effectively identify
true environmental health hazards? The fact that a random probability

theory model is *consistent with* the patterns does not prove that there are no causal effects. But we are undoubtedly wasting a lot of public funds responding to emotionally and symbolically important events and discovering many false correlations between clusters and their contexts. The strategy of analyzing individual clusters and looking for correlations with some environmental cause is called the "Texas sharpshooter fallacy" by epidemiologists, after the story about a rifleman who shoots a cluster of bullet holes in the side of a barn and then draws a bull's-eye around the holes. This is a case where we should go with the advice of statistically sophisticated experts and only respond when there are good a priori reasons to hypothesize an environmental cause or truly extraordinary statistical patterns. The much-publicized case of the cancer cluster in Woburn, Massachusetts, described in the book and movie *A Civil Action,* was never resolved by the identification of a scientifically credible causal pathway relating the pollutants from the Riley Tannery to the incidences of cancer in the neighborhood surrounding the factory.

8.3 REGRESSION TOWARD THE MEAN

The final problem with representative thinking about events with a random (unknown causes) component is that it leads to nonregressive predictions. To understand why, it is necessary first to understand regressive prediction.

Consider very tall fathers. On average, their sons are shorter than they are. Also, the fathers of very tall sons are, on average, shorter than their sons. That may seem paradoxical at first, but it can be understood by looking at Figure 8.2. What you see is a simple averaging effect. Because the heights of fathers and sons are not perfectly correlated (for whatever reasons), there is *regression*. In fact, the technical definition of regression toward the mean is just

regression = perfect relationship – correlation.

Consider another example (from Quinn McNemar, a psychologist who was one of the first to point out this statistical result and its implications for research on human behavior): Suppose that an intelligence test is administered to all the children in an orphanage on two occasions, a year

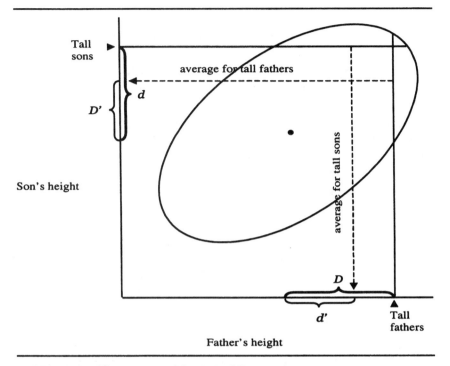

FIGURE 8.2. Illustration of Statistical Regression

apart. Assume, plausibly, that the group mean and standard deviation are the same on both tests, but that the correlation between scores on the two tests is not perfect (a good guess is that the correlation would be about +.80). Now consider only the children with the highest scores on the first test; their scores on the second test will be, on average, lower (since the correlation is below +1.00, we expect some change; since the two distributions of scores are the same, the first test high scorers must be lower on average). The same is true for the children with the lowest scores—the average of the lowest-scoring children on the first test will be higher on the second. What if we reverse time and look backward from the second to the first test? The same relationships will apply: Extreme scores will be less extreme. Regression toward the mean is inevitable for scaled variables that are not perfectly correlated.

Perhaps it is easiest to understand regression by considering the extreme case in which we obtain perfect regression. Toss a fair coin eight times; now toss it another eight times. No matter how many heads are obtained in the first sequence of tosses, the expected (average) number of heads in the second sequence is four. Because the coin is fair, the number of heads in the first sequence is totally uncorrelated with the number in the second—hence the average of four. That is total "regression to the mean." As variables become more predictable from each other, there is less regression; for example, on average, the sons of very tall fathers are taller than the average person, but not as tall as their fathers. It is only when one variable is perfectly predictable from the other that there is no regression. In fact, the (squared value of the) standard correlation coefficient can be defined quite simply as the degree to which a linear prediction of one variable from another is not regressive.

On the other hand, when we match the predicted extremity of one variable with the extremity of another, we make a *nonregressive* prediction. Some of the subsequent errors can be quite subtle. For example, when Daniel Kahneman was explaining to Israeli defense force flight instructors in the mid-1960s that reward is a better motivator than punishment, he was told that he was wrong (quoted in McKean, 1985, p. 24):

> With all due respect, Sir, what you are saying is literally for the birds. I've often praised people warmly for beautifully executed maneuvers, and the next time they almost always do worse. And I've screamed at pupils for badly executed maneuvers, and by and large, the next time they improve. Don't tell me that reward works and punishment doesn't. My experience contradicts it.

This flight instructor had witnessed a regression effect. People tend to do worse after a "beautifully executed maneuver" because performance at one time is not perfectly correlated with performance the next (again, for whatever reason). They also tend to improve each time after "badly executed maneuvers"—once more, simply because performance is not perfectly correlated from one occasion to the next. (The easiest way to obtain an award for "academic improvement" is to be right near the bottom of the class the semester prior to the one for which such awards are given, and the way to be labeled an "underachiever" is to score brilliantly on an aptitude test.) Unfortunately, as the flight instructor anecdote illustrates, teachers who do not understand regression effects may be systematically reinforced (by regression to better performance) for punishing students and disappointed (by regression to worse performance) for rewarding them. (A deeper explanation of people's general preference for punishment over reward as a means of behavior control may be unnecessary.)

The rational way of dealing with regression effects is to "regress" when making predictions. Then if there is some need or desire to evaluate discrepancy (e.g., to give awards for "overachievement" or therapy for "underachievement"), compare the actual value to the *predicted* value—not to the actual value of the variable used to make the prediction. For example, to determine patient "improvement" by comparing MMPI profiles at time 1 and time 2, first correlate the profiles to determine a (regressed) predicted score for each patient at time 2; then compare the actual profile with this predicted score, not to the score at time 1. Otherwise, patients who have high (pathological) profiles at time 1 may be mistakenly labeled improved ("They had nowhere to go but down"), whereas those with normal MMPI profiles may be mistakenly regarded as unresponsive to treatment. Representative thinking, in contrast, leads to comparing discrepancies without regressing first, and the results are predictable. For example, "Of particular significance was the fact that those scoring highest on symptom reductions . . . were those whose symptoms were initially more severe, and who were the less promising candidates for conventional types of therapy." (While one us—Dawes—was a clinical psychologist trainee, he asked the psychologists and psychiatrists at the hospital to dichotomize patients whose improvement was above average at discharge and those whose improvement was below average. Those they categorized as above average in improvement had higher scores on most of the MMPI scales on admission—significantly higher on the major clinical ones.)

Regression toward the mean is particularly invidious when we are trying to assess the success of some kind of intervention designed to improve the state of affairs, such as the flight instructors' efforts to improve student performance by intervening to punish poor performances. The worst-case scenarios for understanding the effects of interventions occur when the intervention is introduced because "we've got a problem." It is almost impossible to accurately assess the causal effects of the introduction of a strict traffic enforcement program *after* a flurry of tragic traffic accidents, or of the hiring of a new CEO *after* several poor corporate performances. The chances are the interventions are going to show improvements, and it is almost certain that some or most of the effect will be due to "regression toward the mean."

REFERENCES

Gawande, A. (1999, February 8). The cancer-cluster myth. *New Yorker,* pp. 34-37.

Gilovich, T., Vallone, R., & Tversky, A. (1985). The hot hand in basketball: On the misperception of random sequences. *Cognitive Psychology, 17,* 295-314.

Kahneman, D. & Tversky, A. (1972). Subjective probability: A judgment of representativeness. *Cognitive Psychology, 3,* 430-454.

Knuth, D. E. (1969). *The art of computer programming: Vol. 2. Seminumerical algorithms.* Reading, MA: Addison-Wesley.

Langer, E. J. (1975). The illusion of control. *Journal of Personality and Social Psychology, 32,* 311-328.

Langer, E. J., & Roth, J. (1975). Heads I win, tails is chance: The illusion of control is a function of the sequence of outcomes in a purely chance task. *Journal of Personality and Social Psychology, 32,* 951-955.

Larkey, P. D., Smith, R. A., & Kadane, J. B. (1989). It's okay to believe in the "hot hand." *Chance, 2*(4), 22-30.

McKean, K. (1985, June). Decisions, decisions. *Discover,* pp. 22-31.

Meisler, S. (1977, December 30). Spain lottery—Not even war stops it. *Los Angeles Times,* p. D1.

Tversky, A., & Gilovich, T. (1989). The "hot hand": Statistical reality or cognitive illusion. *Chance, 2(4),* 31-34.

9

THINKING RATIONALLY
ABOUT UNCERTAINTY

*The actual science of logic is conversant at present only with
things either certain, or impossible, or entirely doubtful,
none of which (fortunately) we have to reason on. Therefore
the true logic for this world is the Calculus of Probabilities,
which takes account of the magnitude of the probability
which is, or ought to be, in a reasonable man's mind.*

—James Clerk Maxwell

9.1 WHAT TO DO ABOUT THE BIASES

One of the goals of this book is to teach analytic thinking about judgment
processes. The best way we know to think systematically about judgment
is to learn the fundamentals of probability theory and statistics and to
apply those concepts systematically when we make important judgments.
Anyone who has taken or taught introductory probability theory realizes
that LaPlace's (1814-1951) dictum that "the theory of probabilities is at
bottom only common sense reduced to calculus," (p. 196) is unhelpful and
certainly false. Probability theory was not invented until recent times and
our minds do not seem to be naturally "wired" to think according to its

precepts. The first eight chapters in this book could be interpreted as a catalogue of cognitive habits of thought that deviate, sometimes radically, from the laws of probability theory. We provide a summary of the basics of probability theory in the Appendix of this book, but in the present chapter we try to convey the essence of elementary probabilistic analysis illustrated with familiar examples.

Ulysses wisely had himself chained to his ship's mast before coming within earshot of the Sirens. He did so not because he feared the Sirens per se, but because he feared his own reaction to their singing. In effect, he took a precaution against himself, because he knew what he would be likely to do if he heard the Sirens. Similarly, the cognitive biases of automatic thinking can lead us astray in a predictable direction. We must take precautions against the pitfalls of such unexamined judgment.

Attempts to train people not to think representatively and not to be influenced by availability or other biases have been mostly unsuccessful. Associations and heuristics are ubiquitous in our thinking processes. Moreover, making judgments on the basis of one's experience is perfectly reasonable and essential to our survival.

Thus what is needed is an alternative way of making these judgments, a method that affirmatively diverts us from relying on intuitions and associations and heuristics, at least when the judgments are consequential. One such precaution against our biases is the use of external aids. For example, a clinical psychologist can record instances (e.g., of suicide threats) on paper or in a computer file and then compile the data, using a symbolic formula or diagram, when he or she wishes to estimate the frequency. A simple charting of "good" and "bad" weeks can reveal a pattern—or the lack of one. Alternatively, simply writing down base rates and trying to apply the ratio rule (from Section 6.3) can help us avoid irrational judgments.

The greatest obstacle to using external aids, such as the ones we illustrate in this chapter, is the difficulty of convincing ourselves that we should take precautions against ourselves as Ulysses did. Most of us, like our government leaders searching for the ultimate nuclear weapons and defense, seek to maximize our flexibility of judgment (and power). The idea that a self-imposed external constraint on action can actually enhance our freedom by releasing us from predictable and undesirable internal constraints is not a popular one. It is hard to be Ulysses. The idea that such internal constraints can be cognitive, as well as emotional, is even less palatable. Thus to allow our judgment to be constrained by the "mere numbers" or pictures or external aids offered by computer printouts is anathema to many people. In fact, there is even evidence that when such aids are offered, many experts attempt intuitively to improve on these aids' predictions—and then they do worse than they would have had they "mindlessly" adhered to them. Estimating likelihood does in fact involve "mere numbers," but as Paul Meehl (1986) pointed out, "When you come out of a supermarket, you don't eyeball a heap of purchases and say to the clerk, 'Well, it looks to me as if it's about $17.00 worth; what do you think?' No, you add it up" (p. 372). Adding, keeping track, and writing down the rules of probabilistic inference explicitly is of great help in overcoming the systematic errors introduced by representative thinking, availability, anchor-and-adjust, and other biases. If we do so, we might even be able to learn a little bit from experience.

9.2   GETTING STARTED
THINKING IN TERMS OF PROBABILITIES

Modern probability theory got its start when wealthy nobles hired mathematicians to advise them on how to win games of chance at which they gambled with their acquaintances (as noted in Cardano's case, the advice was for himself). Perhaps the fundamental precept of probabilistic analysis is the exhortation to take a bird's-eye, distributional view of the situation under analysis (e.g., a dice game, the traffic in Boulder, crimes in Pittsburgh, the situation with that troublesome knee) and to define a sample space of *all* the possible events and their logical, set membership interrelations. This step is exactly where rational analysis and judgments based on availability, similarity, and scenario construction diverge: When we judge intuitively, the mind is drawn to a limited, systematically skewed subset of the possible events. In the case of scenario construction, for example, we are often caught in our detailed scenario—focused on just one preposterously specific outcome path.

    Probability theory starts with a precise vocabulary with which to describe elementary events, sets of events, and the relationships between them. Let's start with the well-defined example of throwing two dice. First, there is the *simplest event,* a value on a single upper face of one die, for example, "I threw a 1." Second, there is a *conjunction* of two simple events, for example, "I threw a 1 *and* a 6" (in either order, on either die). Third, there is a *disjunction* of two simple events, for example, "I threw a 1 *or* a 6, *or both*" (sometimes called the "inclusive or"). Fourth, there are *conditional* events, the occurrence of one event *given* that another has occurred, for example, "I throw a 1 (on either die), *given* that I threw a total of 7 on the two dice." In the case of "perfect dice," we can systematically describe the entire *sample space* of 36 possible, equal probability outcomes: You could throw the numbers 1 to 6 on the first die and the same numbers 1 to 6 on the second; thus there are 6 × 6 possible pairings or equally probable events.

For present purposes, once we have conceptualized the sample space of possible events, we want to assign frequencies and probabilities to the events and relational events in the space. In the case of idealized situations, we can reason logically about the kinds of events, their frequencies, and probabilities. (Dice, card games, and other honest mechanical gambling devices closely approximate these ideals.) Thus, since there is one face out of six that matches the description "1 is thrown," we would say the probability "of a 1" is 1 in 6. And there are 2 outcomes where a 1 and 6 are thrown, out of 36, so we have 2 in 36 probability of throwing that conjunction; and there are 20 outcomes out of 36 where a 1 or a 6 or both are thrown, so we have 20 in 36 probability of the disjunction event. And for the conditional event, "1 on either die given a total of 7," we focus only on the given "total = 7" and calculate the probability as 2 in 6, since there are six events where the total = 7 and for two of them a 1 is thrown on one of the dice.

Now let's work through another, less precisely defined situation: Suppose we are interested in events that involve the occurrence of characteristics of college students. If we pick a student at random from the student body at the University of Colorado, what is the probability that student will be a female? Of the approximately 20,500 undergraduates at Colorado in 1999, 9,840 were women, so the probability a randomly picked undergraduate is a woman is 9,840 in 20,500, or approximately .480. As for the probability of majoring in psychology, 1,433 students declared psychology majors, so the probability of a randomly sampled student being a psychology major is 1,433 in 20,500, or .070. Now what is the probability of the conjunction event of both female and psychology major? Nine hundred and eight-six students were both female and psychology majors, so the probability is 986 in 20,500, or .048. For the disjunction, female or psychology major, or both, 10,287 meet this description, so the probability is 10,287 in 20,500, or .502. And what about a conditional: "Female *given* psychology major?" The result is 986 in 1,433, or .688—we consider only students who are psychology majors (there are 1,433 of them) and then ask, what is the probability a psychology major is a woman? Here's another case where the categories or sets that define the events are well defined (let's assume that femaleness and psychology major can be defined precisely), so we can count relative, empirical frequencies (not the idealized, logical frequencies for the dice game) to infer probabilities.

Notice that the inverse conditional probability, "Psychology major *given female*," is *not* the same (986 in 9,840, or .100) as "female *given psychology major* (986 in 1,433, or .688). In general, a conditional probability is not the same as its inverse, as illustrated by the ratio rule from Section 6.3, for example, p(female | psychology major) ≠ p(psychology major/female).

What about an even murkier situation where we can define sets and categories but there are no obvious frequencies to count? Suppose we were trying to decide whether a Republican would win the presidential election in the year 2000. As we wrote this book (in 1999), the lead candidates for the party nominations were Al Gore (Democrat, incumbent vice president) and George W. Bush (Republican, governor of Texas); but the final candidates had not been selected and we knew that the outcome of the election would be conditioned on many uncertain economic, political, diplomatic, and social events (and, in hindsight, *legal* events) over the next year. The distributional approach is still the best method to analyze the situation and to make predictions. We can list most of the plausible outcome categories, starting with the slates of potential candidates for each party (e.g., Elizabeth Dole, John McCain, and Steven Forbes as front-runners competing with Bush; only Bill Bradley competing with Gore) and the still uncertain events that are most likely to have an impact on the party and electorate's votes (economic condition, personal scandal, health problems, charisma factor, campaign funds . . .). Despite the murkiness, distributional representations and probabilistic analysis are a big improvement over spontaneous judgments. Just explicitly listing the full collection of candidates is likely to improve predictions. But we are unlikely to rely primarily on relative frequencies about this saliently vivid, unique event—although, if we're really at a loss, we might resort to some statistics that *may* be relevant, for example, p(former vice president wins), p(incumbent party wins). Even when we reason based on scenarios and reasons for the possible outcomes, however, a deliberate attempt to represent the problem explicitly and completely improves the coherence and accuracy of our judgments.

Let's consider one more case: Will there be a conflict in the Middle East in the next decade in which *nuclear* weapons are deployed by one nation against another? Here even the outcomes are poorly defined: Is it a nuclear deployment if terrorists (perhaps not even identified with a single nation) detonate a nuclear device in a Middle Eastern country? Our scenarios, really descriptions of concrete possible outcomes, are nebulous: "A minor skirmish between United Nations peacekeeping inspectors and Iraqi soldiers escalates . . . ;" "An assassination attempt on an Israeli leader fails and the reprisal . . . " Now it seems there are no relevant frequencies to count. The future situation in the Middle East will be different from any previous historical situation that comes to mind. But we still believe that the systematic distributional approach is the best method by which to make educated, though vastly uncertain, probability estimates. In fact, there is evidence from psychological studies conducted by Asher Koriat, Sarah Lichtenstein, and Baruch Fischhoff (1980) that simply spelling out many of the relevant events and systematically thinking through the "reasons for" and "reasons against" the occurrence *of each event* increases the quality of judgments under ignorance.

What points do we want to make with these examples?

1. We introduce the basic set membership relationships that are used to describe all events to which technical probabilities can be assigned.

2. We introduce four kinds of situations to which we might want to attach probabilities: (a) situations, like conventional games of chance (e.g., throwing dice), where idealized random devices provide good descriptions of the underlying structure and where logical analysis can be applied to deduce probabilities; (b) well-defined "empirical" situations where relative frequencies can be used to measure probabilities (e.g., our judgments about kinds of students at the University of Colorado); (c) moderately well defined situations, where we must reason about causation and propensities (rather than relative frequencies, e.g., predicting the outcome of the next presidential election), but where a fairly complete sample space of relevant events can be defined with a little thought; and (d) situations of great ignorance, where even a sample space of relevant events is difficult to construct and there seem to be no relevant frequencies (e.g., events in the Middle East in the next decade).

   One of the remarkable characteristics of probability theory is that four simple axioms (see Appendix) provide the rules for how to reason rationally and probabilistically, even though there is massive disagreement about what the numbers refer to. Our four examples were chosen to give a feeling for the spectrum of interpretations of probabilities: as an extension of elementary deductive logic; as real numbers based on frequencies of events in the external world; or as indices of subjective confidence "in our heads," but not "in the external world."

3. Many errors in judging and reasoning about uncertainty stem from mistakes that are made at the very beginning of the process, in comprehending the to-be-judged situation. If people could generate veridical representations of the to-be-judged situations and then keep the (usually) set membership relationships straight throughout their reasoning, many errors would be eliminated. Of course, there are also misconceptions about probabilities and about random processes, but many times judgments under uncertainty are already off track even before a person has tried to integrate the uncertainties. Our advice about how to make better judgments under uncertainty focuses on creating effective external (diagrammatic and symbolic) representations of the situation being judged.

9.3   COMPREHENDING THE SITUATION BEING JUDGED

It may be especially difficult to start from a written description of a novel uncertain situation and to create a comprehensive representation of the situation, although it is probably not much easier to create situation models from direct experience. In an article that focuses on the ambiguities and incompletenesses in verbal probability problems, Raymond Nickerson (1996) has catalogued many of the errors that occur at the comprehension stage. Some of the best-known examples have been enshrined in the popular literature on brain teasers. The following problem was published in the "Ask Marilyn" column of a popular magazine (Deborah Bennett provides a good summary to this problem in her 1998 popular introduction to probability theory, *Randomness*) and received much attention because it provoked disagreements between some famous mathematicians:

> Suppose you're on a game show, and you're given a choice of three doors. Behind one door is a car; behind the others, goats. You pick a door—say No. 1—and the host, who knows what's behind the doors, opens another door—say No. 3—which has a goat. He says to you, "Do you want to pick Door No. 2?" Is it to your advantage to switch your choice? (Vos Savant, 1991, p. 12)

The first difficulty with this brain teaser is the surprising complexity of the situation of "possible events" to which it refers. Try to diagram the situation by systematically listing each of the relevant events: There are three doors that the contestant could pick; there are three possibilities for where the car is located; there are several options for which door the host could open (and they differ in number depending on which of the first nine "situations" is encountered); and then there is a further complexity created by which policy (stay or switch) is followed by the contestant. Altogether, there are between 18 and 36 situations to keep in mind— *depending on which representation of the problem* a solver has settled on.

There is a further difficulty with this brain teaser because of the ambiguity of the written statement concerning the *host's rule for choosing a door to open;* unless this ambiguity is resolved, there is not a unique sample space representation of the problem. There are at least three plausible interpretations of the host's rule given the problem statement. One rule is that the host always opens one of the nonchosen doors at random (e.g., by tossing a coin to choose door 2 or door 3 in the situation described in the written problem above). This means that sometimes he will open a door and reveal the car—presumably then he (and the audience) will just laugh at you for having chosen the wrong door and the game is over. But there is a second rule for the host that is also consistent with the written problem statement: Suppose the host always selects a door concealing a goat, never opens the door selected, and when the contestant has chosen the car picks a door at random. Now there is a more complex dependency between the contestant's choice and the door opened by the host. An even more complex third rule has also been proposed: Suppose the host always selects a door concealing a goat, never opens the door selected by the contestant, and when the contestant has chosen the car has a bias to pick the remaining door with the lowest number (and there are other possible biases for this kind of rule). The underlying probabilities are different for each of these three rules, but all three rules are consistent with the original verbal problem statement.

The most popular solution of the problem is to interpret the problem statement to mean that the host always opens a door other than the one chosen originally by the contestant, and never opens a door revealing the car (i.e., follows rule 2 or rule 3); then it is possible to say that the "switch doors" strategy may increase and will never decrease the probability of getting the car. Under these representations of the problem, the answer is the contestant should switch. But the point is that representation is the essential, determinative first step in probabilistic reasoning. In the case of the three doors problem, much confusion and controversy and many academic journal articles ensued from the ambiguity in the problem statement.

Let's look at another problem that has been the subject of research on probabilistic reasoning (introduced to psychology by Maya Bar-Hillel and Ruma Falk, 1982; play the game and make a personal estimate before you read on):

Three cards are in a hat. One is red on both sides ("red-red"), one is white on both sides ("white-white"), and one is red on one side and white on the other ("red-white"). A single card is drawn at random and tossed into the air and lands red side up. What is the probability that it is the "red-red" card? (p. 119)

A common response is 1 in 2, or .50 (given by 66% to 79% of the participants in various experiments conducted by Bar-Hillel). Interviews with participants revealed that a typical justification for this answer is, "Well, since the card landed red side up, we know it's not the 'white-white' card. There are two cards left, so it's 50-50 whether it's the 'red-red' card." The implication is that the written problem led these subjects to create a first three, then two cards remaining problem representation. But this problem is not ambiguous (like the three door problem) and the (unambiguously) correct representation is in terms of the *sides* of the cards, not the whole cards (Brase, Cosmides, & Tooby, 1998, make this point). Thus the possible sample space includes the three events where a red side ends facing up: "red-white" (red up), "red_{side1}-red_{side2}" (red_{side1} up), or "red_{side1}-red_{side2}" (red_{side2} up), with the correct answer 2 in 3; in two of the three equally probable events the card is truly "red-red."

One more example (from Hillel Einhorn, 1980):

Imagine you are a military general in a politically tense area and you are concerned that your enemies will invade your country. Furthermore, from past experience it is known that when enemy troops mass at the border, the probability of invasion is .75. However, you don't have direct access to information about enemy troops massing at the border, so you must rely on a report of such activity from your intelligence sources. As it turns out, every time your intelligence sources report the troops are massing at the border, they really are there. Now, you receive an intelligence report that the troops are at the border: What is the probability of invasion? (p. 7)

Most people answer confidently that the probability of invasion given the report of troops at border is .75. But here the problem is incompleteness: There is not enough information in the problem statement to answer the question. The probability could be as low as 0.00! The catch in the problem is that it is possible that the troops only allow themselves to be seen (and mass at the border) when they do *not* plan to invade. Thus the information about intelligence reports is true: Whenever there is report of massing, massing has occurred. But the wily troops only allow themselves to be seen when they are not planning to invade.

This is an error that occurs because the situation to be judged is incompletely defined, but the person making the judgment (we or you) fills in the gaps and constructs a more complete situation model than is warranted by the information in the problem statement. Of course, this is not a habit that is uniquely associated with probability brain teasers or with verbal judgment problems: We "go beyond the information given to our senses" to create situation models all the time.

There are plenty of examples of important judgments that are wrong because the initial situation has been misconstrued; sometimes this is interpreted as "asking the wrong question"—and then answering it. One publicized failure to keep probabilities straight occurred in a televised statement by Harvard law professor Alan Dershowitz, a member of the defense "Dream Team" in the O. J. Simpson murder trial. Simpson's defense did not contest his prior history of spousal abuse of his deceased ex-wife Nichole Brown Simpson. Dershowitz said, "Among men who batter their wives, only one tenth of one percent go on to murder them" (p[husband murders wife | husband had battered wife]; quoted in Good, 1995, p 541). But in a letter to the scientific journal *Nature,* the statistician I. J. Good pointed out that the relevant probability is that among husbands who batter their wives *and* whose wives are subsequently murdered. Using Dershowitz's own assumptions (no one knows what the true probabilities are in this situation), Good (1995) calculated the relevant probability, concluding that in more than one half of such cases, the husbands are the murders: p(husband murders wife | husband had battered wife *and* wife was murdered). Good went on to enthusiastically assert:

> Of course, this argument applies much more generally than to the O. J. Simpson trial. It shows once again, and dramatically, that the simple concept of Bayes factor is basic for legal trials. It is also basic for medical diagnosis and for the philosophy of science. It should be taught at the pre-college level! (p. 541)

One major benefit of enrollment in probability and statistics courses is to provide practice in translating situations into more precise and complete representations. This first step is important and difficult to master. We will return to this theme of how to represent to-be-judged situations "distributionally" after we review what we've learned about the nature of common errors in judgment under uncertainty.

9.4   TESTING FOR RATIONALITY

We have repeatedly commented that some judgments are inaccurate or irrational. On what basis can we make such evaluations? The conditions necessary to conclude a judgment is *inaccurate* are relatively straightfor-ward: (a) We need to have some measurable criterion event or condition in mind that is the target of the judgment. (b) We need to be sure the person making the judgment is in agreement with us on the nature of the target and is trying to estimate, predict, or judge the same criterion value that we have in mind. (c) We also want to be sure that the judge is motivated to minimize error in the prediction and that the "costs" of errors are symmet-ric so the judge will not be biased to over- or underestimate the criterion (e.g., my judgments of acquaintances' ages [the criterion] are inaccurate and they tend to be systematically too low; but it is also important to know that this bias is *deliberate* to avoid offending people who are sensitive about being viewed as older than they really are). This logic for assessing the quality of judgments, which has been dubbed the "correspondence framework" for accuracy, is the framework that underlies the lens model that we introduced in Chapter 3. (See Hastie & Rasinski, 1988, and Hammond, 1996, for further discussion.)

We talk about irrationality or "incoherence" in judgments when it is not obvious that a correspondence test can be applied. For example, we said that people who ranked "Linda is a feminist bank teller" as more probably true than "Linda is a bank teller" were irrational and making judgment errors, even though we know there is no real Linda out there whose occupation and attitudes could be measured to provide a criterion for a correspondence test of accuracy. In these cases, we are evaluating the quality of judgments, and we can only apply the approach to two or more judgments by considering their coherence or logical consistency with one another; we might say we are evaluating the judgments with reference to their adherence to the laws of logic and probability theory, which we accept as a standard of rational reasoning. By the way, if we are sure that a collection of judgments is incoherent, we can be sure that some are also inaccurate, although we often cannot say exactly which of the individual judgments is in error. (And more generally, as noted in Chapter 2, that which is self-contradictory cannot constitute a true description of the world.)

Another convincing argument that the judgment errors we have iden-tified are truly irrational is that experimental participants shown their own responses and told the rule they have violated often conclude, "I made a mistake," or even, "Boy, that was stupid, I'm embarrassed." Kahneman and Tversky (1982, 1996) (who first identified most of the errors we discussed) label these judgment errors *illusions*, because they are behavioral habits that we know are mistakes when we think carefully about them, but which still persist when we do not exercise deliberate care to counteract our intuitive tendencies—very much like the many familiar, but still irresistible, optical illusions.

This dissociation of deliberately analytic reasoning and intuitively guided behaviors is one of the mainstays in arguments for the postulation of separable analytic, explicit versus intuitive, implicit reasoning and memory processes. Seymour Epstein and his students (Denes-Raj & Epstein, 1994) have reported several studies in which some of the errors demonstrated by Kahneman and Tversky, such as in the Linda problem and other probability brain teasers, were reduced or eliminated by simply instructing experimental participants to answer "how a completely logical person would respond." They aptly titled their article, "When do people behave against their better judgment?" In general, however, simply instructing someone to "behave logically" is not sufficient to induce rational thinking.

Once we have committed ourselves to using logic, mathematics, and decision theory as the standards to evaluate rationality in judgments and choices, there is still work to be done. First, it is not always obvious how to represent a decision situation objectively so that rational principles can be applied. Even when we have compact verbal descriptions, as in the brain teasers described at the beginning of this chapter, there is still often incompleteness, ambiguity, and even contradiction in our knowledge about the to-be-analyzed situation. When people are trying hard to communicate clearly or when they are immersed in the critical situation (maybe even worse when they're in the situation), there is ambiguity and confusion. Thus, even if we have a well-specified standard for rationality, there can be problems in deciding if and how a response is irrational.

Second, it is impractical to focus on the short-run performance of a fully informed person with plenty of time to think in an ideally quiet environment. We should be more interested in performance in the long run over many judgments, made in noisy environments with distractions, interruptions, and missing information. It may well be that the optimal, ideally rational judgment calculation is not the *adaptively* best judgment process under more realistic conditions. This theme has been developed recently by researchers led by John Payne (Payne, Bettman, & Johnson,

1993), by Lola Lopes and Gregg Oden (1991), and by Gerd Gigerenzer (Gigerenzer, Todd, & ABC Research Group, 1999). These groups of scientists have argued that "fast-and-frugal" algorithms or heuristics for judgments and choices may be more robust and sturdier and have better survival value than optimal calculations that are superior only when information, computational capacity, and time are generously available.

So far we have presented the "behavioral side" of our story, illustrating these judgment errors in the previous four chapters, organized according to the cognitive processes and heuristics that underlie these judgments and produce the errors. Now we discuss the judgment errors with reference to the rules of probability and logic that are violated, with some advice about how to avoid these irrationalities. We should warn the reader that sometimes it is difficult to infer exactly which rule of probability theory was violated first in a person's judgment process. Because the rules are all inextricably interrelated, it is difficult to be sure whether the primary error is a misrepresentation of the set membership relations among the events being judged, an error in assuming two different contingencies or probabilities are the same, ignoring a critical piece of judgment-relevant information such as a background base rate, or something else.

9.5 HOW TO THINK ABOUT INVERSE PROBABILITIES

We have given several examples of judgment errors that arise because people (we) are not careful to keep separate the easily confusable inverse probabilities: p (pot smoking | hard drug usage) versus p (hard drug usage | pot smoking); p (successful executive | childhood pet) versus p (childhood pet | successful executive); and, most recently, p (invasion | troops reported) versus p(troops reported | invasion). Let's spend some time dissecting a detailed example (reported in a news article by Gay McGee, 1979).

> BAY CITY, MICHIGAN, 1979: A surgeon here is one of a handful in the country who is taking a pioneering approach to the treatment of breast cancer. Charles S. Rogers, M.D., is removing "high-risk" breasts before cancer has developed.
>
> The risk factor is determined by mammogram "patterns" of milk ducts and lobules, which show that just over half of the women in the highest-risk group are likely to develop cancer between the ages of 40 and 59. The mammogram patterns are the work of Detroit radiologist John N. Wolfe, M.D.

The surgery, called prophylactic (preventive) mastectomy, involves removal of the breast tissue between the skin and the chest wall as well as the nipple.

Reconstruction of the breast with the remaining skin is usually done at the time of the mastectomy. Silicone implants and replacement of the areola (the pigmented skin around the nipple) leave the patient "looking like a woman," according to the surgeon.

He has performed the surgical procedure on 90 women in two years.

The rationale for the procedure is found in the surgeon's interpretation of studies by radiologist John Wolfe. The newspaper article continues:

In his research Wolfe found that one in thirteen women in the general population will develop breast cancer but that one in two or three DY (highest-risk) women *will develop it between the ages of 40 and 59.* [Italics added. Wolfe did *not* find that; what he discovered is explained in the next paragraph.]

The low-risk women (NI) account for 42 percent of the population, but only 7.5% of the carcinomas. By examining the DY women and those in the next-lower risk groups, P1 and P2, Wolfe felt that 93% of the breast cancers could be found in 57% of the population.

One remedy to these confusions is to shift to systematic symbolic representations. Translating each to-be-judged situation into probability theory notation and then carefully applying basic rules from probability theory can help. (See the discussion of the useful ratio rule in Section 6.3 and the more general discussion of probability theory in the Appendix.) Let's look at that approach applied to the breast cancer example. Using Rogers's figures, it is possible to construct results for 1,000 "typical" women; see table in Figure 9.1. No other numbers satisfy the constraints. Note that $499 + 71 = 570$, or 57% of the population, which is the stated proportion in the high-risk category. Also, $71/(71 + 6) = .92$. Thus, as stated, 92% of the cancers are discovered in 57% of the population. The overall breast cancer rate of the population is $(71 + 6)/1,000 = .077$, which at the time was approximately 1 in 13. And so on.

By the way, it is usually helpful to think about these kinds of ratios concretely in terms of *frequencies* of individuals in the relevant subgroups.

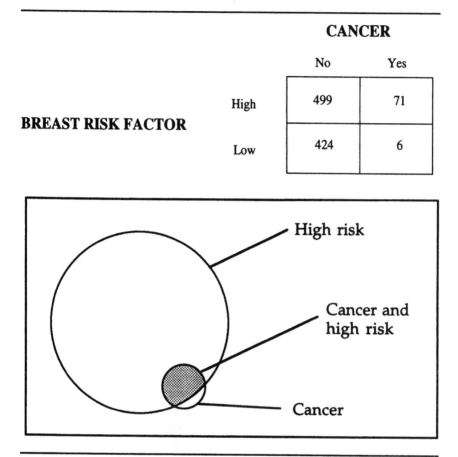

FIGURE 9.1. Table and Venn Diagram Summaries of the Relationships Among Risk Factors and Disease States in Rogers's Analysis of the Probabilities of Developing Breast Cancer

People are much better able to keep track of the relationships between the constituent partitions of the overall population when they imagine frequencies of individuals, objects, or events. In fact, some of the errors of judgment we presented in the previous chapters are reduced dramatically when people are encouraged to represent the situations in terms of frequencies instead of probabilities. For example, the conjunction error for the "Linda the feminist bank teller" problem was committed by 86% of the college students in the original probability format, but when Klaus Fiedler (1982) re-expressed the problem in a "frequency format" (e.g., "Suppose that there are 100 people who fit Linda's description, how many of them are bank tellers? bank tellers and active in the feminist movement?") the error rate dropped to about 20%. Gerd Gigerenzer and his colleagues (e.g., Gigerenzer & Hoffrage, 1995) have studied frequency formats and provide some extremely helpful suggestions for representing probability problems with tutorials that provide practice with their "represent-and-solve" methods; we will rely on some of their developments when we give some advice about pictorial representation schemes below.)

To return to Rogers on breast cancer: Although it is true that 93 % of the cancers are found in the high-risk group, *the estimated probability that someone in this group will develop a cancer is only 71 in 570, or .12.* (Remember, these calculations are based on Rogers's own proportions.)

The .12 figure can be determined even more easily by applying the ratio rule. According to Wolfe's figures, p(cancer) = .075, p(high risk | cancer) = .93, and p(high risk) = .58. Thus,

$$\frac{p(\text{cancer}\,|\text{high risk})}{.93} = \frac{.075}{.580}$$

therefore, p(cancer|high risk) = .12.

The most informative statistic is negative—the estimated probability of developing breast cancer if the woman is from the low-risk group being 6 in 430, or .014. It is not possible based on the newspaper article to evaluate the claim about the very highest risk group, DY.

Rogers does not stress the value of a negative inference. After urging *all women* over 30 to have an annual mammography examination, he is quoted as saying,

> The greatest danger is in having a mammogram without a medical exam by a doctor. There are too many times when the surgeon feels a lesion that wasn't picked up on a mammogram. . . . This is definitely a case where one plus one equals more than three.

Agreed. But incidentally, his mammogram advice is also based on a confusion of inverse probabilities. Roughly 20% of cancers were not detected by mammography—that is, surgeons discovered a lesion "that wasn't picked up on a mammogram." But that is much different from the percentage of times women have cancer given a normal ("negative") mammogram result; $p(\text{cancer} \mid \text{negative}) \neq (p(\text{negative} \mid \text{cancer})$. In fact, this former figure at the time the article was written was approximately .5% (1 in 200) according to figures from the Hartford Insurance Project that had just been completed and published—which most of us would not regard as a "great danger." (In fairness to Rogers, it must be pointed out that the article did not specify how seriously high risk the "high-risk" breasts would have to be before Rogers would operate. The point of the present critique is that his *reasoning* used to justify the procedure *at all* should—from a rational perspective—be highly unpersuasive.)

In general, words are poor vehicles for thinking about inverse probabilities. It is clear that some verbal links are not symmetric, for example, "roses are red" does not mean that all red flowers are roses. Other verbal links however, are symmetric; "zeppelins with hydrogen gas are the type that explode" means, as well, that the type of zeppelins that explode are filled with hydrogen gas. It is easy to confuse symmetric and asymmetric verbal links. In fact, linguistic links are notorious for their ambiguity. (Does "the skies are not cloudy all day" mean that the skies are cloudy for only a portion of the day or never cloudy?) And it is possible to express sincere belief in a linguistic phrase without knowing what it means. (How many school children singing our national anthem know that *o'er* refers to "over" rather than "or"? Or when asked, "How many animals of each kind did Moses take on the Ark?" how many of us confidently answer "two?" without noticing that it was Noah, not Moses, who was supposed to have survived the Biblical flood on an ark?)

But it is difficult for many people to think without words. In fact, some eminent thinkers maintain that it is virtually impossible. "How do we know that there is a sky and that it is blue? Should we know of a sky if we had no name for it?" (Max Müller). "Language is generated by the intellect and generates intellect" (Abelard). "The essence of man is speech" (the Charodogya Upanishad). "In the beginning was the word . . ." (Genesis 1:1). But perhaps the advice of the Lankavatara Sutra is more useful and correct: "Disciples should be on their guard against the seduction of words and sentences and their illusive meaning, for by them the ignorant and dull-witted become entangled and helpless as an elephant floundering around in deep mud." Or perhaps we should cultivate nonverbal thinking patterns such as those of Albert Einstein, who wrote, "The words or language, as they are written or spoken, do not seem to play any role in my mechanism of thought." But concrete visual images are often no better

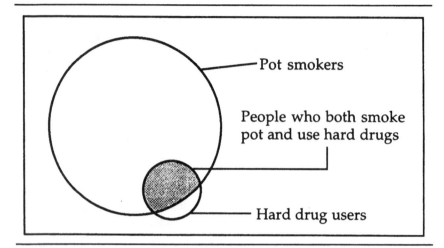

FIGURE 9.2. Venn Diagram to Summarize the Judgment Situation
(Sample Space) to Answer Questions About the
Probability That a Pot Smoker Is Also a Hard Drug User

than words. For example, the expert's image of a breast cancer victim is indeed of a woman with high-risk breasts, because most of the cancer victims the expert encounters have high-risk breasts.

Symbolic, especially algebraic, representations are effective, but many people are not adept with algebra. Fortunately, there is another method—a systematic one proposed by the 19th-century mathematician and logician John Venn (1834-1923). Intersecting circles can be drawn to represent sets of objects or events. Such circles are called Venn diagrams. The area of each circle represents the simple probability that an outcome is from it, and the overlap of the circles represents the probability that the outcome is from the corresponding compound event. Conditional probabilities (e.g., p[invasion | report of troops massing]) are thereby represented by the ratio of the area in the overlap to the area in the larger circle representing the "given" event. When representations are made in this way, it is clear that conditional probabilities are not symmetric. Moreover, it is obvious that their ratio is equal to the ratio of the areas in the two "given" probabilities—expressed algebraically by the ratio rule. The Venn diagram in Figure 9.2 represents the relationship between pot smoking and hard drug usage. Clearly, being a pot smoker does not imply with high probability that a person is a hard drug user, but being a hard drug user does have such an implication for pot smoking.

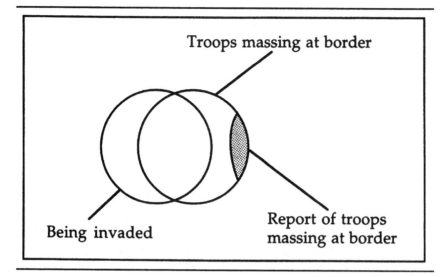

FIGURE 9.3. Venn Diagram Summarizing the "Troops at the Border"
Judgment Problem

Or consider the situation of judging the likelihood of an invasion
given we heard that troops are massing on our border. Here there is some
ambiguity; several possible set relationships are consistent with our background knowledge and the information in the problem statement. But
once we realize that the diagram in Figure 9.3 is consistent (though not
uniquely so) with the situation described in the written problem, we real-
ize that p(invasion | report of troops massing at the border) is not necessar-
ily .75, and could be as low as 0.00.

9.6   AVOIDING SUBADDITIVITY
AND CONJUNCTION ERRORS

One flagrant error we have described in judgments, especially those that
depend on our sense of similarity and involve category memberships, is
the habit of making estimates of several exclusive event probabilities that
add up to more than 100%. For example, the probabilities that your car has
failed to start because the battery is dead, or because a wire is loose, or
because the gas line is plugged, or because the gas tank is empty, or
because there is a seat belt security bar on the ignition sum to 1.55. In its

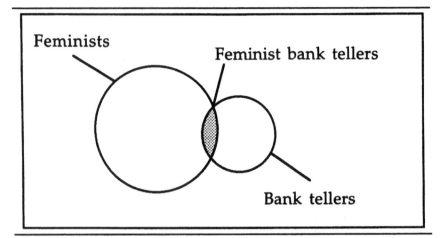

FIGURE 9.4. Sample Space Venn Diagram for the Judgment: Is Linda a Feminist Bank Teller?

extreme form, subadditivity involves estimating that the probability of a subset, nested event is greater than the probability of a superset, superordinate event in which it is nested (e.g., that Linda is more likely to be a feminist bank teller than any kind of bank teller at all). The problem is termed *subadditivity* because the probability of the whole is judged to be less than that of the sum of its parts—in the case of the conjunction fallacy, less than that of a single part.

The diagrammatic approach seems certain to reduce the rate of Linda problem errors to zero. If we draw a Venn diagram of the relationship between "bank tellers" and "bank tellers who are feminists," it is unlikely we will judge the probability (or frequency) of "feminist bank teller" to be higher than "bank teller" (Figure 9.4).

Similarly, if we diagram the exclusive subset relations for "reasons our car didn't start" we are much less likely to distribute more than 100% of the probability space across the subset events. In fact, just reminding people verbally at the time they are making multiple subevent judgments that the sum of mutually exclusive events must not exceed 1.00, if they are using probability numbers correctly, is sufficient to induce more rational, comparative reasoning about event probabilities. Lori Van Wallendael and Reid Hastie (1990) asked college students to solve some whodunit mysteries. Students who had not been reminded that the guilt judgments for different, mutually exclusive suspects needed to sum to unity, exhibited massive subadditivity. When they learned about new incriminating evidence, they increased their beliefs in the guilt of the most relevant suspect without decrementing their suspicions about other suspects. But when they were reminded of the "hydraulic" property of the mutually exclusive events, then they were much more additive, and they traded off guilt and innocence judgments much more consistently than without the reminder.

9.7   THE OTHER SIDE OF THE COIN: THE PROBABILITY OF A DISJUNCTION OF EVENTS

Consider a set of events $1, 2, \ldots, k$. Suppose moreover, that these events are *independent*—that is, whether or not one occurs has no effect on whether any of the others occurs, singly or in combination. (For a more precise definition of *independence,* see the Appendix.) Let the probabilities that the events occur be $p_1 \times p_2 \times \ldots \times p_k$. What is the probability that *at least one* will occur? That is, what is the probability of the *disjunction* (as opposed to the conjunction) of these events? The probability of disjunction is equal to one minus the probability that none will occur. But the probability that the first will not occur is $(1-p_1)$, the probability that the second will not occur is $(1-p_2)$ and so on. Hence the probability that none will occur is $(1 - p_1) \times (1 - p_2) \times \ldots \times (1 - p_k)$. (This, also, is explained in the Appendix.) The product may be quite small, even though each $(1 - pi)$ is quite large, because each pi is small. For example, let the probabilities of six events be .10, .20, .15, .20, .15, and .10, respectively. Then the product of the $(1 - p_i)$s is, once again, $.90 \times .80 \times .85 \times .80 \times .85 \times .90 = .37$, so the probability that at least one of these events will occur is $1-.37 = .63$. Again, the result occurs even though each separate event is quite improbable (the average is .15).

Just as we tend to overestimate the probability of conjunctions of events (to the point of believing in the conjunction probability fallacy), we tend to *underestimate* the probability of disjunctions of events. There seem to be two reasons for this. First, our judgments tend to be made on the basis of the probabilities of individual components, but, as illustrated, even though those probabilities may be quite low, the probability of the disjunction may be quite high. We attribute this error primarily to the anchor-and-(under)adjust heuristic estimation process. Second, any irrational factors that lead us to underestimate the probabilities of the component events—such as lack of imaginability—may lead us to underestimate the probability of the disjunction as a whole. Occasionally, this underestimation problem is well understood, at least on an implicit basis. For example, in their summations lawyers avoid arguing from disjunctions in favor of conjunctions. (There are not many closing arguments that end, "Either the defendant was in severe financial straits and murdered the decedent to prevent his embezzlement at work from being exposed or he was passionately in love with the same coworker and murdered the decedent in a fit of jealous rage or the decedent had blocked the defendant's promotion at work and the murder was an act of revenge. The State has given you solid evidence to support each of these alternatives, all of which would lead to the same conclusion: first-degree murder.") Rationally, of course, disjunctions are *much* more probable than are conjunctions.

There is evidence for a *disjunction probability fallacy* comparable to the conjunction probability error—such a fallacy consisting of the belief that a disjunction of events is *less* probable than a single event comprising it (Bar-Hillel & Neter, 1993). But of course, logically when the probability of A and B is higher than the probability of A (the conjunction fallacy), then the probability of not-A would be less than that of not-A or not-B. This is because the probability of not-A is one minus that of A and the probability of not-A or not-B is one minus that of A and B. Does the former fallacy imply the latter? In fact, if we can arbitrarily decide what we call A and not-A (e.g., call A not being a feminist and not-A being one) and B and not-B (call B not being a bank teller and not-B being one), then aren't the two fallacious inequalities equivalent? Our answer is that they are logically but not psychologically equivalent. We think in terms of categories, not their complements (negations). To a trained logician, not-A is as well defined a category as A is, but As (which may have many associations) rather than not-As (which tend to have few) crowd our minds. It takes a Sherlock Holmes to understand that the fact that the dog *did not bark* constitutes a crucial clue (implying that the dog was familiar with the criminal)—that is, to treat *not barking* as an event.

9.8 CHANGING OUR MINDS: BAYES' THEOREM

A very common judgment problem arises when we receive some new information about a hypothesis that we want to evaluate and we need to update our judgment about the likelihood of the hypothesis. Consider a medical example that was introduced by physicians interested in how doctors and patients would interpret the new information provided by medical tests (Casscells, Schoenberger, & Graboys, 1988):

> The prevalence of breast cancer is 1% for women over age 40. A widely used test, mammography, gives a positive result in 10% of women without breast cancer, and in 80% of women with breast cancer. What is the probability that a woman in this age class who tests positive actually has breast cancer? (p. 999)

When David Eddy (1988) presented this problem to practicing physicians, an amazing 95 out of 100 responded "About 75%." That estimate is dramatically incorrect—and in a context where these physicians deal with this type of judgment on a daily basis and where the numbers in the problem reflect the actual conditions surrounding mammography test results. What is the correct answer? About 7.5%! An order of magnitude lower than the physician's modal answer.

One way to calculate the correct answer is symbolic, algebraic. If we study the rules of probability, it is not difficult to see that the following formula applies to this question (an informal derivation is provided in the Appendix, Section A.5):

$$p(\text{cancer} \mid \text{positive test}) = \frac{p(\text{cancer}_{\text{before the test}}) \times p(\text{positive test} \mid \text{cancer})}{p(\text{positive test}_{\text{with or without cancer}})}$$

The original problem statement gives us the probabilities we need to plug in on the right-hand side of the equation: $p(\text{cancer}_{\text{before the test}}) = .01$; $p(\text{positive test} \mid \text{cancer}) = .80$; and $p(\text{positive test}_{\text{with or without cancer}}) = .107$. The last term requires a little precalculation: If the person has cancer (1% of the women we are concerned with), the numerator gives us the probability .008 (= .01 × .80); if the person does not have cancer (99% of the women we are concerned with), we get the probability .099 (= .99 × .10); and since the only possibilities are having cancer or not having cancer, we add those two probabilities, .099 + .008 = .107. If we put all the numbers into the right-hand side of the equation, we get the answer .075:

$$\frac{.01 \times .80}{.107}$$

That conclusion follows from the even simpler one that $p(\text{cancer} \mid \text{positive test}) \times p(\text{positive test}) = p(\text{cancer}) \times p(\text{positive test} \mid \text{cancer})$.

This famous and useful formula is the most general and practical rule for updating beliefs about a hypothesis (e.g., that an event is true or will occur) given evidence. It is named Bayes' theorem after Thomas Bayes (1702-1761), the British clergyman who derived it algebraically in his quest for a rational means to assess the probability that God exists *given* the (to him) abundant evidence of God's works. (By the way, almost any reader of this book could derive this profound theorem from the four basic principles of probability theory, once the derivation problem has been clearly stated; see Appendix.)

What systematic errors do people make as they try to update their beliefs about an event when they receive new information relevant to the judgment? We want to repeat our admonition that it is often difficult to figure out exactly which part of the judgment under uncertainty process is the fundamental error and even harder to assign the error to a specific misconception or misapplication of probability theory. In the mammography example, we would describe the error as a failure to consider the alternative hypothesis, and instead to ignore the probability that the evidence would be observed even if the hypothesis is false; that is, what we symbolized as p(positive test | no cancer) in our example above is often ignored. This focus on the salient hypothesis is a general habit of our attention and reasoning systems; we might even attribute it to the general bias for available, salient information to dominate judgments (Raymond Nickerson, 1988, provides a thorough introduction to this "confirmation bias"). A second error is to ignore the base rates of occurrence of simple events (e.g., to underweight the fact that only 1% of the patients walking into the clinic are going to have breast cancer—before we know the results of any test).

We've encountered the bad habit of ignoring base rates before, most obviously in Section 6.1 where we found errors in judging Penelope's major field of study and errors in judging occupations of engineers versus lawyers were due to a reliance on similarity between personality and sketches and social stereotypes. But conceptualizing the errors with reference to probability theory instead of psychology, we'd say people were underusing or ignoring background base rates. Here's another example judgment from Maya Bar-Hillel (1980, p. 211) in which it is obvious that base rates are being ignored (again, make your own judgment before you read our analysis):

> Two cab companies operate in River City, the Blue and the Green, named according to the colors of the cabs they run. 85% of the cabs are Blue and the remaining 15% are Green.

A cab was involved in a hit-and-run accident at night. An eye-witness later identified the cab as Green. The Court tested the witness's ability to distinguish between Blue and Green cabs under nighttime visibility conditions. It found the witness was able to identify each color correctly about 80% of the time, but he confused it with the other color about 20% of the time.

What do you think is the probability that the cab in the accident was Green, as the witness claimed?

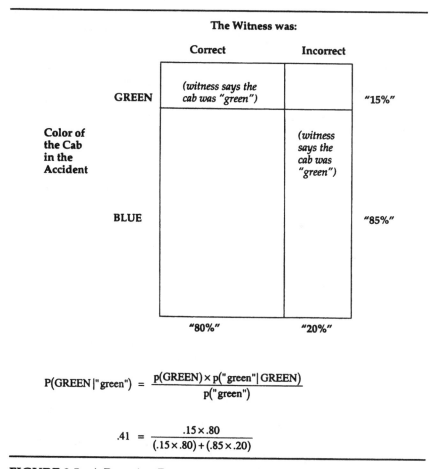

$$P(GREEN \,|\, "green") = \frac{p(GREEN) \times p("green" \,|\, GREEN)}{p("green")}$$

$$.41 = \frac{.15 \times .80}{(.15 \times .80) + (.85 \times .20)}$$

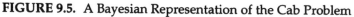

FIGURE 9.5. A Bayesian Representation of the Cab Problem

In this problem, the most relevant base rate corresponds to the proportions of green and blue cabs on the streets and it should used as the starting point for the judgment, the "prior probability" of green before any case-specific evidence (e.g., the witness's testimony) is heard. What Maya Bar-Hillel (1982) found when she presented the problem to a varied sample of people was almost universal failure to consider the base rate; once they heard about the concrete case-specific eyewitness testimony the base rate is faded into the background. Thus Bar-Hillel found that the modal response was the eyewitness's accuracy rate (.80), with no adjustment for the base rate information. If we plug the numbers into the Bayes' theorem formula (in Figure 9.5), it is easy to calculate the correct answer: .41. (We should acknowledge that there is ambiguity in the written problem statement—Is the witness accuracy already a posterior probability because the witness was tested under "15% green cabs" conditions? And there are other interpretations that depart from the information in the problem statement by assuming that readers import various kinds information into their problem representations from their background experiences with taxi cabs or traffic accidents or eyewitnesses; cf. Birnbaum, 1983. But there is no direct evidence that these alternative representations are conceived of by anyone except experts intent on criticizing Maya Bar-Hillel's conclusions by speculating about possible representations. In fact, unpublished data collected by one us [Hastie] is most consistent with the hypothesis that college students comprehend the problem in the Bayes' formula format presented above, but underuse base rate information.)

How can these errors be remedied? First, we noted in Section 6.4 that when the problem statement links the base rate information more strongly to the outcomes in the situation, especially when causal relationships make the connection, then people are likelier to incorporate the base rates into their judgments. Bar-Hillel created a version of the cab problem that stated, "Police statistics show that in 15% of traffic accidents involving taxi cabs, a Green cab was involved." With this causal connection, the majority of people presented the problem used the base rate information to adjust down from the 80% value implied by the witness's testimony, although the adjustment (as we would expect) was insufficient. Perhaps this finding can be interpreted as a vote for the underlying rationality of our natural tendency to create and rely on situation models in the form of causally-glued-together narratives. We speculate that causal scenario-based reasoning may be an intuitive way to keep track of the most important relationships among events—important when we need to make predictions or diagnoses or just update our "situation models." But spontaneous scenario-based reasoning cannot be sufficient by itself; most of the probability errors we have discussed are prevalent when this mode of judgment is adopted.

Second, use of symbolic algebraic representations, like those we provide above, has a big impact on judgments. In medical diagnosis situations, there are now software decision aids that query physicians for relevant "prior probabilities" and "evidence diagnosticity" estimates and then compute the posterior probabilities. These systems improve performance in repeated clinical judgment situations, although there still seems to be a psychological mismatch between physicians' intuitive reasoning and the systems' response formats. People have difficulty estimating about the probability of observing the evidence (test result, witness, testimony, symptom) *given* the condition or disease was *not* present. But if a person making a judgment can deliberately spell out the problem in terms of the Bayes' equation and then identify all the relevant information, performance improves. Even if the person is only able to use the (correct) formula to organize his or her thinking, we expect improvements from (a) identification of incomplete and ambiguous descriptions of the judgment problem, (b) consideration of nonobvious information necessary to make the calculation, and (c) motivation to search for specific information and to think about focal-hypothesis disconfirming information (e.g., the probability that the witness says "green," *given* the cab was really blue; the probability that the test is positive, *given* that the patient did not have cancer; the probability of a DNA match, *even if* the defendant was not the criminal).

Third, and most helpful, we recommend the use of diagrams to represent the to-be-judged situation and to guide information search, inferences, and calculations. (We rely heavily on Gerd Gigerenzer and his colleague Peter Sedlmeier's experiments with various representational systems; a tutorial in their "BasicBayes" method is available in Sedlmeier, 1997.) For example, consider the mammograph diagnostic test situation: The prevalence of breast cancer is 1% for women over age 40. A widely used test, mammography, gives a positive result in 10% of women without breast cancer and in 80% of women with breast cancer. What is the probability that a woman in this age class who tests positive actually has breast cancer? First, we recommend thinking about the situation in terms of frequencies; for example, imagine that 1,000 women are tested. Second, for many Bayesian updating problems, a tree diagram summarizing the possible "states of the world" (given various events occur or do not occur) is helpful (Sedlmeier calls these "frequency trees"). We recommend ordering the tree from top to bottom with reference to the temporal sequence of the events relevant to the judgment. In the case of the mammography diagnosis, see Figure 9.6. Similarly, for the cab problem, start by imagining

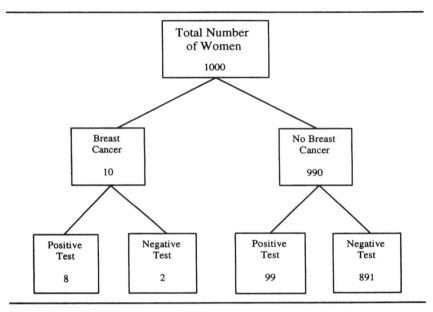

FIGURE 9.6. Diagrammatic Summary of the Relationships Between Test Results and Disease Conditions in the Breast Cancer Diagnosis Problem

that there are 1,000 cabs in the city, 150 green cabs and 850 blue cabs, and then add the witness testimony results, conditioned on whether the cab in the accident was green or blue (Figure 9.7).

The task of reasoning coherently and rationally about probabilities is not a academic homework problem any more. All of us are more and more likely to encounter probabilistic evidence, presented as probability numbers in courtrooms and hospitals. Consider the months of testimony and debate about DNA match and blood type evidence in the O. J. Simpson criminal (and civil) trial. Or consider the plight of a woman reporter's story about a consultation with her physician after a mass was discovered in her breast:

> "I'd like you to get a xeromammogram. It's a new way to make mammograms—pictures of the breasts."
>
> "Is it accurate?"
>
> He shrugged, "Probably about as accurate as any picture can be. You know," he warned, "even if the reading is negative—which means the lump isn't malignant—the only way to be certain is to cut the thing out and to look at it under a microscope."

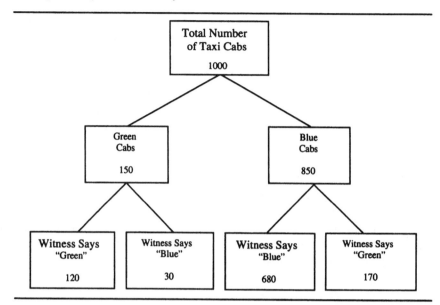

FIGURE 9.7. Diagrammatic Summary of the Relationships Between the Witness's Evidence and the Possible Outcomes in the Cab Problem

The woman then discussed the problem with her husband.

"What did the doctor say?"

"He wants to do a xeromammogram. Then, whatever the result is, the lump will have to come out."

"So why get the X-ray in the first place?"

"It's something to go on, I guess. And our doctor says it's right about 85 percent of the time. . . . So, first I've scheduled an appointment to have a thermogram. If that's either positive or negative, and if it agrees with the Xerox pictures from the mammogram, the statistics say the diagnosis will be 95 percent reliable." (Kushner, 1976, p. C1)

Is there any possibility that this patient will not have the tests? Or that the lump will be biopsied *no matter what the test results?*

9.9 CONCLUDING COMMENT ON RATIONALITY

If a scientific theory cannot state when an event will occur, a skeptic might ask what good it is. In fact, a dedicated behaviorist (if any still exist) might critique this entire book on the grounds that since the phenomena discussed are not controllable, descriptions of them—and the mechanisms hypothesized—are of no scientific value. The answer is that insofar as we are dealing with mental events and decisions of real people in the booming, buzzing confusion of the real world, we can neither predict nor control them with perfect accuracy. The argument of ceteris paribus ("other things being equal") always applies to these phenomenon. The uncertainty of predicting actual outcomes in the world is intrinsic to the problem of decision and the consequences of decision. Of course, it may be said that true scientists should not investigate such uncertain phenomena— they should perhaps limit themselves to investigating the rate at which a rat presses a bar in an environment in which the only moving part is the bar. (What other than the consequences of manipulating the one thing that can be manipulated could shape the rat's behavior?) But if all scientists followed this rule and stayed in their antiseptic ivory towers, we would not have meteorology, agricultural science, computer science, and many other useful applied sciences.

What we have attempted to do is to point out factors and thinking styles that lead us all to make irrational judgments and choices (based on those judgments). People will not necessarily engage in these thought processes, any more than a swimmer who panics necessarily attempts to keep his or her head above water; like a swimmer with survival training, we can learn to counteract the intuitive response and to be more rational— but as with the swimming example, it takes knowledge, self-control, and effort. From a normative perspective, however, becoming able to specify conditions that facilitate or inhibit certain types of behavior or to distinguish between productive and nonproductive ways of thinking is quite an accomplishment for psychologists or other behavioral scientists. Finally, as is pointed out in the concluding chapter, people who attempt to grasp the totality of situations in order to predict or control exactly what will happen seldom fare as well as those who seek the more modest goal of determining what we can influence. A person who attempts to understand everything can easily end up understanding nothing. An understanding of irrational forms of thinking is not nothing, even though we cannot predict exactly when such irrationality will occur or always how to control it.

REFERENCES

Bar-Hillel, M. (1980). The base-rate fallacy in probability judgments. *Acta Psychologica, 44*, 211-233.

Bar-Hillel, M., & Falk, R. (1982). Some teasers concerning conditional probabilities. *Cognition, 11*(2), 109-122.

Bar-Hillel, M., & Neter, E. (1993). How alike is it versus how likely is it: A disjunction fallacy in probability judgments. *Journal of Personality and Social Psychology, 65*, 1119-1131.

Bennett, D. J. (1998). *Randomness*. Cambridge, MA: Harvard University Press.

Birnbaum, M. H. (1983). Base rates in Bayesian inference: Signal detection analysis of the cab problem. *American Journal of Psychology, 96*, 85-94.

Brase, G. L., Cosmides, L., & Tooby, J. (1998). Individuation, counting, and statistical inference: The role of frequency and whole-object representations in judgment under uncertainty. *Journal of Experimental Psychology: General, 127*, 3-21.

Casscells, W., Schoenberger, A., & Graboys, T. B. (1978). Interpretation by physicians of clinical laboratory results. *New England Journal of Medicine, 299*(18), 999-1001.

Denes-Raj, V., & Epstein, S. (1994) Conflict between intuitive and rational processes: When do people behave against their own better judgment? *Journal of Personality and Social Psychology, 66*, 819-829.

Eddy, D. (1988). Variations in physician practice: The role of uncertainty. In J. Dowie & A. S. Elstein (Eds.), *Professional judgment: A reader in clinical decision making* (pp. 200-211). Cambridge, UK: Cambridge University Press.

Einhorn, H. J. (1980). Learning from experience and suboptimal rules in decision making. In T. S. Wallsten (Ed.), *Cognitive processes in decision and choice behavior* (pp. 1-20). Hillsdale, NJ: Lawrence Erlbaum.

Fiedler, K. (1982). Causal schemata: Review and criticism of research on a popular construct. *Journal of Personality and Social Psychology, 42*, 1001-1013.

Gigerenzer, G., & Hoffrage, U. (1995). How to improve Bayesian reasoning without instruction: Frequency formats. *Psychological Review, 102*, 684-704.

Gigerenzer, G., Todd, P. M., & ABC Research Group. (1999). *Simple heuristics that make us smart*. New York: Oxford University Press.

Good, I. J. (1995). When batterer turns murderer. *Nature, 375*, 541.

Hammond, K. R. (1996). *Human judgment and social policy: Irreducible uncertainty, inevitable error, unavoidable injustice*. New York: Oxford University Press.

Hastie, R., & Rasinski, K. A. (1988). The concept of accuracy in social judgment. In D. Bar-Tal & A. W. Kruglanski (Eds.), *The social psychology of knowledge* (pp. 193-208). Cambridge, UK: Cambridge University Press.

Kahneman, D., & Tversky, A. (1982). On the study of statistical intuitions. *Cognition, 11*, 123-141.

Kahneman, D., & Tversky, A. (1996). On the reality of cognitive illusions. *Psychological Review, 103,* 582-591.

Koriat, A., Lichtenstein, S., & Fischhoff, B. (1980). Reasons for confidence. *Journal of Experimental Psychology: Human Learning and Memory, 6,* 107-118.

Kushner, R. (1976, March 24). Breast cancer—the night I found out. *San Francisco Chronicle,* p. C1.

LaPlace, P. S. (1814/1951). *A philosophical essay on probabilities* (F. W. Truscott & F. L. Emory, Trans.). New York: Dover.

Lopes, L. L., & Oden, G. D. (1991). The rationality of intelligence. In E. Eels & T. Maruszewski (Eds.), *Poznan studies in the philosophy of the sciences and humanities* (Vol. 21, pp. 225-249). Amsterdam: Rodopi.

McGee, G. (1979, February 6). Breast surgery before cancer. *Ann Arbor News,* p. B1 (reprinted from *Bay City News*).

Meehl, P. E. (1986). Causes and effects of my disturbing little book. *Journal of Personality Assessment, 50,* 370-375.

Nickerson, R. (1996). Ambiguities and unstated assumptions in probabilistic reasoning. *Psychological Bulletin, 120,* 410-433.

Nickerson, R. S. (1998). Confirmation bias: A ubiquitous phenomenon in many guises. *Review of General Psychology, 2,* 175-220.

Payne, J. W., Bettman, J. R., & Johnson, E. J. (1993). *The adaptive decision maker.* New York: Cambridge University Press.

Sedlmeier, P. (1997). BasicBayes: A tutor system for simple Bayesian inference. *Behavior Research Methods, Instruments, and Computers, 29,* 328-336. (See also Sedlmeier's Web site: http://www.psycho.uni-paderborn.de)

Van Wallendael, L. R., & Hastie, R. (1990). Tracing the footsteps of Sherlock Holmes: Cognitive representations of hypothesis testing. *Memory and Cognition, 18,* 240-250.

Vos Savant, M. V. (1991, February 17). Ask Marilyn. *Parade Magazine,* p. 12.

EVALUATING CONSEQUENCES: SIMPLE VALUES

*We hold these truths to be self-evident, that all men
are created equal; that they are endowed by their Creator
with certain inalienable rights; that among these are
life, liberty, and the pursuit of happiness.*

—Declaration of Independence
of the United States of America

10.1 WHAT GOOD IS HAPPINESS?

The philosopher Jeremy Bentham (1748-1832) referred to pleasure and pain as the "sovereign masters" that "point out what we ought to do as well as determine what we shall do." Many people would say that *the* goal of decision making is to get outcomes that will make the decision maker happy. But when decisions are driven by the "pursuit of happiness," it is not the *experiences* of pleasure and pain that are most important. At the time of decision, what is most important is our *predictions* of what will make us happy *after* we make a decision. Daniel Kahneman, Peter Wakker, and Rakesh Savin (1997) call this anticipated happiness-unhappiness "decision utility," to contrast it with "experienced utility" (the "sovereign master" of behavior referred to by Bentham). Most deliberate decisions involve the prediction of how we will feel about the outcomes that we think will occur if we choose one course of action or another. When we make a decision about what to study in school, we think about how we will enjoy the experience and the opportunities we expect will follow; when we decide to get married, we predict how much we will like spending the rest of our life with that partner; and when we choose a medical option, we evaluate how we feel about living or dying with the results.

In a moment, we will explore what is known about the prediction and experience of pleasure and pain and the evaluation of consequences from decisions. But it is important to realize that happiness and related feelings of well-being are not the only considerations in the evaluation of consequences. Many times, we focus on other aspects of the expected consequences of our actions and sometimes we appear to make decisions in a nonconsequentialist manner: "I didn't decide to put my newspaper in the recycle basket, I'm just the kind of person who doesn't litter." "I didn't vote because I thought I would have an impact on the outcome of the election, I voted because I think every good citizen should do so." And of course, impulsivity can play an important role in such decisions: "I didn't decide to tailgate the car in front of me, I was just trying to get to the airport in time for my flight." "I didn't decide to have sex, I did it because I could."

But back to our exploration of decision utility and the manner in which people predict, at the point of decision, what will make them happy or unhappy as a consequence of the actions they choose. First, past experience, learning, and memory play a dominant role in predictions of the future. If an outcome made us happy in the past, then we are most likely to predict it will make us happy in the future and to prefer the course of action that led to good outcomes in the past. Thus remembered pleasures and pains play a major role in our choices that lead to future outcomes. Of course, another reason that memory for past pleasures and pains is important is because it is a contributor to our summary feelings of satisfaction. These feelings in turn may have consequences for our behavior in social settings and as citizens who support or oppose their political leadership. Second, when memory does not provide a clear answer, we have a collection of judgment strategies that we use to predict our satisfaction with possible outcomes. We call these *evaluation heuristics* by analogy with the judgment estimation heuristics we've already introduced in Chapters 4 to 7. Third, it is possible that some evaluative reactions are "wired in"; these are evaluations with obvious survival value in ancestral environments, and interpersonal liking (mate preferences) and food and habitat preferences are probably partly determined by evolutionary selection pressures.

Psychologists are just beginning to uncover the processes that underlie subjective feelings of pleasure and pain, what we're calling experienced utility. These processes are especially mysterious because many evaluative reactions occur very rapidly, preceding full cognitive analysis and recognition by the perceptual system. We often use the term "gut reaction" to describe an evaluative response, because we have difficulty explaining the basis of the response at a conscious level. There is nothing uncognitive about this kind of unconscious response process. Any cognitive response that involves retrieval from memory or perceptual analysis is partly implicit; this includes any response of interest to judgment and decision researchers.

Aristotle urged people to seek "the golden mean" between extremes, "moderation in all things" (which we interpret as including moderation in the pursuit of moderation). But why should this golden mean in general be desirable? Clyde Coombs and George Avrunin (1977) have enunciated a very simple principle that implies moderation: *Good things satiate and bad things escalate.* This principle has reference to choosing between alternatives that *vary in amount.* Food is an obvious example. After deprivation, an individual derives both important nutritional value and pleasure from initial amounts of food. As amount increases, however, nutritional importance decreases, and the pleasure in each mouthful decreases as well. These good things *satiate.* On the other hand, the possibly pernicious effects of calories, additives, processed sugars, fats, and so on increase as food consumption continues. Moreover, these pernicious effects *escalate.* For example, 500 extra calories per day is more than twice as bad for the eater as 250 extra calories per day (just as being 30% overweight is more than twice as bad as being 15% overweight).

Another of Coombs's examples is the length of a vacation. The first few days of getting away from it all are delightful. Soon, however, the vacationer begins to adapt to the new environment, and its positive qualities become less salient. The 200th view of a mountain or a palace or a Rembrandt painting is less thrilling than the third. In addition, interesting challenges gradually become hassles. At the same time, the amount of drudgery on returning home necessary to make up for lost time begins to mount. Because drudgery is an escalating phenomenon (2 hours devoted to drudgery is more than twice as bad as 1 hour), this bad characteristic of vacations also escalates with time (amount). The principle that "good things satiate and bad things escalate" can be visualized with the simple graph in Figure 10.1.

When the good, satiating characteristics (+) are added to the bad, escalating characteristics (–), the result is a *single-peaked function* that has a maximum value of a moderate amount (the dotted line in Figure 10.1). Net welfare (positive combined with negative) is maximized at moderate amounts. Coombs and Avrunin (1977) have proved that if (a) good characteristics satiate (the function relating goodness to amount has a slope that is positive and *decreasing*), and (b) bad things escalate (the function relating bad characteristics to amount has a slope that is negative and decreasing—becoming more negative), and (c) the negative function is more rapidly changing than the positive one, then (d) the resulting sum of good and bad experiences (i.e., the sum of the good characteristics function and the bad characteristics function) will *always* be single-peaked. (In fact, a single-peaked function results from any additive combination in which the sum starts off positive from zero and the absolute value of the slope of the utility for bad characteristics is greater everywhere than the absolute value for good characteristics. The flat nature of this peak in Figure 10.1 is common.)

The important point here is that many experiences exhibit a single-peaked preference function relating the amount of the experience (food consumed, days on vacation) to the associated pleasure (and pain); in other words we have personal "ideal points" on amount-of-experience dimensions. And notice that different people are likely to have different locations for that ideal peak: Mary doesn't like much sugar in her coffee at all, Ken likes a ton of sugar; 11 days vacation for Mary, 3 days for Ken; two children is just right for Mary, four is Ken's preferred number . . .

Furthermore, most experiences probably evoke positive evaluations and negative evaluations in parallel, followed by an integration of the two more primitive reactions, just as Coombs and Avrunin hypothesized. The evidence for this two-channel hypothesis comes from research conducted by Tiffany Ito and John Cacioppo (1999) in which they presented pictures of evaluatively evocative scenes to experimental participants while they recorded their brain activity. Physiological studies suggest pleasure and pain involve different neural circuits and different neurotransmitters (the family of dopamines associated with pleasure, the family of acetylcholine transmitters associated with pain). Consistent with this notion, Ito and Cacioppo found that some evaluative reactions are massively ambivalent (a recovering alcoholic's reactions to a glass of whiskey; a dieter's reaction

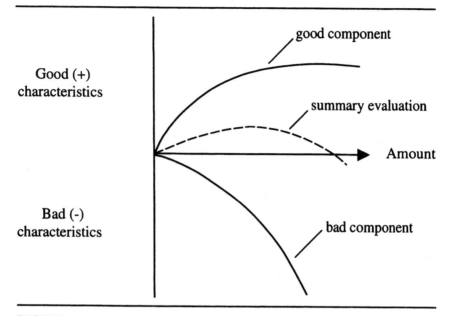

FIGURE 10.1. Coombs and Avrunin's Hypothesis About the Two
Components Underlying Single-Peaked Preferences

to a rich dessert) and illustrate the workings of both channels simultaneously, independently, and in parallel.

Another discovery about evaluations of experience is that even immediately after they occur, the sum of the momentary evaluations is not
equal to the summary remembered from the experience. Donald Redelmeier and Daniel Kahneman (1996) asked people undergoing painful
medical procedures (e.g., a colonoscopy in which a medical instrument
the size of a small baseball bat is inserted into the victim's rectum) to
report on their current levels of pain throughout the procedure. Then
immediately after, they asked for a global rating of the painfulness of the
whole experience. They found that a general "peak-end" evaluation rule
applied to pain and pleasure experiences, such that only the level of
the most intense part of the total experience and the final level of pain/
pleasure needed be considered to predict the summary evaluation. A corollary of the peak-end principle is "duration neglect." People tend to be
surprisingly insensitive to the length of the experience. Putting these principles together, Kahneman, Redelmeier, and their colleagues (1993) conducted a neat demonstration of the power of duration neglect and the

"end" of the experience to determine overall evaluation. Experimental participants were exposed to two unpleasant ice water immersion experiences: (a) immersion for 60 seconds at 14° Celsius, and (b) immersion for 60 seconds at 14° C with an unannounced shift to 30 more seconds at 15° C. When given a choice between which of the two unpleasant experiences to repeat, a majority (65%) of the participants chose the longer experience—not noticing that it must have been objectively worse than the shorter experience that was embedded in it!

The search is on for systematic biases in hedonic prediction. One such systematic misprediction is called the "diversification bias." Itmar Simonson (1990) asked students to choose one of six snacks to be consumed at each of three future class meetings. When the students made their choices by placing an order for all three snacks at one time in the first class meeting, they chose much more variety (from different snack categories) than when they chose sequentially at each class meeting. Furthermore, those who chose in advance and were then allowed to express their preferences at the later meetings (when they were already committed to a snack), showed considerable regret that they had not chosen more uniformly. This kind of study has been repeated with choices among other objects and experiences with similar results; people do not realize how similar their desires will be on different occasions.

A form of *nonregressive prediction* occurs in judgments of future happiness-unhappiness as it does in judgments of other magnitudes and quantities (see Section 8.3). If we do not appreciate regression effects, we systematically overestimate how positively we will feel about good consequences and overestimate the negativity of the bad consequences. Daniel Gilbert, Elizabeth Pinel, Tim Wilson, Stephen Blumberg, and Thalia Wheatley (1998) demonstrated this tendency to expect more extreme evaluative reactions and emotions than we actually experience. They asked people to predict how they would respond to personally important uncertain events that might occur in their near futures. For example, the researchers asked junior faculty members how they would react if their academic departments decided to deny or grant them promotion to senior, tenured faculty status. The respondents' predictions were much more extreme than their posttenure ratings of specific and general well-being. In short, they expected to be elated or devastated, but a few months after the outcome, they felt pretty much the way they had felt before. These same researchers created an experimental analogue to this situation by promising college students a desirable summer job but then disappointing them. Hedonic reactions, like perceptual and cognitive responses, are very adaptive. These researchers labeled this adaptive habit "immune neglect," by analogy with quickly adapting biological immune systems; neglect refers to the tendency to neglect this adaptiveness when predicting future states.

A third collection of important hedonic judgment errors can be grouped under the label *bounded self-control* (reviewed by George Loewenstein, 1996). Contrary to the inspiring story of Ulysses' self-control tactics, most of us exhibit bounded self-control when we make decisions (not just "bounded rationality"). And as the story of Ulysses suggests, the boundedness can be blamed on our failure to predict how we will react, later in time, when we are tempted (Oscar Wilde encapsulated this precept in the aphorism "The only thing I cannot resist is temptation"). People underestimate the power of the situation, of immediately available gratification, to control their behavior. Consequently, people consistently mispredict how they will behave in the future when they are sexually aroused, crave drugs, or are hungry. It is likely our predictions about behavior in social ("This time I'm really going to give my boss a piece of my mind") and consumer ("I'll resist buying the expensive shoes") situations are also subject to the illusion that we will choose according to our higher natures and not succumb to our visceral desires. But the evidence is that these predictions are too optimistic, and we end up not using the condom, injecting the drug, and eating the unhealthy dessert when we are confronted by the actual choice situation.

Psychologists have made some interesting proposals for personal programs to increase overall personal happiness. The basic problem stems from the notion of hedonic relativism. As Philip Brickman and Donald Campbell (1971) put it, "How can we get off of the hedonic treadmill?" (p. 300). One psychologist, Allen Parducci (1995), has invented a "happiness game" in which players choose amounts of play money to receive and are taught, via feedback, to sample according to the author's *range-frequency theory* of happiness. Another, David Lykken (1999), provides a catalogue of "happiness thieves" with advice on how to protect against them. Given what we know about feelings of well-being in general, our best advice is not to overemphasize predicted happiness in making decisions, but rather deliberately to consider other aspects of decision alternatives and their consequences (we give more advice on how to decide in Sections 11.5, 12.4, and 12.5). For most people, an ambient sense of well-being is a moderately stable individual difference. Some people are usually a bit more optimistic and happy than others, others usually a bit below the norm, but for most of us there are modest perturbations up and down around a fairly stable "happiness set point"; in other words, global feelings of personal well-being seem to behave a lot like our body weight.

10.2   THE ROLE OF EMOTION IN CHOICE

Everyone knows that emotions play a significant role in decision making and choice. But it has been difficult to make progress in specifying that role. One obstacle to progress is that there is little consensus on a precise definition of the concept of emotion. Paul Ekman and Richard Davidson (1994) surveyed their colleagues' views in an attempt to identify points of consensus. They titled their concluding section "What *Most* Students of Emotion Agree About" (italics added) and comment, "We originally did not include the word 'most' in this title of this section" (p. 412). They explain that they could not find any topics on which all agreed.

We don't hope to solve the problem of a universal definition of "emotion," but for present purposes we think four concepts will be useful: emotions, feelings, moods, and evaluations. We define *emotion* as reactions to motivationally significant stimuli and situations, usually including three components: a cognitive appraisal, a "signature" physiological response, and phenomenal experiences. We would add that emotions usually occur in reaction to perceptions of *changes* in the current situation that have hedonic consequences. Second, we propose that the term *mood* be reserved for longer-duration background states of our physiological (autonomic) system and the accompanying conscious *feelings*. Note that the implication is that emotions and moods are not always conscious, that the phenomenal experience component is not a necessary element of an emotional reaction. Finally, we suggest that the expression *evaluation* be applied to hedonic, pleasure-pain, good-bad judgments of consequences.

Judgment and decision making researchers have only recently begun to study the distinctive role of emotions in decision-making processes. Decision making had long been viewed as a rational, perhaps cognitive, process. Emotion, if considered at all, was just one more "input" into a global evaluation of utility. We would still assign a major role to anticipated emotional responses in the evaluation of the value or utility (either decision utility or experienced utility) of a course of action; we usually do try to predict how we will feel about an outcome and use that inference to evaluate and then decide. But even in the category of decision utility, anticipatory emotional responses seem to play a distinctive role.

One way to avoid the confusions surrounding the concept of emotion is to study a simple situation in which operational definitions are generally accepted. Thus some of the most illuminating research, especially on the relationships between behavioral and neural-physiological substrates, has been conducted in the well-defined fear conditioning paradigm with nonhuman subjects. The operational definition is with reference to a fear conditioning paradigm in which the experimental subject, usually a rat, is presented with a novel stimulus, usually a sound, paired with an unpleasant, mild electric shock. After the sound has been paired with (and signals or predicts) the electric shock on several trials, the sound alone produces a variety of fearful responses (freezing, defecating, suppression of pain responses, stress hormone release, and reflex potentiation; one of the strengths of the fear conditioning paradigm is the great diversity of reactions that are produced in the animal, a diversity that is best explained with reference to a central "fear" response). Joseph LeDoux (1996), Edward Rolls (1999), and other neuroscentists have made impressive progress tracing out the neural and biochemical systems that underlie conditioned fear responses in rats and other animal models. These scientists have mapped the mostly noncortical "circuits" and have assigned a central role to the amygdala in anxiety and fear responses.

One important message from this research is that the precursors of many emotional responses are unconscious, and these emotions are often mysterious to the person experiencing them. How often are we puzzled by an inexplicable reaction to a situation or person or even deny a strong emotional reaction that is obvious to everyone except ourselves: "I am NOT angry," he screamed. The primary function assigned to the emotions by these researchers is to be a fast emergency response system. LeDoux (1996) writes that the subcortical fear system processes information more quickly than the conscious cerebral systems and that this "quick and dirty pathway . . . allows us to begin to respond to potentially dangerous stimuli before we fully know what the stimulus is" (p. 274).

More generally, there seems to be agreement on the conclusion that an early, primitive reaction to almost any personally relevant object or event is a good-bad evaluative assessment. Many behavioral scientists have concluded that an evaluation occurs very quickly and includes emotional feelings and distinctive somatic-physiological events. Robert Zajonc (1980) was one of the first to emphasize the theme that, in the words of mathematician Blaise Pascal (1623-1662), "the heart has its reasons which reason knows nothing of." In support of his claims, Zajonc cited anecdotal and experimental evidence for a dissociation between analytic, cognitive responses and intuitive, emotional responses. He started with examples from memory-based judgments: How often have you been reminded of a book or a movie and know instantly that you liked it, a lot, but are unable recall any specific details from it to explain your evaluation? In subsequent, experimental research studying on-line judgments, Zajonc demonstrated that evaluative reactions occurred very quickly and often before or instead of cognitive recognition.

Cognitive neuroscientists have attempted to describe the properties of the neural-physiological processes that underlie these rapid evaluations. Tiffany Ito and John Cacioppo (1999) have argued that there is a *bivariate* evaluative response system with two neurally independent circuits, one (dopamine mediated) assessing positivity and one (acetycholine mediated) assessing negativity. Of course, the bivariate hypothesis is exactly consistent with the Cooms and Avrunin (1977) two-factor interpretation of the single-peaked preference phenomenon (Section 10.1 above). Much of Cacciopo and Ito's evidence for the bivariate, two-channel hypothesis is behavioral demonstrations of the properties of simultaneous, joint, positive + negative reactions to unitary stimulus images. But they have also recorded the electrophysiological responses of their subjects' brains and found some suggestive hemispheric asymmetries that converge with the results of Richard Davidson and his colleagues, who study long-term individual differences in affective style (Davidson, Jackson, & Kalin, 2000). The tentative conclusion is that people with relatively active right-hand prefrontal hemispheric areas tend to exhibit more negative, depressive ambient moods and react more negatively to stimulus events, whereas left prefrontal activation is associated with more positive moods and emotional reactions.

In the context of decision making per se, perhaps the most fascinating results concerning the role of emotion come from the laboratory of Antonio Damasio at the University of Iowa. Damasio, a world-renowned neurosurgeon, was intrigued by the historical medical case of a construction worker named Phineas P. Gage. In 1848, Gage was working on the construction of a railroad track when he was injured by a dynamite blast that sent an iron crow bar through the front of his head. (Gage suffered a massive trauma, we could call it an extirpation, of a small portion of his orbitofrontal cortex, the part of the brain centered between and behind the eye sockets.) The remarkable result, described as a "Wonderful Accident" in a newspaper headline, was that Gage seemed to be barely injured, was able to stand upright and walk unassisted a few hours after the accident, and then subsequently seemed to be fully competent intellectually. Gage's physician, John Harlow, impressed by the apparently miraculous recovery, provided detailed descriptions of his postinjury behavior. Although Gage was not physically disabled, his character and temperament changed: From a formerly temperate, model citizen he became

> fitful, irreverent, indulging at times in the grossest profanity which was not previously his custom, manifesting but little deference for his fellows, impatient of restraint or advice when it conflicts with his desires, at times pertinaciously obstinate, yet capricious and vacillating, devising many plans of future operation which are no sooner arranged than they are abandoned. (Harlow, 1868, p. 333)

Neurologist Damasio (1994) focused on Gage's loss of decision-making abilities: "Gage had once known all he needed to know about making choices conducive to his betterment . . . after the accident, he no longer showed respect for social convention; ethics were violated; the decisions he made did not take into account his best interest . . . there was no evidence of concern about his future, no sign of forethought" (p. 11).

Damasio and his colleagues Daniel Tranel and Antoine Bechara invented a risky gambling task, designed to capture some of the decision-making deficits that he hypothesized would be produced by injuries like that sustained by Phineas Gage (Bechara, Damasio, & Damasio, 2000; Damasio, 1994). In Damasio's gambling task the subject, called the "Player," is presented with four decks of cards labeled A, B, C, and D (see Figure 10.2). The Player is given a stake of play money and instructed that turning over cards will win or lose money. The goal of the experimental game is to win as much money as possible, by choosing cards from the four decks. The Player is ignorant of the composition of the decks or when the game will terminate. The compositions of the decks are summarized in Figure 10.2, where it should be clear that the best strategy is to choose from decks C and D, both of which have positive expected values, whereas persistent choices from decks A and B will lose money in the long run. But decks A and B are attractive because they pay a larger per card bonus, a gain of $100, compared to the cards in decks C and D, which pay a steady $50. The "catch" is that the deceptively attractive decks A and B also contain larger punishment cards, with catastrophic losses as large as $1,250 in deck B.

	Deck A	Deck B	Deck C	Deck D
Reward Amount (on every card in deck)	$100	$100	$50	$50
Punishment Amounts (on only some cards)	$150-350	$1,250	$25-75	$250
Probability of Punishment	0.5	0.1	0.5	0.1
First punishment appears at card:	3	9	3	10
Expected Value	-$25	-$25	+$25	+$25

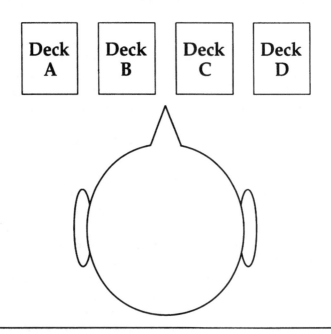

FIGURE 10.2. A Summary of Damasio's Card Selection Gambling Task

What Damasio and his colleagues had designed was a situation to test whether the Player would prudently learn to avoid the high gain-high loss decks A and B and choose from decks C and D. He found that patients with orbitofrontal cortex injuries like Phineas Gage's did not learn to choose wisely across a sequence of 100 choice trials, whereas nonpatients with intact prefrontal cortexes learned to avoid the negative expected value decks. Further studies found that normal nonpatient Players developed a skin conductance response that preceded choices that they made from the more punishing decks—essentially they started to sweat before choosing from decks A and B—whereas the patients did not develop this anticipatory fear response. These findings led Damasio to hypothesize that the orbitofrontal cortex was a part of the brain where linkages between factual, cognitive knowledge made contact with subcortical bioregulatory (emotional) information. If this location was damaged, a person would still comprehend the situation cognitively, but this image would not retrieve the emotional reactions that could warn the person of potential danger or loss. Damasio (1994) asked his readers to imagine a situation in which they are confronted by several options or courses of action (like the Player presented with the four decks of cards in the experimental gambling game):

> The key components unfold in our minds instantly, sketchily, and virtually simultaneously, too fast for the details to be clearly defined. But now, imagine that *before* you apply any kind of cost/benefit analysis to the premises, and before you reason toward the solution of the problem, something quite important happens: When the bad outcome connected with a given response option comes into mind, however fleetingly, you experience an unpleasant gut feeling. Because the feeling is about the body, I gave the phenomenon the technical term *somatic* state ("soma" is Greek for body); and because it "marks" an image, I called it a *marker*. Note again that I use somatic in the most general sense (that which pertains to the body) and I include both visceral and non-visceral sensation when I refer to somatic markers.
>
> What does the *somatic marker* achieve? It forces attention on the negative outcome to which a given action may lead, and functions as an automated alarm signal which says: Beware of danger ahead if you choose the option which leads to this outcome. The signal may lead you to reject, *immediately*, the negative course of action and thus make you choose among other alternatives. The automated signal protects you against future losses without further ado, and then allows you *to choose from among fewer alternatives*. There is still room for using cost/benefit analysis and proper deductive competence, but only *after* the automated step drastically reduces the number of options. (p. 173)

Thus the primary adaptive function attributed to the fast somatic marker reaction is to simplify or winnow large choice sets to a smaller size, containing fewer options, to allow a more thoughtful cost-benefit evaluation. (Joseph LeDoux, 1996, and Robert Zajonc, 1980, attributed similar functions to fast emotional reactions.) Note that under this hypothesis emotional reactions are not just another input into the evaluation of an alternative; they occur before a summary evaluation and determine which alternatives remain in the choice set that is evaluated.

An alternative functional interpretation in the decision making literature is that fast emotional reactions serve a crucial override function that operates when necessary to interrupt the course of an ongoing plan or behavior sequence to respond quickly to a sudden emergency or opportunity (Simon, 1967). Under either functional interpretation, anticipatory emotional responses play a special role in decision making.

Damasio's hypothesis is still controversial, as is the analysis of the roles of other emotions in the decision process. Two experienced utility postdecision emotions have received special attention from decision researchers. They are sometimes called *counterfactual emotions* because they depend on the comparison of the outcomes that were experienced with outcomes that did not occur but might have. Regret (disappointment) and rejoicing (elation) have figured in several nonexpected utility theories of decision making. Essayist William Hazlitt (1778-1830) singled out these emotions as distinctively human in his famous observation: "Man is the only animal that laughs and weeps; for he is the only animal that is struck with the difference between what things are, and what they ought to be."

There is no doubt that experienced utility is intensified if it produces regret or rejoicing, and especially if it is a surprise too. Barbara Mellers and her colleagues designed a neat experimental task to capture these reactions (Mellers, 2000; Mellers, Schwartz, & Ritov, 1999). In their experiments, subjects are either told or not told the payoffs returned by nonchosen gambles in addition to being given the outcomes from those chosen. This method allowed Mellers to produce regret effects (e.g., when the nonchosen gamble pays off with a much better outcome than the chosen one, and even more so if the payoff probability for the nonchosen gamble was low) and rejoicing effects (e.g., when the nonchosen gamble turned out much worse than the one chosen). But it is not so clear under what conditions people actually infer and consider counterfactual emotions at the time they make the decisions, that is, under what conditions regret and rejoicing affect decision utility as well as experienced utility.

In spite of the progress that is being made studying and incorporating emotions into theories of decision making, emotion is the least understood of the many systems involved in decision processes. Some of the biggest surprises come from what George Loewenstein (1996) calls "immediate emotions," emotions being experienced at the time a decision is made that may even have nothing to do with the decision itself, in other words, that appear to be involved in neither decision utility nor experienced utility. When the emotions of anger, love, fear, or greed are strong enough at the time of decision, we often choose poorly or get hung up in a dysfunctional loop of indecision. And sometimes, when emotions are very intense, they override cognitive processing, as when people report that they "are out of control" or "just couldn't help themselves."

10.3   HOW WE SENSE VALUES: FROM THE JUST NOTICEABLE DIFFERENCE TO PROSPECT THEORY

In the 1923 edition of *Webster's International Dictionary*, the first definition of *value* is the quality of a thing or activity according to which its worth or degree of worth is estimated; subsequent definitions concern intrinsic desirability, and later ones talk about market equivalent in terms of money or goods. By the 1968 edition, in contrast, the first five definitions explicitly concern *monetary equivalents:* "1. A fair or proper equivalent in money . . . fair price. 2. The worth of a thing in matter of goods at a certain time; market price. 3. The equivalent (of something) in money. 4. Estimated or appraised worth or price. 5. Purchasing power." Only the sixth 1968 definition corresponds to the first 1923 definition. Hence, even in everyday usage, value has come to be almost synonymous with *monetary equivalent*. The more general concept of the degree of worth or desirability specific to the decision maker, as opposed to mere money, is better termed *utility*. Even that term is ambiguous, however, because the dictionary definition of utility is "immediate usefulness," and that is not what decision theorists have in mind when they discuss utility. Our own preferred general term is *personal value*—to the decision maker. Nonetheless, most of the examples we discuss in this chapter involve personal values assigned to money, although the findings we describe apply to personal value more generally.

The standard account of valuation by economists and philosophers focuses on what a psychologist would call the psychophysical relationship between objective dimensions of experience and the subjective value derived from it. (Coombs's single-peaked curve, discussed above, is in that tradition, although it is relatively modern in its derivation and conception.) To understand the psychophysical approach to values and utilities, it helps to take brief historical excursion, going back to the 1850s. In that period, many psychologists asked a simple question: How much must the physical intensity of a stimulus be augmented for people to notice the difference? For example, if people are first given a one-gram weight, how much heavier must another weight be for them to notice that it is in fact heavier? Psychologist Ernst Heinrich Weber (1795-1878) noted that, in general, the amount the stimulus must be incremented (or decremented) physically for people to notice a difference is proportional to the stimulus magnitude itself; that is, it must be incremented (or decremented) by a certain *fraction* of its physical intensity to achieve what is technically termed a *just noticeable difference*, or "j.n.d." (The standard procedure currently used for determining the j.n.d. is to require people to judge which of two stimuli is more intense and then to define this noticeable difference as occurring whenever the subjects are correct 75% of the time; that figure is chosen by defining the j.n.d. as the intensity at which people can note a difference 50% of the time and assuming that when they cannot note it they guess correctly 50% of the time; 50% + [50% of 50%] = 75%.)

The proportion that stimuli must be incremented or decremented to obtain a just noticeable difference in intensity has been termed a *Weber fraction*. The Weber fraction for weight, for example, is approximately 2.8%. The fact that this fraction is more or less constant for any particular type of intensity has been termed Weber's law. It does not hold exactly over all dimensions and ranges of intensity, but it is useful in research and practice as a rough approximation.

In the 1880s, psychologist Gustav Fechner (1801-1887) proposed that just noticeable differences could be conceptualized as units of *psychological intensity*, as opposed to physical intensity. It immediately follows that psychological intensity is a logarithm of physical intensity. The proposal that psychological intensity is the logarithm of physical intensity became known as Fechner's law. Again, it does not hold over all dimensions and ranges of intensity, but it is a good approximate rule. In fact, it has been so well accepted that when the psychological intensity of noise was measured

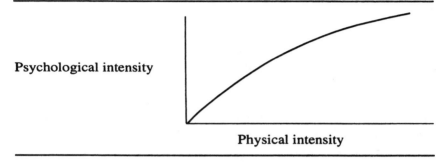

Psychological intensity

Physical intensity

FIGURE 10.3. An Illustration of the Logarithmic Functional Relationship Summarized in Fechner's Law and Later Proposed
by Daniel Bernoulli as a General Utility Function

in bells and decibels, these units were defined as the logarithm of the
physical amplitude. (A *bell* is a tenfold increase in physical amplitude; a
decibel is an increase of 1.26; $1.26^{10} = 10$; hence the logarithm of $1.26^{10} = 10$
times the logarithm of 1.26, i.e., 10 decibels to a bell.) This logarithmic
function is illustrated in Figure 10.3.

The logarithmic function follows what may be termed the "law of
diminishing returns," or the "law of decreasing marginal returns." Independently, economists have proposed that this law also describes not only
sensory intensities, but also the *utility* of money and possessions for individuals. Two million dollars would be worth less (have a lower personal
value) than twice the value of $1 million to the reader of this book—even
when these two amounts refer to money after taxes. This diminishing
return characteristic of what is termed the *utility function* for money need
not yield a precise logarithmic pattern.

This function (Figure 10.3) was originally proposed for utilities by
Daniel Bernoulli, a Swiss mathematician and physicist who lived in the
18th century. His proposal is the first clear statement of the principle that
subjective satisfaction is not directly (linearly) related to objective amounts,
and it is enormously appealing intuitively. Who would disagree that the
difference between nothing and $10 is much more salient, palpable, and
pleasure producing than the difference between $100 and $110 or between
$1,000 and $1,010? (It is tempting to try to relate this function to Coombs
and Avrunin's derivation of the single-peaked preference curve. Certainly
Coombs and Avrunin had the general principle of diminishing returns in
mind when he proposed the "good things satiate" portion of his model.
But it is more correct to suppose that the Bernoullian utility function reflects

both positive and negative substrates and to imagine that it is single-peaked, too. This would mean that there is such a thing as too much money—a point at which harassment; social enmity; threats of kidnapping; and other antiwealth, anticelebrity actions would become so aversive that the curve would peak and more wealth would be less desirable.)

The assumption of a diminishing marginal returns utility function relating dollar gains to utilities has been a cliché in economic theorizing and most research shows that our evaluations of gains show a negatively accelerating, diminishing returns pattern. In 1979, Daniel Kahneman and Amos Tversky proposed what they termed prospect theory as a descriptive theory of decision behavior. A basic tenant of this theory is that the law of diminishing returns applies to *good and bad* quantitative consequences of decisions. There are many components of this theory, which we discuss extensively in Chapter 13, but only three of them need concern us here:

1. An individual views monetary consequences in terms of changes from a *reference level,* which is usually the individual's status quo. The values of the outcomes for both positive and negative consequences of the choice then have the diminishing returns characteristic.

2. The resulting value function is steeper for losses than for gains. This implies *loss aversion;* equal-magnitude gains and losses do *not* have symmetric impacts on the decision. Losses hurt more than gains satisfy; most empirical estimates conclude that losses are about twice as painful as gains are pleasurable.

3. The curve is concave for gains and convex for losses, implying that decision makers will be *risk averse when choosing between gains and risk seeking when choosing between losses.*

The addition of a moveable reference level is the major difference between prospect theory and traditional economic utility theories. Although in many situations it seems obvious how the context of a decision problem determines a reference point, the specification of behavioral principles to predict reference point locations is one of the most urgent research problems confronting modern prospect theory.

Now consider the following choices: Imagine you have just received $200. Which of the following options would you prefer?

Option 1: You receive an additional $100.

Option 2: A fair coin is tossed. If it lands heads, you receive an additional $200; if it lands tails, you receive nothing more.

Most people prefer Option 1, the sure additional $100.

Now consider a variation on the first pair of options: Imagine you have just received $400, but there is a penalty attached. You must choose one of the two penalty options.

Penalty Option 1: You must give back $100.

Penalty Option 2: A fair coin is tossed. If it lands heads, you must give back $200; if it lands tails, you may keep all of the money ($400).

Presented with the penalty options, most people prefer the second alternative.

If we apply the prospect theory principles summarized above, we can see that a gain of $100 has, by the diminishing returns characteristic of the value function, greater than half the value of a gain of $200; hence people prefer the certainty of $100 to the 50% chance of $200. But at the same time, a loss of $100 is *more than* half as negative as the loss of $200, so the people prefer a 50% chance of giving back $200 to a certainty of giving back $100. This pair of preferences is irrational; the irrationality enters because people do not look at the final outcomes of their choices but, rather, allow the reference level to change and make judgments relative to that labile reference. When they have been told they are given $200, they accept that status quo as their reference level; when they are told they have been given $400, they accept that. Thus they make contradictory choices even though the final outcomes are identical in both problems ($300 profit for the Option 1 sure things; $300 expected value for the Option 2 gambles).

As Kahneman and Tversky (1979) point out, the psychological justification for viewing consequences in terms of the status quo can be found in the more general principle of *adaptation* (also derived from historical developments in the study of sensory psychology). They write:

> Our perceptual apparatus is attuned to the evaluation of changes or differences rather than to the evaluation of absolute magnitudes. When we respond to attributes such as brightness, loudness, or temperature, the past and present context of experience defines an adaptation level, or reference point, and stimuli are perceived in relation to this reference point. . . . Thus, an object at a given temperature may be experienced as hot or cold to the touch depending on the temperature to which one has adapted. The same principle applied to non-sensory attributes such as health, prestige, and wealth. The same level of wealth, for example, may imply abject poverty for one person and great riches for another— depending on their current assets. (p. 277)

The difference between prospect theory and the standard economic theory of diminishing marginal utility is that the latter assumes that decision makers frame their choices in terms of the *final* consequences of their decisions. The diminishing return shape of the utility function guarantees that *any gamble* between two negative outcomes is *less* negative, worth more in terms of utility than the corresponding certainty, and the utility for *any gamble* between the positive outcomes is worth less than the corresponding certain outcome. (Ironically, stockbrokers often advise poorer people to be conservative and wealthier ones to take chances, which makes no sense at all from this framework—especially given that poorer people who invest their money conservatively are virtually destined to remain poor, whereas the wealthy have nowhere to go but down.)

Panel (a) in Figure 10.4 presents the standard economic analysis, and panel (b) illustrates the prospect theory analysis of the option choice problems. Recall that both choices are between a final outcome of $300 versus a 50-50 chance of $200 or $400. These final outcomes form the basis of the standard expected utility theory analysis. If there is marginal decreasing utility for money, the average of the utility for $200 and that for $400 is less than the utility for $300. This average is indicated by a point on the line connecting the $200 point and the $400 point; the shape of the curve dictates that this line will always lie entirely *beneath* it. If the decision maker has a positive asset level that is added to the options in determining final consequences, the line connecting these points still lies entirely beneath the curve—as they are moved to the right—so the certainty of $300 is still preferred. In fact, a line connecting *any* two points will lie entirely beneath the curve; which, in general, implies people will be "risk averse" when thinking about gains.

Now consider the choice framed in terms of being given $200 and then asked for a preference between $100 more for sure versus a 50-50 chance of $200 more or nothing. According to prospect theory, the decision maker does not look at the final outcomes ($300 vs. a 50-50 chance of $200 or $400) but, rather, views each choice between options in terms of gains or losses from his or her status quo (reference level). The $200 has been incorporated into that reference level, and because the shape of the utility postulated by prospect theory is also marginally decreasing, the decision maker again opts for the additional certainty of $100. Like classic utility theory, prospect theory makes the general prediction that people will be risk averse when thinking about gains.

Suppose now that the choice is framed in terms of being given $400 and being required to either give back $100 or take a 50-50 chance of

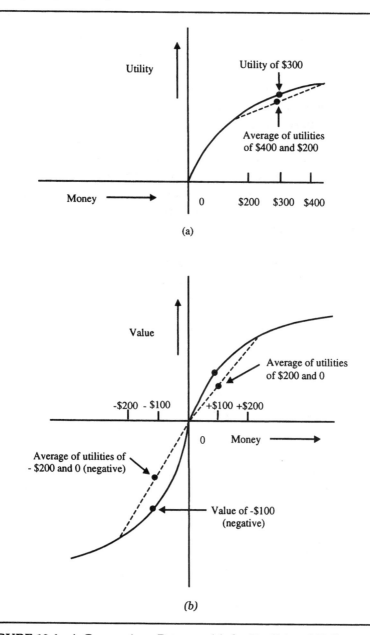

(a)

(b)

FIGURE 10.4. A Comparison Between (a) the Traditional Utility
Analysis, and (b) the Prospect Theory Analysis of
Relationships Between Objective Consequences and
Experienced Utility, or Value

giving back nothing or $200. The final outcomes remain the same. According to prospect theory, however, the decision maker analyzes the options in terms of losses from the status quo (the reference level has shifted to include the $400). Given the (hypothesized) marginally decreasing utility function for losses as they get more severe (Figure 10.4b), the average of the disutility of –$200 and nothing is not as bad as the disutility of –$100. (This result is illustrated by the point on the line connecting the relevant outcomes; on the negative side a marginally decreasing utility function guarantees that the line connecting any two points lies wholly *above* the curve, which has the general implication that behavior will be "risk seeking" for losses.) The prediction, according to prospect theory, is to choose the 50-50 risky gamble, and that is in fact the most common choice when people are presented with this problem.

Before discussing examples outside a gambling context, we illustrate prospect theory predictions with the example used in Chapter 1 to illustrate expected utility theory. It involved choice between two pairs of gambles:

(a) With probability .20, win $45, otherwise nothing.

(b) With probability .25, win $30, otherwise nothing.

and

(a′) With probability .80, win $45, otherwise nothing.

(b′) Win $30 for sure.

As pointed out in Chapter 1, options (a) and (a′) have higher *expected values*, than options (b) and (b′), respectively (e.g., the expected value of [a] is $9, whereas that of [b] is $7.50). Nevertheless, the marginally decreasing shape of an individual's utility function may lead to a choice of (b) and (b′). What is incompatible with classic utility theory is a choice of (a) and (b′) or of (b) and (a′). It is still possible, however, to choose (a) and (b′) or (b) and (a′) without violating the criteria of rationality presented in Section 1.5.

Now consider a choice between two options:

(a″) With probability .75, fail at Stage I of the gamble and receive nothing, but if Stage II is reached, win $45 with probability .80; otherwise, win nothing.

(b″) With probability .75, fail at Stage I of the gamble and receive nothing, but if Stage II is reached, receive $30.

If Stage II becomes a functional status quo, prospect theory predicts that (b") may be chosen in preference to (a") by subjects who would choose (b') over (a')—and in fact most subjects do. But (a") is logically equivalent to (a) (because .25 × .80 = .20) and (b") to (b) (because .25 × 1 = .25), so that a choice of (a) and (b") or of (b) and (a") violates rationality itself. Such patterns of choices are common in research on preferences among gambles. This phenomenon has been labeled *pseudocertainty*. The prospect theory explanation is that the chooser adopts a particular stage or hurdle in a probabilistic process as a psychological status quo and consequently becomes risk averse for gains and risk seeking for losses following it (the complete prospect theory explanation is a bit more complex). If the stage is actually reached, there is nothing irrational about preferring the $30 certainty ([b'] to [a']) while, prior to reaching it, preferring the uncertain option with the higher expected value ([a] to [b]). But that violates classic utility theory. The irrationality here is that pseudocertainty leads to contradictory choice prior to knowledge of the outcome, depending on whether the choice is viewed in its totality (which might lead to a choice of [a] in preference to [b]) or sequentially by components (which might lead to a choice of [b"] in preference to [a"]).

Note that Coombs and Avrunin's "good things satiate, bad things escalate" principle is in direct conflict with prospect theory, which (like Fechner's law and classic economics) includes a decreasing marginal returns principle for negative as well as positive outcomes. One possible resolution is that the moderation principle is a *realistic* generalization from past experience (although often an implicit one), whereas the framing effects of prospect theory involve *imagination* of future consequences. A nuclear war that killed two thirds of a population would be more than twice as bad as one that killed one third, even though an individual decision maker in a particular crisis situation may choose a 50-50 risk of a nuclear war that would kill two thirds to avoid losing one third for sure. This interpretation is consistent with the irrationality of framing effects in that a person choosing among alternatives that can equally well be framed positively or negatively cannot consistently frame them both ways according to a negatively accelerating function. For example, if a person normally sleeps 8 hours a night and regards the first 4 hours as the most important, then the last 4 hours of sleep lost must also be the most important; a *positively* accelerating function for the disutility of lost sleep is implied. An alternative interpretation is that it's not true in many contexts that "bad things escalate." As pointed out earlier, this principle is *sufficient* for producing a single-peaked function, but it is not *necessary*.

10.4   MENTAL ACCOUNTING

In modern societies, money can be used as means to obtain an enormous variety of outcomes and experiences (there may even be some truth in the saying "The surest way to get people to love you is to save your money"). Economists refer to this broad usefulness of money with the term *fungibility*: A dollar can be perfectly substituted to pay any (financial) account. Food, health, clothing, shelter, entertainment—even sexual favors, addictive drugs, or murder can be purchased with the same dollar. But people violate the principle of fungibility: Money in one *mental account* is not perfectly substitutable for money in another mental account.

Richard Thaler (1999) tells the story of a trip to Switzerland a few years ago when the Swiss franc was at an all-time high relative to the U.S. dollar. Everything was exorbitantly expensive. Fortunately, the conference he was attending paid Thaler a substantial fee for his presentation (on mental accounting, we presume). He and his wife then used the fee to cover the expenses of their weeklong postconference travel in Switzerland. Thaler noticed that if he had received the same fee for a talk in, say, New York a week before the stay in Switzerland he would have found the vacation much less enjoyable.

Another example (also from Thaler), that rings true to most of us: A friend was shopping for a bedspread. She went to a department store and was pleased to find a perfect quilt on sale. The usual prices for the quilts were $200, $250, and $300 for double, queen, and king sizes, respectively, but during the sale all sizes were priced the same at $150. The friend bought the king-sized quilt and was delighted at the price, although the quilt did bunch up on the floor of her bedroom surrounding her double bed.

Or consider the experimental dilemmas posed by Chip Heath and Jack Soll (1996) to experimental participants: Suppose you are offered a $50 theater ticket to a play that you would really like to see. But earlier that week you spent $50 on tickets to a basketball game. How likely would you be to purchase the theater ticket? Now consider the same theater ticket, but earlier in the week you spent $50 to pay for a parking ticket. Now how likely are you to purchase the theater ticket? The overwhelming response in these kinds of situations is to purchase the ticket *if* you have not spent any money recently *in that mental account* (the "entertainment account" in this example), but to forgo the tempting theater ticket if you've already spent money on entertainment. Mental accounting is closely related to the sunk costs fallacy we introduced in Chapter 2; people seem to be concerned about where money comes from and where it was intended to go in a manner that violates the principle of economic fungibility.

In the most general terms, mental accounting is the study of how we organize, plan, and keep track of financial activities. It explains many anomalous saving and spending habits we have that appear to be contrary to our economic self-interest. Why do we exert a great deal of energy to make a proportionally large savings on a small purchase (e.g., go to a second store to save $5 on the purchase of $25 in pet supplies), but forego the same savings on a larger budget item (don't go to a second store to save $5 on the purchase of a $250 CD player)? Why do we "decouple" the costs of items we purchased long ago from our evaluation of the cost of consumption now: Thaler gives the example of a person who purchased wine in a futures market for $20, then 3 years later is considering drinking a bottle of the wine, which could now be sold at auction for $75. The typical answer to the question of how much do you *feel* the wine cost you is "Nothing," or, "I felt I was making money." The economically realistic answer is $75.

Of course, the most insidious decoupling device is the modern credit card, which insulates the purchase decision from the feeling of loss as it combines modest individual purchases into a sum total against which any one purchase seems like a barely perceptible loss. Consider the demonstration experiment conducted by Drazen Prelec and Duncan Simester (1998) on their colleagues at the Sloan School of Business at M.I.T. They offered tickets to a Boston Celtics basketball game as prizes in a sealed bid auction (every participant submits one sealed bid; the highest bid wins). Half the participants were told that they had to pay for the tickets in cash; the other half were told they had to pay with a credit card. The average credit card bid was approximately twice as much as the average cash bid.

Another failure to maximize economic earnings occurs because of the common reliance on aspiration levels to determine how much and how hard we work. Cab drivers do not work longer hours on high-demand days (e.g., rainy weather days); rather, they usually work until a fixed aspiration-level amount has been earned and then quit (Camerer, Babcock, Loewenstein, & Thaler, 1997). This is, of course, bad for the passengers (who get soaked), and it is inefficient for the drivers, who spend many idle hours on a typical low-demand day. (The question of how aspiration levels are chosen, analogous to the question of how reference points are set, is a major open question in current research.)

Mental accounting may also be an important factor in the consistency with which many people lose on gambling excursions. They set aside a certain amount of money with which to play and they (often) stop after losing that amount. They have, however, no equivalent rule for stopping when they are ahead. Filled with fantasies of the big payoff, they continue to gamble, and because the long-run odds favor the house, they eventually lose. Now consider the situation of a friend of ours who had budgeted $250 for the gambling occasion but by luck gets ahead by $1,000. At that point, our friend's total asset position is $1,000 more than before gambling. Had that $1,000 been obtained by some means other than gambling, our friend would still have been willing to invest only $250 in the excursion. ("Blow $1,250 at the tables? You're kidding! I can't afford that!") But by framing the $1,000 as different from other money, this friend has no compunction about losing all of it, plus—of course—the $250 already budgeted for the process. It's a sure way to lose while simultaneously congratulating yourself on your self-control.

People, particularly less affluent ones, are urged by various real and purported financial experts to budget their money. Such budgeting may occur "concretely" in a family ledger; occasionally, it is "psychic." A certain amount is to be set aside for food, a certain amount for shelter, a certain amount for entertainment, and so on. Insofar as budgeting helps people meet their needs, such budgeting advice is fine. It discourages overspending without one's having to consider the financial consequences of each purchase in detail. But it can lead to irrationality, for example, the potentially disastrous results of allowing small expenditures because they involve only a small fraction of your total assets. And it would not be very rational to buy a Ferrari because the automobile budget is in a state of excess while simultaneously depriving oneself of warm clothes during a northern winter because the clothing budget has been depleted.

Prospect theory is meant to describe behavior; thus it incorporates irrationality when it occurs. The theory describes choices made as the result of intuitive, automatic processes, for example, as the result of accepting our status quo as a basis for our choices, rather than framing them in terms of changes from our fixed asset level. Prospect theory does not describe everyone's decision-making behavior all the time; for example, some people some of the time will *not* make the contradictory choices resulting from the pseudocertainty effect. But it is one of the most successful, if not *the* most successful, descriptive theory of decision making today (in 2001).

Classic economic utility theory, in contrast, is interpreted as a normative theory of how we *should* choose and only sometimes a description of how we *do* choose. A central thesis of this book is that our intuitive, automatic thinking processes can lead us to choose one alternative while analytic, controlled thought leads us to choose another. If we could not choose differently "on reflection," there would be little point in studying the normative theory of decision making. Although we should not always be bound by the normative theory's implications, we should be aware of them and violate them only self-consciously for a compelling reason.

REFERENCES

Bechara, A., Damasio, H., & Damasio, A. R. (2000). Emotion, decision making, and the orbitofrontal cortex. *Cerebral Cortex, 10,* 295-307.

Bentham, J. (1948). *An introduction to the principles of morals and legislations.* Oxford, UK: Blackwell. (Original work published 1789)

Brickman, P., & Campbell, D. T. (1971). Hedonic relativism and the good society. In M. H. Appley (Ed.), *Adaptation-level theory: A symposium.* New York: Academic Press.

Camerer, C., Babcock, L., Loewenstein, G. F., & Thaler, R. H. (1997). Labor supply of New York cabdrivers: One day at a time. *Quarterly Journal of Economics, 112,* 407-442.

Coombs, C. H., & Avrunin, G. S. (1977). Single-peaked functions and the theory of preference. *Psychological Review, 84,* 216-230.

Damasio, A. R. (1994). *Descartes' error: Emotion, reason, and the human brain.* New York: Putnam.

Davidson, R. J. (1999). The neuroscience of affective style. In M. S. Gazzaniga (Editor-in-Chief), *The new cognitive neurosciences* (pp. 1149-1159). Cambridge, MA: MIT Press.

Davidson, R. J., Jackson, D. C., & Kalin, N. H. (2000). Emotion, plasticity, context, and regulation: Perspectives from affective neuroscience. *Psychological Bulletin, 126,* 890-909.

Ekman, P., & Davidson, R. J. (Eds.). (1994). *The nature of emotion: Fundamental questions.* New York: Oxford University Press.

Gilbert, D. T., Pinel, E., Wilson, T. D., Blumberg, S., & Wheatley, T. (1998). Immune neglect: A source of durability bias in affective forecasting. *Journal of Personality and Social Psychology, 75,* 617-638.

Harlow, J. H. (1868). Recovery from the passage of an iron bar through the head. *Publications of the Massachusetts Medical Society, 2,* 327-347.

Heath, C., & Soll, J. B. (1996). Mental budgeting and consumer decisions. *Journal of Consumer Research, 23,* 40-52.

Ito, T. A., & Cacioppo, J. T. (1999). The psychophysiology of utility appraisals. In D. Kahneman, E. Diener, & N. Schwarz (Eds.), *Well-being: The foundations of hedonic psychology* (pp. 470-488). New York: Russell Sage Foundation.

Kahneman, D., Fredrickson, B., Schreiber, C. M., & Redelmeier, D. (1993). When more pain is preferred to less: Adding a better end. *Psychological Science, 4,* 401-505.

Kahneman, D., & Tversky, A. (1979). Prospect theory: An analysis of decision under risk. *Econometrica, 47,* 263-291.

Kahneman, D., Wakker, P. P., & Sarin, R. (1997). Back to Bentham? Explorations of experienced utility. *Quarterly Journal of Economics, 112,* 375-405.

LeDoux, J. E. (1996). *The emotional brain: The mysterious underpinnings of emotional life.* New York: Simon & Schuster.

Loewenstein, G. F. (1996). Out of control: Visceral influences on behavior. *Organizational Behavior and Human Decision Processes, 65,* 272-292.

Lykken, D. (1999). *Happiness: What studies on twins show us about nature-nurture, and the happiness set-point.* New York: Golden Books.

Mellers, B. (2000). Choice and the relative pleasure of consequences. *Psychological Bulletin, 126,* 910-924.

Mellers, B., Schwartz, A., & Ritov, I. (1999). Emotion-based choice. *Journal of Experimental Psychology: General, 128,* 332-345.

Parducci, A. (1995). *Happiness, pleasure, and judgment: The contextual theory and its applications.* Mahwah, NJ: Lawrence Erlbaum.

Prelec, D., & Simester, D. (1998). *Always leave home without it.* Working Paper, Sloan School of Management, MIT, Cambridge, MA.

Redelmeier, D., & Kahneman, D. (1996). Patients' memories of painful medical treatments: Real-time and retrospective evaluations of two minimally invasive procedures. *Pain, 116,* 3-8.

Rolls, E. T. (1999). *The brain and emotion.* New York: Oxford University Press.

Simon, H. A. (1967). Motivational and emotional controls of cognition. *Psychological Review, 74,* 29-39.

Simonsen, I. (1990). The effect of purchase quantity and timing on variety-seeking behavior. *Journal of Marketing Research, 32,* 150-162.

Thaler, R. H. (1985). Mental accounting and consumer choice. *Marketing Science, 4,* 199-214.

Thaler, R. H. (1999). Mental accounting matters. *Journal of Behavioral Decision Making, 12,* 183-206.

Zajonc, R. B. (1980). Feeling and thinking: Preferences need no inferences. *American Psychologist, 35,* 151-175.

COMPLEX VALUES
AND ATTITUDES

De gustibus est disputandum.

—Anonymous

11.1 THE CONSTRUCTION OF VALUES

If the rational model of decision making is to be of any practical use, it must assume that tastes do not change often or capriciously. Economists George Stigler and Gary Becker (1977) argue vociferously for the general principle that tastes are stable and uniform and there are few, if any, important variations in preferences that cannot be accounted for with reference to prices and incomes. Baruch Fischhoff (1991) has labeled this paradigm the *philosophy of articulated values;* and attributes to it the core assumption that people have the ability to articulate and express values on almost any topic because they already possess "true" values or preferences on many specific issues. Fischhoff contrasts this position with a paradigm he labels the *philosophy of basic values,* which holds that people lack values for all but a few basic issues.

In practice, when survey researchers or laboratory psychologists attempt to measure their respondents' evaluations of everything from the quality of the air they breathe to support for the death penalty to desire to play a monetary gamble, they often find there is unreliability and apparent instability. Proponents of the articulated values view explain these phenomena by asking if the respondents have been queried with the right questions in a context in which sincere responding is encouraged. Proponents of the basic values view point to a basic unreliability in the inferential process that underlies the generation of answers to the evaluative questions (Kahneman, Ritov, & Schkade, 1999). As so often happens, we believe that both camps have some pieces of the puzzle that explains why evaluations of complex entities are so often unreliable.

Survey researchers with backgrounds in cognitive psychology have proposed a belief sampling model for the generation of survey responses from information in long-term memory. The model can be applied usefully to explain unreliability in evaluations of many types. As the name suggests, the heart of the model is a (memory) sampling process. Thus, when a respondent is asked for an opinion, for example, about a political issue (e.g., the death penalty), about a political candidate (e.g., Al Gore), or about a consumer product (e.g., General Electric toasters), the label of the topic serves as a probe to retrieve information from the respondent's long-term memory. Many of the items of information retrieved from memory will be associated with or evoke molecular evaluative reactions of their own, and these elementary evaluations are integrated on the fly to yield a summary evaluation. The general properties of any cognitive memory system, namely fluctuations in the availability of information from memory, explain unreliability in the system. Human memory retrieval is highly context dependent, and the specific information retrieved varies with small changes in the encoding of the retrieval probe and other changes in activation of parts of the system. For example, if a question about abortion or about Bill Clinton follows a question about individual freedom or about John F. Kennedy, the evaluation is likely to be different from what it would have been if the preceding context had activated ideas about family values or about Ronald Reagan.

Roger Tourangeau, Lance Rips, and Ken Rasinski (2000) have formalized this belief sampling process in an explicit model for survey responding that we summarize in Figure 11.1. They distinguish four stages in the evaluation process: comprehension of the question, retrieval of value-laden information from long-term memory, integration of the retrieved evaluations, and response generation. Parts of the model are consistent with precepts from the articulated values position, especially its analysis of the important roles played by question comprehension and response generation. Other parts are consistent with the basic values position,

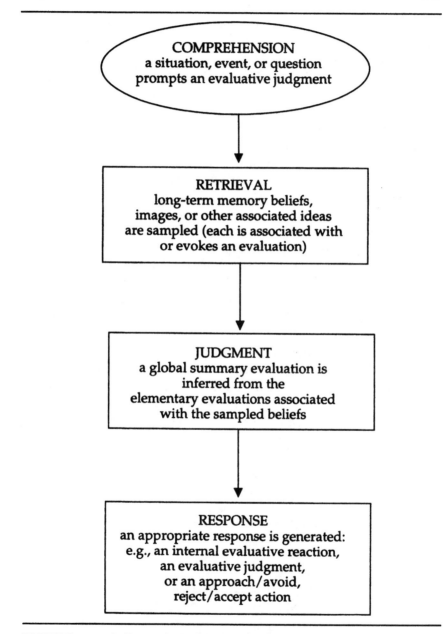

FIGURE 11.1. A General Model of the Belief Sampling Process for
the Construction of Evaluations and Attitudes for
Complex Multifaceted Objects, Individuals, and Events
(based on Tourangeau, Rips, & Rasinski, 2000)

especially the emphasis on variability in the memory sampling process. The retrieval and judgment stages of the model can be described by the anchor-and-adjust process model that we summarized in our Figure 5.1. Tourangeau and his colleagues have assumed that the integration process can be described by the weight-and-add principle of a linear equation, and we pointed out that the anchor-and-adjust process is also essentially a weighted averaging operator (Section 5.2). The serial, integrate-one-retrieved-evaluation-at-a-time depiction of the anchor-and-adjust process describes the sampling and evaluation process in the model too.

The notion that memory sampling is more like skimming the croutons off the surface of a bowl of boiling soup than like the orderly search for a location by address in a quadrilateral grid of city streets explains many of the troublesome phenomena that plague the important business of survey polling. Decades ago, political scientist Philip Converse (1962) identified what he called "nonattitudes," political issue and candidate evaluations that shifted unpredictably from one panel to the next when individual citizens were polled repeatedly. Such unpredictability would be a natural result of the unreliable memory retrieval process at the heart of the belief sampling model. The model can also account for context effects, *systematic* shifts in the evaluations when the prior question changes or when other factors that would impact memory retrieval vary (e.g., mood effects; Seymour Sudman, Norman Bradburn, and Norbert Schwarz [1996] have identified many such effects). When the context or mood shifts from poll to poll, the information retrieved will change and so will the ultimate evaluation.

Thus we suggest that many evaluation tasks involve the construction of a value by retrieving elementary values from long-term memory and then integrating them to infer a summary evaluation. Sometimes, however, especially in consumer choice situations, the constructive process is more systematic, although not always more rational.

11.2 DELIBERATE CHOICES
BETWEEN COMPLEX ALTERNATIVES

We have just reviewed most of what is known about the psychology of fundamental valuation processes. But many important choices don't involve split-second, visceral reactions or reasoning about quantities indexed on a single dimension of dollars; nor are they strictly memory based. Many important choices are made more deliberately from choice sets available to inspection and containing several multiattribute options. When we need to choose between apartments to rent, courses to enroll in, mountain bikes to purchase, vacations to commit ourselves to, or job offers to accept, we rely on "choice strategies" that are directly analogous to the judgment heuristics we studied in Chapters 4 through 7.

These choices are complex because they involve the integration of many small valuations into a global evaluation. For example, when considering which apartment to rent, each of an apartment's attribute values (the lousy location, the low rent, the rickety shower, etc.) are evaluated and then combined into a global assessment. The evaluations of individual attributes depend on current goals. If we are making choices to compose a softball team or a software development team or to pick a roommate, an identical set of candidates (with identical attributes) will be valued differently. We assume that the elementary evaluations have been made (perhaps via the belief sampling process and a visceral response), and the question we address is, how are the pieces put together into a global evaluation?

What makes choices difficult is that often there are many alternatives to consider and each alternative has many important, consequential attributes. The most difficult choices occur when there are "negative correlations" between the values of the attributes across the alternatives: Cheap apartments are usually small, noisy, and poorly furnished; easy-to-reach vacation spots tend to be crowded; popular, useful courses are often crowded and hard to achieve an A grade in.

John Payne and his colleagues Jim Bettman and Eric Johnson (1993) have conducted a systematic analysis of choice strategies and compiled a catalogue of the strategies in a typical adult's "cognitive toolbox." Like judgment heuristics, these strategies are adaptive. Robust when choices need to be made quickly under low and unreliable information conditions, they "work" even when the chooser is distracted by other cognitive tasks or by emotional stresses; and many of the strategies demand only modest amounts of attention and other cognitive resources. Gerd Gigerenzer (Gigerenzer, Todd, & ABC Research Group, 1999) labels some of the most common choice rules "fast-and-frugal heuristics" because they approach optimality, but are frugal, requiring the consideration of relatively little information about the alternatives, and hence fast. Figure 11.2 lists the major strategies identified thus far by behavioral

	Mental Effort	Compensatory vs. Noncompensatory?	Whole vs. Part?	Exhaustive?
DOMINANCE	MEDIUM	NONCOMP	ALTERNATIVE	YES

Search for an alternative that is at least as good as every other alternative on all important attributes and choose it or find an alternative that is worse than any other alternative on all attributes and throw it out of the choice set. Consistent with prescriptions for rational choice, but will only "work" to select a unique best alternative if there is a "superalternative" that beats all others in the choice set. Often used as a first-stage strategy to weed out the weakest "dominated alternatives" in a large choice set.

ADDITIVE LINEAR (MAUT)	VERY HIGH	COMPENSATORY	ALTERNATIVE	YES

Weight all the attributes by their importance (with reference to the current goals of the decision maker). Then consider each alternative one at a time and calculate a global utility by valuing each attribute, weighting it by its importance, and adding up the weighted values. A rigorous version of Benjamin Franklin's advice to a decision maker and the strategy prescribed by economic theories for rational choice. Tends to find the uniquely "best all around" alternative in the choice set, but requires a great deal of effort and time for complex choice sets.

ADDITIVE DIFFERENCE	VERY HIGH	COMPENSATORY	ATTRIBUTE	YES

Consider two alternatives at a time; compare attribute by attribute, estimating the difference between the two alternatives; and sum up the differences across the attributes to provide a single overall difference score across all attributes for that pair. Carry the winner of this comparison over to the next viable alternative and make the same comparison. At the end of this process, the best alternative is the one that has "won" all the pairwise comparisons. This strategy should pick the same ultimate winner as "additive linear" or MAUT, strategy, but the calculation process is different. Common in the final stages of everyday choices, e.g., among consumer goods. Often appears in a qualitative form, where the comparison only "counts" the number of winning attribute comparisons. In this form, it is sometimes called a "voting rule" for choice (in a pairwise comparison ["election"] each attribute pairing has one "vote"). In the qualitative form, the order in which alternatives are considered has a big impact on which is the ultimate winner. (This choice strategy is formally analogous to an election, and certain "voting paradoxes" known to occur in elections occur when an individual makes a personal choice by following this strategy.)

"SATISFICING" (CONJUNCTIVE)	LOW	NONCOMP	ALTERNATIVE	NO

First, set "acceptability" cutoff points on all important attributes; then look for the first alternative that is at least as good as the cutoff values on all important attributes or use the strategy to select a set of good-enough alternatives (all above the cutoff points) for further consideration. Tends to select a homogeneous subset of "good" alternatives and is often used as a first-stage strategy to screen out "losers" or in a general "satisficing" strategy to find the first alternative that is "good enough." Very common in consumer choice.

DISJUNCTIVE	LOW	NONCOMP	ALTERNATIVE	NO

First, set "acceptability" cutoff points on the important attributes; then look for the first alternative that is at least as good as the cutoff value on any attribute or use the strategy to select a set of alternatives that are each very good on at least one dimension for further consideration. Tends to select a heterogeneous subset of "specialists."

LEXICOGRAPHIC	MEDIUM	NONCOMP	ATTRIBUTE	NO

First, review the attributes and pick the one most important attribute; then choose the best alternative on that attribute. If there are several "winners" on the first attribute, go on to the next most important attribute and pick the best remaining alternative(s) on that attribute. Repeat until only one alternative is left. Common in everyday choices and can produce intransitivities; also there is an opportunity for "manipulation" in that the order in which attributes are considered has a

(continued)

FIGURE 11.2. Major Choice Strategies

233

	Mental Effort	Compensatory vs. Noncompensatory?	Whole vs. Part?	Exhaustive?

big effect on the final choice—there is often a possible attribute order that will result in choosing any option in the set. This strategy is similar to Gerd Gigerenzer's highly successful "take the best" fast-and-frugal heuristic (successful in choice and judgment environments that reflect the distributions of alternatives and attribute values in real, everyday environments). The only adjustment to our description would be to substitute the word "validity" (predictive accuracy) for "importance"; order the attributes considered by their past validity in discriminating between good and bad alternatives.

ELIMINATION BY ASPECTS	MEDIUM	NONCOMP	ATTRIBUTE	NO

Pick the first attribute that is salient and set a cutoff "acceptability" point on that attribute. Throw out all alternatives that are below the cutoff on that one attribute. Then pick the next most attention-getting attribute, set an "acceptability" cutoff on that attribute, and again throw out all alternatives that are below the cutoff. Repeat until only one alternative is left. Often used to screen out "losers." The order of attributes considered (aspects) is heavily dependent on momentary salience, and there are the same possibilities for manipulation as in the lexicographic strategy (i.e., if you apply this strategy considering the attributes in one order and then apply it again considering attributes in a different order, you are likely to end up choosing different alternatives).

RECOGNITION HEURISTIC	LOW	NONCOMP	ALTERNATIVE	NO

In some choices, people are so poorly informed about the alternatives that they simply rely on "name recognition." They choose the first alternative that they recognize. Gerd Gigerenzer has shown that in many realistic choice and judgments (choosing the city with a larger population; choosing the stock that is likeliest to increase in price) the "fast-and-frugal" recognition choice heuristic behaves surprisingly well.

FIGURE 11.2. Continued

234

researchers. The columns in this figure indicate some of the important dimensions along which the strategies differ from one another.

Imagine trying to decide which of several available apartments to rent and also suppose that the apartments are described by lists of their attributes (rent, location, size, furnishings, noisiness, etc.) as attributes often are in *Consumer Reports*, on many commercial Web sites, or perhaps in a rental property directory. Now imagine relying on one or another of the strategies listed in Figure 11.2 to understand some of the overarching dimensions that distinguish between the strategies.

The amount of cognitive effort—measured subjectively or objectively— varies across strategies. Effort also depends on the structure of the choice set. If the set is large, requires a lot of trade-offs across dimensions and across alternatives, lacks critical or reliable information, or includes a lot of similar alternatives, most of the strategies will demand a lot of effort. Research shows that people are sensible, perhaps exhibiting a kind of metarationality, about which choice strategies they use: If the choice is consequential, people rely on more thorough and more demanding strategies, those that are also more likely to identify the best alternatives in the choice set. Furthermore, Daniel McAllister, Terrence Mitchell, and Lee Roy Beach (1979) found that when the chooser was more "accountable" to a superior for his or her choices, that more demanding strategies were chosen and the alternatives selected were better.

Some strategies can involve across-attribute compensatory trade-offs, while others do not. The good location of an apartment can *compensate* for the high rent and lead to an overall good evaluation; the reliability or safety of an automobile can compensate for its dumpy appearance. But some strategies, called *noncompensatory*, are unforgiving: If the rent is over $500 per month, the apartment is rejected, no matter how good its other features; if the automobile doesn't comfortably seat a family of four, it's not considered further. Such strategies are usually easier to follow, and they often yield quick answers. However, these cognitive savings come at a cost, and noncompensatory strategies are likely to miss "balanced, all-around good" alternatives and sometimes terminate the search before a truly dominant "winner" is found.

Because our attention is limited, strategies tend to guide information search. A useful distinction is between *alternative-based* strategies versus *attribute-based* ones. In alternative-based strategies, attention is focused on one alternative at a time, its attributes are reviewed, and a summary evaluation is performed of that item before attention is turned to another alternative. The contrasting organizational principle is in terms of attributes: An attribute (e.g., price, location) is selected and several alternatives are evaluated, usually comparatively, on that attribute. Then attention turns to the next attribute. Alternative-based strategies tend to be more cognitively demanding than attribute-based strategies.

Finally, although there is some dependence on the structure of the set of choice alternatives, the strategies differ in terms of the amount of information each is likely to consume in the choice process. Some are *exhaustive* and require perusal of all relevant information (and even deploy inference processes to fill in the missing-information gaps); others are likely to make a choice after a *small subset* of the total accessible information has been covered. Obviously, more information means more cognitive effort for most choice situations, and exhaustive strategies are exhausting.

The most thorough, systematic, cognitively demanding choice strategy is the Multi-Attribute Utility Theory (MAUT) evaluation process that is essentially the linear weight-and-add, lens model judgment policy applied to valuation (i.e., to predict or estimate our "internal" reaction to the object of choice). Most efforts to improve choice habits focus on inducing people to use strategies that are more like this method. For example, Benjamin Franklin's advice (described briefly in Section 1.1) was aimed at helping his friend Joseph Priestley make a choice. Franklin (1772/1987) wrote:

> When these difficult Cases occur, they are difficult, chiefly because while we have them under Consideration, all the Reasons *pro* and *con* are not present to the Mind at the same time; but sometimes one Set present themselves, and at other times another, the first being out of sight. Hence the various Purposes or Inclinations that alternatively prevail, and the Uncertainty that perplexes us. To get over this, my way is to divide half a Sheet of Paper by a Line into two Columns; writing over the one *Pro*, and over the other *Con*. Then, during three or four Days Consideration, I put down under the different Heads short Hints of the different Motives, that at different Times occur to me, for or against the Measure. When I have thus got them all together in one View, I endeavor to estimate their respective Weights; and where I find two, one on each side, that seem equal, I strike them both out. If I find a Reason *pro* equal to some two Reasons *con*, I strike out the three. If I judge some two Reasons *con*, equal to some three Reasons *pro*, I strike out the five; and thus proceeding I find at length where the Balance lies; and if, after a Day or two of further Consideration, nothing new that is of Importance occurs on either side, I

come to a Determination accordingly. And, though the Weights or Reasons cannot be taken with the Precision of Algebraic Quantities, yet when each is thus considered, separately and comparatively, and the whole lies before me, I think I can judge better, and am less liable to make a rash Step, and in fact I have found great Advantage from this kind of Equation, in what may be called *Moral or Prudential Algebra*. (Vol. 19, pp. 299-300)

We'll return to the issue of advice on choosing wisely after we consider some implications of the fact that we often rely on less demanding heuristic strategies when we choose, even when the choices are consequential.

11.3 ORDERING ALTERNATIVES

Since we cannot think of our all of decision options—and their possible consequences—simultaneously; we must do so sequentially. (Notice how Benjamin Franklin's comments on difficulty in choosing agree with our discussion of bounded cognitive capacities, especially working memory limits.) The resulting order in which we consider options and consequences may have profound effects on decision making. Because many of the ways in which we order alternatives in our minds are automatic, irrational choices are common. Here's a simple example.

Richard Nisbett and Timothy Wilson (1977) asked people to state their preference from an array of merchandise (dresses and stockings). The items were arranged in a single row facing the subject. Nisbett and Wilson discovered that no matter where the individual items were placed, the subjects tended to choose the item at the far right. The subjects were not aware that the positioning of the items had an effect on their choice, and certainly they would have rejected an explicit decision rule to "choose whatever happens to be on the far right."

Nisbett and Wilson observed that most subjects scanned the products from left to right—a habit that may well be related to the fact that we read from left to right. (It would be interesting to repeat the experiment in Israel, where sentences are read from right to left.) Why did the subjects tend to prefer the product on the far right? One possibility is that each new product seen possesses desirable characteristics that the one previously scanned does not, but there is no product on the right of the one at the end of the row to bring attention to desirable characteristics that it lacks. (This interpretation is bolstered by the plausible assumption that any product must have a desirable characteristic that others don't in order to be on the market—for long anyway.)

In Nisbett and Wilson's experiment, people at least looked at all the alternative choices. A very severe problem with the ordering of alternatives is that it may *exclude* consideration of certain possibilities. Herbert Simon (1955, 1956) made a strong impact in the fields of individual and organizational decision making by demonstrating that far from making optimal choices, individuals often search through the set of possible alternatives until they find one that satisfies an aspiration level and then they terminate their search. Such a procedure yields a satisfactory decision, but not necessarily an optimal one. Simon used the Scottish word *satisficing*—as opposed to *optimizing*—to describe this process.

The strategy of searching through possible alternatives only until the first satisfactory one is found has important implications in the study of the rationality of choice. It means the *order* in which people search may be of paramount importance. But order can be determined by many factors having very little to do with the consequence of choice (e.g., left-to-right bias) or can even be manipulated by a clever person with control of the agenda of a discussion. The strategy we are describing is not rational, because it operates independently of considerations of the desirability of the consequences of alternative choices. A search in one manner may lead to one decision, whereas a search in another may lead to a different decision.

Decisions that would be rational if they were not influenced by factors not directly tied to consequences—such as the order in which alternatives are considered—have been termed *bounded* by Simon. Decision theorists now speak of "bounded rationality" to characterize a wide range of choice processes (most of the strategies in our Figure 11.2) that do not adhere strictly to principles of rationality but may or may not approximate them. In later work, Simon (1978, 1979) has pointed out that such bounds on rationality are often the most important determinants of choice.

Bounded rationality can have desirable consequences. First, there are situations in which it is not possible to specify all of the alternatives, their attributes, and their consequences in advance. In such a situation, a very reasonable strategy is to collect information in a predetermined manner over a specified period of time and then select the alternative that appears best up to that point. This strategy, however, is not as reasonable as one that constantly revises the manner and time frame of the search on the basis of information as it is gathered, although this is another form of bounded rationality that does not consider all the alternatives. Second, the consideration of all relevant possibilities and consequences involves *decision costs*, which are difficult to integrate with the costs and benefits of payoffs because they are of a qualitatively different type. Let's give two examples—first, one of decision costs.

A visiting professor is contemplating three offers of well-paying professorships, all of which would provide considerable time and support to do the research she loves. From the information she has gathered thus far, there is a clear ranking of how good the offers are, but she needs to collect more information. The situation is complicated by the fact that the offer that appears now to be best is one she must accept or reject within a week; she can postpone a choice between the other two (and any other alternatives that might appear in the meantime) for a month. How much time should she spend collecting information, evaluating possible consequences and their probabilities, and attempting to integrate the information and potential results to reach a decision? There are other things she wishes to do with her time, and there is a deadline; moreover, such decision making is emotionally draining. Should she, as some friends have urged, begin by "bounding" her search by rejecting what appears to be the weakest offer? That clearly has the advantage of allowing her more time and energy to evaluate the other two, but it has the disadvantage of eliminating an option before it has been thoroughly evaluated. Should she make a higher-level decision about how to decide—for example, by adopting a criterion for the decision to reduce the set of three alternatives to two?

These questions are not as easily answered as are those in choices between gambles. What makes this choice particularly difficult, however, is the incomparability of the benefits and costs involved in making the decision with those involved in the jobs themselves. Given the professor's bounds on time and cognitive capacity, she cannot consider the decision costs in a fully rational manner—even if she had some way of integrating them with the consequences of the decision. And then, somewhat paradoxically, even if she could figure out a way to do that, she would have to take into account the probable time and effort involved in figuring it out to determine whether she should attempt to do so in the first place! The rationality of whatever decision she makes will be "bounded." Nonetheless, she must decide something.

An example of not considering all possibilities is someone hiring a secretary for the first time. In some areas of the United States, it is not uncommon for as many as 100 applicants to apply for such a position. The decision is particularly difficult for someone who has only secondhand knowledge of what is required of secretaries and how to evaluate secretarial skills. Applications pour in over days. Should the employer wait until 100 applications have arrived and evaluate these in as thorough a manner as possible? That would require an enormous amount of time. Should the employer evaluate all 100 quickly in a superficial manner and then evaluate 20 in depth? Could better information be gained by evaluating a few in depth? Let's suppose the employer uses a very bounded strategy: Evaluate the first 20 applicants in depth and choose the one that appears to be best. How bad is this decision-making procedure relative to one of judging all 100 in depth?

We can evaluate one aspect of this strategy quite specifically. Let's suppose that the employer would be quite satisfied with any of the five best applicants. How likely is it that out of the potential 100, 1 of these 5 will appear in the first 20? Assuming the order of applications is random with respect to secretarial quality (i.e., there is no systematic bias by which the better secretaries apply earlier or later), the probability is .68. In fact, there is a probability of slightly over one half that 1 of these good secretaries will be among the first 15 applicants. Thus although the strategy of evaluating only the first 20 in depth does not satisfy the criterion of looking at all possible alternatives in terms of their consequences, it does not do badly—at least on the criterion of having access to a top-notch secretary. (Whether the employer will correctly judge the worth of one of these applicants is yet another matter.) The strategy has the advantage of cutting down on the decision time and effort, and it allows the employer to find out what the applicant pool is like in order to determine what qualities should be considered in evaluating applicants.

A similar procedure is to estimate the qualifications of a good candidate in this pool by sampling from the pool and using that information to set a criterion for a final choice. For example, suppose the employer examines 15 randomly chosen applicants and then continues the search until finding 1 that is better than any of those. Doing so would result in a probability of .83 of picking 1 of the top 5, with an expected search length of 29 subsequent applicants. (It is a well-known mathematical result that if 37% [$1/e$, or approximately $1/2.718$] of candidates are randomly sampled from a pool and the search is continued until one better than any of these is chosen, the probability of choosing the best candidate is maximized.)

If the employer knew in advance how to judge the qualifications of potential secretaries, he or she could simply search until finding one in the top 5%. Then an average of 17 applicants would have to be screened.

As pointed out by Amitai Etzioni, all three of the search procedures just described are "boundedly rational" or "satisficing" (personal communication, November 3, 1986). The first involves simply truncating the search because there are too many alternatives to consider; the degree to which that procedure is desirable depends on the degree of truncation, the trade-off between the costs of reaching the decision and the costs and benefits resulting from the decision itself, and the degree to which the chooser can avoid a pernicious bias in conducting the search. The second procedure involved using the first part of a search to determine what constitutes a desirable alternative, and the third involved a predetermined "aspiration level." The desirability of the latter two procedures is determined by the same three factors as that of the first one.

According to Richard Cyert and James March (1963), organizations as well as individuals often use bounded search procedures to arrive at satisfactory, but not optimal, solutions to many problems. Moreover, the characteristics that define the goodness of a solution may consist of a mix of those chosen at the beginning of the search and those that become more noticeable as it proceeds.

Another procedure for simplifying a search procedure involves concentrating on *aspects* of alternatives rather than on the alternatives themselves. For example, as Amos Tversky (1972) has proposed, decision makers often *eliminate* alternatives by aspects. The *elimination by aspects* strategy involves choosing a desirable aspect, eliminating all alternatives that do not have it (or enough of it), then choosing another desirable aspect and eliminating all those alternatives not containing it, and so on, until either a single alternative is left or so few are left that they can be evaluated thoroughly. In the secretary choice, for example, familiarity with keyboard skills and prior training with a particular software tool might be aspects by which to eliminate candidates.

If the aspects are considered in the same order as their desirability, this form of bounded rationality results in reasonably good choice—although it involves no compensatory mechanism. If the aspects are chosen probabilistically in proportion to their importance, the procedure is less successful. And if they are chosen ad hoc on the basis of the ease with which they come to mind, it is a decidedly flawed procedure. Advertisers often try to manipulate the appeal of their products by highlighting specific aspects on which their product beats the competition.

One of the most important insights provided by Payne, Bettman, and Johnson's (1993) systematic analysis of the characteristics of the choice strategies was a test of the comparative success of each strategy under different constraining conditions. Even when there were no limits on computational resources or available information, many of the less cognitively demanding strategies did almost as well as the ideal Multi-Attribute Utility Theory (MAUT) evaluation (with reasonable choice sets and no missing information). When a choice deadline was imposed on the strategies, the MAUT strategy was prone to deadlock, or "crash," whereas some of the other "bounded" strategies still performed close to optimally. Gerd Gigerenzer and his research group (1999) have conducted a parallel analysis of his "fast-and-frugal choice algorithms" and reached the same conclusions. For example, the "recognition heuristic" and the "take the best heuristic" can outperform the much more cognitively demanding strategies under some realistic performance conditions. The implication is that these efficient, but nonoptimal, strategies may even be adaptively most successful in noisy, stressful, and unforgiving environments.

Is there a contradiction between the bounded rationality of terminating searches and the findings of Nisbett and Wilson? No, because there is a crucial difference in the choice problems. In the Nisbett and Wilson (1997) study, the subjects were aware of all the choice options—the items were physically lined up in front of them. The problem with the satisficing procedure is that certain choices may not even be considered, including those that may be the best one or better ones for the decision maker (with greater or lesser probability, depending on the situation).

11.4   GROUPING ALTERNATIVES

Adaptation is one of the basic processes of human life. It affects judgment and decision, for example, in framing alternatives relative to a status quo. Another basic phenomenon that affects judgment and decision is sensitivity to *context effects*. Just as a particular visual stimulus (e.g., a gray ring) appears different in different contexts (e.g., against a yellow or a blue background), a particular choice alternative may appear different to a decision maker when it is considered in different contexts. Specifically, it may be evaluated as more or less desirable when it appears in different choice sets. The more judgmental the evaluation, the greater is the importance of context effects. For example, despite the differences with which we perceive a color depending on the colors surrounding it, we experience a great deal more "color constancy" than would be expected from a simple analysis of light frequency on an object and its surroundings; the light that illuminates an object does not have much effect on our perception of the object's color. When evaluating an alternative course of action and its possible consequences, however, we often do not experience such constancy. In fact, the influence of competing alternatives can lead to a contradictory choice, even when the competing alternatives are never chosen.

One principle of rationality that most theorists accept is that choice should be *independent of irrelevant alternatives*. That is, if alternative A is preferred to alternative B when the two are considered alone, then A should be preferred to B when alternative C is considered along with them; the presence of C should be irrelevant to the preference between A and B. Of course, if C is the preferred alternative in the set consisting of A, B, and C, we have no way of knowing whether its existence has reversed the preference for A over B. Hence, to demonstrate that choice may violate this principle of rationality, we must show that the choice of A over B is reversed in a situation where C is not chosen.

Can that happen? Yes, and its occurrence is due to context effects. Joel Huber and Christopher Puto (1983) asked people to make choices between consumer items like batteries, clothing, and beverages. Consider their example for calculator batteries:

Battery A: lasts 22 hours and costs $1.80

Battery B: lasts 28 hours and costs $2.10

Now add a third choice, Battery C: lasts 14 hours and costs $1.50. No one chooses the third battery. It looks similar to Battery A, but inferior—A lasts many more hours for a slight price increase. With Battery C in the set, most consumers prefer Battery A (more than 60%). Now consider A and B with a different third alternative, Battery D: lasts 32 hours and costs $2.70; now Battery B looks similar, but is a "better deal," and a majority (about 60% again) now prefer B to A. These "decoy alternative" effects are common in consumer choice and in social choice and political election situations.

Another interesting choice reversal was illustrated by Michael Harrison and Albert Pepitone (1972). Student subjects were asked to train a rat by administering electric shocks. In one condition, only two alternatives were available: shocks labeled "mild" and "slightly painful." In the others, however, a third shock level, labeled either "moderately painful" or "extremely painful," was available. The subjects were told not to use this more severe level, and none did; thus the only two alternatives were "mild" and "slightly painful." Nevertheless, although the "slightly painful" shock level was chosen only 24% of the time when no third alternative appeared, it was chosen 30% of the time in the presence of the irrelevant "moderately painful" alternative and 36% of the time in the presence of the irrelevant "extremely painful" alternative. Thus, by changing contexts with the introduction of an irrelevant alternative, the experimenters changed the proportion of choice between the relevant alternatives.

11.5   HOW TO MAKE GOOD CHOICES

As for practical advice on choosing, we rely on the robust beauty of linear, weighting-and-adding models explained in Chapter 3 of this book. This is Benjamin Franklin's "Prudential Algebra" method described in Section 11.2. Of course, there are problems. How do we determine and define the reasons or values in the analysis? Might not many of them be related? For example, in assessing a possible job, should we list money, status, and autonomy as separate characteristics? How do we know they are important to us? Aren't they related? Isn't it true that "high-level" jobs tend to be high on all three, whereas "low-level" jobs are low on all? If so, shouldn't we just list "job level" rather than its separate components?

The answer to the question of importance is rather easy. It is up to the decision maker. In constructing a weighting scheme, we list the variables that are important to us, given our current goals. If, for example, we think of "job level" in a global and amorphous way, then we should list it. If, on the other hand, money, status, and autonomy each strike us as psychologically distinct and important, then we should list them separately. Franklin advised his friend not *what to* decide, but *how to* decide it. When suggesting a list he was not advising what should be on it but, rather, how to become explicit about what is important to the decision maker. Research indicates that when specific variables are known, a linear model predicts better than global intuitive judgment. (In fact, simply determining the attributes often makes the choice obvious.) Moreover, the weights assigned to the attributes are those of the individual making the choice. If, for example, sexual compatibility is more important to a person choosing a mate than is character, altruism, or sanity, then there is no reason why the person should not choose on that basis—and live with the consequences. Again, the point of this book is not *what* but *how*. Thus the answer to the related variables question may be found in a distinction made by Wendell Garner (1974) between integral and separable dimensions. The fact that two dimensions are correlated in nature (such as height and weight) does not imply that they are not psychologically separable and independent for the perceiver. If they are distinct to you, think about them as separable.

Once we have determined the attributes, we face the problem of evaluating and weighting them. To do so, we must assume that we have some insight into our values and value systems—and in particular into how we compare conflicting values. Research has demonstrated that this insight need not be total or profound; evaluations and weights that are reasonable provide outcomes very close to those based on optimal ones. Granted these assumptions, the decision is then *decomposed* so that each variable can be considered separately, and the results are combined according to a linear ("weight and add") scheme. The reason—once again—for believing that such decomposition can work well in a choice situation that lacks a criterion for evaluating the outcome is that it works in situations where one is present (see results in Chapter 3).

Of course, it is not always a simple matter to determine values. In fact, there are systematic cognitive biases in achieving valid decomposition, just as there are governing automatic choice. Thus, Amos Tversky, Shmuel Sattah, and Paul Slovic have shown that when matching procedures are used to determine the relative importance of identified attributes, the result is that a systematic underestimation of the degree of discrepancy is inferred from choice situations. For example, most baseball experts consider batting average to be more important than home run hitting. Their implicit weighting of the two variables can be determined by asking them to match two players by assigning a value to one of the two variables so that the players have equal value in their estimation. This could be done, for example, by deciding on the number of home runs a player with a batting average of .310 would have to hit per year to be of the same value as a player who has a .334 batting average and hits 15 home runs per year. But such matching judgments *systematically underestimate* the importance these judges ascribe to batting average relative to home runs when they are asked to choose the more valuable player among pairs.

Which procedure is better for determining true value? For that matter, what *is* such value? This chapter—and indeed this book—is not addressed to those very difficult questions. What *can* be concluded is that the procedure of looking first *within* each attribute and then comparing across by some weighting system is superior to that of making global intuitive judgments *across* attributes regarding each choice in isolation.

REFERENCES

Converse, P. E. (1962). Changing conceptions of public opinion in the political process. *Public Opinion Quarterly, 51,* 12-24.

Cyert, R. M., & March J. G. (1963). *A behavioral theory of the firm.* Englewood Cliffs, NJ: Prentice Hall.

Fischhoff, B. (1991). Value elicitation: Is there anything in there? *American Psychologist, 46,* 835-847.

Franklin, B. (1975). *The papers of Benjamin Franklin* (W. B. Willcox, Ed.). New Haven, CT: Yale University Press. (Original letter to Joseph Priestley written on September 19, 1772, and contained in Vol. 19, pp. 299-300)

Garner, W. R. (1974). *The processing of information and structure.* Potomac, MD: Lawrence Erlbaum.

Gigerenzer, G., Todd, P. M., & ABC Research Group. (1999). *Simple heuristics that make us smart.* New York: Oxford University Press.

Harrison, M., & Pepitone, A. (1972). Contrast effect in the use of punishment. *Journal of Personality and Social Psychology, 23,* 398-408.

Huber, J., & Puto, C. (1983). Market boundaries and product choice: Illustrating attraction and substitution effects. *Journal of Consumer Research, 10,* 31-44.

Kahneman, D., Ritov, I., & Schkade, D. A. (1999). Economic preferences or attitude expressions? An analysis of dollar responses to public issues. *Journal of Risk and Uncertainty, 19,* 203-235.

McAllister, D., Mitchell, T. R., & Beach, L. R. (1979). The contingency model for selection of decision strategies: An empirical test of the effects of significance, accountability, and reversability. *Organizational Behavior and Human Decision Performance, 24,* 228-244.

Nisbett, R. E., & Wilson, T. D. (1977). Telling more than we can know: Verbal reports on mental processes. *Psychological Review, 84,* 231-259.

Payne, J. W., Bettman, J. R., & Johnson, E. J. (1993). *The adaptive decision maker.* New York: Cambridge University Press.

Simon, H. A. (1955). A behavioral model of rational choice. *Quarterly Journal of Economics, 69,* 99-118.

Simon, H. A. (1956). Rational choice and the structure of the environment. *Psychological Review, 63,* 129-138.

Simon, H. A. (1978). Rationality as a process and as product of thought. *American Economic Review, 68,* 1-16.

Simon, H. A. (1979). Rational decision making in business organizations. *American Economic Review, 69,* 493-513.

Stigler, G. J., & Becker, G. S. (1977). De gustibus non est disputandum. *American Economic Review, 67,* 76-90.

Sudman, S., Bradburn, N. M., & Schwarz, N. (1996). *Thinking about answers: The application of cognitive processes to survey methodology.* San Francisco: Jossey-Bass.

Tourangeau, R., Rips, L. J., & Rasinski, K. (2000). *The psychology of survey response.* New York: Cambridge University Press.

Tversky, A. (1972). Elimination by aspects: A theory of choice. *Psychological Review, 79,* 281-299.

Tversky, A., Sattah, S., & Slovic, P. (1988). Contingent weighting in judgment and choice. *Psychological Review, 95,* 371-384.

A NORMATIVE, RATIONAL
DECISION THEORY

*There is nothing more profitable for a [person] than to take
good counsel with [oneself]; for even if the event turns out
contrary to one's hopes, still one's decision was right.*

—Herodotus

12.1 A FORMAL DEFINITION OF RATIONALITY

Some experts have defined rationality as compatibility between choice
and value: Rational behavior is behavior that maximizes the value of consequences. But as should be clear by now, the question of what constitutes
a value is not easily answered, and we think that rationality of choice is a
matter of the process of choosing, not of what is chosen. Nevertheless,
some very important research in decision theory is concerned with the
relationship between decisions and the values of the decision makers.
This is the work of John von Neumann and Oskar Morgenstern, in particular, their classic analysis described in *Theory of Games and Economic
Behavior* (the second edition, published in 1947; first mentioned in our
Section 1.6). Subjective expected utility theory is the most general and
popular description of rational choice in the mathematical and behavioral sciences (an extension, by Leonard J. Savage, 1954, of the original

von Neumann and Morgenstern framework). We introduce this framework and relate it to the psychology of decision making in this chapter.

We have mentioned several times that we (and most psychologists) believe that rational theories are at best an approximate description of how humans really behave. Although people seem to realize that their actual behavior and rational standards diverge, they still want to make good decisions. They want to avoid contradictions in their reasoning and in their behavior; they usually want to behave consistently with the principles of rationality laid down in the subjective expected utility theory we describe in this chapter. Just as we saw in connection with probability theory, as a species we are not endowed with a natural, intuitive sense of these principles. This lack of a clear intuition provides a good reason for an examination of the von Neumann and Morgenstern theory: It doesn't come naturally, so we need to study it to understand its implications for our behavior. To that end, we also present a perspective on how subjective expected utility theory can be used for *improving* the quality of decision making.

Von Neumann and Morgenstern's work was purely mathematical. They demonstrated that if a decision maker's choices follow certain (rational) rules ("the axioms"), it is possible to derive *utilities*—real numbers representing personal values—such that one alternative with probabilistic consequences is preferred to another if and only if its *expected utility* is greater than that of the other alternative. Let's break their argument up into a series of steps:

1. We begin by assuming that a decision maker's choices among alternatives with probabilistic consequences "satisfy the axioms" defining rational choice.

2. Then it is possible to associate a real number with each consequence, which can be termed the *utility* of that consequence for that decision maker.

3. The *expected utility* of a particular alternative is the expectation of these numbers—that is, the sum of the numbers associated with each possible consequence weighted by the probability that each consequence will occur.

4. The conclusion is that a decision maker will prefer outcome X to outcome Y if and only if the expected utility (number) associated with X is greater than that associated with Y.

The axiomatic system achieves several important goals. First, it spells out succinctly and precisely a list of principles of rational decision making. Of course, even at the normative, philosophical level, these principles are a hypothesis about the essence of rational decision making. Other philosophers and mathematicians have proposed alternative systems to prescribe rational decisions, although there is no question but that the von Neumann and Morgenstern system is the current champion. Second, if the axioms are satisfied, then a scale of utilities can be constructed in which the real numbers represent the values of consequences in an orderly manner. In a moment, we will develop an analogy to scales for physical weight; it should be obvious how useful to progress in science and practical applications it is to have such a scale. (Imagine modern physics, chemistry, and engineering without numerical scales.) Third, although it is not specified in detail in the axioms, they provide a method to scale utilities, using human preferences for various outcomes as the inputs.

Many decision theorists who concentrate on the relationship between values and action define rationality as making choices that are consistent with these axioms and further hypothesize that real human choices are also described by the axioms. A rational decision maker would then be one who prefers alternative X to alternative Y whenever the expected utility of X is greater than that of Y. Of course, the system itself does not require a decision maker's choices to satisfy the axioms; the axioms are a hypothesis about ideal rational choices. In fact, much of the psychology of judgment and choice, already reviewed in the first 11 chapters of this book, implies that people do *not* satisfy the axioms in many decision-making contexts.

There is also nothing in subjective expected utility theory that states that the person making the decision has any insight into his or her utilities. But, because humans are sentient, active agents (unlike the physical material to which geometry is relevant), there is a special confusion that arises between analytic and synthetic interpretations of the axioms. When expected utility theory is applied *analytically* (usually by economists), actual choices are interpreted as revealing preferences and these revealed preferences are interpreted as implying utilities. The application has a postdictive flavor; as the psychologist Lola Lopes (1987) puts it,

> In the modern [analytic] view, utility does not precede and cause preferences; it is instead merely a convenient fiction that can be used by the practitioner to summarize the preferences of those who, by choice or

chance, follow the dictates of the von Neumann and Morgenstern axiom system. (p. 286)

In contrast, the theory can be applied *synthetically*. A person is asked to make judgments about his or her utilities and probabilities, and then those judgments can be combined according to the axioms to predict that person's decisions. For most of us, this sequence makes the most sense: When we make a decision, we usually first try to figure out what we want and how to get it, and only then do we decide what action to take and what choice to make—first our goals and values, then choices and actions. The analytic sequence—first we observe what we choose and then we infer what we must have wanted and expected—seems backward. There are some exceptions, however, as in psychoanalysis, where we attempt *analytically* to discover what our behavior implies about its precursors in desire and belief. And we must remember that the analytic interpretation is as valid as—and more popular than—the synthetic interpretation, among the experts in economics and mathematics who are the primary users of the theory.

Nevertheless, as Tversky and Kahneman (1974) point out in a classic article, even the probabilities are often estimated first and then "used" to make decisions. They write:

It should perhaps be noted that, while subjective probabilities can some-times be inferred from preferences among bets, they are normally not formed in this fashion. A person bets on team A rather than on team B because he believes that team A is more likely to win; he does not infer this belief from his betting preferences. Thus, in reality, subjective proba-bilities determine preferences among bets and are not derived from them, as in the axiomatic theory of rational decision. (p. 1130)

Early conceptions of utility in economics (e.g., Jeremy Bentham's ideas, 1789/1948) had a psychological quality, but modern utility theories have eliminated most of the psychology and retained only the behavioral principle that people choose what they prefer. There has been a major shift in the past decade, however, with the psychologists Daniel Kahneman, George Loewenstein, and others enriching the economic conceptualization with psychological content concerning the cognitive and emotional sources of value judgments (see discussion in Sections 10.1 and 10.2).

When most of us talk about personal values, we have a far broader concept in mind than the concept of utility in the von Neumann-Morgenstern theoretical system. For example, we believe that people can verbalize their personal values or value systems; we do not infer these from behavior alone. Otherwise, our language system would not include such concepts as "hypocrisy," which refers to a discrepancy between a stated value and a particular behavior. Moreover, we believe that values exist independent of both verbalization and behavior. In ordinary language, we regard values as an important existential dimension on which we can place objects, actions, and other phenomenon. For example, we say, "He values freedom," as easily as we say, "He went to work yesterday." In fact, we often treat statements of value as if they were statements of fact, even though many philosophers make a strong distinction between these two types of statements, and only after studying philosophy do most of us become confused by our own beliefs that we or others value certain objects or actions. (Some logical positivists have argued that statements that refer to values are arbitrary or at least that such statements have no empirical referents.) Perhaps we should (another value!) be less cavalier in our everyday thinking and speaking. The research reviewed in Chapters 10 and 11 should certainly warn us that many intuitive beliefs about our personal values are of dubious validity.

Another important characteristic of values is that they transcend particular situations. When we say we value something, we are referring to more than our behaviors, feelings, and beliefs in just a particular, specific situation. "He values freedom," for example, refers to a general set of dispositions, actions, and beliefs—and once again, a set that the individual described can at least vaguely verbalize. In fact, there is a popular personality test, the Rokeach Value Inventory, that asks respondents to rank-order the entries in a list of abstract value terms—equality, freedom, family security, wisdom, religious salvation—and then uses individual rankings to predict individual behaviors. For example, people who give the term "equality" a high ranking are likely also to support political policies such as school integration, affirmative action, and programs to benefit minority group members. Analogously, those ranking "salvation" high are likely to be regular churchgoers. (We would speculate that the predictive power of the Rokeach test derives from the principles we discussed concerning the belief sampling model for the construction of summary values in Section 11.1. The value labels [e.g., "equality"] sample from the same pool of related, evaluatively loaded beliefs that are sampled when we are in relevant situations [e.g., have just been asked to sign a pro-affirmative action petition], hence the predictability stems from a overlap of memories retrieved to the label cue and to the situation cues.)

As an axiom system that leads to derivations of numerical utilities, the von Neumann-Morgenstern theory is of special interest to behavioral scientists because its conclusions have implications about decisions and values as we understand these terms in everyday language and life. Just as the conclusions of Euclidian geometry can be applied to real-world objects, we suppose the conclusions from subjective expected utility theory describe or can be compared to human decision behavior. Otherwise, they would be simply systems of rules for manipulating symbols and deriving numbers that would have little interest for most of us.

To explain the nature of a mathematical axiom system and how such a system can be related to real-world objects and phenomena, we start with a system that is simpler and more concrete than von Neumann and Morgenstern's, but which has an analogous structure. Specifically, let's consider the weights of physical objects. Such weights are *positive real numbers;* they can be added together, as when a 1.37-pound weight and a 7.86-pound weight are put together on a scale to yield 9.23 pounds. Such real numbers have important properties, eight of which are elaborated here.

Property 1. Comparability. Given any two positive real numbers, one is larger than the other or they are equal. That may be expressed algebraically by letting x and y stand for the numbers. Then $x > y, y > x$, or $x = y$. To avoid expressing all of the following properties in terms of both inequality and equality, we will usually use the "weak" form of comparability: "greater than or equal to," symbolized $\geq$. Thus we can express comparability as meaning that for any two real numbers x and y, $x \geq y, y \geq x$, or both, in which case they are equal.

Property 2. Ordering. The relationship "greater than or equal to" determines the transitive ordering of the numbers, that is, if $x \geq y$ and $y \geq z$, then $x \geq z$.

Property 3. Additive Closure. When we add two positive numbers, we get a third positive number, that is, if x and y are positive numbers, $z = x + y$ is a positive real number.

Property 4. Addition Is Associative. The order in which we add numbers is unimportant, that is, $x + (y + z) = (x + y) + z$. "The sum of the sums equals the sum of the sums."

Property 5. Addition Is Symmetric. The order in which two numbers are added is unimportant, that is, $x + y = y + z$.

Property 6. Cancellation. When a third number is added to each of two numbers, the order of the two sums is the same as the order of the two original numbers, that is, $x + z \geq y + z$ if and only if $x \geq y$.

Property 7. The Archimedean Property. This property is often termed the *Archimedean* property (although it is credited to Eudoxus, circa 408-355 B.C.). In effect, it asserts that no positive real number is infinitely larger than any other, that is, that no matter how much smaller one number is than a second number, there is some multiple of the first number that is larger than the second number.

Given any two numbers, there always exists an integer-value multiple of one that is larger than the other, that is, if, $x \geq y$, then there exists an n such that $ny > x$. Here, ny simply refers to y added to itself n times; this axiom does not involve the general concept of multiplication, since multiplication is unnecessary when we combine integers. (Note that the Archimedean property implies that there is no largest or smallest positive real number: Consider any two numbers x and y with $x \geq y$; x cannot be the largest number, because there exists an n such that $ny > x$. Similarly, y cannot be the smallest, because $y > x/n$ with that same n.)

Property 8. Solvability. If $x \geq y$, there exists a z such that $x < y + z$.

The German physicist and mathematician, Otto Hölder (1901; see Michell & Ernst, 1996, for an English translation of the relevant sections) recognized that the way in which objects behave on a pan balance corresponds perfectly to the eight axioms of this system, where $x R y$ indicates that object x outbalances object y and the operation O corresponds to placing two objects together on the same pan ("concatenating" them). Readers should confirm for themselves that the behavior of objects on a pan balance satisfies these eight properties restated as abstract axioms where R refers to the tilt of the balance and O refers to placing objects in the same pan. (This correspondence is *conceptual;* any particular pan balance may not be large enough to hold all objects that have weight or may be subject to errors in its actual operation.) Thus Hölder demonstrated mathematically the correspondence between his axiom system and the positive real numbers and noted the empirical correspondence between the axiom system and the behavior of objects on pan balances. The result is that the behavior of objects on pan balances may be used to assign them real number measures, called *weights.*

Then, Hölder demonstrated something quite profound. Using knowledge from a branch of mathematics called *measurement theory,* he showed that if a system has these eight properties ("the axioms are satisfied"), then real numbers can be associated with the elements of the system, and these real numbers are unique except for multiplication by a positive constant. A measurement scale with these properties is technically called a *ratio scale.* That is, he restated these eight properties in terms of axioms in which an abstract relationship R replaced the $\geq$ and an abstract operation O replaced addition. He subsequently demonstrated that if the elements of the system related by R and combined by O satisfy these eight axioms, then it is possible to associate a positive real number with each such that (a) the real number associated with $x \geq y$ if and only if $x R y$, and (b) $z = x + y$ whenever $z = x O y$. Moreover, any two sets of real numbers associated in this manner have the relationship that one set is a positive multiple of the other. For example, the number of ounces assigned to an object is 16 times the number of pounds. These numbers are termed *measures;* the measure associated with the entity x is often symbolized $m(x)$. Just as a 1 is the unit of measurement in the real numbers, the "standard gram" or "standard pound" is the unit of measurement for weights. Finally, the fact that we measure weights in pounds, ounces, or grams—all of which are multiples of each other—corresponds to the conclusion that two sets of measures assigned to the entities satisfying the axiom system are positive multiples of each other.

12.2   SUBJECTIVE EXPECTED UTILITY THEORY

The axiomatic method, stating the essentials of a theory as an elegantly simple set of postulates that include all and only the necessary definitions and assumptions from which the entire theory can be derived, is a brilliant intellectual invention (usually attributed to the Greek philosopher and mathematician Euclid, who axiomatized plane geometry). Although the method is far from universal in the sciences, we believe it is reasonable to propose the axiomatic formulation as an eventual goal for the expression of all significant theories in any scientific discipline. Even in domains where it may be useful to implement theories in computer programming languages, a summary of the essential principles on which the simulation program is based is absolutely necessary for comprehension and evaluation of any theory with which we are familiar (cf. Hastie & Stasser, 2000). There is not a unique axiomatization for each theory; usually different, but logically equivalent, axiom systems can be stated. Our choice of the particular eight properties of numbers, and hence the translation into the eight axioms of weight, is based on our judgment of which axioms readers will find easiest to understand. Other authors cite different systems, many of which are more elegant. In the case of the von Neumann and Morgenstern utility theory, there are many axiomatizations. We have chosen the one that we believe is most comprehensible to an intelligent reader who is not an expert in mathematical logic.

The basic *entities* of the von Neumann-Morgenstern system can be conceptualized as *alternatives* consisting of probabilistic consequences— often referred to as *gambles*. The basic relationship is one of *preference*, which induces an order on the alternatives; we will settle for the *weak ordering*, $\gtrsim$, which might be expressed as "is indifferent or preferred to" behaviorally. (Note that expression is rough; a more precise interpretation of $\gtrsim$ is "is not unpreferred to," because both $A \gtrsim B$ and $B \gtrsim A$ are possible, in which case $A \sim B$. That usage is quite awkward, however. To be technically precise, we should distinguish between strong preference [>] and weak preference [$\gtrsim$]; the reader wishing such precision can translate by considering weak and strong preference separately.) The basic *operation* for combining the alternatives (analogous to placing more than one object on a balance pan) may be conceptualized as a *probability mixture* of alternatives. Thus, if A and B are alternatives, ApB refers to receiving alternative A with probability p and alternative B with probability $(1 - p)$. Note the probability of receiving B is implicit; we only consider binary, two-alternative gambles when discussing the theory, and so given the probability of A (e.g., p), the probability of B will be 1 minus that value, or the *complement*. To illustrate some relationships that will be prescribed by the axioms, consider the evaluation of a complex multiple-stage gamble. The following results will be explicated when we discuss the interpretation of individual axioms (especially Axioms 3, "Closure," and 4, "Distribution of Probabilities Across Alternatives"). Because the alternatives specify the consequences with particular probabilities, the probability mixture of alternatives is synonymous with a probability mixture of the consequences, that is, if alternative A consists of consequence x with probability r and consequence y with probability $(1 - r)$ whereas alternative B consists of consequence z with probability s and alternative w with probability $(1 - s)$, then ApB consists of consequence x with probability rp, consequence y with probability $(1 - r)p$, consequence z with probability $s(1 - p)$, and consequence w with probability $(1 - s)(1 - p)$. An alternative with a single consequence is conceptualized as one in which the consequence occurs with a probability of 1.

We find it helpful to represent alternatives, consequences, and probability mixtures in the decision tree diagram format, as in Figure 12.1 (this format was introduced in Section 2.2). These diagrams are useful when theoretical gambles are to be compared (e.g., to grasp the implications of the axioms or the structure of experimental stimulus gambles) and especially when the system is to be applied to analyze actual personal decisions.

What von Neumann and Morgenstern (1947) proved is that when their axioms are satisfied, a numerical measure can be associated with each consequence—termed a *utility* of that consequence (analogous to the numerical weight of a physical object)—and that the alternatives themselves can be ordered according to their expected utility. In other words, the basic result is that a preference between the alternatives can be represented by an ordering of their numerical expected utilities. (Because a single consequence can be conceptualized as an alternative in which that consequence occurs with the probability of 1, and vice versa, the axioms can be stated in terms of either consequences or alternatives. We chose to present the axioms in terms of alternatives because we think they will be easier to understand in that form.)

We can summarize the analogy between the von Neumann and Morgenstern system and Hölder's (1901) axiomatization of physical weight: Alternatives in a choice set are analogous physical objects to be weighed, weak preference is analogous to the "weighs the same as or more than" result from a pan balance test, and the "probability mixture" concatenation operation (mixing two alternatives together in a binary gamble) corresponds to placing more than one object on a pan at the same time. In both systems, if the axioms are satisfied, the result is a real number scale, of utility or of physical weight.

Here, at last, are the von Neumann and Morgenstern axioms for subjective expected utility theory:

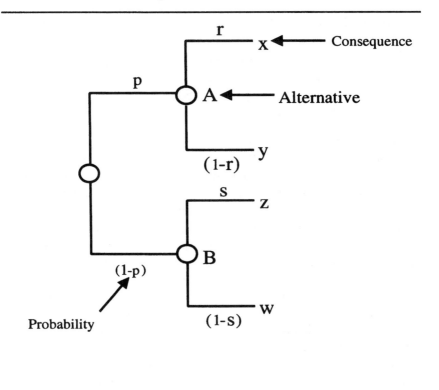

$$A \; p \; B$$

$$A \equiv x \, r \, y$$

$$B \equiv z \, s \, w$$

FIGURE 12.1. Example Decision Tree Representation of a Gamble That Might Be Abbreviated in the von Neumann and Morgenstern Axioms

Axiom 1. Comparability. If A and B are in the alternative set S, then either $A \succeq B$ or $B \succeq A$, or both, in which case $A \sim B$.

Axiom 2. Transitivity. If $A \succeq B$ and $B \succeq C$, then $A \succeq C$.

Axiom 3. Closure. If A and B are in alternative set S, then ApB is as well.

Axiom 4. Distribution of Probabilities Across Alternatives. If A and B are in S, then $[(ApB)qB] \sim (ApqB)$.

Axiom 5. Independence. If *A*, *B*, and *C* are in *S*, *A* ≳ *B* if and only if *(ApC)* ≳ *(BpC)*.

Axiom 6. Consistency. For all *A* and *B* in *S*, *A* ≳ *B* if and only if *A* ≳ *(ApB)* ≳ *B*.

Axiom 7. Solvability. For all *A*, *B*, and *C* in *S*, if *A* ≳ *B* ≳ *C*, then there exists a probability *p* such that *B* ~ *(ApC)*. This axiom is crucial to the construction of the utility scale.

If numbers are substituted for the alternatives and probabilities for the *p*s and *q*s, then it is clear that these axioms are satisfied whenever the number associated with an alternative is equal to its expectation. What von Neumann and Morgenstern did was prove the converse: If these axioms are satisfied, then it is possible to construct a measure for each alternative equal to its expectation in such a way that the order of the alternatives corresponds to the order of the expectations. Moreover, the origin and units of these measures are arbitrary (as in the familiar scale of temperature). The number associated with an alternative is termed its *expected utility*; that number associated with a consequence, which is equivalent to an alternative that has that consequence with probability 1, is the utility of that consequence. Because only the origin and the unit of measurement are arbitrary in such utility assignments, any different assignments are related in a linear manner, meaning any two scales of utility across a set of alternatives will plot as a straight line in x-y graphic coordinates. Technically, this is called an *interval scale* because both the units of measurement and the "zero point" are arbitrary (remember we called the weight scale a *ratio scale*, because the zero point was *not* arbitrary, although the units [e.g., ounces, pounds, grams] were).

The arbitrary origin and unit of measurement allow us to use the solvability axiom to determine the utility of a third alternative whenever the utilities of two others are known. Suppose, for example, *A* ≳ *B* ≳ *C*. We can allow the utility of *A* to equal 1 and the utility of *C* to equal 0. Now, according to the solvability axiom, there exists a probability *p* such that the utility of *B* is equal to the utility of *ApC*, which is simply *p* times the utility of *A* plus $(1 - p)$ times the utility of *C*, which is $p \times 1 + (1 - p) \times 0 = p$. Thus, as noted, the solvability axiom is crucial in determining the actual numerical values of these utilities. Because all possible scales and utilities are linear functions of each other, we can assign 1 as the utility of the most preferred alternative in each set *S*, and 0 as the utility of the least preferred alternative, and then solve for the utilities of all the remaining alternatives, locating their utilities in the 0-1 interval. Notice the probability scale in the probability mixture operation is the means to scale the utilities (the laws and scale of probability will be preserved in the decision maker's preferences *if* "the axioms are satisfied"—an assumption that may be hard to satisfy behaviorally if the empirical results reported in Chapters 8 and 9 are valid).

Von Neumann and Morgenstern's system is conceptually beautiful. At the risk of being redundant, we state again that the *utilities* derived analytically from these axioms do not necessarily correspond to our intuitive or verbal notions of personal value, any more than the measures of weight derived from behavior of objects in pan balances necessarily correspond to our intuitive notions of weight. Nevertheless, just as a concept of weight that did not relate to our intuitions about which objects are heavier than which others would be a very strange notion indeed, the concept of utility is meant to have a relationship to subjective value. In fact, it is because the utilities derived according to the von Neumann and Morgenstern system *do* bear some relationship to our notions of personal value that they are of interest to psychologists. And this is the justification for our attempt to explain how they can be used to *improve* our decision-making capabilities at the end of this chapter. Most people, perhaps after some thought, acknowledge that each axiom individually seems to be acceptable as part of a general definition of rationality and even as a prescription for how they wish they made their choices. Let's discuss each axiom in more detail.

Axiom 1. Comparability

If A and B are in the alternative set S, then either $A \gtrsim B$ or $B \gtrsim A$ or both, in which case $A \sim B$.

Axiom 1 states that when faced with two alternatives, the decision maker should have at least a weak preference. The strongest rationale for this axiom is the fact that a decision maker faced with alternatives must choose one of them. But it also equates inability to make such a choice with indifference. Is someone who maintains that he or she cannot choose between two alternatives necessarily indifferent? Consider, for example, the choice discussed in Chapter 11 of the professor trying to decide what job to take. If she were to conclude that she could not make a choice, would that really mean that she is indifferent, that she does not care? Jay Kadane, Mark Schervish, and Teddy Seidenfeld (1999), for example, maintain that not having a preference is *not* equivalent to being indifferent. And in some circumstances where "protected values" are perceived to be at stake, people refuse to make choices—which is, of course, a choice too. Jonathan Baron and Mark Spranca (1997) cite situations in which many people refuse to choose. For example, when considering personal or policy alternatives where trade-offs between lives and money are demanded, many citizens appear to avert their gaze and "choose not to choose." But is it reasonable to say that these nonchoices express a true indifference between 65 mph speed limits and inexpensive automobiles versus the deaths of approximately 50,000 fellow citizens?

Apples and oranges are, however, fruit, and if one must choose a fruit from a dish of apples and oranges, it will be either an apple or an orange. Could not the choice itself define the preference analytically? Economists refer to such a choice as a "revealed preference" and assume utility theory to infer that, for example, our highway safety preferences imply a dollar value of approximately $3 million per human life. Moreover, isn't it true that when people say they have no idea why they made a choice, subsequent questioning often reveals that there really *is* a preference involved. For example, if the professor in 11.3 maintained that she really was incapable of choosing between jobs but "just happened to pick" one of them to be near (or away from) relatives, would not proximity to relatives be an important consideration in her choice? Perhaps she would be simply unaware of this factor at the time she made the choice—or perhaps embarrassed to discuss it, because she might not consider it a good reason for choosing one job over another. Our own position is that people really do have preferences, except in rare instances such as predicting the outcome of a coin toss, in which case they are truly indifferent. We do not, however, accept the revealed preference position—that the preference is inherent in the choice—for the reasons outlined in the previous chapters. Choice may be truly irrational and hence contradictory. Thus it follows that there may be a discrepancy between choice in a particular situation and the preferences of the individual making the choice.

Although revealed preference can be rejected on the basis of the cognitive difficulty of choice, the most common reason for rejecting the apparent evidence is that people sometimes do things they do not *want* to do, that is, choose alternatives they do not prefer. For example, William James (1842-1910) noted that people with toothaches often prod the painful area of their mouth with their tongue, although they clearly prefer lack of pain to the pain that results from prodding. Clearly, people do not always do what gives them greatest pleasure or what they want to do.

The counterargument from the revealed preference theorist is that the very act of prodding the area of a toothache indicates that the individual has a greater positive value for the information gained that the tooth is still hurting than negative value for the pain experienced. Such values may appear "stupid," because toothaches tend not to go away on their own without treatment, and when a given part of our mouth is aching we can be more than reasonably sure that it will be more painful if we touch it with our tongue, *without* actually doing so. The revealed preference theorist, however, has the counterargument that *de gustibus non disputandem* ("There's no disputing matters of taste"). The fact that the sufferer prods the tooth reveals that even such redundant information is worth the pain.

Because what constitutes pleasure and pain to an individual cannot be known unambiguously, the argument that people often do what they really dislike doing is fairly ineffective against the revealed preference position. In contrast, knowing that the choices are often contradictory for *cognitive* reasons undermines this position.

Axiom 2. Transitivity

If $A \succeq B$ and $B \succeq C$, then $A \succeq C$.

The primary justification for Axiom 2 is that individuals who violate it can be turned into "money pumps." Suppose that John Dolt preferred alternative A to alternative B, alternative B to alternative C, and yet C to A. Assume further that he is not indifferent in his choice between any of these alternatives. Consequently, he should be willing to *pay something* to trade a less preferred alternative for a more preferred one. Now suppose John is given alternative B *as a gift*. Because he prefers alternative A to B, he should be willing to pay something to have A instead. Subsequently, John should be willing to pay something to have alternative C substituted for A, and finally to pay for the substitution of B for C. Then John will have paid for the privilege of ending up with the alternative he was given in the first place. By repeating this cycle indefinitely, John (hypothetically anyway) would pay an indefinite amount of money to get nowhere.

The response to the money pump argument is that an individual with intransitive preferences would simply refuse to play that game. Choices are, after all, not made repeatedly, but in a particular context. A choice between two alternatives does not have to be one by which the individual is bound for all time and in all circumstances. The noted economist Paul

Samuelson is quoted as saying that in a particular decision-making situation most people will "satisfy their preferences and let the axioms satisfy themselves" (cited in Daniel Ellsberg, 1961, pp. 655-656). Consider the hiring of a new secretary. Suppose that the employer has three criteria for making a job offer: (a) clerical skills, (b) organizational ability, and (c) willingness to run errands and do other jobs not specifically in the position description. Suppose that the rank of three prospective secretaries (A, B, and C) on clerical skills is A, B, C; on organizational ability is B, C, A; and on willingness is C, A, B. Thus applicant A is superior to applicant B on two of these three dimensions (clerical skill and willingness), B is superior to C on two (clerical skill and organization), and C is superior to A on two (organization and willingness). A decision based on the principle that one applicant is preferred to another whenever that applicant is superior on two of three dimensions results in intransitivity (this is the qualitative additive difference, or "voting" choice strategy, in Figure 11.2). What will happen is that the *order* in which the applicants are considered will be crucial, with the applicant considered last being the one chosen.

Is this consequence necessarily a bad one? Even though the employer could in principle become a money pump, no one is going to make him or her one—by giving him or her one of the secretaries and then demanding payment for subsequent substitutions. But we suspect that many of our most frustrating decision experiences occur when we encounter alternatives that are important and where each alternative has some good and some bad attributes, forcing us to consider compensatory trade-offs and sometimes inducing intransitivity-producing strategies ("Okay, I'm going to take the high-paying job; but, no, I don't want to give up the much more flexible vacation options in the second job; but, wait, I don't want to live in the Midwest; but the chance for advancement is much better in the third job . . .") and sometimes producing great personal discomfort and leading to an inability of make a choice.

We believe that choices *should* be transitive. This idea is part of a general argument that choice is superior when it is made as if the decision maker *were* bound by that choice in a broader context and across time. This argument is from Immanuel Kant (1724-1804), who proposed that individuals should make choices as if they are formulating a *policy* for all people at all times. There is empirical evidence showing that when a criterion is available according to which we can decide whether choices are good or bad, choices made in accord with Kant's principle are in fact superior to those made in the narrower context of considering only the options immediately available.

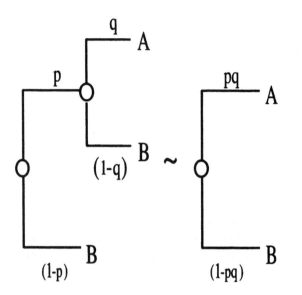

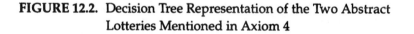

FIGURE 12.2. Decision Tree Representation of the Two Abstract Lotteries Mentioned in Axiom 4

Axiom 3. Closure

If *A* and *B* are in alternative set *S*, then *ApB* is as well.

Axiom 3 simply requires that the decision maker be capable of conceptualizing a probability mixture of alternatives as itself an alternative. If people were incapable of doing so, there would be little point in theorizing about decision making.

Axiom 4. Distribution of Probabilities Across Alternatives

If *A* and *B* are in *S*, then *[(ApB)qB] ~ (ApqB)*.

Basically, Axiom 4 requires that people follow the principles of probability theory (see Appendix). This axiom is illustrated in the decision trees in Figure 12.2; the two-stage gamble on the left must be treated as equivalent to the one-stage gamble on the right to satisfy the axiom.

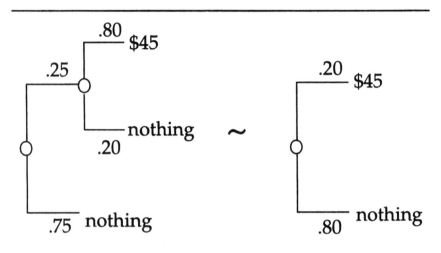

FIGURE 12.3. Decision Tree Representation of a Concrete Pair of Gambles Illustrating an Equivalence Implied by Axiom 4

Of course, people may violate the axiom without disputing it; for example, it is violated by the person who reacts differently to a consequence of receiving $45 with probability .20 than to a two-stage consequence in which the person receives nothing with probability .75 in the first stage and then receives $45 with probability .80 if the second is reached (since [1.00 − .75] × .80 = .20, the distribution axiom requires that the two lotteries be treated as identical; see Figure 12.3).

Von Neumann and Morgenstern discuss probabilities as if they were objective (their ps and qs are supposed to be probabilities measured on an absolute scale, although the concept of accuracy or objectivity in probabilities is complex and controversial). Leonard J. Savage (1954) relaxed this assumption in the subjective expected utility theory we present here. Thus, Axiom 4 allows for subjective, nonobjective probabilities, but these probabilities must still be internally coherent and consistent with the laws of probability theory (see Appendix). If the decision maker attempts to deal with future uncertainty by making probability assessments, these must be made according to rules of probability theory; otherwise contradictory choices can result. In Chapter 13, we will explore prospect theory (introduced in Chapter 10), an axiomatic "nonexpected utility theory," in

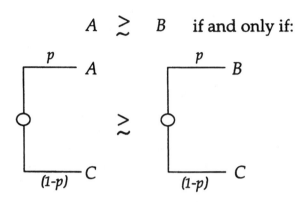

FIGURE 12.4. Decision Tree Representation of the Situation Described by Axiom 5

which nonobjective and incoherent decision weights replace probabilities. Prospect theory is similar in overall structure to the von Neumann and Morgenstern theory, but it is intended to be descriptive of human decision behavior and *not* a model of rational choice.

Axiom 5. Independence

If A, B, and C are in S, $A \gtrsim B$ if and only if $(ApC) \gtrsim (BpC)$.

Axiom 5 is crucial. In fact, many decision theorists have investigated at length the effects of violating it or of omitting it from a set of rules governing choice. At first reading, it appears innocuous. If one alternative is preferred to another, shouldn't that preference remain even though, with some specified probability, the decision maker receives neither, but a third instead? That is all this axiom states. Figure 12.4 summarizes the axiom graphically.

Warning: Some students are confused because they misread the axiom to refer to a situation as one of *joint receipt*—the chooser *receives both A and C or receives both B and C*, but the correct situation is a *probability mixture* of receiving *A or B* compared to a *probability mixture* of receiving *B or C*, where *or* is exclusive—meaning *not* both. If the situation was joint receipt, then the axiom wouldn't make much sense. Of course, we might have little desire to receive a right shoe *or* a left shoe, but to receive both a right shoe *and* a left shoe might be very attractive—depending on the shoes, of course.

Consider a "pseudocertainty" effect: Most people prefer a .20 probability of receiving \$45 to a .25 probability of receiving \$30 (Panel 1 in Figure 12.5), yet simultaneously they prefer \$30 for sure to an .80 probability of receiving \$45 (Panel 2). Now let A be the alternative of receiving \$30 for sure and B be that of receiving \$45 with the probability of .80. A is preferred to B (as in Panel 2). Let C be the alternative of receiving nothing. Now let p equal .25. Then $(A .25 C)$ is an alternative consisting of receiving \$30 for sure with probability .25 versus receiving nothing with probability .75 (left-hand side of Panel 3), which—by the distribution of probabilities axiom—is just the alternative of receiving \$30 with probability .25 (left-hand side of Panel 4). In contrast, $(B .25 C)$ is the alternative consisting of a .25 probability of receiving \$45 with probability .8 and a .75 probability of receiving nothing (right-hand side of Panel 3), that is, receiving \$45 with probability $.80 \times .25 = .20$ (right-hand side of Panel 4). Thus the typical preference summarized in Panel 1 implies the opposite ordering of that summarized in Panel 2. Therefore, anyone who has the Panel 1 and Panel 2 preferences (most people) both exhibits the pseudocertainty effect and violates the independence axiom.

The pseudocertainty effect describes choices that are influenced by the way the consequences are framed, rather than solely by the consequences themselves. Is such irrationality the only reason for violating the independence axiom? There is another reason. Axiom 5 implies that the decision maker cannot be affected by the *skewness* of the consequences, which can be conceptualized as a probability distribution over personal values. Figure 12.6 shows the skewed distributions of two different alternatives. Both distributions have the same average, hence the same expected personal value, which is a criterion of choice implied by the axioms. These distributions also have the same variance. (For a description of the mean and variance of a probability distribution see a good introductory statistics text, e.g., *Statistics* by David Freedman, Robert Pisani, Roger Purves, and Ani Adhikari, 1991.)

If the distributions in Figure 12.6 were those of wealth in a society, most people would have a definite preference for distribution (a); its positive skewness means that income can be increased from any point—an

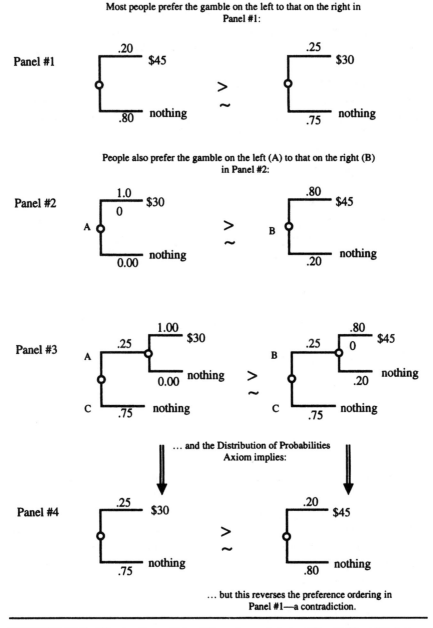

FIGURE 12.5. Illustration of the "Pseudocertainty Effect" That Violates Axioms 4 and 5

incentive for productive work—and incidentally it is the distribution that describes wealth in industrialized societies. Moreover, those people lowest in the distribution are not as distant from the average as in distribution (b). In contrast, in distribution (b), a large number of people are already earning a maximal amount of money, and there is a tail of people in the *negatively skewed* part of this distribution who are quite far below the average income. If we have such concerns about the distribution outcomes in society, why not of the consequences for choosing alternatives in our own lives? In fact, many of us do not like alternatives with large negative skews. Note also that popular lotteries, gambling devices, and competitive tournaments generally have positive skews (i.e., small probabilities of winning a lot). There are substantial individual differences in preferences for distributions of multi-outcome gambles or lotteries; in experimental studies in which money lotteries are evaluated, positive skewed lotteries (like distribution [a] in Figure 12.6) are the modal favorites for lotteries composed of both gains and losses (Lopes & Oden, 1999).

Axiom 6. Consistency

For all A and B in S, $A \gtrsim B$ if and only if $A \gtrsim (ApB) \gtrsim B$.

Axiom 6 states that if we prefer one alternative to another, then we prefer at least some chance of receiving that alternative rather than the other one (see Figure 12.7). This axiom appears indisputable.

Axiom 7. Solvability

For all A, B, and C in S, if $A \gtrsim B \gtrsim C$, then there exists a probability p such that $B \sim (ApC)$.

Axiom 7 is similar to the Archimedean property in Hölder's axiom system for physical weights. What it states in effect is that no alternative is so much better or worse than another that some probability mixture of alternatives on either side is not regarded as equivalent to the original alternative (see Figure 12.8). Consider, for example, three alternatives A, B, and C with the preference order $A \gtrsim B \gtrsim C$. The axiom states that there will be *some* probabilistic way of combining A and C such that the individual is indifferent to choosing B or this combination.

Now if A were incomparably more attractive to the decision maker than any of the other alternatives, then *any* probability of receiving A rather than C might lead to a preference for ApC over B. The same argument

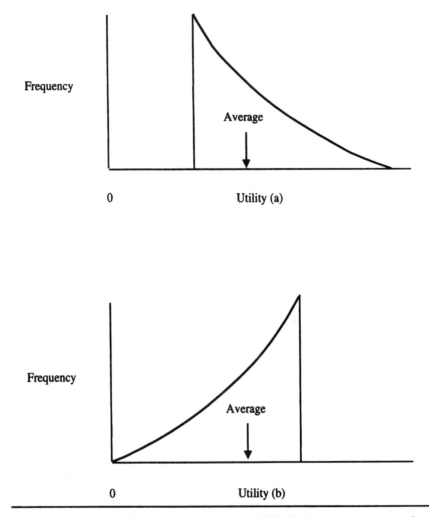

FIGURE 12.6. Two Skewed Distributions With the Same Average and Variance

would hold *mutatis mutandis* if alternative C were incomparably worse than B. The axiom states that no such alternatives exist. Well, what about eternal bliss in Heaven? Or, conversely, sudden death? Would not any alternative involving even the slightest probability of eternal bliss be preferred to some other alternative with drabber consequences—so that the

$$A \succsim B \quad \text{if and only if:}$$

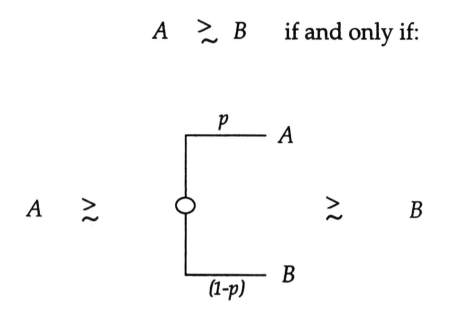

FIGURE 12.7. Decision Tree Representation of the Relationship
Summarized in Axiom 6

individual could never be indifferent in choosing between the drab alternative and a probability mixture involving such bliss? Or do we not
eschew completely those alternatives involving some probability of
death? (We cannot discuss eternal bliss, because we cannot even conceptualize it.) It is clear from our behavior that we dread death and attempt to
avoid it, at least for as long as we have hope that the positive aspects of life
and the future outweigh the negative. Do we not, then, avoid all alternatives that involve some probability of death? The answer is no. Everyday
life involves some risk of death, even such trivial actions as crossing a
street to buy a newspaper. Sometimes this probability is more salient than
at other times—as when people who fear airplane trips still fly tens of
thousands of miles a year. But it is always there. Even staying in bed all
day to avoid what appears to be the risk of death would involve a risk of
physical deterioration, perhaps leading to death. In addition, there are
clear examples of thoughtful decisions that involve a high probability of

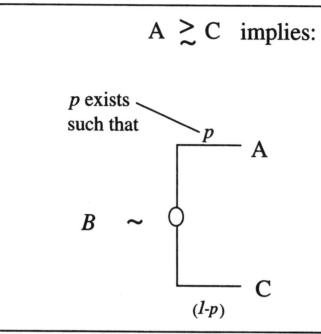

FIGURE 12.8. Decision Tree Representation of Axiom 7; the Axiom
Implies There Exists a Probability (*p*) That Satisfies
the Equivalence Relationship Between the "Certainty
Equivalent" (B) and the Gamble

death—for instance, a decision to join an underground resistance movement during a military occupation or the deliberate choice of a high-
paying, but dangerous, profession such as industrial deep sea diving.

All of the axioms appear quite reasonable. In fact, if we assume comparability, we can violate only the independence axiom without becoming
outright irrational. The axioms, however, have strong implications, as do
other mathematical results. Believing the Pythagorean theorem, for example, we anticipate the length of a third side of a right-angled triangle when
we know the length of two sides. If physical measurement does not confirm our expectations, we conclude that the triangle is not a right-angled
triangle; we rarely or never conclude that the theorem is true—that the triangle has a right angle and our measurements are correct—but that the
logic of mathematical deduction just doesn't apply. The demanding
aspect of the von Neumann and Morgenstern axioms is that if we accept

them, we are bound to evaluate alternatives in a choice situation in terms of their expected utility. That is, numbers exist that describe the utility of each consequence of alternative choices. (Such numbers are, once again, those associated with alternatives that have that particular consequence with probability of 1.) Using the solvability axiom, these numbers can be determined by some choices; they then require that other choices as well be made in terms of the expected utilities computed. Other characteristics describing the distribution of consequences, for example, its skewness, are irrelevant.

The solvability axiom is especially useful if we want to design a method to scale a person's utilities for outcomes. A review of measurement and scaling methods is beyond the scope of this text (see Dawes & Smith, 1985, for an introduction), but here is an example to convey the basic method. For simplicity, consider three outcomes (which could be money dollars, but let's consider something less quantitative): a one-week vacation in the city of Boulder (Colorado), Pittsburgh (Pennsylvania), or Lubbock (Texas). Suppose further that our decision maker prefers them in that ordering, Boulder over Pittsburgh, Pittsburgh over Lubbock ($A \gtrsim B \gtrsim C$ as required by the solvability axiom). Now where in the interval between Boulder and Lubbock is the decision maker's utility for Pittsburgh? Relying heavily on solvability, we can assign the most favored and least favored options the values of 1.0 and 0.0 (or for that matter, because the scale origin and units are arbitrary, +100 and −100) and present the decision maker with a series of gambles, mixing a trip to Boulder with a trip to Lubbock, until we find a gamble that is judged indifferent compared with the trip to Pittsburgh (in Figure 12.8, the left-hand "sure thing" term would correspond to the trip to Pittsburgh, the right-hand gamble would correspond to the mixture of a trip to Boulder with a trip to Lubbock). Then, if the axioms are satisfied, we can use the probability mixture number from the gamble as a scale value for Pittsburgh's utility. For example, if a decision maker is indifferent between one week in Pittsburgh for sure and an .80 chance of ending up in Boulder mixed with a .20 chance of spending the week in Lubbock, we would scale the utility value for Pittsburgh at .80 on a 0.0-1.0 scale with Boulder and Lubbock as endpoints. This method can be generalized to scale any number of outcomes on an interval utility scale (and this method of eliciting "preference probabilities" is frequently used in applied decision analysis).

There are many studies in which utility functions are scaled, especially for the utilities of money. The forms of these functions are often used to interpret, and even to predict, the behavior of people from whom they've been derived. For example, a concave curve (negatively accelerating, with diminishing marginal returns) is sometimes interpreted as implying that the person who exhibits it is risk averse in the domain of such a curve, whereas the reverse, convex curve is interpreted as implying a risk-seeking attitude. According to the theory, such curves summarize, analytically, and predict, synthetically, behavior in choosing real-money gambles to play in the laboratory and they are even associated with the occupational choices of business executives. Executives in financially volatile businesses are more likely to exhibit convexity in their utility curves than executives in more placid financial environments (MacCrimmon & Wehrung, 1986; see additional discussion of the interpretation of utility curves in Section 10.3).

12.3   TRADITIONAL OBJECTIONS TO THE AXIOMS

The axioms were not presented as descriptions of actual behavior but, rather, as conditions of *desirable* choices. Are they? After the publication of von Neumann and Morgenstern's book, several theorists suggested that the axioms placed unreasonable constraints on choice behavior and that they should *not* be satisfied. The best-known objections consisted of two paradoxes, both originally stated as conceptual puzzles and later validated in experimental studies. One of these objections was raised by Nobel laureate economist Maurice Allais and the other by the decision theorist Daniel Ellsberg (who achieved notoriety by releasing the *Pentagon Papers*, which exposed the U.S. government's secret objectives in the Vietnam War).

The Allais Paradox

The Allais argument is that the expected utility principle which results from the axiom system is too restrictive. Consider, for example, the choice between alternatives A and B involving millions of dollars:

Alternative A: Receive $1 million with probability 1.00 (i.e., for certain)

Alternative B: Receive $2.5 million with probability .10, $1 million with probability .89, and nothing with probability .01

When presented with this (hypothetical) choice, most people choose alternative A. That means that if they abide by the axioms, it is possible to assign utilities to the consequences of receiving $1 million, $2.5 million, or nothing in such a way that the choice of A implies a higher expected utility for it than for B. Specifically,

U($1 million) > .10 U($2.5 million + .89 U($1 million) + .01 U(nothing).

By the solvability axiom, we can set U($2.5 million) = 1.0 and U(nothing) = 0.0. The conclusion then is .11 U($1 million) > .10.

Now consider the choice between two different alternatives:

Alternative A': $1 million with probability .11, otherwise nothing

Alternative B': $2.5 million with probability .10, otherwise nothing

The expected utility of alternative A' is .11, whereas that of alternative B' is .10, because we have set the utility at $2.5 million equal to 1.0. Thus the choice of A over B requires the choice of A' over B'. Allais argued that it was nevertheless reasonable to choose A over B *and* B' over A', which is in fact the choice most people make when presented with this hypothetical pair of decisions. Why accept a 1 in 100 chance of receiving nothing when you can receive a million dollars for sure? Conversely, given that the most probable outcome in the second choice is to receive nothing at all, why not accept a 1 in 100 risk of getting nothing to increase the potential payoff by a factor of two and one-half times?

The mathematician Leonard J. Savage (1954, pp. 101-103) gave a compelling analysis of those questions. Consider his suggestion that the probabilities of the various outcomes are brought about by randomly drawing a chip out of a bag containing 100 chips. One of these chips is black, 10 are blue, and 89 are red. Alternative A can then be conceptualized as paying $1 million no matter which chip is drawn. In contrast, an individual choosing alternative B receives $1 million if a red chip is drawn, $2.5 million if a blue chip is drawn, and nothing if the black chip is drawn. Now it does not matter to the decision maker which alternative is chosen if a red chip is drawn, because in either case he or she receives $1 million; hence a choice of A over B implies that the possibility of receiving $1 million rather than nothing if the black chip is drawn from the 11 chips that are not red is preferred to the possibility of receiving $2.5 million rather than nothing if one of the 10 blue chips is drawn. (Sometimes the choice is interpreted as a desire to avoid the potential regret of getting nothing: "Well,

BALLS IN URN

		89 Red	1 Black	10 Blue
	A	$1 million	$1 million	$1 million
CHOICE				
	B	$1 million	nothing	$2.5 million
	A'	nothing	$1 million	$1 million
CHOICE				
	B'	nothing	nothing	$2.5 million

FIGURE 12.9. Illustration of Savage's Analysis

dear, I had a sure million dollars, but I decided to try to 'maximize' my expected value and I gambled . . . unfortunately, I lost."). But that preference is violated if the individual also chooses B ' over A'. Once again, the outcome will be the same if a red chip is drawn, but the individual is now showing a preference for receiving $2.5 million if a blue chip is drawn and nothing if the black one is drawn over receiving $1 million if either a blue or the black is drawn.

Savage's example is basically a restatement of the independence axiom in concrete terms; it makes this axiom quite compelling. Savage's argument is illustrated in Figure 12.9. In the figure, it is obvious that the event of drawing a red chip, with a constant .89 probability across the gambles, should be irrelevant to the choice, because its payoff is constant in each choice set pair (the lefthand column in Figure 12.9).

The Ellsberg Paradox

Ellsberg's (1961) problem focuses attention on the nature of the uncertainty presented by different gambles, but again it is an assault on the acceptability of the independence axiom. Imagine an urn containing

90 colored balls, 30 red balls, and 60 black or yellow balls. You do not
know the exact proportion of blacks and yellows, only that there are total
of 60. One ball will be drawn at random from the urn. Which of the following gambles would you prefer?

Alternative I: Receive $100 if the ball drawn is red, nothing otherwise

Alternative II: Receive $100 if the ball drawn is black, nothing otherwise

Most people choose Alternative I; the obvious interpretation is that they
would rather bet on a precise, known probability of winning than on an
ambiguous uncertainty.

Now consider another pair of gambles. Again, which would you
prefer?

Alternative III: Receive $100 if a red or a yellow ball is drawn, nothing if a
black is drawn

Alternative IV: Receive $100 if a black or a yellow ball is drawn, nothing if a
red is drawn

Now most people choose IV, again because they prefer the well-defined
risk (60 in 90 balls) over the ambiguous uncertainty. (The chances of winning in alternative III could range from 31 in 90 to 89 in 90.)

The catch with this pattern of choices is again that it violates the independence axiom. Figure 12.10 makes this clear. The payoffs resulting from
drawing a yellow ball are identical in each pair, so the preference should
depend only on the pattern of payoffs for the red and black draws; the yellow outcome should be irrelevant. But the red and black patterns are identical across the two pairs, implying there should be no change in preferences from the first pair to the second, but most people do exhibit strong
preferences for reversed red and black patterns between the two pairs.
Another way to express the contradiction is to note that in the first pair,
the chooser prefers to bet *on* red rather than black. But in the second pair,
the chooser prefers to bet *against* red rather than black. These choices
imply that the chooser believes red is more likely than black *and* that not-
red is more likely than not-black. Moreover, the chooser is acting as
though *red or yellow* is less likely than *black or yellow,* but at the same time as
though *red* is more likely than *black.* It is impossible to assign probabilities,
numbers consistent with the principles of probability theory, to the outcomes given these choices.

BALLS IN URN

		30	┌─ 60 ─┐	
		Red	Black	Yellow
CHOICE	I	$100	nothing	nothing
	II	nothing	$100	nothing
CHOICE	III	$100	nothing	$100
	IV	nothing	$100	$100

FIGURE 12.10. The Gambles Presented in Ellsberg's Paradox

12.4 THE SHOULD'S AND DO'S OF THE SYSTEM

For several reasons, people do not always choose in accord with von Neumann and Morgenstern's axioms. First, there are the irrationalities of judgment and valuation that have been described in the previous chapters of this book. Second, without being irrational in the sense defined in this book, people often make choices that contradict the axioms—as when they are faced with the Allais and Ellsberg paradoxes. In fact, Savage noted in discussing these paradoxes that his own initial choices sometimes violated the axioms, another dissociation of intuitive versus analytic thinking. It follows that since we do not necessarily satisfy the axioms in our actual choice behavior, we do not *behave* as if we assign utilities to consequences and alternatives and then pursue the alternative that has greater subjective expected utility.

Should we make only choices satisfying the axioms of the system? Our answer to that question is a qualified yes. The qualification is that although we should not be *bound* by the axioms, we should *consider* them when making choices. Although it is difficult to determine whether a particular decision per se satisfies or violates an axiom or a set of axioms, the fact that the axioms are true if and only if choices are made according to expected utility provides a method for considering alternative decisions. For example, consider a husband and wife with children whose decision to fly on separate airplanes indicates (according to the theory) that the couple felt that the death of both of them would be more than twice as bad as the death of either one alone. We will analyze this example in the von Neumann and Morgenstern framework.

There are three distinct consequences: Both die, one dies and one lives, or neither dies. Because the assignment of two utility values is arbitrary (given that all utility scales are related to each other in a linear manner), we can arbitrarily assign the utility -1 to the consequence that both die and 0 to the consequence that neither dies. Now let p be the probability that one airplane crashes; whether we estimate this probability objectively by looking at the airline's safety statistics or on the basis of our subjective hunch, our conclusion is that the probability that both airplanes independently crash is $p \times p$, or p^2. This is the probability that both parents will die if they fly separately. In contrast, the probability that they both will die if they are in the same airplane is simply p. Now let the utility that *exactly one* of them dies be symbolized x (which will be a *negative* number). The choice of flying separately is interpreted in the von Neumann and Morgenstern framework as

$$p(-1) < 2p(1 - p)x + p^2 - 1.$$

The first term on the right side is x times the probability that one parent will survive the trip and the other will not (which is equal to the probability that the first plane will crash and the second will not *plus* the probability that the first one will not and the second one will, that is, twice the probability that only one plane will crash). The second term is the probability that both will die on independent trips multiplied by -1, the arbitrarily assigned utility of the *both die* consequence.

Dividing by p and rearranging terms yields $x > -\frac{1}{2}$. After the p is canceled out, move the remaining $-p$ on the right side to the left side, which yields $p - 1 < 2(1 - p)x$; dividing by $(1 - p)$ yields $-1 < 2x$. Hence $x > -\frac{1}{2}$ means that the death of exactly one has less than half the (negative) utility of both dying.

Our advice is that the couple might be well advised to consider whether the death of one of them is less than half as bad as the death of both. In this example, that would probably not change the decision; in fact such consideration would most likely reinforce it. What we have done in this example is to assume that people have at least *partial* appreciation of the utility as specified by the framework. There is nothing in the framework itself that requires such insight—just as there is nothing in the physics framework for measuring the weight of objects that requires that the numbers obtained should correspond to our subjective ideas of which objects are heavier than which. Nevertheless, just as weights measured by pan balances do correspond—at least partially—to our subjective experience of these weights, so might the utilities in the system correspond to our subjective conceptions of personal value. In fact, if there were no such correspondence in either case, there would be little reason to be interested in either axiom system.

Consider another example, this one from a medical context involving the diagnosis of a renal cyst versus a tumor on the basis of X ray evidence. In his doctoral dissertation, Dennis Fryback studied decisions at a university hospital to test whether a kidney abnormality that appeared on an X ray could be a cyst or a tumor (summarized in Fryback & Thornbury, 1976). The standard procedure was for patients who appeared to be suffering from a kidney disorder to be X-rayed, and if an abnormality appeared the radiologist interpreting the X ray made a probability judgment about whether that abnormality was a cyst or a tumor. Then the patient would be tested directly by an invasive procedure. No procedure existed at that time, however, that tested for both a cyst and a tumor. Moreover, because there was always the possibility that an X-ray abnormality is a "normal variant," a negative result on the test for one of these two pathologies required a subsequent test for the other. The decision Fryback studied was which test to do first. This decision was important to the patient, because the nature of the tests is quite different.

The test for a cyst is termed *aspiration*. It consists of inserting a large needle through the patient's back to the location of the abnormality and determining if fluid can be drawn from it; if fluid can be drawn, the abnormality is a cyst. The procedure can be accomplished in a doctor's office with a local anesthetic; the risk of a blood clot is very low; and the cost is not great.

The test for a tumor is termed *arteriography*. A tube is inserted into the patient's leg artery and manipulated up to the kidney, at which point a device on the end of the tube removes a sample of tissue from the suspected spot; this tissue sample is then subjected to a biopsy. At the time of

Fryback's study, this procedure required one day of hospitalization in preparation for the operation and at least one day's hospitalization after the operation. The probability that a blood clot would develop was approximately 10 times as great as that with the aspiration procedure; the patient experienced considerable discomfort in the days following the operation; and it was much more costly than the aspiration test.

Fryback found that in general the aspiration test was done first if the radiologist believed that the probability was greater than 1 in 2 (½) that the abnormality was a cyst rather than a tumor; otherwise the arteriography test was conducted. He also found that the patients, doctors, and potential patients from the general public he questioned all thought that the arteriography test was at least 10 times worse than the aspiration test. (Interestingly, discomfort, lost work days, and probability of formation of a blood clot were the major determinants of this judgment; cost was considered irrelevant—perhaps given the assumption that "insurance pays"—which is why we do not specify the cost difference in the above description.) Fryback then conducted an expected utility analysis on the assumption that the disutility of the arteriography test was 10 times that of the aspiration test. For the purposes of this analysis, we can conditionalize probabilities on the assumption that the patient has *either* a cyst or a tumor, even though the requirement that the second test be given if the first is negative arises because the patient may have *neither*, that is, we can let p be the probability that the patient has a tumor *given* the abnormality is not a normal variant, and hence $(1 - p)$ is the probability that the patient has a cyst given that the abnormality is not a normal variant. Again, we can arbitrarily set the utility of no test at all at 0; then setting the utility of the aspiration test at –1, the utility of the arteriography test is –10, and hence the utility of doing both tests is approximately –11.

Let the probability that the radiologist interpreting the X ray believes the problem to be that of a tumor be p. If the arteriography test is done first, the expected disutility of the entire testing procedure is

$$p(-10) + (1 - p)(-11).$$

The second term in the expression occurs because both tests are required if the abnormality is not a tumor. In contrast, the disutility of doing the aspiration test first is

$$(1 - p)(-1) + p(-11).$$

The expected utility of doing the arteriography test first will be greater than that of doing the aspiration test first (i.e., the disutility will be *less negative*) whenever

$$-10p - 11(1 - p) > -(1 - p) - 11p.$$

This is true if and only if

$$11p > 10 \text{ or}$$

$$p > 10/11.$$

In other words, doing the arteriography test first is better in a subjective expected utility framework only under those conditions in which the probability of a tumor relative to that of a cyst is greater than 10 in 11, that is, when a tumor is 10 times more likely. Recall that the people questioned believed that the disutility of the arteriography test was *at least* 10 times that of the aspiration test; it follows that the 10 in 11 figure is a *lower bound*. Yet the procedure at the hospital was to use the arteriography test first whenever the judged probability was greater than 1 in 2 (½).

This example involved at least a partial equating of the utilities in the von Neumann and Morgenstern system with the personal values expressed by people when asked. Nevertheless, believing people can assess such utilities seems to be quite reasonable; in fact, when this conclusion was communicated to the hospital physicians, the procedure was changed. An interesting sidelight is that when the radiologists' probability judgments were checked against the actual frequencies with which cysts and tumors were found on testing, these judgments turned out to be quite accurate. Simultaneously, however, the analysis indicated that they were also usually irrelevant, because it implied that the aspiration tests should be done first except in those rare cases in which the radiologist was at least 10 times more certain that the aberration was a tumor rather than a cyst.

The new—since 1970—field of applied decision analysis makes use of the von Neumann and Morgenstern approach in an attempt to aid decision makers in their choices (Clemen, 1996; Hammond, Keeney, & Raiffa, 1999). It is based on the premise that people do have some insight into their personal values, but that these values may not be reflected in single choices in a particular context—especially those that tend to be made intuitively or according to a standard operating procedure. What the applied decision analyst does is to question the decision maker at length about values and probabilities in hypothetical situations as well as the situation in which the choice of interest is to be made. After having done so, the analyst proposes an expected utility analysis that would allow the decision maker to systematize the alternatives in making subsequent choices. Such applications can have a profound effect, as when the hospital decided to change its order of tests.

Another example is provided by a man who owned a company in a small town and was considering automation. His family had owned the company for many years, and the factory provided employment to a substantial number of people in the community. After receiving an economic report on the probable increase in profits that would follow automation of many of the factory jobs, he was uneasy about implementing automation, but he was not sure why. He hired a consultant who worked as an applied decision analyst in such situations. After questioning the business owner at length, the consultant concluded that the owner's real utilities in running the business had very little to do with the profit he made. Instead, the owner derived great satisfaction from providing employment to so many people in the town; doing so provided him with status and a feeling of doing something important for the community. According to the consultant's analysis of expected utility, automation would be a very poor choice, one that would decrease rather than increase the utility this man derived from running his business. When the owner was presented with the results, his response was "Aha!" He then understood that providing employment was exactly what he wanted to do. In fact, his reluctance to automate in face of rather conclusive data that it would increase his profits was, he now understood, due to that desire. In addition to reinforcing his gut impression that something was amiss with the automation plan, the consultant's analysis provided him with a rationale for explaining his refusal—both to himself and to those who might regard him as a poor businessperson for having bypassed the opportunity to increase his profits.

Such decision analysis is a form of psychotherapy because it helps people to change their behavior to be consistent with their personal values. The von Neumann and Morgenstern framework does not dictate what choice must be made, but it is an important tool for such therapy. Moreover, it can help prevent more basic irrationalities, because a decision made in this framework cannot be irrational. Consider, for example, an individual who is reluctant to abandon a sunk cost; because expected utility analysis concerns only the expectation of *future* consequences, sunk costs are not entered in the analysis. In effect, the individual who is tied to the sunk costs broadens his or her framework in such a way that the original motive—the perception of waste in abandoning the sunk costs—disappears when the person realizes that honoring sunk costs conflicts with the more important motive of behaving in a rational manner.

The decision analyst starts with the assumption that there are conflicts between a client's attitudes or dispositions to choose in certain ways in particular decision-making situations and more general dispositions. The analyst tries to identify, even quantify, the conflicts and then hopes that the client can resolve them in a manner more compatible with his or her basic goals.

12.5   SOME BUM RAPS
FOR DECISION ANALYSIS

A popular misconception is that decision analysis is unemotional, dehumanizing, and obsessive because it uses numbers and arithmetic to guide important life decisions. Isn't this turning over important human decisions "to a machine"—sometimes literally a computer—which now picks our quarterbacks, our chief executive officers, and even our lovers? Aren't the "mathematicizers" of life, who admittedly have done well in the basic sciences, moving into a context where such uses of numbers are irrelevant and irreverent? Don't we suffer enough from the tyranny of numbers when our opportunities in life are controlled by numerical scores on aptitude tests and numbers entered on rating forms by interviewers and supervisors? In short, isn't the human spirit better expressed by intuitive choices than by analytic number crunching?

Our answer to all these concerns is an unqualified no. There is absolutely nothing in the von Neumann and Morgenstern theory—or in this book—that requires the adoption of "inhuman" values. In fact, the whole idea of utility is that it provides a measure of what is truly *personally* important to individuals reaching decisions. As presented here, the aim of analyzing expected utility is to help us achieve what is really important to us. As James March (1978) points out, one goal in life may be to discover what our values are. That goal might require action that is playful or even arbitrary. Does such action violate the dictates of either rationality or expected utility theory? No. On examination, an individual valuing such an approach will be found to have a utility associated with the existential experimentation that follows from it. All that the decision analyst does is help to make this value explicit so that the individual can understand it and incorporate it in action in a noncontradictory manner.

Nor is decision analysis an obsessive, equivocating activity. In fact, some conclusions mandate action rather than thought. As mentioned earlier, there is a great deal more in von Neumann and Morgenstern's (1947) classic *Theory of Games and Economic Behavior* than has been presented here. One particularly intriguing section of that book concerns optimal play in poker games. There are 2,598,960 possible poker hands, and because no two of these hands are tied, drawing a particular hand is equivalent to drawing some number between 1 and 2,598,960. Since a hand is won by the person with the highest number, the question is what constitutes good betting strategy, so von Neumann and Morgenstern considered a simplified form of poker in which only two people play. Each person must ante, one person bets, and the other has the opportunity to either match the bet or raise it, at which point the first person may respond by matching the raise. What von Neumann and Morgenstern proved mathematically is that according to the principle of maximizing expected utility, a player should either bet the maximum amount immediately or fold. (If the player is the first bettor, he or she may "check".) Our point is that this is a rigorous demonstration, in the context of the theory, that hesitant behavior is poor strategy. It implies the exact opposite of obsessing about a decision. In this context, dynamic decision making is supported. Absolutely nothing in the theory encourages people to obsess, procrastinate, or postpone.

REFERENCES

Baron, J., & Spranca, M. (1997). Protected values. *Organizational Behavior and Human Decision Processes, 70,* 1-16.

Bentham, J. (1948). *An introduction to the principles of morals and legislations.* Oxford, UK: Blackwell. (Original work published 1789)

Clemen, R. T. (1996). *Making hard decisions: An introduction to decision analysis* (2nd ed.). Pacific Grove, CA: Duxbury.

Dawes, R. M., & Smith, T. L. (1985). Attitude and opinion measurement. In G. Lindzey & E. Aronson (Eds.), *Handbook of social psychology* (Vol. 1, pp. 509-566). New York: Random House.

Ellsberg, D. (1961). Risk, ambiguity, and the Savage axioms. *Quarterly Journal of Economics, 75*, 643-669.

Freedman, D., Pisani, R., Purves, R., & Adhikari, A. (1991). *Statistics* (2nd ed.). New York: W. W. Norton.

Fryback, D. G., & Thornbury, J. R. (1976). Evaluation of a computerized Bayesian model for diagnosis of renal cysts versus tumor versus normal variant from exploratory urogram information. *Investigative Radiology, 11*, 102-111.

Hammond, J. S., Keeney, R. L., & Raiffa, H. (1999). *Smart choices: A practical guide to making better decisions*. Cambridge, MA: Harvard Business School Press.

Hastie, R., & Stasser, G. (2000). Computer simulation methods in social psychology. In C. M. Judd & H. Reis (Eds.), *Handbook of research methods in social psychology* (pp. 85-114). New York: Cambridge University Press.

Hölder, O. (1901). Der Axomie der Quantität und die Lehre vom Mass. *Berichte über die Verhandlungen der Königlich Sächsischen Gesellschaft Wissenschaften zu Leipzig, Mathematisch-Physische Classe, 53*, 1-64.

Kadane, J. B., Schervish, M. J., & Seidenfeld, T. (1999). *Rethinking the foundations of statistics*. Cambridge, UK: Cambridge University Press.

Lopes, L. L. (1987). Between hope and fear: The psychology of risk. *Advances in Experimental Social Psychology, 20*, 255-295.

Lopes, L. L., & Oden, G. C. (1999). The role of aspiration level in risky choice: A comparison of cumulative prospect theory and SP/A theory. *Journal of Mathematical Psychology, 43*, 286-313.

MacCrimmon, K. R., & Wehrung, D. A. (1986). *Taking risks: The management of uncertainty*. New York: Free Press.

March, J. G. (1978). Bounded rationality, ambiguity, and the engineering of choice. *Bell Journal of Economics, 9*, 587-608.

Michell, J., & Ernst, C. (1996). The axioms of quantity and the theory of measurement. Translated from Part I of Otto Hölder's German text, "Die Axiome der Quantität und die Lehre vom Mass." *Journal of Mathematical Psychology, 40*, 235-252.

Savage, L. J. (1954). *The foundations of statistics*. New York: John Wiley.

Tversky, A., & Kahneman, D. (1974). Judgment under uncertainty: Heuristics and biases. *Science, 185*, 1124-1131.

von Neumann, J., & Morgenstern, O. (1947). *Theory of games and economic behavior* (2nd ed.). Princeton, NJ: Princeton University Press.

A DESCRIPTIVE, PSYCHOLOGICAL DECISION THEORY

Human life occurs only once, and the reason we cannot determine which of our decisions are good and which are bad is that in a given situation we can make only one decision, we are not granted a second, third, or fourth life in which to compare various decisions.

—Millan Kundera

13.1 NONEXPECTED UTILITY THEORIES

Both the economists' paradoxes and psychologists' experiments have repeatedly shown that subjective expected utility theory is not a valid descriptive theory of human behavior. Most efforts to create a more adequate descriptive theory have the basic form of the rational expectations principle (Section 2.3), and accordingly they are sometimes called *non*expected utility theories as a reminder that they are derived from the expected utility framework.

But why should we work within the general expected utility framework? First, the framework includes the ingredients that our intuitions and experience tell us are essential to deliberate decision making. Second, the framework provides a roughly accurate descriptive account of decision behaviors in many situations. Some economists call it a "positive theory," because it relates inputs and outputs (psychologists might say stimuli and responses) in decision behavior to one another approximately correctly. And third, the framework captures the essence of rationality (as best our culture can define it), and it is likely that we are adapted to be approximately rational in our behaviors. Our optimistic hypothesis is that people are at least half-smart in achieving their personal goals.

However, as almost every paragraph in this book implies, human beings are far from the paragons of rationality and optimality demanded by fully rational behavior. Thus a valid descriptive theory will not be exactly the same as the best normative theory. The most influential, successful, and interesting of these descriptive variants is Kahneman and Tversky's prospect theory (1979; Tversky & Kahneman, 1992; introduced in Section 10.3, this volume). Like traditional decision theories, prospect theory adopts an algebraic formulation to represent decision processes: A *prospect* is an alternative or course of action defined by one or more *outcomes*, (i) which result in consequence *values* (v_i) which are weighted by *decision weights* (π_i), which are related to the objective probabilities for each outcome's occurrence. The *overall value* (V) for that prospect is

$$V = \Sigma(\pi_i \, v_i)$$

which is the same essential equation as the rational expectations principle at the heart of expected utility theories.

There are two phases in the prospect theory decision process: editing the alternatives, which involves constructing a cognitive representation of the acts, contingencies, and outcomes relevant to the decision, and evaluation, in which the decision maker assesses the value of each prospect and chooses accordingly. The evaluation phase can be broken down into three steps for each prospect: (a) valuation, in which the value function is applied to each consequence (*i*) associated with each outcome; (b) decision weighting, in which each valued consequence is weighted for impact by a function based on its objective probability of occurrence; and (c) integration, in which the weighted values across all the outcomes associated with a prospect are combined by adding them up. Let's look at each part of the process separately.

Prospect theory goes beyond traditional decision theories to describe some of the cognitive processes involved when the decision maker comprehends a decision situation. Comprehension results in a cognitive representation that includes the prospects' outcomes and events, contingencies between them, associated values, a reference point, and perhaps links to other information (in long-term memory or in the immediate environment) relevant to the assessment of values or decision weights.

The first major editing operation that is hypothesized to occur is *setting a reference point* on the objective valuation scale. In the case of money and health, the current status quo is the most likely candidate for the reference point that will define zero on a personal gain-loss scale. The location of the reference point is central in explanations for many value-related phenomena as it determines what is a gain and what is a loss and predicts where the decision maker will be most sensitive to changes in value (near the zero reference point). But the reference point is not always the status quo, Tversky and Kahneman (1981) write:

> A diversity of factors determine the reference outcome in everyday life. The reference outcome is usually a state to which one has adapted; it is sometimes set by social norms and expectations; it sometimes corresponds to a level of aspiration, which may or may not be realistic. (p. 456)

The most common reference point studied in psychology other than the status quo is *aspiration level*. This point not only defines success for many people—particularly those high in need for achievement—but is often related to the length of time we search for alternatives yielding desirable outcomes. As we noted in Chapter 11, such satisficing strategies are not optimal and we would expect aspiration level to interact with the order in which we encounter or consider prospects to determine how well the strategy works. An example of an aspiration level effect is the observation that long-shot bets are especially popular at the end of the day at racetracks. This phenomenon probably results from losing bettors' attempts to recoup their losses before they leave the track for the day. These bettors act and talk as though they have an aspiration level of "breakeven." Of course, this means that the higher odds bets on favorites are a better value for those last races. And some bettors, casino players, and on-line stock investors of our acquaintance at least talk about quitting point aspiration levels: "If I'm ahead $1,000, I quit for the day and go jogging."

The labile, adaptive reference point concept is troubling to many economists (though it was first proposed by an economist). Like all of the framing subprocesses proposed in prospect theory, it is not highly constrained, making it difficult to derive a priori predictions or to formally estimate post hoc parameters, such as the location of the reference point. Some progress has been made on these technical problems. Lola Lopes and Gregg Oden (1999) have conducted several interesting experiments studying participants' preferences for experimental lotteries and identified the locations of special, sensitive points on the value continuum. When asked to think aloud about their choices, the participants make remarks like the following (p. 304):

> I picked the [long-shot lottery] because winning any amount of money would be exciting for me. If I picked $50 that would be great but if I picked any other number it automatically gives me more money in comparison with the other lottery choices.

> Excluding the extreme, the $190 top lottery prize in the [short-shot lottery] and the $50 lottery prize in the [long-shot lottery] it appears that if you win, the prize will be for more money in the [long-shot lottery]. A better payoff for not that much more risk.

Lopes and Oden concluded that three locations play key roles in people's evaluations of uncertain prospects: a reference point, an aspiration level ("What are the chances that I will achieve my goal of . . . ?"), and a security level ("What is the chance that I will lose . . . or more?"). Their interpretation is that there are individual differences in security-mindedness (loosely analogous to risk aversion) and potential-mindedness (analogous to risk seeking). These individual differences are stable across time (e.g., from experimental session to experimental session), at least in the financial domain, and they may correspond to "cautious" or "risky" personality types, speaking *very* loosely. The aspiration level for an individual is hypothesized to be much more labile and dependent on situational factors. Lopes and Oden interpret these individual parameters as indirect measures of attention deployment, and eye movement measures confirm that they are related to perceptual orientation and information search in the experimental lottery choice tasks. (We recommend Lopes and Oden's SP/A theory as an alternative to prospect theory, but a full coverage of competitors in the contest to propose a winning nonexpected utility formulation is beyond the scope of this book.)

James March and Zur Shapira (1987) find that business decision makers consider other critical amounts as well. They frequently refer to the "downside risk," by which they mean the maximum amount that could be lost in a business venture. They also discuss "breakeven points" and "survival points" (the amounts necessary to continue doing business). We suspect that careful studies of the behavior of these executives would reveal that they are especially sensitive to differences in the neighborhood of these attention-drawing reference points.

The second major editing operation hypothesized in prospect theory involves *combining or segregating* outcomes. This is predicted to happen as part of "mental accounting" (see Section 10.4), because money or some other resource comes from or is intended for particular mental accounts. It is hypothesized, although there is scant empirical evidence, that people group gains and losses to increase their overall satisfaction. People certainly have beliefs about what will feel better or hurt more. For example, most people judge that they would gain more pleasure from receiving two separate money gifts than from receiving one lump sum gift; for example, two separate tax refunds of $100 each would be more satisfying than one larger refund of $200. And most people would rather take one big loss than several smaller losses; for example, a single traffic fine of $200 dollars hurts less than two $100 fines. These intuitions are consistent with the theoretical principle that we are most sensitive to gains and losses near our reference point (it would be the status quo in these examples)—two small movements up or down from the zero point on a diminishing returns value function would have a bigger impact on our satisfaction levels than one larger movement. Remember, the theory also assumes that the reference point shifts rapidly; otherwise two small gains or losses in sequence would be no different from one large gain or loss.

Valuation involves inferring the personal values for the consequences attached to each outcome. The *value function* (see the lengthy discussion in Section 10.3; also Figure 13.1) summarizes prospect theory's assumptions about the translation of an objective measure of consequences into personal values for a typical person making a decision. The theory acknowledges that there will be individual differences in the basic function form and, sure enough, when the functions have been measured they do vary across individuals and across decisions, although there is considerable consistency too. Each consequence is identified as part of the framing process and then translated into a personal value according to the value function. An illustrative equation for this function can be written as follows:

$$v(x) = \begin{cases} x^\alpha \text{ if } x > 0 \\ \\ -\lambda(-x^\alpha) \text{ if } x < 0. \end{cases} \qquad \text{(with a typical } \alpha = 0.88 \text{ and } \lambda = 2.25)$$

This process has three major characteristics:

1. Reference level dependence: An individual views consequences (monetary or other) in terms of changes from the *reference level*, which is usually that individual's *status quo*.

2. Gain and loss satiation: The values of the outcomes for both positive and negative consequences of the choice have the diminishing returns characteristic. The α term in the value function equation captures the marginally decreasing aspect of the function. Empirical studies estimate that α is typically equal to approximately .88 and always less than 1.00. When the exponent $\alpha < 1.00$, the curve will accelerate negatively (if $\alpha = 1.00$, the function would be linear; and if $\alpha > 1.00$, it would accelerate positively).

3. Loss aversion: The resulting value function is steeper for losses than for gains; losing $100 produces more pain than gaining $100 produces pleasure. The coefficient λ indexes the difference in slopes of the positive and negative arms of the value function. A typical estimate of λ is 2.25, indicating that losses are approximately twice as painful and gains are pleasurable. (If $\lambda = 1.00$, the gains and losses would have equal slopes; if $\lambda < 1.00$, gains would weigh more heavily than losses.)

If we take this value function seriously, we can calculate predicted personal values for various options. For example, to understand loss aversion, we could calculate the prospect theory value for a sure gain of $100 and compare it to the value for a sure loss of $100: $V_{+\$100} = \$100^{.88} = 57.54$ versus $V_{-\$100} = -2.25(\$100^{.88}) = -129.47$. Obviously, the loss hurts much more than the gain pleasures. To understand the effects of segregating and aggregating consequences, we can calculate the personal value of receiving two gifts of $100 versus one gift of $200: $(V_{+\$100} + V_{+\$100}) = 115.08$ versus $V_{+\$200} = 105.90$. And the same for losses: $(V_{-\$100} + V_{-\$100}) = -258.94$ versus

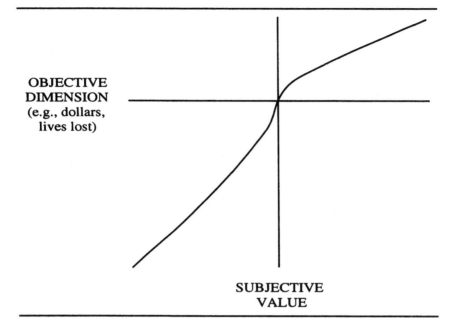

FIGURE 13.1. The Prospect Theory Value Function

$V_{-\$200}$ = \$238.28. The impact of segregated consequences is greater than the impact of a lump sum consequence, whether the outcomes are good or bad.

Prospect theory includes a decision weighting process, analogous to the weighting of outcomes by their probabilities of occurrence or expectations in expected utility theories. Again, prospect theory relies on a mathematical function to summarize the relationship between objective and subjective continua, translating probabilities into decision weights. The modal decision weight function (again, typical for most individuals in most decision situations) looks like the S-shaped curve in Figure 13.2. A useful rule of thumb to interpret these psychophysical functions is that when the curve is steeper, it implies the decision maker will be more sensitive to differences on the objective dimension: If the curve is steep, there is relatively more change in the psychological response to any difference on the objective dimension, as compared to where the curve is flatter. Several mechanisms have been postulated as explanations for the differences in steepness or slope, for example, differential attention, differences in sense

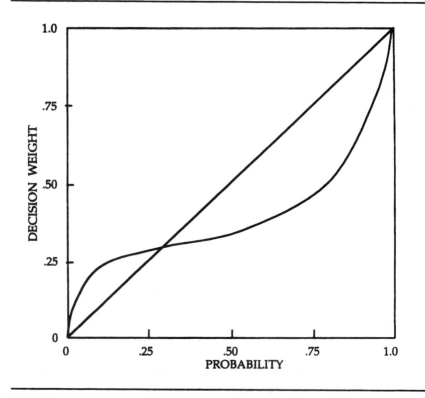

FIGURE 13.2. The Prospect Theory Decision Weight Function

organ sensitivity, and differences in the reactivity of neural-biochemical substrates.

An illustrative equation for this function can be written as follows:

$$\pi(p) = \frac{p^{\gamma}}{\left(p^{\gamma} + (1-p)^{\gamma}\right)^{\frac{1}{\gamma}}} \quad \text{(with a typical } \lambda = 0.64\text{).}$$

Let's walk through the characteristics of the decision weight function.

1. Near the zero point, the curve is steep, implying that people are very sensitive to the difference between impossibility and "possibility-hood." This steepness is consistent with people's overreactions to small probability risks and is also part of the explanation for why people purchase

incredibly long shot state lottery tickets. The business of industrial and governmental risk management is complicated by people's willingness to pay exorbitant amounts to completely eliminate low probability threats. U. S. Supreme Court Justice Stephen Breyer (1993) refers to the "unnecessary and unproductive attempt to remove the 'last 10 percent' of risk" from toxic spills, asbestos exposure, and disease susceptibility (p. 75). Breyer quotes administrators of the Environmental Protection Agency (EPA) in support of the contention that about 95% of toxic material could be removed from almost all hazardous waste sites in a few months, but years are spent trying to remove the last little bit. Removing that last little bit involves high cost, devotion of considerable societal resources, large legal fees, and endless argument. A former trial judge, Breyer cites a memorable example from his own experience, arising out of a 10-year effort to force the cleanup of a toxic waste dump in southern New Hampshire (*United States v. Ottatti & Goss*, 1990):

> The site was mostly cleaned up. All but one of the private parties had settled. The remaining private party litigated the cost of cleaning up the last little bit, a cost of about $9.3 million to remove a small amount of highly diluted PCBs and "volatile organic compounds" (benzene and gasoline components) by incinerating the dirt. How much extra safety did this $9.3 million buy? The forty-thousand page record of this ten-year effort indicated (and all parties seemed to agree) that, without the extra expenditure, the waste dump was clean enough for children playing on the site to eat small amounts of dirt daily for 70 days each year without significant harm. Burning the soil would have made it clean enough for the children to eat small amounts daily for 245 days per year without significant harm. But there were no dirt-eating children playing in the area, for it was a swamp. Nor were dirt-eating children likely to appear there, for future building seemed unlikely. The parties also agreed that at least half of the volatile chemicals would likely evaporate by the year 2000. To spend $9.3 million to protect non-existent dirt-eating children is what I mean by the problem of "the last 10 percent." (Breyer, 1993, p. 12)

The problem is not that people want to be safe but that their overreaction to many of these hazards means that funds are not available for other protective or constructive social programs. Each $9.3 million we spend on a useless cleanup will be $9.3 million less to spend on mitigating more important hazards.

2. There is a crossover point at about .20 on the objective probability dimension where, in many gambling situations (e.g., cards, dice, horse racetrack betting), people are well calibrated in terms of their sense of "objective" probabilities.

3. In most of the central portion of the curve, people are "regressive," the curve is "too flat," and substantial changes in objective probabilities produce small changes in decision weights. People are insensitive to differences in intermediate probabilities. This portion of the function implies that people will be superadditive for events associated with these objective probabilities: The sum of a set of decision weights will be smaller than the sum of the objective probabilities.

4. Finally, at the high end of the objective probability scale the curve becomes steep again as a high probability changes to certainty. This phenomenon is sometimes called the "certainty effect." It provides part of an explanation for the observed pattern of preferences between gambles in the Allais paradox (discussed in Section 12.3). It is important to people to be certain of getting the big prize, so important that the shift from .99 to 1.00 is worth more to the experimental subject than the shift from .10 to .11. The cleverly designed Allais paradox bets lead people to violate the independence axiom of subjective expected utility theory.

Figure 13.3 is a summary of the decision processes proposed by prospect theory. We have taken some liberties by ordering the three preliminary substages (editing, valuation, and decision weighting) in a temporal sequence. The theory itself is not explicit about the order of the computations. Furthermore, like most scientific theories, the formulation is revised to accommodate new empirical findings. The most recent version of the theory (as we write in 2000) has a more complex "decumulative" weighting process than the one we describe here (Tversky & Kahneman, 1992). Let's take a look at some recent behavioral findings, especially those that discriminate between traditional subjective expected utility theory and prospect theory.

13.2   GAIN-LOSS FRAMING EFFECTS

The influence of the frame for the outcomes in a decision problem can be demonstrated by creating two versions of the problem, two different statements that describe identical decision situations in different words.

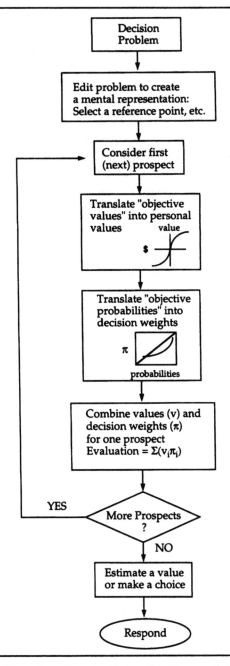

FIGURE 13.3. Flowchart Summarizing the Stages of Decision Making
According to Prospect Theory

When the two problem statements are presented to experimental participants and different choices are made, the *framing effect* is demonstrated. We will consider examples in which alternate statements of a single problem affect the location of the chooser's reference point, but other violations of "invariance" have also been demonstrated (invariance is implied, e.g., by Axiom 4 of subjective expected utility theory: A gamble that can be represented in an extensive tree format should be evaluated identically to the same gamble presented in a collapsed, "normal" format). The reference point manipulation affects the perception of some of the component outcomes so that an identical outcome seems like a gain when compared to a low reference point, but seems like a loss when compared to a high reference point.

Imagine that you have just been given $1,000. Which prospect would you prefer?

> PROSPECT A: You receive $500 for sure.
>
> PROSPECT B: A fair coin is tossed; heads and you receive $1,000, tails and you receive nothing more.

Now imagine you have just been given $2,000. Which prospect would you prefer?

> PROSPECT A': You must pay back $500 immediately.
>
> PROSPECT B': A fair coin is tossed; heads and you give back nothing, tails and you give back $1,000.

In the first pair, the status quo reference point is the money in your pocket plus $1,000, and all outcomes are framed as gains. Accordingly, with the diminishing returns value function for gains, most people prefer the sure thing (prospect A). But in the second pair, the reference point is your pocket money plus the $2,000 (imaginary, but the adaptation is remarkably fast; it works!) and all outcomes are framed as losses. Now the diminishing returns property of the value function for losses makes most people want to gamble and they choose prospect B'. When all four prospects are written down next to each other, most people change their preference from prospect A' to prospect B', although A and A' are identical (certain gain of $1,500) and so are B and B' (lottery with a .50 chance of gaining $1,000 and a .50 chance of gaining $2,000). This is irrational—an essential

criterion of rationality is that choices be made on the basis of the consequences of behavior—yet with identical consequences people choose different courses of action. This result is problematic for traditional decision
theories: How can we reliably change our preferences when making two
formally identical choices? This result implies that it will be impossible to
measure our utilities on an invariant scale.

For the sake of clarity, let's look at the prospect theory valuations of
each prospect using numerical calculations based on the value function
and decision weight equations presented in Section 13.1:

$$V_{\text{PROSPECT A}} = \pi_{1.00}(v_{+\$500}) = 237.19$$

$$V_{\text{PROSPECT B}} = \pi_{.50}(v_{+\$1000}) + \pi_{.50}(V_0) = 198.18$$

$$V_{\text{PROSPECT A'}} = \pi_{1.00}(v_{-\$500}) = -533.67$$

$$V_{\text{PROSPECT B'}} = \pi_{.50}(V_0) + \pi_{.50}(v_{-\$1000}) = -442.36.$$

In the first pair, prospect A has a higher overall "gain" value; in the second
pair, prospect B' has a higher "loss" value (the lesser loss is in B'); thus
people's choices are predicted to reverse from the first pair to the second,
as they do for most individuals.

Another example of a gain-loss framing effect is from the consequential domain of medical decision making. When describing a medical procedure, which is more correct: to indicate its efficacy by presenting the
survival rates or the mortality rates for those receiving the treatment? It
shouldn't matter, but Barbara McNeil, Stephen Pauker, Harold Sox, and
Amos Tversky (1982) found that it does, both to physicians and to their
patients (pp. 1260-1261).

> You have been diagnosed with a life-threatening medical condition.
> Which procedure do you prefer?
>
> - Surgery: Of 100 people having surgery for this condition, 90 live
>   through the postoperative period, 68 are alive at the end of the first
>   year, and 34 are alive at the end of 5 years.
>
> - Radiation Therapy: Of 100 people having radiation therapy for this
>   condition, all live through the treatment, 77 are alive at the end of
>   the first year, and 22 are alive at the end of 5 years.

You have been diagnosed with a life-threatening medical condition. Now which procedure do you prefer?

- Surgery': Of 100 people having surgery for this condition, 10 die during surgery or in the postoperative period, 32 die by the end of the first year, and 66 die by the end of the 5 years.
- Radiation Therapy': Of 100 people having radiation therapy for this condition, none die during treatment, 23 die by the end of the first year, and 78 die by the end of 5 years.

The first problem statements frame the treatments in terms of survival rates, and only 18% of respondents choose radiation. But in the second, the mortality frame, 44% of the respondents chose radiation. Apparently, the reduction from 10 dead postoperatively for surgery to zero dead for radiation therapy looms much larger in the mortality frame. The framing effect was clear for physicians, medical students, patients, and college students.

These discrepancies have become more important due to the increase in the latter part of the 20th century of the medical practice of sharing with patients diagnoses, prognosis, and likelihood of subsequent results given various possible treatments. The purpose of this practice is to allow patients themselves to decide which treatment option to choose, or at least to provide *informed consent* for choosing the one recommended by the doctor. Previously, doctors gave orders, and patients were often not even permitted to ask in hospitals about the content of the pills they were told to take; moreover, it was common practice not to tell the patients about potentially devastating diagnoses (e.g., of cancer), or the likelihood of death, or when it is likely to occur (a practice that seems to still be common, according to interviews conducted by Elizabeth Lamont and Nicholas Christakis, 2000, with 258 physicians who were treating terminally ill cancer patients. Their conclusion: "We infer that direct, explicit, and frank verbal communication between physicians and terminally ill patients about prognosis probably occurs at most only one third of the time"; p. 1). This reluctance to be frank with patients is a barrier to patients' ending their lives in the manner they desire. But in any case, the question arises about how prognoses and the likely results of various options should be shared with patients. Clearly, from a logical perspective, discussing such matters in terms of the probability of survival is equivalent to discussing them in terms of the probability of not surviving. But now it turns out that these two types of framing have different effects on decision making.

Thus, if the doctor is supposed to present information in the most neutral possible manner and allow the decision to be made by the patient, how should this information be presented? McNeil and her colleagues (1982) suggested presenting all this information in both survival and mortality frameworks. The problem there is that such presentation might be confusing, and some people may not even be able to understand the equivalence of the two frames. Another possibility is to present the information *visually*. For example, if a graph is constructed where the number of years is presented visually on the x axis, then *both* the survival rate (e.g., in blue) and the mortality rate (e.g., in red) can be presented in the same pictorial representation. In the current example, one such graph could be constructed for surgery and the other for radiation. Then the actual or potential patient is asked to choose between these two procedures, and given that all the information is available in both graphs, any decision to focus on living or dying is made by the patients or potential patients themselves, not by the physician supplying the information.

Now consider a choice, which is like the ones that social policymakers must make, posed to diverse samples of respondents by Kahneman and Tversky (1984, p. 343).

Imagine that the United States is preparing for an outbreak of an unusual Asian disease that is expected to kill 600 people. Two alternative programs to combat the disease have been proposed. Scientific estimates of the consequences of the programs are as follows:

If Program A is adopted, 200 people will be saved.

If Program B is adopted, there is a 1 in 3 probability that 600 people will be saved and a 2 in 3 probability that no people will be saved.

Which program would you favor? Seventy-two percent of the original sample of college students chose program A. The alternatives were presented in terms of gains—lives saved—and the subjects were risk-averse. A second group of respondents, however, was presented with the same situation but a different description of the alternative programs:

If Program C is adopted, 400 people will die.

If Program D is adopted, there is a 1 in 3 probability that nobody will die and a 2 in 3 probability that 600 will die.

Which program would you favor? Only 22% of the students chose program C, while 78% chose program D. Yet program C is identical to program A (400 people dying being exactly equivalent to 200 living), and program D is equivalent to program B. The difference in the way the programs were presented led to a whopping 50% difference in their endorsement.

Again, let's run the prospect theory calculations using the equations from Section 13.1:

$$V_{\text{PROGRAM A}} = \pi_{1.00}(V_{+200}) = 105.90$$

$$V_{\text{PROGRAM B}} = \pi_{.33}(V_{+600}) + \pi_{.67}(V_0) = 96.96$$

$$V_{\text{PROGRAM C}} = \pi_{1.00}(V_{-400}) = -438.53$$

$$V_{\text{PROGRAM D}} = \pi_{.33}(V_0) + \pi_{.67}(V_{-600}) = -349.55.$$

The calculations predict that people will choose program A in the first pair, as its overall (gain) value is higher than program B's, but will choose program D in the second pair, because its loss is less (the overall value is higher) than program C's. Thus here is another reversal of choices for identical comparisons as a result of framing.

Competent debaters have always realized that such framing is an important component of persuasion, but it is only in the past 20 years that psychologists have investigated framing effects systematically. Moreover, psychologists have discovered that framing effects are particularly strong in matters regarding life and death. Why? Because the first life saved is the most important, just as is the first life lost. Thus decision makers are risk averse when questions are framed in terms of saving lives and risk seeking when the identical questions are framed in terms of losing lives. The number of lives lost plus the number of lives saved, however, must equal the number of people at risk for death. Hence the contradiction.

In fact, the contradiction concerning saving versus losing lives is even deeper than indicated by the inconsistent responses. Paul Slovic, Baruch Fischhoff, and Sarah Lichtenstein (1982) asked people not only to make such hypothetical choices, but also to enunciate general policies concerning death from various causes. In a typical study, members of the League of Women voters were asked both to make hypothetical choices and to state their overall philosophies. With great consistency, they opted for avoiding risk when questions were framed in terms of saving lives. But when they were asked to state how serious it would be for various numbers of people in society to lose their lives, they consistently indicated that such seriousness *accelerated* with the number of lives lost. Thus a large airplane accident was seen as more than twice as serious as a smaller one with half the fatalities (which presumably would have less than half the disruptive effect on society). In a more extreme situation, it is probable that most of us would agree that a nuclear attack involving 80 million casualties would be more than twice as bad as one involving 40 million, and, at the greatest extreme, a nuclear war annihilating all life on earth would be more than twice as bad as one annihilating "only" half.

These *positively* accelerating concerns for loss of life are inconsistent with risk aversion for saving lives. For example, if 600 deaths is more than three times as bad as 200, then it is contradictory to opt for 200 of 600 people being saved for sure rather than a 1/3 chance of saving all 600. Nevertheless, people appear consistently risk averse when presented with single choices in which the alternatives are phrased in terms of lives saved.

The same accelerating concern for possible deaths is implied by parents who fly on separate airplanes when their children are not with them. By doing so, they reduce the probability that both of them will be killed while simultaneously increasing the probability that *at least one* of them will be—since the probability that one of two planes will crash is greater than the probability that either alone will crash. As was rigorously demonstrated in Section 12.4, this choice to fly on separate planes also implies, according to the von Neumann and Morgenstern theory, that the implicit *disutility* of both dying is more than twice as great as the disutility of one of them dying.

Another realm in which framing effects are deliberately manipulated is the courtroom when attorneys are arguing about the amounts that should be awarded to compensate a plaintiff for harm suffered as a result of the defendant's actions. Defense attorneys frame the award as a gain: "How much should the defendant pay to make the plaintiff whole again?" whereas plaintiff's attorneys favor a loss frame: "How much would you have to be paid to suffer an injury like the harm done to my client?"

Is framing merely verbal trickery? The answer is no for two reasons. First, framing effects can be explained by simple psychological principles; they make sense in the context of a complex web of validated psychological principles. And second, people who make such contradictory choices often stand by them when the inconsistency is pointed out. One of us (Dawes) and two colleagues, Eric Johnson and Scott Hawkins, showed that framing effects can lead individuals to make such inconsistent choices (Hawkins, Dawes, & Johnson, 1987). They found, for example, that over half of their research participants were inconsistent in hypothetical life versus death problems like Kahneman and Tversky's "Asian disease" problem. Most important, the degree of inconsistency was as high within single choosers (who responded to identical questions framed in two different ways within 5 minutes of each other) as between choosers. Another colleague, Scott B. Lewis, asked participants to comment on their choices and found that the modal response was to stand by the original, contradictory choice. Whereas verbal tricks lose their effectiveness once they are understood, framing effects are durable.

People buy insurance. Why? The easiest explanation is that when considering insurance they no longer view their status quo as neutral, but rather they view their possessions on the positive side of zero (and a good insurance salesperson encourages that view); hence they are willing to take a small financial loss to avoid a risk of being wiped out. Again, the principle is that the expected utility of the gamble when dealing with positive amounts will always be less than the expected amount defined in monetary terms. But in fact, defined purely in monetary terms, individuals should expect to lose when they purchase insurance; after all, insurance companies make money.

Now consider people's unwillingness to use automobile seat belts unless state or national legislation requires them to do so. According to prospect theory, people tend to adopt their status quo as the reference point. Due to the shape of the value function, small gains become very important. People believe that not wearing seat belts yields a small gain in comfort. On the other hand, due to the diminishing returns shape of the value function for negative outcomes, the objective consequences of a catastrophic auto accident are undervalued. Hence, viewed in prospect theory terms, not wearing seat belts appears to be a reasonable behavior.

The deeper point is that people's decisions may be changed by changing the reference level. As Norman Gutkin (personal communication) has pointed out, people might be more willing to use seat belts if their status quo was made positive. Instead of emphasizing all the terrible things that could result from an accident, seat belt campaigns might better be framed in terms of how well off people are prior to the drive, in which case they would regard seat belt use as a form of insurance—insurance that they remain in their happy state. Gutkin suggested that seat belt advertising should not emphasize the terrible results of a serious automobile accident but, rather, should rather show a happy and affluent young couple reminding themselves that they don't wish to lose their pleasant lives as a result of an avoidable injury. (The impact of gain-loss framing of self-help messages is complex; see research by Peter Salovey and his colleagues for some recent findings; e.g., Rothman, Martino, Bedell, Detweiler, and Salovey, 1999.)

A similar analysis can be made of propaganda from peace groups that wish to change people's attitudes about nuclear armament and proliferation. These groups typically show films of how awful nuclear war would be, but the psychological impact of objective awfulness diminishes, according to Fechner's law, prospect theory, and the entire tradition of diminishing returns utility. For example, the expectation that nuclear winter may last 2 years rather than 6 months can hardly have much psychological impact. In contrast, if these groups emphasized how well off most Americans are—that is, portrayed us as *above* the reference level provided by the life of most people in the world—some limitations on armaments, and consequently power, would be viewed as only a small loss, like the one involved in buying an insurance premium. Usually, it is those opposed to the philosophy of such groups who have successfully sold nuclear buildup as a form of insurance.

Given our propensity to avoid sure losses, insurance sales pitches must be carefully framed. As one of our colleagues points out, a campaign advertising lower premiums that begins, "Reduce your sure loss," would not be likely to sell insurance. We speculate that at least some people buy insurance in part because they can imagine themselves to be "small winners" vis-à-vis the insurance company; if disaster does occur they have won a low-stakes, low-probability-of-big-payoff bet against that company. Fully aware that the expected value of this bet is negative, they make it to ensure peace of mind in contemplating what *might* happen; "At least, my children will be able to make it through college if the wing falls off." The same prospective contemplation of possible outcomes may be one motive for buying lottery tickets with full knowledge of negative expectation.

Of course, sometimes insurance coverage pays off. Reuven Brenner (personal communication) notes that purchases of both insurance policies and lottery tickets may be explained when they are framed in terms of *relative* rather than *absolute* wealth, given that wealth relative to other people's wealth is generally not altered by the small amounts spent on the premiums and tickets. As Brenner sees it,

> They [people] perform both acts for the same reasons: in both cases individuals expect to lose relatively small amounts, either the price of the lottery ticket or the insurance premium. But these small amounts are worth losing since these are the only ways by which people can either change or avoid changing their relative position in the distribution of wealth. Thus people gamble in order to try to become richer and change their relative position in the distribution of wealth, and they insure themselves in order to prevent becoming poorer, thus avoiding a change in their relative position.

13.3 LOSS AVERSION

The basic concept of loss aversion is both intuitively appealing and well supported empirically. Perhaps the most convincing evidence comes from transparently simple *endowment effect* demonstrations. Once people have possessed an object for even a minute, they act as if "losing it matters more than gaining it would have mattered if they didn't have it." Daniel Kahneman, Jack Knetsch, and Richard Thaler (1991) gave half the students in a class gift coffee mugs; the other half were then allowed to bid to purchase the mugs. There were substantial differences between the dollar values placed on the mugs by those who were "endowed" with the mugs and those who were not. Students endowed with the mugs placed much higher selling prices on them than the nonowners' bids. This study has been repeated many times with various commodities and measures designed to more exactly elicit true, sincere valuations, always obtaining the same status quo bias.

The loss-gain asymmetry is important in formal markets, for it predicts the common situation where a seller values his or her commodity more highly than buyers do. The endowment effect is surely part of the explanation for the malfunction of some markets in which trading occurs at inefficiently slow rates. The problem with this interpretation is that there are other plausible explanations for the predicted gap between buying price and selling price valuations. Obviously, it is strategically wise to bid low if you are a potential buyer (e.g., in an auction) and to start high if you are a seller. We all expect that there will be some negotiation and we do not want to miss a bargain by offering too much or selling to cheaply. This is a reason why controlled experiments are important to rule out alternative explanations and to carefully assign credit to different causal factors in a complex situation (see discussion of one "sincere valuation" method in Section 5.2).

What about some more subtle implications of loss aversion? Most of the examples are from the financial world (and are due, again, to Richard Thaler, 1991, 1992, 1999). Why are some many markets "too sticky," inefficient in economic terms because they "settle too slowly" and as a result support a low volume of trading? Part of the answer is surely that there is a psychological gap between willingness to sell and willingness to buy; people truly value a commodity that they possess more than they would the identical commodity if they were bidding to buy it. These surprisingly wide gaps between willingness to buy versus willingness to sell have been documented in many real and artificial markets.

In many universities, faculty members are offered some control over the form of their retirement fund investments. To simplify, they can allocate these funds between a relatively volatile stock investment and a relatively stable bond investment. For the most part (in laboratory and field studies of investment habits), people overinvest in the stable instruments such as bonds and underinvest in volatile instruments such as stocks. Thaler calls this *myopic loss aversion* because, according to his analysis, the volatile investments are much more profitable over the long run. His interpretation is that the up-and-down roller-coaster experience of the volatile investment is very aversive. Every rise feels good, but every fall hurts much more, because the loss arm of the value function is much steeper than the gain arm, and the more the price oscillates, the more pain accumulates relative to pleasure. In the real world, it is difficult to definitively show that the conservative investment is worse than the volatile investment, although Thaler provides convincing numbers on the returns from stock, treasury bill, and bond market investments. Certainly, the historical results from the academics' retirement funds support his contention that the volatile fund is underinvested in. But Thaler has also conducted controlled demonstrations in which the only difference between experimental conditions is in the frequencies with which the current values of the investments are reported (the investments simulated the behavior of bonds or stocks). When reports were frequent (analogous to annual reports), people preferred the conservative, stable bonds, investing a majority of their funds accordingly. When reports were infrequent (analogous to 30-year return summaries), they invested 90% of their funds in the higher-paying volatile stocks.

13.4   LOOK TO THE FUTURE

Prospect theory is the best comprehensive description we can give of the decision process. It summarizes several centuries' worth of findings and insights concerning human decision behavior. Moreover, it has produced an unmatched yield of new insights and predictions of human behavior in decision making. The theory provides a useful catalogue of irrational and anomalous behaviors and relates them to the traditional normative (rational) framework. And it attributes many of these anomalies to underlying psychological processes. But the theory is not complete. We know of almost no intellectual domain that is labeled a science that is not moving forward. There are phenomena that it does not predict or explain. An example is the preference reversals we described in Section 5.2: When presented with individual bets, people place higher prices on those that have high dollar payoffs, but when comparing pairs of bets, people tend to prefer bets that offer a high probability of winning some amount. Thus their preferences are the reverse of their prices, contradicting traditional utility theories and also contrary to prospect theory.

Although some of these behaviors, which are anomalous with reference to canons of rational decision making, can be justified by considerations of information search and decision costs, others such as frames depend on haphazard events and are arbitrary for any predictive purposes. Studying them can leave one with an uneasy feeling about the "course of history"—both personal and social—and the uneasiness is not diminished by considerations of the potential magnitude of the effects of choices in our technologically advanced (nuclear) world. Perhaps framing and other irregularities of the decision process partly explain the lack of predictability of human behavior—in the psychiatric clinic and on the street. People make choices every day, and many of these choices have important consequences (even ones that are considered trivial at the time, such as whether to go to a party where you might happen to meet someone who will have a profound effect on your life). To the degree to which choices are influenced by factors other than considerations of their consequences, such as arbitrary context and framing effects, they are arbitrary.

REFERENCES:

Breyer, S. (1993). *Breaking the vicious circle*. Cambridge, MA: Harvard University Press.

Hawkins, S. A., Dawes, R. M., & Johnson, E. J. (1987). *Intra-individual framing effects*. Unpublished working paper, Department of Social and Decision Sciences, Carnegie Mellon University, Pittsburgh, PA.

Kahneman, D., Knetsch, J. L., & Thaler, R. H. (1991). Anomalies: The endowment effect, loss aversion, and the status quo bias. *Journal of Economic Perspectives, 5,* 193-206.

Kahneman, D., & Tversky, A. (1979). Prospect Theory: An analysis of decision under risk. *Econometrica, 47,* 263-291.

Kahneman, D., & Tversky, A. (1984). Choices, values, and frames. *American Psychologist, 39,* 341-350.

Lamont, E. B., & Christakis, N. A. (2000, May). *Physician's preferences for prognostic disclosure to cancer patients near the end of life*. Paper presented at the annual meeting of the American Society Clinical Oncology (Abstract #1704), New Orleans.

Lopes, L. L., & Oden, G. C. (1999). The role of aspiration level in risky choice: A comparison of cumulative prospect theory and SP/A theory. *Journal of Mathematical Psychology, 43,* 286-313.

March, J. G., & Shapira, Z. (1987). Managerial perspectives on risk and risk taking. *Management Science, 33,* 1404-1418.

McNeil, B. J., Pauker, S., Sox, H., Jr., & Tversky, A. (1982). On the elicitation of preferences for alternative therapies. *New England Journal of Medicine, 306,* 216-221.

Rothman, A. J., Martino, S. C., Bedell, B. T., Detweiler, J. B., & Salovey, P. (1999). The systematic influence of gain- and loss-framed messages on interest in and use of different types of health behavior. *Personality and Social Psychology Bulletin, 25,* 1355-1369.

Slovic, P., Fischhoff, B., & Lichtenstein, S. (1982). Responsibility, framing, and information-processing effects in risk assessment. In R. M. Hogarth (Ed.), *New directions for methodology of social and behavioral science: Question framing and response consistency* (pp. 21-36). San Francisco: Jossey-Bass.

Thaler, R. H. (1991). Quasi rational economics. New York: Russell Sage Foundation.

Thaler, R. H. (1992). *The winner's curse*. New York: Russell Sage Foundation.

Thaler, R. H. (1999). Mental accounting matters. *Journal of Behavioral Decision Making, 12,* 183-206.

Tversky, A., & Kahneman, D. (1981). The framing of decisions and the psychology of choice. *Science, 211,* 453-458.

Tversky, A., & Kahneman, D. (1992). Advances in prospect theory: Cumulative representation of uncertainty. *Journal of Risk and Uncertainty, 5,* 297-323.

United States v. Ottatti & Goss, Inc., 900 F.2d 429 (1st Cir. 1990).

IN PRAISE OF UNCERTAINTY

Accept the fact of uncertainty and learn to live with it.
Since no magic will provide certainty, our plans must
be made without it.

—Roberta Wohlstetter (1962)

14.1 UNCERTAINTY AS NEGATIVE

People abhor uncertainty. A common way of dealing with our experience of the uncertainty in life is to ignore it completely or to invent some "higher rationale" to explain it, often a rationale that makes it more apparent than real. A preacher in Ecclesiastes 9:11 observed, "The race is not to the swift, nor the battle to the strong, neither yet bread to the wise, nor yet riches to men of understanding, nor yet favor to men of skills; but time and chance happeneth to them all." This sounds like an exhortation to expect and adapt to uncertainty. But his views are contradicted by most of the narratives in the remainder of the Old Testament, where people generally get what they deserve, where there is a moral to every tale. The Old Testament Israelites, for example, lose battles when they turn away from Yahweh to worship graven images or to adopt the heathen practices of neighboring tribes; when they mend their ways, they win. False prophets are put to death; true ones triumph—although the heads of some of them end up on a platter first. The battle is to the morally superior and not

313

always to the strong; bread is supplied to the wise and riches to men of understanding, although they may, like Job, suffer first. Uncertainty, randomness are apparent, not real. (Admittedly, exactly which members of Job's first family or the people of Jericho, other than the traitorous prostitute, did deserve their fates is not entirely clear.)

Many who have abandoned traditional religion manifest the same dread of uncertainty in beliefs in astrology, scientology, tarot cards, and innumerable other systems that help many people "make sense" of life's uncertainties, which are believed to be part of some deep, underlying structure that they strive to understand. Fred Ayeroff and Bob Abelson (1976) conducted studies in which they searched for ESP (extrasensory perception) abilities in their college student subjects. They found no evidence for ESP at all in their careful experiments, but they did find plenty of evidence for ESB (extrasensory belief). (There is structure in the universe, but is it related to the course of an individual life?) Shaking off the dread of uncertainty in our lives and the need for denying its existence is extraordinarily difficult; even those who have a profound and compelling *intellectual* belief that the world is not constructed according to human needs cannot help but wonder what they "did wrong" when their children develop leukemia or their aging mother is hit, out of the blue, by a teenager joyriding in a stolen car during the high school lunch hour. And even intellectuals are prone to misconceptions concerning the behavior of random processes, unless they check themselves and analytically apply their school-learned probability theory calculations (see Chapters 8 and 9 and the Appendix).

We noted that people seem eager to interpret chance events in which we have some input (e.g., choosing a lottery ticket or picking numbers in lotto) as if they involved an element of skill (see Section 8.1). Even in domains such as sports and academic test taking, where Ziva Kunda and Richard Nisbett (1986) have found that people's naive statistical intuitions are pretty good, the contributions of chance are underappreciated. People know that there is an element of inexplicable, even random, influence in tests of human ability. Thus, for example, what percentage of variance in athletic outcomes can be attributed to the skill of players, as indexed by past performance records? Bob Abelson (1985) asked knowledgeable fans to consider whether a major league baseball player would get a hit in a given turn at bat. He asked the fans to estimate the relative contributions of skill and chance to this outcome (actually, he asked them to estimate the squared correlation or "proportion of variance explained" by the players' batting averages, widely held to be the most useful summary of skill at batting). The median estimate was around 25%, but the true answer is approximately 0.5%. Even in a familiar domain in which people appreciate chance factors, people overestimated the contribution of skill by a factor of about 50. As Abelson put it, "We as baseball fans are prone to regard a .330 hitter as a hero who will always come through in the clutch, and the .260 hitter as a practically certain out when the game is on the line" (p. 131). (This example has another important message: In many situations, small differences in skill and other biases of behavior add up when the behavior is repeated many times. What is the incremental impact of even tiny biases in judgment when amplified by hundreds of career success evaluations, hundreds of medical operations, or hundreds of prison sentences?)

This illusion of personal control or a hidden causal order is the basis of superstitious behavior. Superstitions are particularly likely to develop when the outcomes of behaviors involve components of both skill and chance (e.g., making a hit in a baseball game) because it is easy to confuse factors based on skill with those based on chance. In fact, if we were to evaluate these behaviors by simply noting what we did and what outcome followed, there would be no way to distinguish between chance and skill components—short of deliberately varying our behavior in a systematic fashion and then conducting a statistical analysis to determine which behaviors are associated with success and which with failure. Neither people nor rats do that, however; instead, both have a strong tendency to adopt a "win-stay, lose-switch" strategy, repeating whatever behavior preceded success and changing whatever preceded failure (e.g., swinging the bat precisely five times in the on-deck circle). Such a strategy has two *logical* consequences: First, it is impossible to evaluate the chance component in success versus failure; and second, the distinction between adaptive and superstitious behavior becomes meaningless. (One simply "did X" and "Y followed.") As pointed out in Sections 1.5 and 2.6, decisions based solely on the outcomes (reinforcements) of past behavior do not satisfy our criterion of rationality, because they are not made with regard to probable future consequences.

A much-trumpeted success of Skinnerian behaviorism was its explanation of superstitious behavior (Skinner, 1948). If the analysis just proposed is correct, this success is based on the fact its principles do not distinguish between adaptive and superstitious behavior. Moreover, even a pigeon or rat (or a human) with expert statistical skills and training would tend to behave superstitiously when its total environment consisted of a Skinner box. Given that nothing can be done in such an environment other than to press a bar or refrain from doing so, and that the only environmental variability involves the appearance of food, a desperately hungry animal (the animals in Skinner's experiments were kept at 70% of their normal body weight) would experience an overwhelming temptation to adopt a "win-say, lose-switch" strategy and hence never learn. Moreover, the problem is confounded by the experimenter's deliberate reinforcement of superstitious behavior, thereby further blurring the distinction between superstition and adaptation.

Often, however, we even fail to understand the probabilistic nature of events in which we have no involvement whatsoever. For example, many psychological experiments were conducted in the late 1950s and early 1960s in which subjects were asked to predict the outcome of an event that had a random component but yet had base rate predictability; for example, subjects were asked to predict whether the next card the experimenter turned over would be red or blue in a task in which 70% of the cards were blue, but the sequence of red and blue cards was totally random (the experimenter simply shuffled the deck before each experiment). In such a situation, the strategy that will yield the highest proportion of successes is to predict the more common event on every trial. For example, if 70% of the cards are blue, then predicting blue on every trial yields a 70% success rate, the highest possible in this task. What subjects tended to do instead, however, was to match probabilities, that is, to predict the more probable event *on the proportion of trials on which it occurred*. For example, subjects tended to predict 70% of the time that the blue card would occur and 30% of the time that the red card would occur. Of course, their accuracy was unrelated to their strategies and matched the prediction of a random probability model. Such a strategy yields a 58% success rate, because the subjects are correct 70% of the time when the blue card occurs (which happens with probability .70) and correct 30% of the time when the red card occurs (which happens with probability .30): $(.70 \times .70) + (.30 \times .30) = .58$. In fact, subjects predict the more frequent event with a slightly higher probability than that with which it occurs, but do not come close to predicting its occurrence 100% of the time, even when they are paid for the accuracy of their predictions. Despite feedback through a thousand trials, even when the subjects are *explicitly told* that only the base rate prediction is relevant—"the sequence is random with no repetitive patterns"—subjects cannot bring themselves to believe that the situation is one in which they *cannot* predict (Tversky & Edwards, 1966, p. 680). Apparently, the uncertainty inherent in this experimental situation is unacceptable, even though failing to appreciate it results in reduced payoffs to the subject. (And once again, it appears to be unacceptable to those of us who develop arthritis or cancer—or lose children or parents.)

When there is a chance component in the outcomes of our own behavior, we tend to treat the chance component *as if* it involves skill. In the probability-matching experiments, subjects responded to a purely probabilistic outcome beyond their control *as if* it were deterministic. (There "must" be some pattern there.) Hillel Einhorn (1986) has suggested that the crucial distinction between clinical-intuitive and probabilistic-statistical approaches to prediction and control is whether or not the predictor treats probabilistic events as if they were deterministic. Regarding probabilistic events as deterministic makes the rules of probability theory—such as the necessary consideration of base rates—irrelevant. For example, if the sequence of events in a probability-matching experiment really were deterministic, the prediction of the low-probability event would be neither counterinductive nor silly. But, it is precisely such counterinductive judgments made by his colleagues that led Paul Meehl—a psychoanalyst as well as a leading researcher in the area of clinical judgment—to be critical of their reasoning capacities, as recounted in his 1976 article, "Why I Do Not Attend Case Conferences." A simple explanation is that, like subjects in probability-matching experiments, these colleagues do not regard the outcomes in the world as inherently probabilistic.

Einhorn (1986) goes on to argue that the probabilistic approach is *superior* to the clinical one, as evidenced, for example, in the studies conducted by Meehl and others summarized in Section 3.3. We concur. Even if the world has some underlying deterministic structure, we do not usually understand it, and in particular we do not comprehend it with respect to the events in everyday life about which we are most concerned. Moreover, subjects' inability to appreciate the probabilistic nature of the probability-matching experiments even after as many as 1,000 trials indicates that the tendency to reject uncertainty is a strong bias—not a consequence of adaptive learning from experience.

Could treating chance as skill be explained on a motivational basis? For example, does the belief that we cannot predict the outcome of coin tossing or batting somehow threaten our ability to cope with the world? Or is it that cognition itself is so inextricably bound with our attempts to predict and control that our judgments about events in the world—no matter how clearly they are randomly determined—implicitly assume predictability? We do not know the answer.

Clearly, there are contexts in which lack of predictability involves threat. For example, the Cable News Network presented an interview with three "experts" while the jury was deliberating during the New Bedford rape trial in 1984. One of these, a psychologist named Lee Salk, proclaimed that one of the worst aspects of such victimization is that the experience undermines the three beliefs on which our ability to cope with the world is based: the belief that we are superior, the belief that we are invulnerable, and the belief that the world is just; moreover, after victimization, "it takes several years to re-establish these beliefs." In contrast, Lord Acton observed in 1887 that "history provides neither compensation for suffering nor penalties for wrong."

14.2   AN ILLUSION OF HEDONIC CERTAINTY

We not only underappreciate uncertainty in the world outside of us, but we are prone to an illusion of consistency, reliability, and certainty about the world inside our own heads. There can be little doubt that we think we are more logical, rational, and consistent than we really are. This book has catalogued dozens of examples of this kind of hubris; we even rewrite our personal biographies to reinforce our beliefs that we "knew it all along" and that we've "always felt this way." But we suspect we have a special blind spot when thinking about what we will want, thinking about *decision utility* in Daniel Kahneman's terms (Section 10.1).

Research on hedonic psychology, especially phenomena relevant to deliberate decision making, is in the early stages, but already there is a sizable catalogue of errors and biases. Without repeating the many examples of bad judgments about hedonic consequences (see Section 10.1), we can state some summary premises concerning our capacities to predict our postdecision, experienced utilities: First, we are at best moderately accurate predictors of our evaluations and emotional reactions to future outcomes. Second, the outcomes themselves (which occur preceding our reactions) are often hard to predict and more complex than our anticipations of them. Third, even if we could predict our reactions to the outcomes, the impact of these outcomes on our long-term global well-being (and domain-specific happiness) is modest, much smaller than we think it is. This last point has been verified many times in research on personal well-being and happiness. The best current theory of well-being proposes that most people have "hedonic set points," ambient levels of ebullience or depression that are a consistent within individuals and that vary reliably across individuals (and that may even be inherited or set by early life experiences).

The image is of people bobbing up and down as the day-to-day events perturb their hedonic levels, but with everyone returning to pretty much where they started on the up-down scale. Hedonically significant events (divorce, losing a job, winning the lottery, getting into your first-choice college) move you up or down, but after 3 months (or at most 6) you're back to normal (David Lykken, 1999, argues that genetics may be an important determinant of your hedonic set point, just as heredity predicts your body weight). What does this mean for decision making? People have erroneous, self-aggrandizing beliefs that they can predict and control how happy they will be. People focus too much on "decision utility," expending too much cognitive energy attempting to predict their future happiness when they make decisions. We are not advocating that people completely ignore what they want, or think they want, when they choose. But one useful tactic is to avoid focusing on global assessments of "how happy will it make me" when we are evaluating our prospects; rather, focus on predicting other important attributes of the consequences you are considering, such as good health, productivity, variety of experience, helping others, and perhaps money, and on bad attributes that can be decreased, such as constraints on time or opportunities and risks of tangible losses.

14.3 THE PRICE OF DENYING UNCERTAINTY

When one of us (Dawes) was training to be a clinical psychologist, he met a patient we'll call Harold. Before his hospitalization, Harold had a shaky marriage held together by concern for his 2-year-old son, and he was doing badly at a job he disliked. One morning, he was fired from his job and he went home. When he arrived, the police were there and his wife was hysterical. His son had run into the street and been killed by an automobile. After his wife had been sedated, Harold wandered back to his former workplace, which was nearby, and into the canteen. An attractive woman motioned him to join a group she was with for a cup of coffee. Drinking coffee was strictly forbidden by his religion. He suddenly realized that this woman was trying to *liberate* him from his compulsive adherence to his religious teachings and that she might be trying to *liberate* him sexually as well. His boss had *liberated* him from his unpleasant job, and the motorist had *liberated* him from his bad marriage. He suddenly realized that all of these people had formed a conspiracy to *help* him! He ended up in the hospital when he mistook strangers for members of that conspiracy. His belief was unshakable; for example, protestations by the hospital staff members that they were trying to cure him from his delusions were simply met with a knowing smile.

When one of us (Hastie) was teaching his judgment and decision-making course for the first time, he encountered an odd-looking, middle-aged student. After a few lectures, the student introduced himself and explained why he was enrolled in the course. As the student told it, he had suffered a series of apparent misfortunes and was also in the midst of a divorce and fighting his employer's efforts to fire him. He said that at first he was confused by the events that were happening to him, but on reflection he realized that he was actually the subject of a huge "psychology experiment" (in fact, one reason he had come to Harvard to study was because he wanted to meet Professor B. F. Skinner, who he believed was the experimenter who was manipulating his life). He went on to cite dozens of instances of inexplicable behaviors and events that only made sense if the hypothesis that he was "in a psychology experiment" was true. Hastie asked for specific examples, but was not much impressed by the strength of the evidence for the student's hypothesis. Most of the examples seemed at least as probable under the alternate hypothesis that the student was *not* in a psychology experiment (e.g., "I was interrupted by my wife, and she spoke exactly the words I was thinking, before I could say them myself"; "I was having a drink with a coworker after work and he mentioned the company was laying off workers, and this happened only 2 days before they told me I was fired"). The bright side of the student's delusional system was that he believed that eventually the experiment would be finished and publicized and that his demonstrated aptitude (for being controlled by the experimenter) would certify his qualities as a leader who would be trustworthy and accountable in a high public office.

Perhaps the most fascinating part of this anecdote concerns the student's explanation for why he had approached Hastie: He was concerned that he not be irrationally deluded in his interpretation of these events. Thus to ensure that he not reach a false conclusion, he was attempting to apply the instructor's advice as carefully as he could. After enrolling in Hastie's class, he realized that he needed deliberately to apply Bayes' theorem to evaluate the posterior probability of the hypothesis, "I am the subject of a huge, secret psychology experiment," with reference to the many items of evidence he had accumulated. He wanted help with his calculations! (We hesitate to draw the obvious conclusions for the readers of this book.) The story did not end that semester. A few months later, the student called on Hastie to testify on his behalf in his lawsuit to retain his job. Psychiatrists for his employer had asserted that he was suffering from massive paranoid delusions (plausible), that the silliness about Bayes' theorem was part of his delusional system, and furthermore that the Reverend Thomas Bayes was a figment of his schizophrenic imagination. (Hastie provided a deposition rebutting the psychiatrists' claims that Thomas Bayes was a delusion, although he acknowledged that he did not fully support the plaintiff's calculations and he was dubious of that posterior probability: 999,999/1,000,000. Of course, the experience of producing the deposition also led Hastie to wonder why *he* was so confident in the existence of a vague historical figure whom he knew of only because a mathematical theorem was named after him.)

Psychiatrist Silvano Arieti (1974) maintained that it is not uncertainty (or pain) per se that creates psychotic disorders, but rather the attempt to make sense of it in a way that does not make sense to others—the "psychotic insight." Of course, not all attempts to reduce uncertainty are pathological. We all attempt to reduce uncertainty. Organizations do it; political decision makers do it; and uncertainty reduction is essential to science, if not all knowledge. It can become pathological, however, if it becomes too important. Such pathology is not limited to those of us socially designated as mentally ill.

There must, for example, be some explanation for a plague. "The Jews are poisoning the wells," some unenlightened people of the 13th century concluded. In fact, such explanations have been resurrected in the lifetime of many of us to explain such other phenomena as an economic depression, students running amok with automatic weapons in our high schools, or the global AIDS epidemic. These explanations can lead to vicious programs. But *it is not* pathological to seek to reduce uncertainty. Such a quest may even lead to knowledge allowing us to understand things that puzzle us today. *It is* pathological to conclude that we *must know now* in situations containing irreducible uncertainty, at least when analyzed in terms of our present knowledge (cf. Hammond, 1996).

A belief that "If I am successful, I must somehow have deserved it" can make a person into an arrogant ass. A belief that "If I am not, I must have done something very bad in the past" can make a person into a depressed masochist. There is evidence, due mainly to the work of Bernard Weiner (1979), that most people ascribe their successes to their own characteristics and their failures to factors beyond their control, such as plain bad luck. Depressed people's thinking does not follow this pattern; if anything, it reverses it, as shown by Chris Peterson and Martin Seligman's (1984) research on explanatory style. Many of our colleagues have subsequently made the inferential leap that it is therefore mentally healthy to ascribe success to oneself and failure to circumstances—and that distressed people should be trained to make these self-aggrandizing but logically unjustifiable attributions. Of course, all outcomes are due to some combination of personal and situational factors, which are extraordinarily difficult to unravel, particularly for a single result.

Multi-cause, multi-effect situations, namely *all* situations, are seductively rich with explanations. On March 24, 1989, the oil tanker *Exxon Valdez* ran aground on Bligh Reef and spilled 11 million gallons of crude oil into Prince William Sound. It was America's worst oil spill. There were many ingredients available to construct causal narratives to explain the event: The ship's captain, Charles Hazelwood, had a history of drinking problems, including hospitalization for treatment; the Coast Guard had recently changed its policies, did not provide a local pilot, and had reduced its monitoring of ship passages; the crew of the *Valdez* had recently been reduced from 33 to 19; an unlicensed third mate was steering the ship when it hit the reef, and he testified he had "spaced out" and missed the turn he had been instructed to make; the *Valdez* was behind schedule and the crew was short of sleep; Hazelwood consumed some amount of alcohol on the afternoon of the ship's sailing; there were seasonal ice floes in the normal tanker traffic lanes and the *Valdez* had diverted its course to miss them; and much more. In such a situation, it is easy, in fact irresistible, retrospectively to construct a coherent causal narrative to account for the disaster.

If we were to undertake a prospective study to identify which of these factors predict the occurrence of tanker oil spills, we would surely find massive uncertainty. There are plenty of instances of each of these precursors being present, but without any oil spills: Many tankers were out of the shipping lanes that night; ice floes are a normal part of ocean environments at that time of year in Alaska; the practice of allowing unlicensed mates to pilot tankers was common. (The Exxon Corporation provided many examples as part of its defense in the resulting lawsuits.) The base rate incidence of oil spills is extremely low, impeding any systematic probabilistic analysis. But intuitive explanation processes usually produce high levels of hindsightful confidence. One of us (Dawes) has argued that such explanations can only be trusted if there is prior or subsequent systematic, ideally experimental, analysis that establishes *general* causal principles that can then be applied to the specific to-be-explained event. Situations with many antecedents and many consequents invite spurious backward searches to find causes. (The details of Dawes's technical analysis are beyond the scope of this book, but see his 1993 article, "Prediction of the Future Versus an Understanding of the Past: A Basic Asymmetry"). One inevitable byproduct of our tendency to construct and tell causal stories is blindness to the extent of our ignorance and a derogation of the role of chance in life.

Again, although some phenomena that we now attribute to chance may eventually be predictable and controllable, they remain chance events from our current perspective. Many of us know people who have suffered some great misfortune who appear to prefer believing they did something to bring it about to believing that it was something that just happened. The price of our retreat from uncertainty is often paid by others. Some individuals believe that if people are poor or on the street or addicted or ill, they must somehow have done something to deserve that fate. In the face of such deservingness, help is futile. Moreover, given the biasing effects of retrospective memory (see Sections 7.5 and 7.7), these victims themselves may accept that judgment, for if they, too, believe in "just deserts," that could play a crucial role in determining their recall of what it is *they did wrong*.

A gross misunderstanding of the role of chance in evolution can lead to cruelty as well as to failure to help. Consider Social Darwinism. Even the strongest adaptationists maintain that it is a *slight* genetic advantage that leads to a slight increase in the probability of success in the struggle for (gene) existence, which over *many* generations can lead to genetic change. But to claim, as some Social Darwinists did, that a single individual's poor situation implies the lack of genetic capacity, viciously underestimates the role of chance in life—viciously because it leads to the conclusion that it is "nature's way" to let such people suffer and die in order to let good genes multiply. Although the threat of uncertainty may cause pain, its denial can be cruel.

Such costs of denying uncertainty are high—too high to justify any feeling of security that this denial may offer. In particular, the pathological consequences of believing in a "just world" are severe—both for others and for oneself (see Melvin J. Lerner's research, 1980). An essential part of wisdom is the ability to determine what is uncertain, that is, to appreciate the limits of our knowledge and to understand its probabilistic nature in many contexts. It follows that an essential part of bravery is eschewing a false sense of security, for example, not believing we are invulnerable or superior or that the world is just.

Some psychologists, however, urge people to develop these beliefs as part of a general effort to reinforce belief in personal control of outcomes, since belief in such control is supposed to be a motivator for desirable choice and putting forth effort. It is true that parents attempt to reward good behavior and punish bad so that their children learn to behave in ways that the parents wish; moreover, children who see little contingency between their own behavior and their rewards and punishments often behave badly, or at least we can improve their behavior by increasing the contingency. In addition, employees who believe that they have control over the rewards they receive for their work are motivated to work hard and be productive. Consequently, employers and supervisors are well advised to establish a contingency between employee accomplishments and rewards. Global, diffuse control is another matter. If we have "put away childish things" when we are no longer children, we should understand that we have more or less control over outcomes *depending on the particulars of the situation.* Illusory control can have the pernicious effects discussed above. Some control theorists, nevertheless, claim that belief in control, illusory or real, is a mentally healthy motivator.

Rationally, it often doesn't matter how much control we have over outcomes—so long as we have some. For example, various alternatives will still have the same ranking in expected value even if a large random component determines the actual outcome (see Section 3.4). Understanding the wisdom of Ecclesiastes should in no way inhibit us from choosing the best possible alternative and pursuing it with all our energy. To maintain that it is necessary or desirable to overestimate the amount of control we have is to maintain that we can function only as children or agents of someone else, not as autonomous adults. Unfortunately, some of our colleagues treat their adult clients as if they really were children and give advice to the entire population on the same basis. (Striking examples of treating the adults as adults may be found in some of the rhetoric of John F. Kennedy. In one speech, he stated bluntly that life is not fair and gave the example that during wartime some people are shot on battlefields while others sit at desks. In his famous American University speech shortly before his assassination, he proclaimed that this country, comprising 6% of the world's population, cannot control everything that happens on the globe and that it would be a tragic mistake to equate national security with such control.)

Shelley Taylor has argued that belief in control is adaptive to coping in threatening situations. Taylor (1983) presents the following anecdote about a woman with breast cancer:

> One of the women I interviewed told me that after detection of her breast tumor she believed that she could prevent future recurrences by controlling her diet. She had, among other things, consumed huge quantities of Vitamin A through the singularly unappetizing medium of mashed asparagus. A year and a half later, she developed a second malignancy. This, of course, is precisely the situation all control researchers are interested in: a dramatic disconfirmation of efforts to control. I asked her how she felt when that happened. She shrugged and said she guessed she'd been wrong. She then decided to quit her dull job and use her remaining time to write short stories—something she had always wanted to do. Having lost control in one area of her life, she turned to another area, her life work, that *was* controllable. (p. 1170)

Taylor presents no evidence that her subjects who attempted to achieve illusory control over the recurrence of breast cancer were better off than those who did not, although the article itself implies that attempting such control is psychologically valuable. Her anecdote, however, can be interpreted in the precisely opposite way. It could serve as an example of how *giving up* the attempt to control is valuable. The woman's shrug was clearly an acknowledgment that she *did not* have control. Perhaps if the shrug had occurred a year and a half earlier, a year and a half of the woman's life would have been devoted to the work she desired rather than to a dull job and mashed asparagus.

14.4 TWO CHEERS FOR UNCERTAINTY

Imagine a life without uncertainty. Hope, according to Aeschylus, comes from the lack of certainty of fate; perhaps hope is inherently blind. Imagine how dull life would be if variables assessed for admission to a professional school, graduate program, or executive training program really *did* predict with great accuracy who would succeed and who would fail. Life would be intolerable—no hope, no challenge.

Thus we have a paradox. Although we all strive to reduce the uncertainties of our existence and of the environment, ultimate success—that is, a total elimination of uncertainty—would be horrific. In fact, it may be that such procedures as testing for AIDS antibodies and predicting the recurrence of breast cancer on the basis of hormonal and now genetic analyses are the results of long medical marches that have taken us to a place we do not wish to be. Imagine the horror of being notified that you possess a gene that invariably leads to Alzheimer's disease. Would that be worse than learning you have a terminal illness? At least, in the latter situation most people feel sick. As we write this, genetic testing is developing at an amazing pace. But in many such situations, people choose *not* to receive the feedback (at least probabilistic feedback) about the implications of their genetic constitution. For example, some people who have a parent with Huntington's disease (due to a single dominant gene) choose not to be tested to determine whether or not they have that gene—which inevitably leads to horrible debilitating and irreversible neurological degeneration.

On the other hand, some people do wish to find out. The results of such discovery were quite interesting. Many doctors and health professionals were opposed to a test for Huntington's disease that usually led to a conclusion with high probability that people either did or did not have the gene, but in which a third result was also possible: The test could be inconclusive. (Now there are tests available that are never inconclusive.) The rationale was that people who found out they probably had the gene might become suicidal. The counterargument was that such people might also choose not to have children, in which case the problem would disappear over a few generations. Both predictions are wrong. Among those people wishing to find out, those who were told that the results of the test were inconclusive were the most distressed. Those who found out they had the gene adapted to the bad news, just as pointed out in our discussion in Section 14.2. Moreover, they did not decide to refrain from having children, which they appeared to regard as equivalent to a wish that they themselves had never been born (and recall that most do not commit suicide). Conversely, those who received the good news that they most probably did not have the gene did not lapse into dysfunctional euphoria. People adapt.

But consistent with the illusion of hedonic certainty, a study of people who tested HIV positive or negative indicated that they grossly exaggerated how the news of their HIV status would affect them. These people were asked to predict how they would fill out a standard mood score 5 weeks after finding out their test results. They were then contacted (as much as possible, given the experiment was done under conditions of anonymity rather than confidentiality) to fill out these mood questionnaires roughly 5 weeks after they did, in fact, find out their test results. In addition, people who claimed to have found out they were HIV positive or negative roughly 5 weeks earlier also filled out these questionnaires. Compared to the anticipation of very negative feelings or very positive ones, the actual feelings were much more neutral. Again, people adapt. The major finding of the HIV study was that people failed to anticipate how much they'd adapt. (For a review of the Huntington's results and a presentation of the HIV testing results, see Sieff, Dawes, & Loewenstein, 1999).

It should be pointed out that these results are valid only for people who had indicated a very clear preference for finding out whether or not they have a condition that leads to extremely negative outcomes. Because these experiments and surveys were conducted in a predominantly free society, it is not possible to sample people at random and simply force information on them about their medical status. Thus it is not possible to determine whether the results concerning Huntington's and HIV status are applicable to the general population at large or only to people who already want to find out whether or not they have a devastating medical condition. Moreover, it is not possible on the basis of sampling such people to determine how large a proportion of the general population they constitute. Because the surveys and experiments can be conducted only on people who volunteer to learn the information, these surveys and experiments themselves do not lead to an estimate of how prevalent these people are. Of course, it would be possible to supplement the work already done by asking the general population of people whether they would want to find out, but that has the problem of equating actual behavior with people's hypothetical statements of how they would wish to behave, and because the original problem stems from the question of whether people can anticipate their future feelings very well, it is their feelings when facing the possibility of taking an actual test that are important.

Knowing *pleasant* outcomes with certainty would also detract from life's joy. An essential part of knowledge is to shrink the domain of the unpredictable. But although we pursue this goal, its ultimate attainment would not be at all desirable.

14.5   LIVING WITH UNCERTAINTY

Without uncertainty, there would be no hope, no ethics, and no freedom of choice. It is only because we do not know what the future holds for us (e.g., the exact time and manner of our own death) that we can have hope. It is only because we do not know exactly the results of our choices that our choice can be free and can pose a true ethical dilemma. Moreover, most of us are aware that there is much uncertainty in the world, and one of our most basic choices is whether we will accept that uncertainty as a fact or try to run away from it. Those who choose to deny uncertainty invent a stable world of their own. Such people's natural desire to reduce uncertainty, which may be basic to the whole cognitive enterprise of understanding the world, is taken to the extreme point where they believe uncertainty does not exist. The statistician's definition that an optimist is "someone who believes that the future is uncertain" is not as cynical as it may first appear to be.

We are optimistic about the contributions to general social welfare from research that will follow the studies and theories reported on in this book. There are many constructive lessons from the body of scientific knowledge that is amassing on judgment and decision making. We know much about important limits on our abilities to make accurate judgments and rational decisions. The reader will recognize many problematic habits and potential pitfalls simply from the insights provided by the huge collection of examples described here. We have several genuinely useful technologies for assessing, aiding, and replacing human decision makers. The key insight is to apply statistics and probability theory whenever you can, if not to calculate numerical solutions, then to structure and guide your decision making. When people deliberately scrutinize their decisions, they are able to identify and correct their own biases and inconsistencies. Finally, our advice is to strive for systematic external representations of the judgment and decision situations you encounter: Think graphically, symbolically, and distributionally. If we can make ourselves think analytically and take the time to acquire the correct intellectual tools, we have the capability to think rationally. But, like Benjamin Franklin, we have not tried to tell you *what* to decide but, rather, *how* to decide.

REFERENCES

Abelson, R. P. (1985). A variance explanation paradox: When a little is a lot. *Psychological Bulletin, 97*, 128-132.

Arieti, S. (1974). *Interpretation of schizophrenia* (2nd ed.). New York: Basic Books.

Ayeroff, F., & Abelson, R. P. (1976). ESP and ESB: Belief in personal success at mental telepathy. *Journal of Personality and Social Psychology, 34*, 240-247.

Dawes, R. M. (1993). Prediction of the future versus an understanding of the past: A basic asymmetry. *American Journal of Psychology, 106*, 1-24.

Einhorn, H. J. (1986). Accepting error to make less error. *Journal of Personality Assessment, 50*, 387-395.

Hammond, K. R. (1996). *Human judgment and social policy: Irreducible uncertainty inevitable error, unavoidable injustice.* New York: Oxford University Press.

Kunda, Z., & Nisbett, R. E. (1986). The psychometrics of everyday life. *Cognitive Psychology, 18*, 195-224.

Lerner, M. J. (1980). *Belief in a just world: A fundamental delusion.* New York: Plenum.

Lykken, D. (1999). *Happiness: What studies on twins show us about nature-nurture, and the happiness set-point.* New York: Golden Books.

Meehl, P. E. (1973). Why I do not attend case conferences. In *Psychodiagnosis: Selected papers* (pp. 225-302). New York: Norton.

Peterson, C., & Seligman, M.E.P. (1984). Causal explanations as a risk factor for depression: Theory and evidence. *Psychological Review, 91*, 347-374.

Sieff, E. M., Dawes, R. M., & Loewenstein, G. (1999). Anticipated versus actual reaction to HIV test results. *American Journal of Psychology, 112*, 297-311.

Skinner, B. F. (1948). "Superstition" in the pigeon. *Journal of Experimental Psychology, 38*, 168-172.

Taylor, S. E. (1983). Adjustment to threatening events: A theory of cognitive adaptation. *American Psychologist, 38*, 1161-1173.

Tversky, A., & Edwards, W. (1966). Information versus reward in binary choice. *Journal of Experimental Psychology, 71*, 680-683.

Weiner, B. (1979). A theory of motivation for some classroom experiences. *Journal of Educational Psychology, 71,* 3-25.

Wohlstetter, R. (1962). *Pearl Harbor: Warning and decision.* Stanford, CA: Stanford University Press.

Appendix

BASIC PRINCIPLES OF
PROBABILITY THEORY

*Say you're thinking about a plate of shrimp. Suddenly
someone says plate, or shrimp, or plate of shrimp. Out
of the blue. No use looking for one either. It's part of
the lattice of coincidence that lays on top of everything.*

—from the film *Repo Man,* written
and directed by Alex Cox, 1984

A.1 THE CONCEPT OF PROBABILITY

The bulk of this book deals with the evaluation of the likelihood, or probability, of consequences of choice. All such future consequences are viewed as uncertain. Moreover, there is empirical evidence that those of us who believe in the uncertainty of the future underestimate it. Thus an absolute essential of rational decision making is to deal constructively with this uncertainty. Irrationality is not constructive, or at least the conclusions that follow from it cannot be true of the world. Thus the bottom line is that likelihoods and probabilities must be assessed rationally.

Uncertainty is commonly expressed in terms of probabilities, or odds. The odds of an event equal the probability of its occurrence divided by one minus the probability, for example, a probability of 2 in 3 equals odds of 2 to 1, that is, $(2/3)/(1/3)$. A set of probabilities (or odds) is consistent if and only if it satisfies four broad algebraic rules. Otherwise, it is contradictory. These rules, which are quite simple, are formally termed the principles of probability, or of "probability theory." This appendix explains each of these principles and some of their many implications. The method of presentation is first to discuss probabilities relevant to each principle in the context of equally likely outcomes, most commonly illustrated by coin tosses and dice rolls, then to present the principles both algebraically and verbally, and finally to discuss them in more general contexts.

Because we evaluate and discuss uncertainty in terms of probabilities, it follows that our view of uncertainty is rational if and only if the probabilities we assign to possible events satisfy the four rules. If the rules are satisfied, our view of uncertainty is termed coherent; otherwise it is incoherent (read "irrational").

Before proceeding, however, four caveats are in order. First, our discussion of probability will be limited to numerical (or vaguely numerical) judgments about future events. For the decision maker, events in the past either have occurred—and thus are not uncertain—or have not occurred— in which case they cannot have probabilities assigned to them. We speak loosely, of course, of the probability of past events. For example, we might speak of the probability that Lee Harvey Oswald was the assassin of John F. Kennedy (or the lone assassin), the probability that a defendant actually committed a crime, or even the probability that a hypothetical coin has rolled off a table and landed heads up. For the purposes of this book, however, such statements about the probability of past events can be interpreted as the probability that we would reach certain conclusions were we to learn the truth, which of course is a possible future event. Sometimes, probabilities are interpreted as "degree of belief," or as objective frequencies over a large number of repetitions. Nevertheless, all students (and developers) of probability theory agree that the four basic rules must be satisfied. (In fact, as an abstract branch of mathematics, probabilities are defined as numbers that follow these rules, and concrete interpretations and other meanings assigned to probabilities are not considered.)

This appendix also considers beliefs about probabilities that order them or categorize them. Such beliefs, as well, may or may not reflect coherent judgment because such beliefs can in fact either satisfy or violate the principles. For example, the belief that the world's best tennis player is more likely to lose the first set of a championship match and win the match than he or she is to lose the first set alone contradicts the principles of probability theory—as does the belief that the probability of a disease given a symptom is necessarily equal to the probability of the symptom given the disease (a belief of equivalence with no specific number proposed).

Only sets of two or more probabilistic beliefs may be irrational (except for the trivial constraint that a probability less than zero or greater than one is irrational). Probabilities cannot be evaluated for rationality in isolation. For example, it is not necessarily irrational to believe that the sun will not rise tomorrow with probability .9. It would be irrational, however, to hold that belief and the belief that you will go to work tomorrow with probability .8 and the belief that you will go to work only if the sun rises— all simultaneously. (What is "simultaneous"? One explanation for irrationality in assessing probabilities—and in decision making in general—is that people fluctuate between different states of mind when viewing different parts of a problem and that conclusions reached in one state are not compared with those reached in another. The same concern has led economists to assume that preferences or the utilities underlying them are stable. Although technically it might not be correct to call someone whose values or expectations are fluctuating rapidly "irrational," it would not be sensible to call them rational or adaptive either.)

A.2 FROM GODS TO NUMBERS

How did probability theory begin? By evaluating gambles.

In Robert Graves's 1943 novel *I, Claudius*, Caligula and Claudius are playing dice prior to Caligula's assassination (and watching bloody games with just enough attention so that Caligula could order losers— and occasionally winners—to be put to death). The four dice they used (termed *astragali*) were made from ankle bones of dogs or sheep and had four faces, each with a different number: 1, 3, 4, 6. The winning throw is a "Venus roll," a roll in which four different numbers are face up. Claudius is winning—a possibly mortal situation for him given Caligula's outbursts of pathological anger. Fearful, Claudius hands Caligula beautiful new astragali that are loaded to yield Venus rolls. When Caligula wins back his money, he is especially delighted, because he interprets his success as a sign that the goddess Venus is favorably disposed toward him that day. In his euphoria, he fails to take the usual precautions departing from the games and is assassinated.

(Most of us now would regard Caligula as superstitious and silly. There is, however, the alternative interpretation. By giving Caligula loaded dice, Claudius deceived him into believing Venus was favorably disposed when in fact she wished him ill—as demonstrated by Caligula's earlier losses. Thus Claudius's deception made him partially responsible for the assassination and his own ascension to the throne.)

How would we determine the probability of a Venus roll? Consider the order of the astragali reading from left to right (from any perspective). The "1" may be in any of the four positions, the "3" in any of the remaining three, the "4" in any of the remaining two, and the "6" in a position then determined. Hence there are $4 \times 3 \times 2 \times 1 = 24$ possible ways of obtaining a Venus roll. The total number of possible rolls, however, is 4^4 (or 256), because any of the four numbers can occur in the first position, in the second, and so on. Thus we conclude that the probability of a Venus roll is 24 in 256, or approximately .094.

There is another way of reaching the same conclusion. Consider the four positions in sequence. Any number face up in the first position is compatible with a Venus roll. Given the number appearing in the first position, the number in the second can be any of the three remaining; the probability of that is 3 in 4. Given that the numbers in the first two positions are different, the number in the third position must be one of the two remaining; the probability of that is 2 in 4 = 1 in 2. Finally, if the numbers in the first three positions are all different, the probability that the number in the last position is the remaining one is 1/4. "Chaining" these probabilities yields $1 \times (3/4) \times (2/4) \times (1/4) = 6/64 = 24$ in 256, or approximately .094.

According to the historian Florence N. David (1972), belief that the outcome of games was due to the influence of gods or goddesses or of supernatural forces ("destiny") was common in the ancient Egyptian, Greek, and Roman civilizations. (And in its implicit form may still be common today among compulsive gamblers.) Moreover, different gambling outcomes were often associated with different gods. In fact, these beliefs about gambling apparently were one reason for its being outlawed by the Roman Catholic Church in the Middle Ages. A monotheistic God did not "play at dice"—and gambling was a catalyst to polytheism.

But some monotheists did appear to rely on gambling for guidance. The following excerpt is from the journal of John Wesley, the founder of Methodism, and refers to his decision to remain single:

> At length we agreed to appeal to the Searcher of Hearts. I accordingly made three lots. In one was writ "Marry." In the second "Think not

of it this year." After we had prayed to God to "give a perfect lot,"
Mr. Delamotte drew the third, in which were the words, "Think of it no
more." Instead of the agony I had reason to expect, I was enabled to say
cheerfully "Thy will be done." (March 4, 1737)

A counting approach to this procedure leads us to conclude that Wesley
had arranged for 2 to 1 odds mandating bachelorhood. His subsequent
lack of agony over the result is understandable.

Of course, not all ancient Greeks and Romans believed that gambling
outcomes were influenced by the gods. In Book 2 of *De Devinatione*, Cicero
wrote:

Nothing is so unpredictable as a throw of the dice [modern translation],
and yet every man who plays often will at some time or other make a
Venus-cast; now and then indeed he will make it twice and even thrice in
succession. Are we going to be so feeble-minded then as to aver that such
a thing happened by the personal intervention of Venus rather than by
pure luck?

Cicero believed luck determined the success of gambling with essentially random devices. He also apparently understood that there was a
relationship between the luck (odds) on a particular throw or set of throws
and long-term frequencies. But Cicero was later executed, illustrating that
rationality does not guarantee success but only increases its likelihood. In
fact, as pointed out earlier, opting for rationality when others do not can
lead to social ostracism.

The major modern development that was not foreseen by Cicero is
that of determining the odds by counting. And counting was possible
only after the development of arithmetic procedures that made complex
computation possible; despite the Greeks' skill in geometry and logic,
arithmetic was not developed in the Western world until the Renaissance.
Such counting was first systematically proposed by the Italian Geronimo
Cardano (1501-1576). Here is how counting leads to the principles of probability theory:

Tossing a coin results in one of two possible outcomes: heads (H) or tails (T).

Tossing a coin twice results in one of four possible outcomes: HH (two heads),
HT (a head followed by a tail), TH, or TT. (See Figures A.1 and A.2.)

Tossing a coin three times results in one of eight possible outcomes: HHH, HHT, HTH, HTT, THH, THT, TTH, or TTT.

And so on.

Outcome is a technical term in probability theory. It refers to a specific result of an experiment such as tossing a coin a certain number of times. An *event* is a collection of outcomes. This concept is crucial to probability theory, and the term event is used throughout this book, even when less stilted English would require another word. *Collection* in this definition does not necessarily mean more than one outcome; that is, an event may consist of a single outcome. Moreover, a collection may consist of all outcomes, that is, the event consisting of all outcomes is a well-defined one. It is symbolized *S*.

Tossing a coin twice results in one of a number of possible events. For example:

A. The event two heads consists of the single outcome HH. (It is equivalent to the event *no tails.*)

B. The event exactly one head consists of the outcomes HT and TH. (It is equivalent to the event *exactly one tail.*)

C. The event at least one head consists of the outcomes HH, HT, and TH. (It is equivalent to the events *at most one tail* and *not two tails.*)

And so on.

In fact, there are 15 (= $2^4 - 1$) events consisting of at least one outcome:

Events consisting of a single outcome

HH

HT

TH

TT

Events consisting of pairs of outcomes

HH, HT

HH, TH

HH, TT

SECOND TOSS

	H	T
H	HH	HT
T	TH	TT

FIRST TOSS

FIGURE A.1. Table Illustrating Possible Outcomes of Two Coin Tosses

HT, TH

HT, TT

TH, TT

Events consisting of triples of outcomes

HH, HT, TH

HH, HT, TT

HH, TH, TT

HT, TH, TT

And the event consisting of all four outcomes

HH, HT, TH, TT

A verbal description may be given to each event. (Try it.)

Note that as a result of tossing a coin twice there are four possible outcomes and 15 possible events consisting of one or more outcomes. Actually, mathematicians define 16 possible events because, for the sake of completeness, they also consider the event consisting of no outcomes. It is termed the null event ("nothing happened"), and it is symbolized Ø.

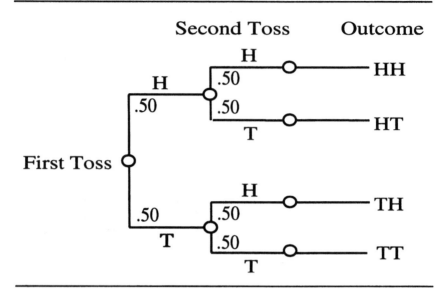

FIGURE A.2. "Tree Diagram" of Possible Outcomes of Two Coin Tosses

Is the null event nothing but the (null) result of an obsessive-compulsive frame of mind? No. The concept of the null event has had the same salutary effect on the development of probability theory that the concept of zero had on the development of our number system. (The concept zero was not introduced into computation in Western culture until about A.D. 900. Prior to that there was one Roman symbol for ten (X), another for twenty (XX), and so on, with the result that it was much more difficult to add and subtract than it is using zeros. For example, X + XXX = XL, rather than 10 + 30 = 40, which is obtained in part by adding 0 to 0 to obtain 0.)

Let's illustrate how probabilities are assigned to events by considering equally likely outcomes and then generalize to other events. Consider two tosses of a fair coin. By fair, we mean that both the following are true:

1. Heads or tails are equally likely on each toss.

2. There is no relationship between the results of successive tosses.

Fairness resides in both the coin and the coin tosser. The first condition states that the coin has no bias and that the coin tosser cannot or does not control the outcome. The second condition states that the coin "has no memory" and once again that the coin tosser cannot or does not control it. (Many "subjectivist" statisticians allege that fairness resides in the beliefs of the observer that the coin and coin tosser satisfy these conditions.) Under these conditions, there are four equally likely outcomes: HH, HT, TH, and TT.

The probability of an event when outcomes are equally likely is equal to the number of outcomes in the event divided by the number of possible outcomes. The number of outcomes is four when a coin is tossed twice.

A. The event two heads consists of only the outcome HH; therefore its probability is 1/4.

B. The event exactly one head consists of the outcomes HT and TH; therefore its probability is $(1 + 1)/4 = 1/2$.

C. The event at least one head consists of the outcomes HH, HT, and TH; therefore its probability is $(1 + 1 + 1)/4 = 3/4$.

And so on.

Following standard notation, events are symbolized by capital letters and their probability by p. For example, if A is the event *all heads* or *all tails*, it consists of the outcomes HH and TT; hence

$$p(A) = (1 + 1)/4 = 1/2.$$

A.3   THE PRINCIPLES OF PROBABILITY THEORY

It should be clear now that probabilities are numbers between 0 and 1. Moreover, $p(\emptyset) = 0$, because there are no outcomes in the null set. Thus the following principles are true for probabilities assigned to events consisting of equally likely outcomes:

Principle I: $0 \le p(A) \le 1$

Principle IIa: $p(S) = 1$

Principle IIb: $p(\emptyset) = 0$

Events can also be combined. The event {A and B}, termed their *intersection* or *conjunction*, consists of all outcomes common to both. For example, the event *at least one head* consists of the outcomes HH, HT, and TH, whereas the event *at least one tail* consists of the outcomes HT, TH, and TT. Thus the event *at least one head and at least one tail* consists of the outcomes HT and TH. (Note that this event is equivalent to the event *one head and one tail*.) Such an event is termed a *compound event* and the probability of such an event is termed a *compound probability*. (Note that any one event may be considered to be a compound event; for starters, each event is equivalent to the intersection of itself and S.)

Another type of combination involves outcomes in either of two events. The event {A or B}, termed their *union* or *disjunction*, consists of all the outcomes in either. (Any overlapping outcomes are included; logically *or* means "in either singly or in both.") For example, the event *at least one head* consists of the outcomes HH, HT, and TH, whereas the event *at least one tail* consists of the outcomes HT, TH, and TT. The event *at least one head or at least one tail* consists of HH, HT, TH, and TT, that is, it is S (because there must be at least one head or at least one tail in any "experiment" or toss).

In these examples, the two events of the intersection or union were partially overlapping. That need not be so, as was indicated, for example, by taking the intersection of an event with S or its union with Ø. We may take the intersection or union of totally disjoint events—those that have no outcomes in common. Or one event may be a distinct part of another— all the outcomes making up the first are in the second as well or the events are identical. An event is a set of outcomes. Linking any two events by *and* or *or* defines a new set of outcomes, an event.

When two events have no outcome in common, they are mutually exclusive. For example, the event *two tails* and the event *at least one head* are mutually exclusive.

Mathematicians and statisticians make use of the null set to express the fact that two events are mutually exclusive—that is, they have no outcomes in common. Briefly, when two events {A and B} are mutually exclusive, the compound event consisting of their intersection is the null set (is devoid of outcomes). Thus {A and B} are mutually exclusive whenever

$$\{A \text{ and } B\} = \varnothing,$$

which by Principle II means that

$$p(A \text{ and } B) = 0.$$

Again, consider tossing a fair coin twice. Let A be the event *two tails* and B be the event exactly one head. These events are mutually exclusive, the first consisting of the outcome TT and the second of the outcomes HT and TH. Moreover, the probability of A is $1/4$ whereas that of B is $2/4 = 1/2$. The probability of {A or B} is $3/4$, because there are three outcomes in A or B, namely TT, HT, and TH. Thus $p(A \text{ or } B) = p(A) + p(B)$.

Whenever any two events A and B are mutually exclusive, the number of outcomes in {A or B} must equal the sum of the number of outcomes in each. If there are n equally likely outcomes in S, m in A and m' in B, then if A and B are mutually exclusive,

$$p(A \text{ or } B) = \frac{m+m'}{n} = \frac{m}{n} + \frac{m'}{n}$$

$$= p(A) + p(B).$$

This observation yields a third general principle of probability theory:

Principle III: If {A and B} = $\varnothing$ (equivalently, $p[A \text{ and } B] = 0$),
    then $p(A \text{ or } B) = p(A) + p(B)$.

Does this principle work backward? That is, if $p(A \text{ or } B) = p(A) + p(B)$, does it necessarily follow that {A and B} = $\varnothing$? This question may be answered by noting that if A and B have at least one outcome in common, $p(A \text{ or } B)$ is less than $p(A) + p(B)$. So, the answer is yes.

The introduction of two more concepts completes this sketch of probability theory. The first is that of the *complement* of an event. The complement of an event A consists of all the outcomes in S that are not in A. The complement of A is often symbolized $-A$ or $\overline{A}$. For example, consider a coin tossed twice:

If A is the event *two heads* (consisting of HH), the complement of A is the event consisting of HT, TH, and TT—the event *at least one tail*.

If A is the event *exactly one head* (consisting of HT and TH), then the complement of A is the event consisting of HH and TT—the event *all heads or all tails*.

If A is the event *at least one head*, then $\overline{A}$ is the event *all tails*.

And so on.

Relationship I: If $\overline{A}$ is the complement of A, then $p(\overline{A}) + p(A) = 1$.

This relationship is established by noting that A and $\overline{A}$ are mutually exclusive; hence by Principle III, $p(A \text{ or } \overline{A}) = p(A) + p(\overline{A})$. But $(A \text{ or } \overline{A})$ is equal to S, because $\overline{A}$ by definition consists of all those outcomes in S not in A. Therefore $p(A) + p(\overline{A}) = p(S)$, which equals 1 by Principle IIa.

Note that Principle IIb, $p(\emptyset) = 0$, was not used in establishing Relationship I; it was established entirely from Principles IIa and III. In fact, Principle IIb itself can be shown to follow from Principles IIa and III via Relationship 1. For since $\emptyset$ is the complement of S, $p(\emptyset) + p(S) = 1$; but since $p(S) = 1$ from Principle IIa, it follows that $p(\emptyset) = 0$ (This is a rigorous proof that the probability of nothing is nothing—zero.)

Finally, it should be noted that the implication in Relationship I cannot be reversed, unlike that in Principle III. It does not follow that if the sum of the probabilities of two events is 1, they are complements of each other. For example, the event *exactly one head* resulting from two coin tosses has probability 1/2 when outcomes are equally likely, as does the event *exactly one tail*. But the probability of *exactly one head or exactly one tail* does not equal 1 (i.e., 1/2 + 1/2); they are not complementary events. In fact, they are identical, both consisting of the outcomes HT and TH.

The final concept is that of *conditional probability*. The essential idea is that the probability of an event A is assessed differently conditional on knowledge of whether another event has or has not occurred. For example, if the events A and B are mutually exclusive, then an outcome in A cannot be in B; thus the probability of A given B's occurrence is 0. At the other extreme, if all the outcomes in B are also in A, then the probability of A given B is 1.

The conditional probability of A given B is symbolized $p(A \mid B)$; it can be expressed verbally in a variety of ways:

1. The probability of A *conditional on B's occurrence*
2. The probability of A *conditional on B*
3. The probability of A *given B*
4. The probability of A *if B occurs*

If outcomes are equally likely, the probability of A *given B* is equal to the number of outcomes in both events (their intersection) divided by the number of outcomes in B. In effect, having been "given" B, we know that the actual outcome must be selected from it, and the probability that an outcome from A occurs is therefore equal to the relative number of outcomes in B that are also in A. The event B now defines the number of possible outcomes; it has, in effect, replaced S.

Let m' be the number of outcomes in {A and B} (i.e., their intersection), and let m be the number of outcomes in B. Then, given equally likely outcomes,

$$p(A/B) = m'/m.$$

Now divide the numerator and denominator of the fraction m'/m by n to obtain

$$p(A/B) = \frac{m'/n}{m/n}$$

But since $p(A \text{ and } B) = m'/n$ whereas $p(B) = m/n$, we conclude

Principle IV: $p(A|B) = \dfrac{p(A \text{ and } B)}{p(B)}$

This principle constitutes the formal definition of conditional probability.

Now let's look at some examples of conditional probabilities resulting from tossing a fair coin twice. The probability of the event two heads given the event at least one head is 1/3 (HH is the only outcome in the event *two heads*, whereas the event *at least one head* consists of the outcomes HH, HT, and TH). Occasionally, this probability is mistakenly believed to be 1/2 rather than 1/3; for example, some people think the probability of a two-child family having two daughters when at least one child is a daughter is 1/2.

In contrast, probability of the event two heads given the event the first toss is a head is 1/2. The common event is again HH, but here the event that is given has only the two outcomes HH and HT. The probability that a two-child family consists of two daughters when the first is a daughter is 1/2, because boys (B) and girls (G) have (roughly) equal probabilities of being born. In contrast, there are three ways to have *at least one girl*: GG, GB, BG; in only one of these (GG) is the other child a girl. Again, the probability of two girls given at least one girl is 1/3, not 1/2.

Principle IV may be reformulated by "multiplying through" by $p(B)$. That is,

$$p(A|B)p(B) = p(A \text{ and } B), \text{ or}$$

Principle IV': $p(A \text{ and } B) = p(A|B)p(B)$.

When expressed in the manner of Principle IV', the conditional probability definition constitutes a *chaining principle* for obtaining the probability of compound events. (Remember the Venus roll example.) For example, the probability that both coin tosses are heads (the event *both heads*) is equal to the probability that the first one is a head multiplied by the probability that the second one is a head given the first one is a head. The reader should verify that both these latter probabilities are 1/2, so that the desired probability of the compound event is 1/4. The probability of drawing two spades randomly without replacement from a deck of cards is equal to the probability that the first draw is a spade (13/52, because there are 52 cards in the deck, 13 of which are spades) multiplied by the probability that the second is a spade given the first is a spade (12/51, because there are 51 cards left of which 12 are spades). The desired probability of this compound event is $(13/52)(12/51) = 3/51$. We could also derive this probability by dividing the number of pairs of spades (78) by the number of pairs of cards (1346), again obtaining 3/51.

Chaining may take place in either direction; $p(A \text{ and } B)$ equals both $p(A \mid B)p(B)$ and $p(B \mid A)p(A)$. Sometimes it is more convenient to chain in one direction than in the other, such as when there is a natural sequence from earlier to later in time.

Finally, *independence* between events can now be defined. The intuitive definition is that A and B are independent if $p(A \mid B) = p(A)$. Accepting this definition, we can multiply both sides by $p(B)$ to obtain

$$p(A \text{ and } B) = p(A)p(B)$$

since $p(A \mid B)p(B) = p(A \text{ and } B)$ by Principle IV'. Moreover, dividing by $p(A)$, we can infer that $p(B \mid A) = p(B)$; hence independence is symmetric. The definition that $p(A \text{ and } B) = p(A)p(B)$ is the one used by mathematicians, because the concept should also be valid if $p(A)$ or $p(B)$ equals 0, in which case division and multiplication would be inappropriate.

Probability theory is now applied in contexts much broader than gambling games. For example, the designs of dikes and dams are based on estimates of the probability that rivers will reach certain flood levels. Engineers clearly don't believe that all flood levels are equally likely, but rather have reference to the frequencies with which certain water levels have occurred in the past. We also may speak of the probability that the Chicago Cubs will defeat the Chicago White Sox in the World Series or the probability of an atomic holocaust prior to the year 3000. In such cases, there is no relative frequency to use, but rather an estimate based on knowledge of baseball, politics, technology—or perhaps on our level of pessimism. When there are neither equally likely outcomes nor frequencies on which to rely, probabilities are often related to "fair" betting odds. For example, if you believe that the probability is 1/3 that the Cubs defeat the White Sox, you should be barely willing to bet $2 on the White Sox against $1 on the Cubs; that is, you should be willing to accept all bets in which you must bet less than $2 to $1 and reject all those in which you must bet more than $2 to $1. That's an assessment of your personal probabilistic belief, and in fact a school of philosophers of probability known as personalists or subjectivists have argued that all probability is ultimately based on personal belief and willingness to bet. (Isn't the fundamental assertion that all elementary outcomes are "equally likely" in a probability analysis one of belief?)

Actually, there has been considerable debate throughout the centuries over whether probability statements refer to facts, individual beliefs about the world, or logical relationships between evidence and belief—or between different beliefs. It is not clear how important this debate is to probabilistic reasoning, but it is clear that people with different understandings about the meaning of the term probability reach the same conclusions about particular probabilities. For example, consider an experiment in which one of two dice is drawn at random from a bag. One of them has four green and two red faces and the other has four red and two green faces. Without examining the die drawn, the experimenter rolls it. What is the probability of a red face showing as a result? All agree it is 1/2. And all agree that the reason is that the probability of drawing each particular die is 1/2.

Some people argue that this latter conclusion follows because we have no reason to believe that we have drawn one particular die or the other; some argue that 1/2 reflects their belief that each die is equally likely; some argue that the concept of "randomness" logically entails a probability of 1/2 that we have drawn either; and still others argue that the equal probability of drawing either is based on a hypothesis about an objective fact whose validity could be assessed by repeated draws. It is even possible to argue that the "real" probability of drawing whichever is actually drawn is l, because nothing ever really occurs at random in the world, but that in our ignorance of all the factors involved and their interaction we must opt for 1/2. All conclude, however, that the probability of drawing either die is 1/2. Then the probability that a red face shows is the sum of the probabilities that the predominantly red-faced die is drawn and that a red face shows, plus the probability that the predominantly green-faced die is drawn and that a red face shows (by Principle III). The first probability is $(1/2) \times (2/3)$, and the second is $(1/2) \times (1/3)$, both by Principle IV'. Hence the probability of a red face is $2/6 + 1/6 = 1/2$. Agreed.

So what, in general, is a probability? First, probabilities refer to numbers assigned to well-defined events. A "well-defined event" is one that can be unambiguously interpreted as occurring or not occurring in the future. Second, probabilities must satisfy the four basic principles, reiterated here:

I. $0 \le p(A) \le 1$

II. $p(S) = 1$

III. If the intersection $(A \text{ and } B) = 0$, then $p(A \text{ or } B) = p(A) + p(B)$

IV. $p(A \mid B) = p(A \text{ and } B)/p(B)$

Without demeaning the philosophers who attempt to find an additional meaning for "probability," we can accept the structural, formal meaning of probability as numbers that satisfy these four principles. For purposes of this book, we have added the additional condition that events shall be in the future.

Note that a single probability cannot violate the principles unless it falls outside the interval between 0 and 1. Thus probabilities refer to sets of numbers describing relationships between sets of events. Of course, people may assert probabilities that violate the principles and insist that they are discussing "probabilities" in the usual sense of the term. But rational or coherent probabilities must satisfy the principles, and this is the only type of probability a mathematician or statistician would accept.

A.4 BELIEFS THAT VIOLATE THE PRINCIPLES OF PROBABILITY THEORY

What is an example of a common "probabilistic" belief that violates these principles? Consider these sequences of events:

1. A star athlete becomes a drug addict, enters a treatment program, and wins a championship.

2. A star athlete becomes a drug addict and wins a championship.

When one or another such sequence of events is presented to people, many judge the first to be more probable than the second. But by the principles of probability it cannot be. To understand why, break the sequences into their constituent events:

A. The athlete becomes an addict.

B. The athlete becomes a champion.

C. The athlete enters a treatment program.

(It is not necessary to label events in the order in which they occur in time.) Now the belief is that:

$$p(A \text{ and } B \text{ and } C) > p(A \text{ and } B).$$

But that is not rational or not coherent according to the principles, which we can demonstrate in two ways.

First demonstration: By the chaining principle (IV') and because the intersection *(A and B)* is just another event, it follows that

$$p(A \text{ and } B \text{ and } C) = p(C \mid A \text{ and } B)p(A \text{ and } B).$$

But since $p[C \mid (A \text{ and } B)] \leq 1$ by Principle I,

$$p(A \text{ and } B \text{ and } C) \leq p(A \text{ and } B),$$

which is a logical contradiction, proving that the original assertion is invalid.

Second demonstration: (A and B) = (A and B and C) joined with *(A and B and C̄)*. But *(A and B and C)* and *(A and B and C̄)* are mutually exclusive. Therefore by Principle III,

$$p(A \text{ and } B) = p(A \text{ and } B \text{ and } C) + p(A \text{ and } B \text{ and } \overline{C}),$$

which means *p(A and B)* must be greater than or equal to the first term—another contradiction. The point is that the athlete could have won the championship by some route other than entering a treatment program. The athlete could have quit drugs for other reasons, the athlete could have been so extremely talented and lucky that it didn't matter, the championship could have been rigged, and so on.

The belief that the likelihood of an unlikely event or combination of events is enhanced by adding plausible additional events to it is termed the scenario effect; such effects have been extensively investigated by Amos Tversky and Daniel Kahneman (1984, see Sections 6.1 and 7.2 in this book). These added events can yield a "good story," even though they in fact restrict the number of possibilities that can lead to the original event or combination. For example, when anthropologists reconstruct from a few bones the nature of a particular prehistoric culture, their reconstructions often seem more believable when they supply details about which they couldn't possibly have any knowledge. And we all know that telling people only known facts is not as persuasive as embellishing our story (e.g., in courtroom summations). It is well documented by cognitive psychologists that the scenario effect results in irrational probability judgments (see Chapters 6 and 7).

Here are two probabilistic beliefs that are wrong but not irrational. Their combination, however, is irrational.

> *The gambler's fallacy:* The more often a coin falls heads (tails), the more likely it will be to fall tails (heads) on the next toss. Thus HT is more likely than HH, HHT is more likely than HHH, and so on. (As noted earlier, such a belief would be correct only if the coin had a memory or if the person tossing it can control it.)

This fallacy occurs in contexts other than coin tossing. Consider the example in the letter to "Dear Abby" reprinted in Section 8.2: "My husband and I just had our eighth child. Another girl, and I am really one disappointed woman. . . . Abby, this one was supposed to have been a boy."

The probability of bearing eight consecutive daughters is (roughly) $1/2^8 = 1/256$. But the probability of bearing a daughter after seven other daughters have been born is about $1/2$. Like coins, sperm have no memories, especially not for past conceptions of which they know nothing. The principle is the same as that in the solution to the game of *balla* referred to in Section 2.6.

> *Distributing ignorance equally across verbally defined categories* (rather than across concrete, equally likely outcomes): Since a coin tossed twice can yield 0, 1, or 2 heads, this pseudo-principle states that each such result occurs with the probability $1/3$.

Suppose that someone believes both in the gambler's fallacy and in distributing ignorance. By the gambler's fallacy,

$$p(HT) \geq p(HH).$$

But by the distribution of ignorance fallacy,

$$p(HH) = 1/3.$$

Therefore, $p(HT) \geq 1/3$, and by a similar argument, $p(TH) \geq 1/3$. Hence their sum is greater than or equal to $2/3$, but their sum must simultaneously equal $1/3$ by the distribution of ignorance fallacy (i.e., "a coin tossed twice can yield 0, 1, or 2 heads").

Such combinations of belief are irrational. Yet people hold them. Choices based on such incoherent probabilistic assessments must themselves be incoherent—and may lead to personal and social harm. The inverse conclusion, that probabilities satisfying Principles I to IV cannot lead to a contradiction, is also true, but proving it lies beyond the scope of this book.

A.5 BAYES' THEOREM

The foundation of Bayesian analyses are far beyond the scope of this book. But we can discuss a simplified example to demonstrate the reasoning involved. The reader should not infer, however, that Bayesian analysis is in any sense vague.

Let's suppose that we have two bookbags containing black and red poker chips. Bookbag A contains 70% red poker chips, and Bookbag B contains 40% red poker chips. Someone rolls a die. If it comes up 1 or 2, he hands us Bookbag B; otherwise he hands us Bookbag A. We are not allowed to observe the outcome of the roll of the die. But we are allowed to sample 10 poker chips from the bag presented. After each observation, we are required to replace the poker chip before drawing again. Our task is to make a probabilistic inference about which bag we are sampling from.

Suppose that we draw 6 black chips and 4 red ones. That would certainly be more "representative" of Boookbag B than of Bookbag A, but on the other hand, we know that as the result of the roll of the die, it is twice as likely that we have been handed Bookbag A. How can we combine the evidence from our sample with our prior belief based on the roll of the die?

One way is to use Bayes' theorem, commonly attributed to the Reverend Thomas Bayes, to derive the probability of having selected a particular bag given the evidence observed. Apparently, Bayes discovered the principle in his quest for a rational method to evaluate the manifest evidence for the existence of God (a Christian God, we suppose). But he was unconfident enough in his derivation that his discovery was communicated only to a friend who published it after Bayes's death in 1761.

Let d stand for the data we have collected—6 blacks and 4 reds. Let A and B refer to the two bookbags. It is easy enough to determine the conditional probability of the data given that we are sampling from either Bookbag A or Bookbag B. We can then calculate the conditional probability that we are sampling from one of the bags given the data if we know both the probability we are sampling from that bag at the outset (which we do) and the probability of obtaining the data, which can be computed. We can illustrate the derivation of Bayes' theorem to compute the specific probability that Bookbag A has been selected given the data we have observed; specifically,

$$p(A \text{ and } d) = p(d \text{ and } A).$$

From the fourth principle of probability, we can infer

$$p(A|d)p(d) = p(d|A)p(A), \text{ or}$$

$$p(A|d) = \frac{p(d|A)p(A)}{p(d)}.$$

Actually, it is simpler to use the ratio rule presented in Section 6.3. To recapitulate in this context:

$$\frac{p(A|d)}{p(d|A)} = \frac{p(A)}{p(d)}.$$

Similarly,

$$\frac{p(B|d)}{p(d|B)} = \frac{p(B)}{p(d)}.$$

Dividing, we obtain

$$\frac{p(A|d)}{p(B|d)} = \frac{p(A)p(d|A)}{p(B)p(d|B)}.$$

As a result of division, we eliminated the troublesome term $p(d)$; our result, in the last equation, is the ratio of $p(A|d)$ divided by $p(B|d)$. Knowing this ratio and that the sum of the two probabilities must equal 1 (we are sampling from just one bag, so, by Principle III, the probabilities sum to 1), we can easily compute both.

In the example, $p(A) = 2/3$, and the probability of obtaining the sample of 6 blacks and 4 reds in the particular order we drew them *given we are drawing from Bag A* is $.3^6 \times .7^4$. Similarly, $p(B) = 1/3$ and the probability of getting the sample in that same order *given we are drawing from Bag B* is $.6^6 \times .4^4$. Thus $p(A|d)$ divided by $p(B|d) = .0001167/.0003981$, or .29. Hence the probability we are drawing from Bag A is .22, and from Bag B, .78. Note that the evidence in this hypothetical experiment has strongly outweighed the *prior odds* of 2:1 that we were drawing chips from Bag A.

In general, Bayesian analysis consists of specifying prior beliefs, by which we mean beliefs that exist prior to the time we sample. In the example, the roll of the die leads to such prior beliefs. Evidence sampled is then combined with prior beliefs according to Bayes' theorem, and they are updated by the rules of probability theory.

A.6 THE POST HOC ANALYSIS OF COINCIDENCE

Everyday life is full of coincidences. Robyn Dawes's older daughter was born on the same day of the year that his mother died, and his younger daughter was born on the same day of the year that his mother was born.

What a remarkable coincidence! A naive analyst might conclude that the probability of that was $(1/365)^2$, or .0000075. But of course, the coincidence could have been reversed, and it would be equally remarkable—so perhaps a more appropriate figure is .000015. And of course, they both could have been born on the same day of the year their grandmother was or both born on the same day of the year she died, so perhaps that figure should be doubled to yield .00003. Then again, the older daughter has visual artistic talent and the younger one writes short stories, and their birthdays could, of course, be the same as those of well-known persons in those respective fields. And then there are the birthdays of people we all know of such as George Washington, Abraham Lincoln, Grover Cleveland, Jack Kennedy—not to mention Omar Khayyám, Mahatma Gandhi, Bertrand Russell, and whoever it was that wrote Ecclesiastes. The point is that we could go on and on; although in retrospect a particular coincidence—such as common birthdays—may appear to be very improbable, it is also very probable that many coincidences will occur.

To understand this principle, consider the probability of death. We will make the simplifying assumption that it is equally probable each day. Then, given a life expectancy of 70 years (25,568 days), the probability of dying on a particular day is .00004, but the probability of dying on *some* day is 1.00. Or consider another example: let's select totally at random a number between 1 and 10,000; the probability that any particular number is chosen is .0001; yet the probability that some number is chosen is, again, 1.00. Interestingly, some philosophers in the 18th century, when probability theory was being developed, equated a probability of .9999 with a "moral certainty." In the death example, that would imply that it is morally certain that we will live through every next day.

These first two paragraphs of this section are meant to illustrate an important principle: Although the probability that a particular event will occur may be close to 0, the probability that nothing at all will happen is exactly 0.

How do we decide, therefore, whether a coincidence is really evidence of ESP? Or whether the finding in a particular study of helping behavior in a subway that tall people are more helpful than short people indicates that there is a correlation between height and altruism? Or whether the fact that between 1900 and 1968, inclusive, the taller candidate always won the presidency indicates that American voters prefer taller men?

The answer to such questions is not easy, but a simplified example might help. Consider, again, drawing a number at random from the numbers 1 through 10,000. If a friend who claims to have ESP says in advance that you will sample the number 973 and you do, you are impressed. If, on the other hand, the friend asks you to draw a number and explains its extrasensory significance after you have announced it is 973, you are not the least bit impressed. It's the same number. Your awe or lack of it is determined by the procedures leading to the claim that 973 has some special significance—specifically the decision-making procedures employed by the friend and consequently by you. By announcing the number in advance, he or she would have led you to consider only the number 973 as a "success." You can specify that decision prior to drawing the number. When the significance is explained to you after the number is drawn, however, you are sufficiently leery of your friend to realize that there are a great many such numbers to which he or she could ascribe some "significance." This principle is illustrated in Figure A.3. The figure presents 16 patterns of heads and tails that can result from six tosses of coin to which some significance could be ascribed post hoc (all heads, all tails, alternation, alternation by pairs, mirror images, etc.). Once the coin has been tossed six times, however, the probability of one of these uniquely interesting patterns occurring is not 1/64 but, rather, 16/64.

Do people make such post hoc judgments? And do people believe such patterns are significant not only in the everyday sense of that word but in the technical, statistical sense as well? Consider the remarks of an astrologer encountered by one of us (Dawes):

> Isn't it remarkable. Among the five of us here there are three Leos and two Cancers, and President Jerry Ford is a Cancer, which makes three Leos and three Cancers. I bet the probability of that is almost zero. Is that the sort of thing you people could figure out?

One method of inflating the apparent significance of such events is the "optional ending point" maneuver described in detail by the statistician (and professional magician) Persi Diaconis (1978). This technique, used by many psychics, involves keeping the naive observer in the dark about exactly what is to be accomplished until it is done. For example, the psychic B.D., whom Diaconis analyzed in some detail, would ask a volunteer to name two cards and then ask two other volunteers to pick small numbers "at random." He would then place two shuffled decks of cards on a table and start turning over the cards in each deck one by one until he reached the larger of the two numbers selected. Of course, if the two cards happened to appear before he turned over the larger of the two numbers, it was a "successful demonstration." If both cards appeared simultaneously, it was clearly a success. If one of the cards named appeared with the larger number, the demonstration was considered a success also. If nothing "unusual" happened, then the cards of one deck were turned over one by one until the smaller of the two numbers selected was reached. By that time, all sorts of outcomes could have occurred. And so on and so on. The "optional stopping trick" is not to tell people in advance how you will manifest your psychic powers. The probability of a coincidence then becomes remarkably large. It helps also to proclaim, as psychic Uri Geller does, that your powers come and go for reasons that are inexplicable to you or that interference is created by skeptical test procedures. Then not finding some striking coincidence in a number of attempts—or even in half of your attempts—is readily understood by the observers.

Would scientists engage in such nonsense? Unfortunately, the answer is yes. (Some analysts have even speculated that scientists, with their capacity to entertain as yet unproven hypotheses, may be especially susceptible to belief in ESP or quasi-sensory communication.) A recent president of the American Psychological Association gave as his presidential address a talk on "torque and schizophrenic viability." In it, he presented some absolutely striking data. Of 52 children who had seen him 10 years earlier who drew circles clockwise, 11 were later diagnosed as schizophrenic; of the 54 who drew circles counterclockwise, only 1 had been diagnosed schizophrenic. This relationship reached the ".01 level of statistical significance." He related his finding to the fact that "the world turns in a counterclockwise direction with respect to the north-south axis" and that "with some exceptions, this 'left-turning' is characteristic of living cells."

Certainly, a finding of this magnitude—particularly when it related to fundamental properties of the earth and of the very unit of life—should have set the psychological world on its ear. At the least, it might have contributed to our understanding of schizophrenia, which is one of the two major mental health problems in this country (along with depression). The average citations by other scientists to that article hovered around three per year in the subsequent 8 years, until it vanished from the charts. Why so few citations? Perhaps the researcher will be neglected for 50

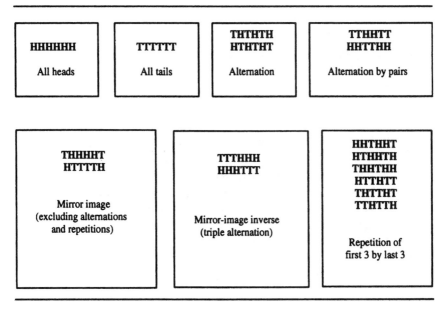

FIGURE A.3. Sixteen Apparent Patterns That Can Occur in Six Random
Tosses of a Coin

years only to be rediscovered as the founder of a modern theory of schizo-phrenia? We think that a more likely explanation is found in part of his talk: "Subjects for this study were 155 children first seen for psychological evaluation at my private psychological clinic." Children seen for such evaluations are given many tests, each of which can be evaluated on a multiplicity of variables. The researcher reported his findings on only one of these in his presidential address. An educated guess is that was 1 out of approximately 200 that he could have easily related to later diagnoses of schizophrenia. (It is important to what follows to note that this guess is based on knowledge of clinical practice, not on the plausibility that he looked at many. But imagine a scenario in which a child enters a psycholo-gist's office, is asked to draw a circle, and is then told to go away.)

How does one evaluate whether one of these very unusual findings might be important? The best answer, of course, is to determine whether it can be repeated. Attempts to replicate such "psychic power" findings have had a dismal history. Absent the possibility of prediction, control, and replication, the best approach is to specify precisely the hypothesis of interest in advance, to specify the conceptual sample space of possible relevant events, and then to systematically collect data, even anecdotes to describe the *entire space* of possible outcomes. Persi Diaconis and Fred Mosteller (1989) have outlined such a strategy and illustrate it with an application to the common experience of encountering coincidental "clusters" of newly learned words in everyday life.

If we look hard enough we're bound to find something; after all, the probability that exactly nothing will happen is indeed exactly zero. And as Diaconis and Mosteller note, "When enormous numbers of events and people and their interactions cumulate over time, almost any outrageous event is bound to occur" (1989, p. 853). Both classical and Bayesian analyses of statistical significance and informativeness are addressed to questions *asked beforehand*. In evaluating research findings to reach rational decisions, it is crucial to determine whether they were hypothesized in advance or simply picked out post hoc—from the imagination of the person purporting to have discovered them.

REFERENCES

David, F. N. (1972). *Games, gods, and gambling: The origins and history of probability and statistical ideas from the earliest times to the Newtonian era.* New York: Hafner.

Diaconis, P. (1978). Statistical problems in ESP research. *Science, 201,* 131-136.

Diaconis, P., & Mosteller, F. (1989). Methods for studying coincidences. *Journal of the American Statistical Association, 84,* 853-861.

Graves, R. (1943). *I, Claudius.* New York: Penguin.

INDEX

ABOUT THE AUTHORS

REID HASTIE is Professor of Psychology and Director of the Center for Research on Judgment and Policy at the University of Colorado. He holds degrees from Stanford University (1968), the University of California at San Diego (1970), and Yale University (1973) in psychology. Previously, he taught at Harvard University and Northwestern University. He has served on review panels for the National Science Foundation, the National Institute of Mental Health, the National Research Council; and on 14 professional journal editorial boards. His research has been funded continuously by the National Science Foundation and the National Institutes of Health since 1975.

His primary research interests are in the areas of judgment and decision making (managerial, legal, medical, engineering, and personal), memory and cognition, and social psychology. He has published over 100 articles in scientific journals on these topics. He is best known for his research on legal decision making (*Social Psychology in Court* [with Michael Saks]; *Inside the Jury* [with Steven Penrod and Nancy Pennington]; *Inside the Juror* [edited]; and *Punitive Damages: How Juries Decide* [forthcoming, multiple authors]) and on social memory and judgment processes (*Person Memory: The Cognitive Basis of Social Perception* [several co-authors]). He is currently studying the psychology of investment decisions; the role of explanations in category concept representations (including the effects on category classification, deductive, and inductive inferences); civil jury decision making (punitive damages and sexual harassment); the primitive sources of confidence and probability judgments; decision making competencies across the adult life span; and neural substrates of risky decisions.

ROBYN M. DAWES is the Charles J. Queenan, Jr., University Professor of Psychology at Carnegie Mellon. After 2 years as a philosophy major at

Harvard (BA 1958), Dawes fled that field to enter clinical psychology at Michigan. After 2 years in clinical psychology, he fled that field to enter mathematical psychology—with a content interest in behavioral decision making, social interaction, and attitude measurement (PhD 1963)—and graduate training in mathematics (to substitute for his linguistic incompetence that made passing the second foreign language requirement an impossibility). He hung around Ann Arbor for 5 years as a research psychologist at the local VA hospital and a member of the university psychology department while his first wife completed her PhD, and then he moved as Associate Professor to Oregon in 1967, where he became Professor in 1971 and served 6 years as a department head (acting, 1972-1973, 1979-1980; regular, 1981-1985). He also worked part-time at the Oregon Research Institute, where he was Vice President in 1973-1974 and fired for insubordination. He moved to Carnegie Mellon University in the fall of 1985, as Professor of Psychology and Chair of the Department of Social and Decision Sciences. He served as that department's head for 5 years and also as acting department head for a 1-year term in 1996.

Dawes is the author of over 150 articles and 5 books, including *House of Cards: Psychology and Psychotherapy Built on Myth*, 1994; *Rational Choice in an Uncertain World*, 1988, recipient of the William James Award, Division of General Psychology of the American Psychological Association; and most recently, *Irrationality: How Pseudoscientists, Lunatics, and the Rest of Us Systematically Fail to Be Rational*. He has served as president of the Oregon Psychological Association, president of the Society for Judgment and Decision Making Research, member of the American Psychological Association's national Ethics Committee, and executive board member of Society for Judgment and Decision Making, the Society for the Advancement of Socio-Economics, and the American Association of Applied and Preventive Psychology. In addition, he has served on the National Research Council's AIDS Research and the Behavioral, Social and Statistical Sciences Committee and has contributed to its reports: *AIDS, Sexual Behavior, and Intravenous Drug Use* (1989), and *AIDS: The Second Decade* (1990).

He has also led a life that might politely be described as "interesting."